SLAVES NO MORE

⌐SLAVES NO MORE⌐

Letters from Liberia 1833–1869

Edited by

Bell I. Wiley

THE UNIVERSITY PRESS OF KENTUCKY

To Joanna Wiley
my beautiful & beloved granddaughter

Library of Congress Cataloging in Publication Data

Slaves no more : letters from Liberia, 1833-1869.

    Bibliography: p.
    Includes index.
    1. Freedmen in Liberia—Correspondence.
2. Afro-Americans—Colonization—Liberia.—Sources.
3. Liberia—History—To 1847—Sources. 4. Liberia—
History—1847-1944—Sources. I. Wiley, Bell
Irvin, 1906-1980
DT633.2.S55   966.6'2'00496073   79-4015
ISBN 0-8131-1388-1

Copyright © 1980 by The University Press of Kentucky

Scholarly publisher for the Commonwealth,
serving Berea College, Centre College of Kentucky,
Eastern Kentucky University, The Filson Club,
Georgetown College, Kentucky Historical Society,
Kentucky State University, Morehead State University,
Murray State University, Northern Kentucky University,
Transylvania University, University of Kentucky,
University of Louisville, and Western Kentucky University.

Editorial and Sales Offices: Lexington, Kentucky 40506

Contents

Acknowledgments

I am especially indebted to the late Dr. L. Minor Blackford of Atlanta, for it was while helping him prepare for publication *Mine Eyes Have Seen the Glory: The Story of a Virginia Lady, Mary Berkeley Minor Blackford* that I was first alerted to the existence of letters written from Liberia by ex-slaves. Dr. Blackford included in his book two letters written from Monrovia by Abraham Blackford, and I found these letters to be so informative and fascinating that I began to search for others. In the twenty-four years since my introduction to the Abraham Blackford letters, I have found more than three hundred letters written from Liberia by other ex-slaves, most of them original manuscripts and most addressed to former masters or members of owners' families.

Many people have assisted me in locating these letters. Professor Clement Eaton told me about the letters written to John Hartwell Cocke by his former slaves. William R. Hogan alerted me to those written to John McDonogh by his ex-slaves. Charlotte Capers informed me of the existence of the correspondence of the Ross-Wade Negroes. William Rachal called my attention to the Page-Andrews letters. The assistance of other individuals and institutions is indicated in the notes.

For assistance in providing copies of letters I am indebted to the staffs of the manuscript departments of the Tennesse State Library and Archives and of the libraries at the University of Virginia, the University of North Carolina, Tulane University, the University of Kentucky, Duke University, the Virginia Historical Society, the North Carolina State Department of Archives and History, the Mississippi State Department of Archives and History, the Chicago Historical Society, the Maryland Historical Society, and the Library of Congress.

The Georgia State University Library made available to me on interlibrary loan a microfilm copy of the files of the *African Repository and Colonial Journal*; the Yale University and University of Wisconsin libraries lent me microfilm of partial files of the *Liberia Herald* for the period 1842-1862; and the University of Georgia Library extended to me through interlibrary loan the use of its microfilm copy of the Library of Congress collection of the Papers of the American Colonization Society.

The Reverend Randolph F. Blackford kindly sent me copies of letters and other materials that had been collected by Dr. L. Minor Blackford. Anastatia Sims, a graduate student at the University of North Carolina, searched the Blackford Family Papers in the Southern Collection of that institution for letters written by James C. Minor, and Bland Blackford Freeman of Williamsburg, Virginia, gave me permission to use those letters. I am indebted to Joseph F. Johnston of Birmingham, John Page Elliott of Alexandria, Virginia, and Mrs. Raymond G. Orf of Bremo Bluff, Virginia, for permission to publish letters from the John Hartwell Cocke Collection at the University of Virginia. Mrs. W. H. Culbertson of Chapel Hill, Tennessee, gave me permission to use letters written by former slaves of Christopher Houston; these letters are now in the Tennessee State Library and Archives.

Professor Randall M. Miller of Saint Joseph's College, Philadelphia, generously shared with me information about the Cocke-Faulcon Negroes that he obtained while doing research for his excellent book *Dear Master: Letters of a Slave Family* published in 1978 by the Cornell University Press. Professor Svend E. Holsoe of the Department of Anthropology of the University of Delaware, drawing on abundant knowledge acquired in his important work on Liberia, during my research patiently and effectively responded to inquiries about emigrants to Liberia. Moreover, his careful reading of the completed manuscript enabled me to eliminate many small errors. I have benefited immensely from the efficient and courteous help given me by members of the reference department of the Emory University Library.

Julie Shelton, now a librarian in West Palm Beach, Florida, was of very great help to me in deciphering and transcribing the difficult writing, original spelling, and unusual sentence structure of the Liberian correspondents. I am grateful to her for her dedication, patience, and efficiency. I am indebted to Professor Myrna Young of Agnes Scott College for helping me translate puzzling Latin quotations appearing in the letters of H. W. Ellis and Henry B. Stewart.

INTRODUCTION

Liberia, its name derived from the Latin *liber*, meaning free, is located just below Sierra Leone on the western coast of Africa. It was created by the American Colonization Society, an organization formed in Washington, D.C., in 1817 to transport freeborn and emancipated American blacks to Africa and help them start a new life in the "land of their fathers."[1]

Between 1820, when the first Negroes were shipped to Liberia, and April 1861, when the Civil War severely curtailed emigration, about 12,000 blacks were transported from the United States to Africa by the American Colonization Society and its affiliates. More than half of these emigrants were ex-slaves.[2]

The American Colonization Society had its origins in the flood of reform sentiment that pervaded the nation in the early years of the nineteenth century, but the motives of those who supported the society were mixed. Many, including Thomas Jefferson, James Madison, and John Randolph of Roanoke, regarded slavery as an evil, inconsistent with the Declaration of Independence; but since they believed it impossible for whites and free blacks to live together in harmony, they regarded colonization abroad as a necessary accompaniment of emancipation. Some supported colonization because of a desire to get rid of Negroes already free, for free blacks were widely regarded as inferior beings—shiftless, prone to theft, and potentially instigative of discontent and insurrection among the slaves. Other colonizationists were interested mainly in using black émigrés as instruments of converting heathen Africans to the blessings of Christianity. Some saw in colonization an effective means of restricting the activities of "slave-catchers" operating on the African coast. Still others were motivated largely by the desire to create in Africa a colony which would produce coffee and other exotic crops and enrich American trade. Thus, as has so often been the case in reform movements, benevolence and the hope of material benefit walked arm in arm.

The first president of the society was Bushrod Washington, nephew of George Washington. Major responsibility for policymaking was borne by a board of managers which in 1838 gave way to a board of directors. The chief administrative officer was the secretary, the most outstanding of whom was the Reverend Ralph R. Gurley, who held the position most of the time from 1822 until 1864.[3] Gurley founded and edited the *African Repository and Colonial Journal* and used it effectively to publicize and win support for the society's activities.[4]

The American Colonization Society assumed responsibility for transporting black émigrés to Liberia and providing them with land, shelter, and subsistence during their first six months in Africa. Land was obtained from local chiefs through a combination of gifts, purchase, persuasion, and force. The organization attempted to maintain security and order by appointing a hierarchy of resident officials, promulgating rules, and providing military training and weapons for defense against hostile natives. The society's top official in Liberia at first bore the title of agent and in the early years his authority was very great.[5] The most outstanding of the early agents in Liberia was Jehudi Ashmun, whose leadership from 1822 until his death in 1828 was an important factor in the colony's survival during one of its most critical periods.[6] In 1839 the board of directors formed the various settlements into a "Commonwealth of Liberia." Under this arrangement the agent was designated governor and the power of the colonial council that advised him was increased. The first governor of the commonwealth was Thomas Buchanan.[7] Not included in the commonwealth was the settlement known as "Maryland in Africa" sponsored by the Maryland State Colonization Society, which in 1833 had broken away from the parent organization.

In 1841 Joseph Jenkins Roberts, a freeborn Virginia émigré who made a fortune as a merchant in Africa, became the first black governor of Liberia. After Liberia proclaimed its independence in 1847 and adopted a constitution modeled on that of the United States, Roberts was elected president of the new nation, which was the first republic established on the African continent.[8] In declaring independence, Liberia was following directions issued by the American Colonization Society, but the United States, because of opposition to accrediting a black diplomat in Washington, withheld recognition of the new country until 1862. The constitution of 1847 excluded whites from citizenship and restricted suffrage to adult black males who owned real estate.

In 1854 Maryland in Africa also became an independent republic but in 1857, after a disastrous conflict with native Africans, the Maryland settlement became a part of the Republic of Liberia.[9]

After creation of the Liberian Republic, the American Colonization Society's role changed from "planter and protector" to "helper and supporter." In terms of money raised and emigrants transported and settled in Africa, the society from 1848 to 1857 experienced the most successful decade of its long career. Following the lean years of the Civil War, the society's activities picked up again for a while, with transportation of blacks averaging 472 persons per year from 1865 to 1869. Afterward the flow of emigrants gradually declined until 1904, when the society ceased to function as a colonizing agency.

Throughout its history the American Colonization Society was beset by enormous problems and discouraging setbacks. From the beginning it was handicapped by lack of funds, and this despite strong endorsement of leading Americans, rapid growth of membership, and government assistance in the form of ships and supplies furnished on the basis of combating the slave trade. In the 1830s, as support for slavery grew in the South and denunciation of the institution increased in the North, the society was caught in the crossfire of the opposing groups. Ardent proponents of slavery accused colonizationists of promoting emancipation while antislavery leaders, and especially William Lloyd Garrison, charged that the society was seeking to strengthen slavery by providing token emancipation to salve guilty consciences and at the same time helping owners to get rid of useless bondsmen. Some free Negroes joined Garrison in attacking the colonization movement on the ground that it was pressuring blacks into migration to Africa instead of working to help them win full rights as citizens in the United States. These attacks influenced some antislavery leaders who had originally supported colonization to join the opposition. Defecting members included James G. Birney, Gerrit Smith, and Arthur Tappan.

The society was handicapped periodically by dissension among its leaders. Most of the controversy grew out of differing attitudes toward slavery, the use of rum as an item of negotiation and trade in Africa, the degree of harshness that should be used in dealing with settlers and natives in Liberia, and the general administration of the society's operations. Dissatisfaction with the society's policies and procedures was the main cause of the Maryland State Colonization Society's breaking away from the parent organization in 1833 and establishing its own colony at Cape Palmas. In 1834 colonizationists of Pennsylvania and New York, openly avowing emancipation as one of their objectives and charging the American Colonization Society with financial indiscretions, collaborated in the establishment of a small settlement at Bassa Cove on the Saint John's River; they did not formally withdraw from the parent organization, but they withheld for their own use a large portion of the funds collected by them. In 1838 Louisiana and Mississippi colonizationists, following the example of New York and Philadelphia, joined forces to establish a settlement called "Mississippi in Africa" at the mouth of the Sinoe River.

In an effort to allay dissension and halt fragmentation, the society in 1838 adopted a new constitution giving the state auxiliaries representation on the board of directors commensurate with the amount of money they contributed and the size of their colonies in Africa. Under the new order, directors representing New York and Pennsylvania gained control of the board and made Judge Samuel Wilkeson president of the board and chairman of the executive committee.[10] Before his retirement in 1841, Wilkeson strengthened the society's control over the state auxiliaries and paid off most of its debts. But his high-handed, dictatorial administration alienated many of the organization's friends. Internal strife persisted into the 1850s and beyond, and the society never again commanded the support that it had inspired in its pioneer years.

While leaders quarreled, ships chartered or acquired by the society continued to deposit cargoes of blacks on the Liberian shore. As the immigrant population increased, the society's agents bartered with local chiefs to extend the boundaries of the Cape Mesurado settlement acquired from King Peter in December 1821 and named Monrovia in honor of President Monroe. Expansion was confined largely to the country lying along the coast. By 1848 the territory claimed by the Republic of Liberia had a coastline of about 285 miles running from the Mafa River to the Grand Cess River and extending inland about 40 miles. The merging of the Maryland settlement with the Republic of Liberia in 1857 extended the coastline southeast to the San Pedro River. Encroachments by the British below Sierra Leone and the French in the southeast in the latter part of the nineteenth century reduced the size of the country considerably. Present-day Liberia with a coastline running from the Mano River on the west to the Cavalla River on the east and with an area of about 43,000 square miles is about the size of Ohio or Pennsylvania.[11]

Territorial expansion was largely responsible for the chronic conflict between natives and settlers that occurred in the years preceding the American Civil War. The tribesmen regarded the newcomers with suspicion from the beginning, and apprehension was intensified as the immigrants increased in number, acquired more land, cut the forests, killed the game, interfered with the slave trade, and sought to impose the Christian religion upon them. Relations were also strained by the attitude of superiority manifested by blacks from America. The immigrants referred contemptuously to the natives as savages and heathens. On April 22, 1840, more than six years after his arrival in Africa, a Virginia artisan, Peyton Skipwith, wrote his former master, John Hartwell Cocke, "It is something strange to think that these people of Africa are calld our ancestors. In my present thinking if we have any ancestors they could not have been like these hostile tribes . . . for you may try and distill that principle and belief in them and do all you can for them and they still will be your enemy."

Conflict between the two groups usually took the form of small nocturnal raids on immigrant huts and storehouses and retaliatory action by the settlers. But occasionally open warfare, involving large numbers and extending over several months, occurred. The first pitched battle was fought on November 11, 1822, when several hundred natives, armed with guns and spears, attacked the Cape Mesurado settlement. Defenders led by Jehudi Ashmun numbered only thirty-five, but they were protected by makeshift fortifications and their weapons included some small cannon. The attackers were repelled when a cannon hurled double charges of grape-shot into their closely formed ranks, littering the ground with casualties. Three weeks later the natives launched a second assault, but this too was repulsed, with timely assistance provided by a British war vessel. Following an armistice arranged by a British officer from Sierra Leone, a long period of relative calm ensued. In 1832, after an aggressive agent, Joseph Mechlin, annexed one hundred miles of coastal country including Grand Bassa and Grand Cape Mount, warfare erupted again. Mechlin restored peace by a successful attack on Dei tribesmen who had imposed import and export duties on tradesmen traversing their territory. In 1838 natives killed the governor of the recently established Mississippi colony at Greenville. A few years later another series of wars occurred, provoked largely by native resistance to continuing expansion of the American colony. Hostilities broke out again in the early 1850s and continued intermittently throughout the decade. Then, as earlier, the turmoil of war interfered with farming and caused shortages of food. On August 14, 1857, a Virginia émigré, Leander Sterdivant, wrote to the daughter of his former owner, John Hartwell Cocke: "We hav had a hard time of wars and famin for 3 years but thank God we hav no wars at this time but the famin is still in the Land."[12]

Conflict with natives was only one of many woes that the settlers had to endure. Far more destructive than encounters with hostile tribesmen were the ravages of disease. A standard part of the breaking-in process was a bout with "African fever." This "mysterious malady" (probably malaria) virtually wiped out the first group of 86 blacks that the American Colonization Society sent to Africa in 1820, and of the total of 1,487 transported in eighteen shipments between 1820 and 1832, it is reported that 230 died of "fever and diseases consequent upon it."[13] Mortality was not so great among those who migrated in subsequent years, owing to avoidance of arrival in the rainy season, improvement of the water supply, location of settlements on higher ground, and provision of better shelter and medical care. But letters written by settlers who reached Africa in the 1850s indicate that fever, tuberculosis, and dysentery were still taking a heavy toll among newcomers.

Geography was another source of discomfort and hardship. Most of the land settled in the period 1820-1860 was in the low, swampy country bordering the Atlantic and lying along rivers flowing through this area. The water was often polluted, and the soil was covered with a thick growth of trees, shrubs, and vines which was difficult to remove; much of the land was hard to cultivate after it was cleared. From late April to the end of October, heavy rains interfered with farming and made life unpleasant. During January, winds blowing from the Sahara sometimes brought dust storms and drought. Throughout most of the year temperatures of 80 to 90 degrees Fahrenheit during the day and 70 to 75 degrees at night were normal, but high humidity, especially in coastal areas, caused temperatures to seem considerably higher than they actually were.[14]

Pests and varmints were more annoying than dangerous, but gardens and crops were damaged by their depredations and insect bites were injurious to health. Snakes, some of them poisonous, caused considerable uneasiness among settlers roaming fields and forests.

Quarreling among the colonists apparently was relatively mild except during closely contested political campaigns. One source of friction, according to an American physician who toured the settlements in 1858, was the assumption of an air of superiority on the part of emigrants from Virginia. Some of the colonists, he stated, "complain of caste and say that the Virginians are most too high-headed and are all the time claiming that they are the *quality* of Liberia."[15]

In their letters settlers complained often about lack of tools and other equipment needed for clearing and cultivating the land assigned to them, for building and repairing houses, and for maintaining themselves and their dependents. Because horses and mules could hardly survive in Liberia, owing to endemic diseases, colonists had to plant and cultivate their crops with hoes. Native livestock consisted largely of chickens, guinea fowls, and goats.

Liberian fields, when properly cultivated, yielded abundant crops of rice, millet, sweet potatoes or yams, peas, beans, okra, peanuts, pepper, eggplant, and two palatable root products known as tania and cassava (popularly termed cassada). Corn and sugar cane or sorghum were grown in limited quantities. Papaw and other wild fruits could be had for the picking, streams abounded with fish, and various types of edible game frequented the forests. But many of the native foods were not relished by the newcomers, and in their letters to friends and relatives in America they often asked for flour, pork, garden seed, nuts, and dried fruit.

Leaders of the American Colonization Society hoped that most of the settlers would become independent farmers. But as a rule emigrants did not take to agriculture. Native crops were strange, land was hard to clear, and there were few if any work animals to lighten the burden of work. Barter with natives was a much easier way to obtain a livelihood, provided desirable items of trade could be procured from America. Correspondence is replete with requests for tobacco, bright-hued cotton cloth, colorful handkerchiefs, beads, trinkets, guns, and hand tools. These items were exchanged not only for food and other articles needed for the comfort and sustenance of the settlers, but also for products that they could use in export trade, such as palm oils, tortoise shells, dye woods, ivory, and leopard skins.

For most of those who settled in Liberia before the Civil War, life was hard. The most difficult period was the first year in Africa when the colonists were going through the acclimatization process and adjusting themselves to a new way of life in a strange land. Much of the hardship during this period of seasoning was due to mismanagement on the part of officials of the American Colonization Society who, owing to lack of funds, ignorance, and inefficiency, failed to provide adequate shelter, subsistence, tools, and protection from the natives. But conditions improved as both officials and settlers acquired experience. Some settlers became so disheartened as to despair of survival in their new home, and a few returned to America. The usual pattern of reaction was initial enthusiasm for the new land and the new life; then, as the novelty wore off and disease began to make its inroads, disillusionment and homesickness became prevalent. Many died during this time of trial. But of those who survived the first year in Africa, most succeeded in achieving a tolerable existence and a few found a degree of success and happiness exceeding anything known by their black friends and relatives in America. Settlers who adapted best to life in Liberia were those who brought with them resourcefulness and skills acquired in America as domestic servants, artisans, and supervisors.

A part of the adjustment process was the establishment of schools and churches. Some of these were founded and supervised by white missionaries sent from the United States, but others were established and conducted by blacks, and in all of them Negroes played an increasingly important role with the passing of time.

All of the letters contained in this volume were written by blacks who had once been slaves and most of them by persons who had been emancipated shortly before their emigration to Africa.[16] Most of the letters were addressed to former masters or to members of masters' families. The correspondence reproduced here is limited to the years 1833-1869 because nearly all of the letters that could be located either in private possession or in public depositories fall within this period. The large collection of papers of the American Colonization Society in the Library of Congress contains a considerable number of letters written after the Civil War but most of these, like those written in the antebellum years, were addressed to officials of the society and as a general rule they are not as informative as those sent to former masters. Some of the letters in the American Colonization Society collection were published *in toto* or in part in the *African Repository and Colonial Journal* but these published versions have been sparingly used here because editors of the magazine in selecting and editing the letters or extracts for publication usually did so with a view to portraying the society and its work in a favorable light.[17] With only a few exceptions, editors corrected spelling and grammar in the transcribing. In a few instances I did include letters transcribed from the *African Repository and Colonial Journal*, such as some of those written by former slaves of Robert E. Lee, because of their importance, and because the original manuscripts could not be found. A careful search was made of the papers of the Maryland State Colonization Society in the Maryland Historical Society in Baltimore, but this yielded very few letters identifiable as the compositions of ex-slaves.

Most of the letters published here were written by blacks or members of their families who had been closely associated with the master class as domestic servants, artisans, drivers, or holders of other supervisory positions. The reason is simple. As a general rule these were the only members of the slave community who were literate. Throughout the South whites were forbidden by state law to teach blacks to read and write. This prohibition was generally effective in the instance of field workers, but some masters schooled their domestic servants in disregard of the law or permitted black juveniles of the favored group to learn to read and write by sharing the books and slates used by white children while preparing their lessons.

Even though these letters for the most part reflect the experiences and impressions of only a small, privileged portion of blacks who had been enslaved, they are still of great importance. Restrospectively they tell much about the character of slavery, the relationship between slaves and masters, and the reactions of blacks recently released from bondage to a new life and a new land. As small and as unrepresentative as it is, this collection of letters becomes one of the largest in print of personal papers produced by American Negroes still in the shadow of slavery.

In their letters from Liberia the blacks revealed much about themselves. Some of them manifested an inordinate propensity for complaining about their plight and finding fault with their associates. Others seemed far more interested in obtaining help from their American correspondents than in supplying their needs by their own exertions. Most of them appear to have been respectable people possessed of an earnest desire to make good in the land of their forefathers. One admirable quality reflected in their correspondence was pride in freedom. Only one of the writers expressed a desire to return to bondage. Abraham Blackford wrote the wife of his former master, shortly after his arrival in Liberia, concerning a call that he made on a white doctor in the employ of the American Colonization Society: "I sets down at his office with surprise which I must say I never enjoy such life as freedom. My conversation is to him when I call him is Dr. Luvenhal [Lugenbeel?] and his to me in a Ripli [is] Mr. Blackford. It is much Bether than to be in the State [where the practice is] for them to call you Boy." This man in a letter to Susan Wheeler, a black woman he had known in Fredericksburg, Virginia, stated: "I am very well pleased. My reason why, is, I can use my own privilieges in every respect. There are a few white people out hear, though they are very polite. . . . The white man never calls me by my name unless they call me Mr. Blackford."

Some indicated that their enthusiasm for settlement in Liberia was due in part to the opportunity it afforded of proving themselves worthy of their freedom. Washington W. McDonogh, one of the blacks emancipated and sent to Liberia by John McDonogh in 1842, wrote four years later to his master: "I will never consent to leave this country . . . for this is the only place where a colored person can enjoy his liberty, for there exists no prejudice of color in this country, but every man is free and equal." Another of the McDonogh Negroes, Henrietta Fuller, wrote in 1849: "Say to them [black friends in Louisiana] that Liberia is the home for our race. . . . Its laws are founded upon Justice & equity. Here we liv under our own vine & Palm Tree. Here we enjoy the same rights and priviledges that our white brethren does in America."

Another quality reflected in the letters is devotion to family. Communications to former masters frequently contained affectionate messages to parents, aunts, uncles, and other relatives. Fathers reported with obvious pride the progress of sons and daughters in Liberian schools or their affiliation with the church. News of the death of near relatives in Africa or America evoked repeated expressions of sadness and grief. Some of the letters written during and after the Civil War to agents of the American Colonization Society were appeals for aid in locating spouses or children unavoidably left behind when the correspondents were sent to Liberia. The concern for close kin manifested in these letters underscores evidence of family strength and stability found in recent studies of American slavery by Eugene Genovese, John Blassingame, Herbert Gutman, and others.

Expressions of devotion to black families were often accompanied by messages indicating continuing affection for former masters and their wives and children. After naming specific whites to whom they wished to be remembered, black correspondents sometimes would extend affectionate greetings to all other members, white and black, of the households to which they had formerly belonged. Matilda Lomax, for example, wrote her former master, John H. Cocke, on September 30, 1850: "Please Remember me very kindly to my Dear Old Grand Mother. . . . Also give my love to my other Grand Mother, Betsey, and all of my relations & friends Both White and Colored."

Another Cocke Negro, James Skipwith, may well have been referring to both black and white members of the Cocke connection when he wrote from Monrovia in 1860: "Jack & his mother [both formerly the property of Cocke] is heair. I will not say much about them. . . . No cats & Gogs [dogs] live worse. [They are] a disgrace to our famely. I do not ond [own] them. They ought to be in the Back side of your cotton farm."

Occasionally, though not frequently, the former slaves revealed a sense of humor in their letters. On April 20, 1853, Matilda Lomax wrote teasingly to her former master's daughter: "I think that it is a hight time for you to be looking out for a beau. I think I mus hount one out for you." Both humor and pride in the white family to which he had belonged are manifested by John Faulcon's comment to John H. Cocke in May 1852: "I See in the colonization Journal your name stiled as vice president [of the society]. Makes me feel like our folks has doings with all and evey good thing. I hope through your influance I may get a Situation."[18]

Other admirable attributes revealed in the letters are dignity, self-reliance, and staunchness in adversity. But none shines through with greater consistency and resplendence than religion. Just as a strong and abiding faith in an omniscient and compassionate God enabled these blacks as slaves to bear the burden of bondage, so did a sincere belief that their lives were directed by a beneficent and unfailing Providence give them strength to endure the peril and tribulation that they experienced as freedmen in Africa. In 1856, Titus Glover, when informing his former master, W. W. Rice, of the death of a child, wrote: "The Lord gave and the Lord taketh, blessed is his kind name." Stephen Rice, another slave whom W. W. Rice had emancipated and sent to Liberia, reported in 1859 that although a recent war with hostile natives had brought considerable hardship, "I donot dispare [for]the Same God that moved your heart to Set us free and Send us to our own Country I hope will keep me from want and Sufferings, and allso raise up friends for me Even in the distant Land of America." Some of the most eloquent expressions of the sustaining power of religious faith came from Matilda Skipwith Richardson, one of the blacks freed and sent to Liberia in 1833 by John H. Cocke. In August 1857, after death had deprived her of her husband and several near relatives and reduced her and her three children to straitened circumstances, she wrote Cocke: "Since the death of my people I some times feel almost broken up and then when I look and think I see that the Lord has not put on me no more than I can bare. I have been in the Baptist Church as a member for eighteen years, and I have [been a] member of Daughters of Temperance for four years [and] Sisters of friendship for five years. . . . Please give my love to Aunt L. Tell [her] I was sorry to hear of the death of her son nedd. Tell her for me that she must remember 'that the Lord Giveth and the Lord taketh away.' "

Since one of the principal merits of these letters as historical documents is the light that they throw on master-servant relationships it was deemed best in most cases to present as a separate chapter those written by former slaves of a particular owner. Letters taken from the *African Repository and Colonial Journal* were, of course, transcribed as edited there, but my guiding rule in editing the other letters has been to preserve as much of their original character and flavor as possible. Hence, no changes were made in spelling and grammar. Some punctuation was added to facilitate reading, but capitalization was altered only to the extent of changing lower case to upper case at the beginning of sentences. Words inadvertently repeated by the correspondents have been silently deleted.

Since the essence of the book is what the migrants wrote of their impressions and experiences in Africa, documentation is sparse. Proliferation of notes to identify persons and places fairly well known or relating only incidentally to the content of the letters, or digressive comments on events hardly requiring explanation, would serve no useful purpose. An attempt has been made to restrict notes largely to instances where they might contribute to a better understanding of what correspondents were trying to communicate.

The letters comprising this volume consist of all that could be found of those written by blacks to former owners, members of owner's families, and to the correspondents' relatives or friends. Those written to officials of colonization societies are a selection of representative communications; to have included all known missives of this category would have resulted in undue repetition and exceeded necessary limitations of space.[19]

Sources treating of Liberia contain variation in the spelling of names— of persons, tribes, places, and things. In some cases I have given variants in parentheses but my general rule has been to adopt the terms most widely used in recent works and to be consistent.

Working with letters written by ex-slaves from Liberia has given the editor an opportunity to pursue an interest extending over the whole range of his scholarly career; namely, the study of the plain folk of America as they revealed themselves in their personal documents. Impressions of the lowly people formed in reading the letters of Johnny Rebs and Billy Yanks and the folk they left at home have been abundantly confirmed by poring over the richly human missives written by ex-bondsmen in Africa. The spelling and grammar of these plain people, black and white, left much to be desired, but the blacks, like their white counterparts, were ambitious for their children, were intimately acquainted with hardship, bore their misery with a minimum of complaint, and demonstrated an enormous capacity for suffering. Some were deficient in courage and in character but the majority were resourceful, well-intentioned, generous, compassionate, and reliable. To them and their kind, America and Liberia owe much of their strength and their greatness.

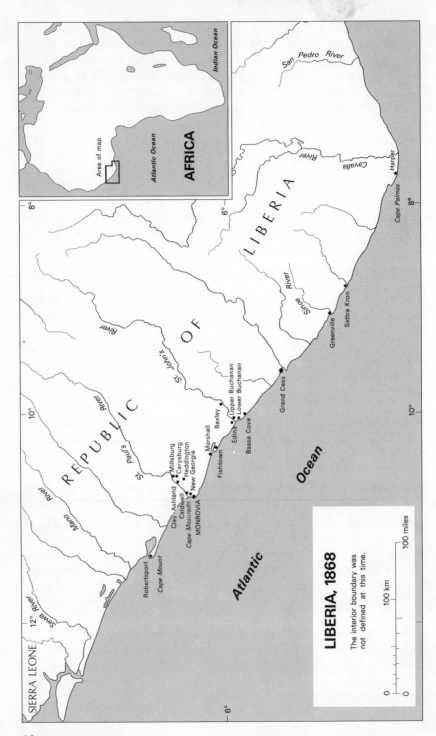

LIBERIA, 1868

The interior boundary was
not defined at this time.

AFRICA

Area of map

Atlantic Ocean

Indian Ocean

REPUBLIC OF LIBERIA

SIERRA LEONE

San Pedro River

Cavalla River

Harper
Cape Palmas

Settra Kroo

Greenville

Sinoe River

Grand Cess

Lower Buchanan
Upper Buchanan
Bassa Cove
Edina
Bexley
Marshall
Fishtown

St. John's River

St. Paul's River

Millsburg
Carysburg
Heddington
New Georgia
Clay-Ashland
Caldwell
Cape Mesurado
MONROVIA

Robertsport
Cape Mount

Mano River

Sewa River

Atlantic Ocean

0   100 km
0   100 miles

12

1/LETTERS OF THE MINOR–BLACKFORD NEGROES

The three blacks whose letters comprise this chapter were freed and sent to Liberia by John Minor and his sister Mary Berkeley Minor Blackford, wife of William M. Blackford, both of Fredericksburg, Virginia. John's and Mary's support of emancipation and colonization derived largely from views passed on to them by their mother, Lucy Landon Carter Minor, widow of General John Minor. Lucy Minor regarded slavery as a great evil. When the American Colonization Society was formed she not only became an enthusiastic member of that organization but she also influenced her children to follow her example. In 1837 one of her sons, Lancelot B. Minor, shortly after his graduation from the Virginia Theological Seminary, went to Liberia as a missionary and there he died, May 29, 1843, of tropical fever. Despite financial difficulties resulting from debts inherited from her husband, Lucy Minor in 1826 freed nine of her slaves and sent them to Liberia.[1]

Mary Blackford, Lucy's daughter, became as staunch an opponent of slavery as her mother. She and her husband were zealous members of the Fredericksburg auxiliary of the American Colonization Society. In 1833 she wrote in her journal: "Disguise it as thou wilt, Slavery thou art a bitter draught. . . . I am convinced that the time will come when we shall look back and wonder how Christians could sanction slavery."[2] She often and openly denounced slavery to her associates in Fredericksburg. Many of them did not share her views but they respected her sincerity and earnestness and never ostracized her. Her hostility to slavery did not prevent her from supporting the South during the Civil War; with her blessing, all five of her sons entered Confederate service.

Thirteen of the seventeen letters contained in this chapter were written by James Cephas Minor and two by his mother, Mary Ann Minor. Both mother and son before their emancipation were the property of John Minor, Lucy's son. On December 26, 1828, a short time before James Cephas left for Liberia, Lucy Minor wrote Ralph R. Gurley of the American Colonization Society:

My son John Minor has for some twelve months past been preparing a man servant of his, who is about twenty years of age, for the Colony. He has been that length of time at the printing business [for the Fredericksburg newspaper, the *Political Arena*, owned by John Minor] and can read and write and is approved to becoming a printer in consequence of which we have concluded to send him immediately lest he might form some connections which would forbid his removal. He is a boy of some principles, perfectly honest, understands all family work, but is not remarkable for his industry; this last is all that can be laid to his charge. He has been raised partly with my children, and I think I can say that he is a very upright, honest man. We wish to send him by the ship which is now going.[3]

James Cephas made the trip to Liberia in 1829, on the *Harriet*. A letter of William M. Blackford to Ralph R. Gurley, May 6, 1830, stated that James was working in Liberia as printer for the *Liberia Herald* at a salary of twenty dollars a month and that he was happy in his new situation.[4] James's early letters were lost, but the first to be preserved, dated February 11, 1833, is a well-written communication, giving interesting details on recent immigrant arrivals, including Burwell Minor, former slave of Lucy Minor, whom James was helping to get established in Africa. Concerning Burwell he made the interesting comment: "When he first arrived, he acted like a young horse just out of the stable—he tested [his] freedom. I gave him the best instruction I could."

Other letters of James Cephas to his master and to Mary Blackford indicate that he took an active interest in all the migrants who came from the Fredericksburg area. These letters also show that he was a person of exceptional initiative and ability and that he commanded the respect of his associates. In one of his communications he thanked John Minor for sending him Blackstone's *Commentaries* and intimated that he was planning to become a practicing attorney. He became a member of the Masonic order and, in anticipation of elevation to higher degrees in his lodge, he requested his former master to send him appropriate regalia. In a letter to John Minor, January 15, 1853, he proposed the establishment of a business partnership with Minor for the sale in Liberia of merchandise sent from Virginia.

In his letters to agents of the American and Maryland colonization societies, James Cephas indicated that he was a key member of the *Liberia Herald*'s staff and that he was in close touch with the country's ruling authorities. His letter of April 10, 1841, to S. Wilkeson of the American Colonization Society, was devoted largely to a defense of Governor Thomas Buchanan against charges of immorality and misconduct. He served as an officer in the militia and was active in public affairs. At the time of his death in 1871 he was serving as judge of the Court of Quarter Sessions and Common Pleas of Monteserrado County.[5]

The experiences of James Cephas Minor afforded further evidence of the importance of both preparatory training and native ability in achieving success in Liberia.

Abraham (or Abram) Blackford, slave of William M. Blackford and his wife Mary, was emancipated at Mary's insistence in 1844 and sent immediately to Liberia.[6] Knowing the importance of preparing the prospective migrant, then about twenty years old, for life in Africa, Mary in 1843 entrusted Abraham to her brother Lucius for a year of intensive training as a farmer and handyman. Before his departure she provided him with some implements and tools and wrote letters to American Colonization Society agents testifying to his honesty and asking them to take an interest in his welfare.[7]

Unfortunately only three letters of Abraham have been preserved. These show that he adapted well to conditions in Africa. He married and applied himself industriously to farming, trading, and other work, and enjoyed relatively good health. In his letter of February 14, 1846, he stated: "I would write you more about fine Africa, but I have a gob of work on hand, and the person [to whom] it belong are in a hurry for it." He manifested great pride in the freedom that was his in Africa and the respect accorded that freedom by both his black and his white associates. The last report of him, given by James Cephas in a letter to Mary Blackford, October 1, 1853, stated that he and his family were living at Cape Mount and getting along well.[8]

1 / JAMES C. MINOR TO JOHN MINOR

Monrovia, Liberia, Feb. 11, 1833

Dear Sir: I received your letter of the 20 inst. by the arrival of the ship Lafayette, with an hundred and fifty-four emigrants. Among the emigrants was Mr. [Burwell Minor] in whose care came your letter and an arithmetic called Colburn's Sequel, a book that is of great service to me, and I am very much obliged to you for it. You also recommend to my care Mr. [Burwell Minor], a young man sent out by your Mother. He is now comfortably situated at Caldwell, one of our Middle Settlements. He is working for 75 cents a day. He was down here on yesterday. He intends working by the day until he can purchase some farmer's tools to commence farming for himself.

We express great joy and thankfulness to your Mother and her offspring for permitting of his liberation and greater thanks to that God who overrules the heavens and the earth and holds in his hand the hearts of the sons and daughters of man and directs their course whithersoever he pleases, even in bringing them across the waters of the great deep. Truely his mind is in obsure darkness, but he seems to see the light of prospect from afar and is cheered.

Affairs of the colony appear quite smooth at present. The war horn is not heard here. The Natives are more friendly with us. Our recaptured Africans seem somewhat persumptuous at times.[1] I thank you for the papers and the book which my worthy friend, Mrs. [Minor] sent me, called the Pilgrim's Progress. All these were received and are much valued by me. I hope many months will not elapse before I shall receive more presents of the same kind from you all. Though I have nothing to send you in return but good will, and that I am trying to live a Christian's life in this dark and benighted land.

On the 16th of January the bark Hercules arrived in our port with an hundred and seventy emigrants from Charleston, South Carolina. They are pretty well. And on the 20th the ship Lafayette arrived with an hundred and fifty-four emigrants from Baltimore, Maryland, all I believe in good health. We have been favoured with the above mentioned numbers to come over on this side the great waters to join this federal head so to speak. We are looking every hour for the arrival of the ship Jupiter. We hope many months will not pass away before we shall see our harbour glittering with ropes [barques] that have been the bearers of the people destined to return to the land of their forefathers.

Let me say something of the above named [Burwell] whom your Mother sent over. When he first approached my presence I had no knowledge of him; but the name he bore, after a little discourse, caused me to recognize him. He is now comfortably situated at Caldwell, the middle settlement, where he can make a crop. When he first arrived, he acted like a young horse just out of the stable—he tested [his] freedom. I gave him the best instruction I could.

There is, as you will see, inserted in the 10th No. of the Liberia Herald, three extensive buildings lately erected solely for the accommodation of new comers. Ho! all ye that are by the pale faces' laws oppressed, come over to the above mentioned destiny. The Charleston people (the most of them) are very intelligent. The major part of them are living in Monrovia, keeping shops.

You are desirous to know the exact number of the Colonists. I will give it as near as I can (counting the two last arrivals), 2829 in all. Good news from Canada.

While I was penning the foregoing lines, my ears were assailed with shouts of praise and hallelujahs to God and the Lamb forever; it is about ten o'clock in the night. They proceeded from a young man who has been for some time under conviction of sin. He lives near us. Suddenly he experienced the love of Almighty God shed abroad in his heart. The same miraculous scene took place in my own heart on the Sabbath day, 29 of January, 1831; Oh, the wonders of redeeming grace! On this subject I could pen nothing but what you are acquainted with.

Remember, I beseech thee, that I wish to become one of the blowers of the Gospel trumpet. That I cannot be without such books as are adapted to prepare me.

Since my exit from death unto life there has been a new church erected, called the Second Baptist Church of Monrovia, the paster of which is the Rev. Colin Teage.[2] Our new church moves slowly, for want of funds to defray the expense. I trust we will not always be in this barren state. I would offer a petition but am doubtful whether or not it would be received or noticed. Nothing do I hear of the coloured inhabitants of the town of Fredericksburg migrating to Liberia. The laws of Virginia surely must be more favourable to the man of color than the laws of South Carolina. Surely they do not shrink back for the fabrications of its enemies. Will they still lay down in Turkish apathy? Africa is a land of freedom. Where else can the man of color enjoy temporal freedom but in Africa? They may flee to Hayti or to Canada, but it will not do. They must fulfil the saying of Thomas Jefferson: "Let an ocean divide the white man from the man of color." Seeking refuge in other parts of the world has been tried; it is useless. We own that this is the land of our forefathers, destined to be the home of their descendants.

You are not aware perhaps that there has recently been a new settlement established at Grand Bassa, under the superintendance of Mr. Wm. Weaver.[3] It is a place that many will resort to. The settlement at Grand Bassa is located in a very good place, and the inhabitants comfortably situated. Our infant commerce is stretching out her hands and inviting the weary wanderers of the Ocean to call. If your readers will peruse the Liberia Herald they will see for themselves the number of vessels that arrive and depart in the course of a month.

I have given you my brightest ideas on things at present that I am capable of doing. Pardon my errors and overlook my inferior discoveries. Remember my best respects to the family and particularly my friend, Mrs. [Minor]. I remain your friend,   J.C.M

2 / JAMES C. MINOR TO RALPH R. GURLEY

Monrovia, Liberia, Ocb. 12, 1833 [?]

De[ar] Rev. Sir: In behalf of the Colonial printing office of Liberia I embrace this opportunity of addressing the Board of Managers of the American Colonization Society to inform them that we are yet in want of some Buckskin or Ball [?] Stocks for the use of the Col[onial] Print Office and if we cannot get them in short we cannot do anything without them.[1]
Yours humble servent,   James C. Minor, Col. Printer

3 / JAMES C. MINOR TO RALPH R. GURLEY

Monovia, Liberia, April 6th, [18]34

Rev. and Dear Sir: I embrace this opportunity of informing the Board of Managers of the American Colonization Society through you that I have been for the last four years in the government employ, and found that it is a mere living from hand to mouth, and have come fully to the determination to desist from the office as Colonial Printer on or before the first of June next [18]34, unless my present salary is raised from $25.00 per month, or $300.00 per annum. It does not give bread to eat Scarcely, much less any thing else, and the manner in which I received my payment is so irregular that I cannot pay my debts.

Perhaps I may stop the Press on the close of the fourth vol. of the Herald. With much Respect Yours,

James C. Minor, C[olonial] P[rinter]

4 / JAMES C. MINOR TO SAMUEL WILKESON

To Honorable S. Wilkeson,   Monrovia, April 10th, 1841
Gen. Agt. of the Am. Col. Socty

Sir,   you may be somewhat astonished at receiving a communication from the undersigned, having never previously written to you, but it may not be less my duty than that of any other of the citizens of this commonwealth to write on a subject so important and so interesting to us all as the one on which I say a few words in support of the gentlemanly conduct of our present Governor, and in contradiction of some of the most flagrant charges set up against him; which seem to have had their origin in the hot bed of the recent excitement in our heretofore peaceful community. These charges have been trumpetted to the world as worthy of everlasting remembrance and to be handed down to posterity. They have been lifted high by the towering pole of confusion.

Whereas, there has been a multiform catalogue of misrepresentation (and false ones too) alledged by sundry persons residing in these colonies against Thomas Buchanan, Esq., Governor of this commonwealth, and among which misrepresentations he is accused of habitual intoxication, nocturnal reveling, a common stroller in the street, ludeness and in fact of every thing that characterizes the immoral man, and to these is added the accusation of his drawing his sword from his cane in the court house while presiding as Chief Judge, and threaten the jury with the arm of his power, if they did not bring in a verdict to suit his own notions and interpretation of the law, contrary to their own judgment.

To the foregoing misrepresentations and accusations as set forth by some [and] entertained and cherished by others, I pronounce that I am an entire stranger and have no personal knowledge of such a course of conduct pursued by His Excellency Governor Buchanan. But to the contrary, so far as my knowledge goes, both his private and public deportment has been pursued with even tenor; he has acted the perfect gentleman. He has received from [some] of our citizens, in our public meetings (the occasion is well known to you) the unkooth and vulgor terms, "it is an untruth," "it is a falshood," but he did not return them.

He has been vigilent in having the laws of the Colony passed by the Colonial legislature and given to him regularly enforced (though, by me, some of them were thought severe). He has been faithful in making known at each annual session of the Council the proceedings of his official acts during the year. He has manifested his friendship for us, and deep interest he has in our welfare, by his vigilence, and active zeal in defending our rights, and in addition to that, offered, as it were, in Gatoom-ba's woods, his life in the defence of our colony.[1] He has affected amicable treaties with the ruthless and turbulent tribes around us. He has been the means of spreading the fame of the Colony far and wide and won [on] her behalf the affections of many who heretofore stood aloof, but are made nigh by the influence of a man of standing among his own nation.

I have been a resident here for more than 12 years and have witnessed the conduct of every Governor that has governed since my arrival here, and previous to his arrival as governor of this commonwealth, and can say of a truth, and that too with the full assurance of the sanction of this community, none has ever pursued a more even tenor of their way or governed with more wisdom or promptness than our present governor; he has done honor to himself, and to Colony; he has checked the stalking ingress of the Spaniards in our towns; he has been seen in the battle field, on the parade ground, in the house of worship, at the table of the Lord's Supper, in his private as well as public capacity, and he has always been the gentleman, and have now or in no one instance descended below that Standard.

In addition to his other usefulness, some have learned the correctness of speech and measurably the bounds of ettiquette; otherwise they would have been reduced to the necessity of going to some famous house of learning. Now may it please your honor not to publish my letter. I am willing that you should make any remarks that you may think proper but not to publish this letter unless you publish it without my name, or with the letter M—but not my name more than M.

Having thus given you the history and conduct of our worth[y] Governor, as far as I am competent to do [and] hoping you pardon all errors and redundancies. I have the honor to be yours, With Much Respect,   James C. Minor

5 / JAMES C. MINOR TO RALPH R. GURLEY

To Rev. R. R. Gurley,   Monrovia, January 27, 1844
General Agent of the American
Colonization Society

Sir,   you may be somewhat astonished at seeing my name at the bottom of a communication addressed to you, though doubtless you may have seen it in the Herald of Liberia; but from the nature of some existing circumstances I am induced to address you with a few lines making certain inquiries, setting forth and shewing my reasons for thus writing.

I herewith transmit to you a copy of the Special Ordinances of the Board of Managers of the American Colonization Society, respecting real estate in Liberia passed February 27th 1832. Now these ordinances have been regarded and observed by all of the Executive Officers that have ever governed here from the time it arrived here until the present administrator, Governor Roberts, who favors the opinion that the Board has virtually repealed these ordinances by granting the Maryland Code as the legal principals in the Colony, when in every deed they have said nothing about the repealing of these ordinances in no way whatever; but in their adaptation of the Code, they have only submitted it for such parts of it to be taken out and annexed to the colonial laws as did not conflict with any of their existing laws of the Colony; and not that the Board intended that any of their special ordinances or acts should be annulled by the authority of this commonwealth, which is minor to that of the Board.

Was not these ordinances intended to secure to all who were then citizens and all who should hereafter become so, the right of maintaining a spot of ground to rest the sole of their feet upon? Is it not plainly said to all in these Ordinances that after a certain day, namely, the first of January 1833, that you shall not sell the land or real property of persons for debts incurred after that time? Unless these Ordinances be revived, if ever they have been annulled, the people here will soon, many of them I mean, have no house nor home. Now in the general rage of affairs and by the interpretation of the Laws by the Governor, the Sheriffs are making havoc among the people by selling of land. In short there will be orphans pilled [piled] upon orphans entirely destitute of house, home, friends or the wherewithal to be maintained when the very courts that ought to be their father and friend takes away from the orphans the last remains of their support, notwithstanding the Ordinances referred to guarantee the possessor of real property the entire right of willing his property to whom he will. Governor Buchannan, though he had the Maryland Code as sanctioned by the Board, gave Credit to and sealed these ordinances and regarded them as being too far above his control for him to annul, and how can his successor do otherwise is a mystery to me. In the case of David White's two orphans is a fair specimen of approaching destruction of which circumstances you will doubtless be informed by the Executor of that estate. The Governor has refused to give me any farm land. Am I entitled to any or not? I came to this country in the ship Harriet, 1829, while under age and now I think I ought to have my farm land. Please inform me. Excuse my bad writing. Yours truly,

James C. Minor

6 / ABRAHAM BLACKFORD TO MARY B. BLACKFORD

Monrovia, Liberia, Sept. 9, 1844

Dear Madam: I am well at present hoping these few lines may find you enjoying good health. I embrace the opportunity of telling you of my travels. When I left Fredericksburg for Richmond, I put up to the Exchange hotell; ther is the place I lodge at night. In going the next morning to settle my bill, expressing myself to the landlord where I was going, he charge me nothing. I set oft to Norfolk next morning and arrived ther that evening. I was very politely ask up to Mr. Bell's house where I was accommodated until Friday Evening, which I had directions from Mr. McClain to see all of the passioners on bord by three o'clock, which I did. So after I saw all on board, me and Mr. McClain came ashore again, which he advise me when I got to Monrovia to set me out some coffee trees, which I has not done as yet, being I has not had the opportunity. When we arrived to the Jolucal Mountain we did not meat the Govner; he was in the States, but I will make it my Business to do so as soon as he coms. I has not been up the River as yet, but I has been inform that the land up thir is very good, but I am in hopes when I Goes up that I will make a living which it is my desires, for I believe an industrious person can live here. I wish you would Rite to Mr. McClain, as he Requested me to Rite to him how these passioners was. Th[e]y is some as smart a people as I would wish to be in company with and some bad enough to pay for it. Since some of them has been a[s]hore th[e]y has been stealing, but I am in hopes that I shall never be guilty of that. Th[e]y is some of them silly enough to say they wish themselves Back. And ther is a great many a going to school. I am included in that number, but I has Regret very much that I refuse when I was there. Mr. McClain give me a letter to the assistant govner which I has to visit. I finds him to be a fine man. I amuse myself, after I has said my lesson to Mrs. James C. Minor and [went] to Doctor J. W. Luvenhal office, a white gentleman which Mr. McClain give me a letter to. I sets down at his office with surprise which I must say I never enjoy such life as freedom. My conversation is to him when I call him is Dr. Luvenhal and his to me in a Repli [is] Mr. Blackford.[1] It is much Bether than to be in the state [where the practice is] for them to call you Boy. I has not seen Mr. James C. Minor as yet, but I am in hopes I shall in a few days. He has Received your letter and has giving me free access to his house. Mr. Minor sends Respect to you and family especially to your Mother. He is not in town; that is the Reason he has not riting you all, but he says he will by the next opportunity. Please to give my respects to the family, particular to Mr. Blackford. I am afraid I cannot return thanks anought to him for his kindness, and also to you. Please to give my respects to all enquiring friends. Mr. Freeman, the gentleman that will give you this letter, I has advise him to stop and see you and give a free estimation of Africa. He is so much please with the place, he is goin back after his family. He is a very fine man. I am in hopes you will give him an invitation to unkle James Wess house so that he can give him an estimation of Africa. I dont think it worth while for me to relate to you what is heare. Mr. Freeman will give you an estatement of it. Please to give my respects to Mr. Lusious H. Minor and family when you return to him. When I left Norkford I was in low spirit about eight days, but after the captain put me as steward over the black and white, which I received from the captain $20.00 after my arrival. He insisted me to go to Calcutta, Being he was so please with me, but I felt loft [loth] to leave my old country and I did not go. I see they is a great deal of religious person heare. I has attended meeting very regular. Th[e]y is a Presbyterian church and Baptist and also the Methodist church. Th[e]y is a great revival with the Methodist. I was a coming home one night from the Methodist Church and I heard a crying over the street and when I come to find out, th[e]y has been a woman died very sudden which was supposed to be well about half hour ago. She was not prepared for death, I think, and I am a stud[y]ing about it every day. Nothing more at present to say, but remainds your acquaintance.

Abram Blackford

P.M. Th[e]y is a plenty out here for to eat, namely: potatoes, butterbeans, cassada and every other thing I see in your garden.   A.B.

7 / ABRAHAM BLACKFORD TO SUSAN WHEELER

Africa, Monrovia, Sept. 10, 1844.

My Dear Miss Susan Wheeler: I take this opportunity of writing you these few lines to inform you that my health is good, and I hope these few lines may find you in the same state. I am now in a new country and am about to settle myself. I left Norfolk on the 14th of June and arrived here the 4th of August. Our passage was longer than we expected, though very safe. I am very well pleased. My reason why is, I can use my own privileges in every respect. There are a few white people out hear, though they are very polite. I meet them sometimes in the streets and they steps one side of the pavements and touch their hats. I call at their dwelling in the course of the day and sets down at large and talks a great deal about the States and about Religious subjects. The white man never calls me by my name unless they call me Mr. Blackford.

There are a great many pretty young ladies here and I amuse myself in visiting the young ladies when the schoole is out, and in going to the church.

There are three churches here, Methodist, Baptist, Presbyterian. There is a great revival here among the Methodists where I go both night and day and where we should all go to try to get acquainted with God. It is necessary we all should have an introduction to him.

You must write to me by the first opportunity. I would send some of this fruit but the passage being expected to be long, therefore I thought it would spoil before it reached you. Your friend,   Abram Blackford

8 / JAMES C. MINOR TO MARY B. BLACKFORD

Monrovia, Liberia, West Africa, February 12, 1846

Much Esteemed Marm: By the reception of these few lines you will know that I am still surviving the wreck of time. There arrived here on the 8th of December last the ship Roanoke with emigrants from Norfolk, 96 in number, among whom was George and James Marshall, two young men from Fredericksburg whom I was glad to see; they, myself and Abram gets together and sits down and cherishes the recollection of home and the remembrance of old acquaintances. The Marshalls talk of returning home. They had expected to have gone back in the vessel that brings this letter; but they have forgone their intention for the present. George, however, was much inclined on returning, but James was not. I have advised them to be content and turn their attention to some sort of occupation. I have not as yet learned the particulars of Mr. Hayes' people but as soon as I do I shall communicate the facts to you.

I cannot at this time give you the detailed account of our colony and Governor, but will, be assured of it, that if God spare my life, give you an account of the whole affair, as far as I am capable, from the war with Gatoomba in 1841, up to the present time.

Has Mr. Blackford gone away from home again or not? Where is your brother John, James, Lewis, and Lucious? Please write me where they all are, and how your dear mamma is; give all of our respects to her and to all of your family.

You have doubtless heard of the arrival of the *Pons* of Philadelphia, in our harbor, with 756 slaves on board, captured by the Yorktown. Capt. C. H. Bell, of[f] Cabend, to the leeward of us.[1] Yours with abundance of respects, James C. Minor

9 / ABRAHAM BLACKFORD TO MARY B. BLACKFORD

Monrovia, Feb. 14, 1846.

Dear Madam: As an opportunity offers, I now embrace it and drop you a few lines by way of remembrance, hoping that they may find you enjoying good health, as they leave me and my family at present. I am doing tolerable well at present, and I like the place very well, insomuch that I have married, trusting that I may do as well as those who has come to this country years before me and are doing as well as can be expected.

As regards sickness, or this being a very sickly climate, it is not so, for I never has enjoyed better health in my life than I has enjoyed since here I have lived. It is very true [that] most all of the people who immigrate from America here has to undergo a acclimating process. I mean by that, that they have the fever, and in many instances it is very slight, only lasting not more than two or three days. And if I were to go entirely by my own feelings, I can assure that I have not lost three days on account of sickness since here. I have had none, properly speaking, since I had the fever. Tell all those who want to come, come. A fine country this is, fine malicious [delicious] fruits grow here, enough to attract the most noblest minds. People speaking about this country tell them to hush their mouths if they are speaking anything disrespectful of it. If any man be a lazy man, he will not prosper in any country, but if you will work, you will live like a gentleman, and Africa is the very country for the colored man. There are a great many colored persons I here that have the liberty to come, but will not come. It is those to whom I speak. Mr. James and George Marshall arrived here in December last, in the ship Roanoke from Fredericksburg, Virginia. And the immigrants that came out at that time has already planted their produce and eating of the same. And out of two hundred and more immigrants there has not more than three or four of them died, and they was old persons. I would write you more about fine Africa, but I have a gob of work on hand and the person [to whom] it belong are in a hurry for it, and the vessel by which this letter is to go is expected to sail in a few hours. Please to give my best respects to Mr. Blackford and tell him that I would have wrote to him, but not knowing where he is. You will please to inform me in your next. You will give my best respects to all the family and also Mr. Lucius Minor, also give my respects to all my friends and acquaintances, and tell them I would have wrote to them, but I do not know where they live. They must write to me so that I may know where they are, and I will certainly answer their letters. Give me all the news in your next. Will you please to be so kind as to write to my mother and tell her that I am well. I want to write to her, but I do not know where she lives. She must write to me so that I may know where to direct my letters to her. Capt. C. H. Bell of the Yorktown took a slaver with nine hundred and fifty slaves on board, about three degrees south of the equator. I very often see Dr. Pattin and Capt. Cunigum, they talk with me much about old home. I will be very glad for you to send me some cloth and tobacco, which articles demands [a] pretty good price, also flour and pork. Such articles demand at times a pretty good price, as I am keeping a little shop and such things I want very much. The freight shall not cost you anything. If Mr. James Marshall returns on a visit, as he expects to do, I will send you the money. I remain yours with much respect,   Abraham Blackford

10 / JAMES C. MINOR TO AGENT, MARYLAND STATE COLONIZATION SOCIETY

Monrovia, Liberia, W[est] A[frica], September 28th, 1850

Dear Sir: Your order on Mr. J. B. McGill by the Liberia Packet was duly received and have been paid;[1] but in behalf of the proprietors of the Liberia Herald I, as conductor of that paper, are authorized to say that the annual subscription to the Liberia Herald is $2.00; the nos. for the new series of our paper will be forewarded on to you; and if you wish the nos. for the whole year, we shall expect the other dollar. The Herald is printed at present by me, and edited by a gentleman whose name, you will know by and bye. We forward you 5 nos. of the Herald. Your &c.,   Jas. C. Minor

11 / MARY ANN MINOR TO AGENT, MARYLAND STATE COLONIZATION SOCIETY

Sept 23, 1851

Dear Sir: It is with much Pleasure I have Embrace this hapay opportunity of writing you A few Lines to inform you of my health is good at Present & I Sincerely hope thesse few Lines May find you the Same.

Der Sir, I Desier you to assist me to come home to bear part of My Expenses. I want to get Some of my people. If you please, Sir, you fill fod [afford] me with much satisfaction by Soding [so doing]. I Send A Letter to My mother. Will you please Sent it to her on Eastern Shore. I have been at Africa A Long time & I wish to come home if I can possibel. You will please Send me an answer. I am doing well as can be expected. Old Grany Rachel is Living yet. This is all at present. You will please pardon all misstakes, yours,   Mary Miner

12 / JAMES C. MINOR TO MARY B. BLACKFORD

Monrovia, October 17th, 1851

Very dear, and much esteemed Madam,   by the reception of these few lines, you may know that myself and family are still surviving the wreck of nature and are in tolerable good health, thank God. We hope that you and your dear family are all well. Of necessity, this letter will be short, for the following reasons.

I have not failed to transmit to you regularly by every opportunity both letters and papers, and have not received any answers at all; and again it has now been a great while since I heard from any of you. Consequently, I do not know who to write to, nor where to write. I have not been able to learn where your husband, sons, brothers, mother, daughters & grandchildren are. Then how can I tell who to write to, or where to write? Please inform me on these points, for I have much to write about.

Mr. Abraham Blackford is well and trying to do well. We have now quite a revival of religion going on. Respectfully yours &c.,

James C. Minor

13 / JAMES C. MINOR TO MARY B. BLACKFORD

Monrovia, Liberia, West Africa, Monrovia [space in copy] 1852
To Mrs. Mary B. Blackford:

Dear Madam: Your favor, under date of the 29th April, last, came safe to hand, by the arrival of the Barque Ralph Cross, from Baltimore, on the 13th of June last. It was received and read with much pleasure, and was glad to hear that health prevailed among the family, but was very sorry to hear of the poor health of your dear mother; we hope that she is now much better. It would have afforded me much pleasure to have been present at the assembling of your brothers and sons and daughters, and grandchildren.

Bishop Payne was at my office, and gave me much interesting intelligence of the whole family.[1] He spoke of the personal interview which he had with you and some of your brothers. He spoke of the healthy appearance of your brother, John, now that he had lived to be a man of an advanced age; his head was white, and withal, he had not married. He spoke of the improvement that was going on in Lynchburg and Fredericksburg. He called the names of many of the residents of Fredericksburg, (the scene of youthhood); many of them I recognized as old acquaintances; others, I had no recollection of. Very often, by reflection, I can take a view of Fredericksburg—Toppen Castle, Edgewood, and many other places, over which I have walked in your beloved country in the days of early youthhood.

The barque Ralph Bross, Capt. Seale, anchored in our roadstead on the night of the 12th of June 1852, from Baltimore, having 156 immigrant passengers and Bishop Payne of the Protestant Episcopal Church, after a passage of 33 days. She sailed from this for Grand Bassa and Cape Palmas. It was the expectation of the Captain not to have been gone more than three weeks. But on arriving at Grand Bassa (it being on the wrong time of the moon, as we call it here), the bar and beach was so bad that the vessel was detained there much longer than was anticipated; however, after a detention of about four weeks, caused by the violence of the seas, the immigrants and their stores were landed in safety. She then sailed for Cape Palmas where the remainder of the immigrant passengers were to be landed. While there, from some unforeseen cause or accident, this fine vessel was wrecked on the beach at Cape Palmas, on the 19th of June [18]52, and unladened portion of her cargo, including about $8000 for government, was totally lost, as far as we have been able to learn. This sad intelligence was brought us by the arrival of our Government schooner "Lark" from Cape Palmas.

From the time that our Independence was declared to the present moment, we have moved on smoothly, with as even a tenor of our course as could be expected, from the encounters that our government have had to contend with during the five years of national career. Soon after the arrival of Mr. Hanson, the British Consul here, he offered an insult to the Government and the principal functioneer and subbalterns, by a jesuistic communication filled with inuendoes and criminations, a copy of which was published in one of the numbers of the Liberia Heralds, sent to you. The magnitude of that offence continued to augment until it reached the notice of the Legislature, who ordered the removal of H.B.M. Consul from this Government. The particulars of the atrociousness of the conduct of this vile person will some day be made known.

On Saturday, the first day of May, last, His Excellency, President Roberts left the Government on a tour to England, with a view to sustain the character of the Government and People of Liberia, by successfully refuting the base, false, and foul slandrous reports that have been charged upon her by Mr. Hanson and the unprincipled english traders that have frequented [the] coast, for the purpose of trade, and who have basely taken the advantage of the leniency of our Government with regard to the manner of controlling their trade with citizens and natives.

We have now a Brazillian Charge de Affairs living among us at present; but really, madam, I am not able to tell you what is his business here farther than by report, and that is that he wishes to negotiate with our Government for a tract of land to colonize the worn out, and unruly Brazillian slaves—a people that we do not want among us at all. He has not yet made known to the Government the object of his coming here as yet; for all I know though he has been officially received. The name of this wonderful personage is His Excellency Noterio, Chavallier Brazillian Charge de Affairs, and minister Extraordinary, and minister of Plenipotentiary, and envoy of His Imperial Majesty, the Emperor of Brazil, to the Court of Liberia.

The Government of France have negotiated a treaty with the Government of Liberia, of amity and Peace and Commerce; it has not yet been finally ratified by both governments; it is now undergoing the necessary discussions for ratification before the extra Session of the Senate now in session, convened for that purpose.

The religion, habits, manners, customs and dress of the unattended to portions of the aboriginees among us are so vague and insignificant that the children are imbibing some of the lowest principles. We hope for better, if worse Come.

This communication has to be forwarded by way of England, because the conveyance that was expected by the barque Ralph Cross is blasted by the unfortunate circumstance of that vessel being wrecked. I have the honor to be Yours most Respectfully,   James C. Minor

14 / JAMES C. MINOR TO AGENT, AMERICAN COLONIZATION SOCIETY

Monrovia, Aug. 27th, 1852

Rev. & Dear Sir: In reply to yours under a former date (the letter not being before me) you made some observations respecting the propriety of using lie about the type; that is all very good, but when the hair strokes of the type are worn away, I cannot see how in the name of peace they can make a good impression. We want new type. Those that we have are all well worn out. We want ink & paper. As time will not permit me to enter into a detail of things, I beg to close by saying that I hope you will forward us the necessary materials for carrying on our work, and do not publish my letter, as it is not intended to be. For the Herald,

J. C. Minor

15 / JAMES C. MINOR TO JOHN MINOR

To John Minor, Esq.   Monrovia, January 15th, 1853

Dear Sir: I avail myself of this opportunity of acknowledging the receipt of two volumes of Blackstone's Commentaries, presented to me by you, which came safe to hand by the Rev. Mr. Scott who came out in the barque Shirley which arrived in our harbor on the 1st day of this month; for which I return you many thanks. It shall be my earnest endeavor to make the best proficiency in the act of the study of Same, that I can.

As our community is on the increase, and there arise many cases for adjudication, which comes within the [purview] of some of us who tries to do just between man and man.

I have written to you very often but have never received any answer to any of them; it was not until I received a letter from Mrs. Blackford that I learned where you at present reside. It shall be my constant care to embrace every opportunity to write to you.

The English postal steam line have commenced and will touch here on both their outward and homeward route, and by that means will render the conveyance of letters more convenient than heretofore. One of them, the "Deer" have already touched here on her outward route and will be the conveyance by which this letter will find its way to England and then to its port of destination.

We have at length formed a masonic lodge here. It organized in the fall of 1851 and we have celebrated the 27th of December twice. I was regularly init[iat]ed an E[ntered] Ap[prentice], then passed to the [one word undecipherable] degree of a C[raft] M[ason], then raised [to the] Sublime degree of M[aster] M[ason], so passed on and now, dear Sir, as I have every rea[son] to believe that you are in possesion of de[grees] far above any that I have alluded to and know the full regalia belonging to both the M[aster] M[ason] and P[ast] M[aster] will you send me out the full regalia belonging to both of these degrees and the bill of cost of them. We have no royal arch C[ommandery] as yet but expect to have it some day and should I live and join that I will want regalia for that too.

President Roberts of this Republic of whom you have heard much talk no doubt and who went to England last year for the adjustment of some difficulties between this Government and that of Great Brittain, returned on the 10th of December [18]52, crowned with the success of having amicably adjusted all pending difficulties between [this] government and that.

Our Presidential Election will come off in May next, the first Tuesday; that of yours is over.

Our Legislature, which commenced its session on the first Monday in December, 1852, adjourned on the 3rd inst. after holding a session of about 25 days.

I have been informed that your mother still enjoys bad health. Sorry for that.

I would propose to you [the] propriety of entering into a sort of commercial business, by way of shipping a small lot of assorted domestic goods all fancy of various patterns and kinds, and of provisions, for sale and returns, provided that such [a] proposition is not contratry to the course of your business, as the amount of two or three hundred dollars worth of saleable domestic goods and a varied assortment of fanciables of female and gentlemen's ware and wholesome provisions, would find a ready market here. Should such a course sute, and you make the experiment or venture, you may rely on prompt attention in every respect; the payment, and lone would be as you desire [as would] information in connection with all necessary advice and instructions.

Please receive our regard [for] yourself, and for your dear Mother. Yours truly with much Respect,   James C. Minor

16 / JAMES C. MINOR TO GEORGE SAMPLE

Mr. George Sample   Monrovia, Liberia, April 18, 1853

Dear Sir: By the reception of this letter you may know that I am living, thank God, and hope that you are well. Should you ever take a notion to come to this Republic, I would advise you to bring with you the following named articles in as large quantity as you can conveniently do: pork, beef, flour, fish, assorted; mackerel, herrings, smoked and pickled; codfish, soap, tea, coffee, butter, lard, dry goods, assorted; bleached and unbleached cottons, shirting cotton, domestic plaids, shoes, stockings, table knives and forks, bonnet ribbons, muslins of various patterns, for ladies wear, white muslins, spools of cotton, skeins d[itt]o, pins, needles, toothbrushes, and in fine any and everything that you can. And if you have not the means to purchase these articles you can get some friend to give you a credit of some four or five hundred dollars for a few months, and you can soon sell enough of them to pay for them. In your selection for ladies wear, do get some lady to assist you to make choices, for the ladies here are very flashy and wear no mean dresses. Yours, &c.,

James C. Minor

17 / JAMES C. MINOR TO MARY B. BLACKFORD

Monrovia, October 1st, 1853

Dear Madam: I embrace this opportunity of writing you a few lines to inform you of my health and that of my family, which is tolerably good at present, thank God, and to say that we hope that your health is also very good, and all of the family.

There is nothing strange about which to write you. We have not had any alarming sensation of trouble nor any fearful foreboding of approaching difficulties. Affairs seem to be moving gradually along. A state of quietude and peace seems to be our chief companion now. The general interests of the country seems to engage the attention of the principal men of the Government. Our revenue is, I believe, on the increase. The imports from foreign countries amounts to several hundred thousands of dollars pr annum, and the exports of the products of the country lies not far behind that amount.

Doctors W. W. Davis, and Jas. Brown, both eminently useful men, have been recently called from labor to reward.[1] Their abilities, both in the Legislative Hall and the Pharmacutical department, have been fully tested. They, like the immortal [Colin] Teage, will be missed from their posts of honor. I informed you of the interview that I had with Rev. Mr. Scott, and also with Bishop Payne, which was interesting. Our harbour has been visited lately by several U.S. Naval cruisers, the Constitution of which Mr. John Rudd is Capt. and the U.S. Ship Marion. They are all on the leeward route now. Our communication route is still kept up with England.

Abraham and his family has gone up the country to live, near Cape Mount; he was well when I heard from him last, and beged to be kindly rembered to you all when I wrote again. Please receive our warmest regard and compliments. Yours, &c.,

J. C. Minor

18 / MARY ANN MINOR TO RALPH R. GURLEY

To Rev. R. R. Gurley   Monrovia, August 19th, 1857

Kind Sir: I embrace the present favorable opportunity of writing you, to say how do you do! I [hope] that yourself and family are all well. My health for the last two years has been very poor but at present [is] some what improved.

 I send for your perusal a printed copy of an address delivered by Mr. E. W. Blyden,[1] on the occasion of the 26th, otherwise the 27th of July at the celebration of Liberia's Independence.

The letters written by you, to my son James [have] been received, but I do not know whether they have been answered or not, as he is not at home now, nor has not been for six months.

During the past rainy season the citizens generally suffered much for want of bread stuff for it is very scarce and could not be bought, scarcely at any place, nor at any price. We are now recovering from the severity of want. The farmers in Monsterado County have entered the bowels of the earth with determination, if possible, [before] another rain to beat back so ugly a monster as the Man "Weather."

From the Rev. John Seys you will be able to learn all particulars.[2] Our city has been much improved by the erection of substantial buildings.

I should be much pleased to see you in our City once more.

There is no sound of war heard now among the surrounding tribes. Very Respectfully Yours,   Mary Ann Minor

2/LETTERS OF THE JOHN HARTWELL COCKE NEGROES

John Hartwell Cocke, born near Jamestown, Virginia, September 19, 1780, was the son of a wealthy Virginia planter.[1] He attended William and Mary College where he was influenced by the deistic, natural rights, antislavery ideas popular among that generation of aristocratic Virginians. On his twenty-first birthday Cocke became owner of several thousand acres of land on the James River and more than one hundred slaves. Soon afterward, he married Anne Barraud who before her death in 1816 bore him six children. In 1819, after serving as a general in the War of 1812, he built a mansion on his Bremo plantation in Fluvanna County, and two years later, at age forty-one, he married Louisa Maxwell Holmes, a deeply religious widow who shared his antislavery views. Among the sixteen house servants at Bremo was Lucy Nicholas Skipwith who, as a sort of second mother, helped rear the Cocke children;[2] their intimate playmates were Lucy's progeny, among whom were Peyton Skipwith, who became a stonemason, and George, who in maturity served intermittently as driver and overseer on the Cocke plantations.

In 1817 Cocke became a member of the American Colonization Society. During the debates over emancipation in the Virginia legislature in 1831-1832 he wrote: "I have long and do still steadfastly believe that slavery is the great cause of all the chief evils of our land, individual as well as national. . . . How is it that all will not agree faithfully and honestly about the work of removing this blot upon our national escutcheon—this cancer eating upon the vitals of our commonwealth."[3] Like many of his contemporaries, Cocke thought that colonization was a necessary accompaniment of emancipation. With the view of preparing his slaves for freedom and a new life in Africa, Cocke established a school at Bremo for their education and development. Instruction was given by his wife and by a white teacher imported from the North.

In 1833 Cocke emancipated and sent to Liberia eight of his slaves: Peyton Skipwith, age thirty-one; Peyton's wife, Lydia; and their six children, Diana, Matilda, Felicia, Martha, Nash, and Napoleon. The certificate of emancipation that Cocke gave to Peyton indicated that he chose this family as the first émigrés because he thought them best qualified physically and morally to cope with conditions in Africa. He also stated that one of his motives was to have this Christian family "carry civilization & the blessed Gospel to the benighted land of their fore-fathers."[4]

The hardship experienced by Peyton and his family in Africa confirmed Cocke's opinion that slaves must be thoroughly trained in moral living and self-support before being sent to Liberia. This conclusion caused him to begin to acquire land in Greene County, Alabama, to use as a training place for prospective emigrants. These Black Belt purchases when completed in the 1850s aggregated about 2,000 acres and from them two plantations eventually were formed: Hopewell and New Hope. In 1840 he transferred 49 slaves to the Hopewell site and in 1850 they were joined by 23 more of the Bremo slaves. In both instances the blacks sent to Alabama were persons whom Cocke considered the most promising prospects for emancipation and colonization. Among them were a good representation of artisans, cooks, and spinners, and most of these were hired out to neighboring planters soon after their arrival in Alabama.

In March 1841 Cocke called his Alabama slaves together and disclosed to them his plan for their emancipation. This called for their earning the equivalent of their value, which he estimated to average $1400 per slave. While contributing their share to the freedom fund they were required to be honest and faithful workers, forego strong drink, have daily prayers, and be submissive to their supervisors.

In Alabama Cocke provided a school run by a literate slave woman to promote preparation for freedom. Educational progress was slow, but in December 1854 Cocke reported that seventeen adults and seven children had learned to read the Bible and seven children knew the alphabet.

Cocke hoped that the Alabama blacks would meet his requirements for freedom in a period of from five to seven years. In this he was sorely disappointed. Most of them seemed to have worked reasonably well. But unfavorable weather, recurrent ravages of the army worm, sickness, and poor supervision held plantation profits at a low level. Even more discouraging was the failure of the blacks to live up to Cocke's high standards of moral living. George Skipwith, of whom much was expected as driver and overseer, became a chronic alcoholic and among his associates observance of the rules of chastity left much to be desired.

Not until 1852 did any of the Alabama blacks meet Cocke's requirements for freedom. Late that year he accompanied Sucky [Susan] Faulcon who, he boasted, "had never been charged with prostitution" and her two children Agnes and George to New Orleans and turned them over to officials of the American Colonization Society for transportation to Liberia. In Monrovia Sucky was reunited with her son, John Faulcon, whom Cocke in 1838 had apprenticed to Peyton Skipwith to learn the stonemason's trade.

Later in the 1850s a few more Cocke blacks went from Alabama to Liberia. But the total number graduating from the "school of freedom" before the Civil War was only fourteen.

Meanwhile, in 1842, Cocke had arranged for shipment from Virginia to Liberia of eight blacks emancipated by the will of his deceased sister, Mrs. Sally Faulcon. They were: Robert Leander Sterdivant and his three children Diana, Rose, and William Leander; three brothers, Richard Cannon, James Nicholas, and Peter Jones; and Julia Nicholas.[5]

Until his death in 1866, Cocke followed closely the careers of the blacks whom he had sent to Liberia. They wrote him and members of his household, both black and white, many letters, most of which were preserved in the Cocke Papers, now at the University of Virginia.[6] Fifteen of the letters were written by Peyton Skipwith, a truly remarkable man who, after a period of disillusionment and sickness, adjusted well to Liberia. His wife and his daughter Felicia died early in their Liberian sojourn, but he married another immigrant from America, a widow with two children, and kept working away at his trade of laying stone. He also did some farming and, with tobacco and other items sent to him by his former master, engaged in trade with other Liberians. Peyton became an officer in a militia unit and took part in at least two military campaigns, one against a slave-trading establishment and the other against a native ruler whom he called a "savage king." Two of his daughters, Diana and Martha, attended school in Liberia and were active in the Baptist church. Martha died in 1844. Peyton himself died October 14, 1849; in the last of his letters, addressed to his mother, he stated: "My efforts have been crowned with Success from on high. . . . And I still feels as if the Lord will bless me in all my undertakings if I put my trust in him." Reliance on Divine Providence undoubtedly was a great source of strength to Peyton Skipwith as he made the difficult transition from American slavery to Liberian freedom. For that faith and for the ability to maintain himself and his family in Africa, he owed much to his former master, a fact which he freely acknowledged in his letters to Bremo.

Eighteen letters were written by Peyton's daughter Matilda. Her religious faith and her strength in adversity were comparable to the trust and staunchness of her father. Her first husband, Samuel B. Lomax, was drowned in 1850, and a second, James Richardson, died in 1860, but Matilda bore these and other trials with a minimum of complaint. In her last letter to her former master she stated: "I have seen a great deal of trouble and am now left all in the hands of the Lord."

Peyton's other children wrote few letters to their former master. One of them, Nash, until his death in 1851 assumed responsibility for the maintenance of Peyton's widow and children and several other close relatives. He apparently followed the trade of carpenter-mason and he acquired enough education to lead him in one of his letters to ask Cocke for a shipment of twelve books, including a large dictionary and four volumes of history.

Of the other letters the most interesting are those written by James P. Skipwith, a cousin of Matilda who migrated in 1857, and Sucky Faulcon. Sucky's daughter, Agnes, died enroute to Liberia and the bereaved mother had a hard time adjusting to life in Africa; but her religious faith helped her to bear all her troubles. James Skipwith was at first pessimistic as to his prospects in Liberia, but as he applied himself to farming, church work, and other activities, his morale improved. In his letter of May 31, 1860, he stated that Liberia "is the Best Country for the Black Man that is to be found on the face of the Earth."

19 / PEYTON SKIPWITH TO JOHN H. COCKE

Monrovia, Liberia, Febuary the tenth, 1834

Dear Sir: I embrace this oppertunity to inform you that we are all in moderate health at this time hoping that these few lines may find you and yours enjoying good health. After fifty Six days on the ocean we all landed Safe on new years day and hav all had the fever and I hav lost Felicia but I thank god that our loss is hur gain.[1] As Job Sais the lord gave and he taketh. I thank god that he has mad it possible that we may meet to part no more. I thank god that we are all on the mend. I cannot tell you much about Liberia. I hav not been from Monrovia yet. As it respects my Self and wife we are dis Satis fide in this place. Their is Some that hav come to this place that have got rich and anumber that are Sufering. Those that are well off do hav the nativs as Slavs and poor people that come from america hav no chance to make aliving for the nativs do all the work.[2] As it respects farming their is no Chance for it unless we would get the nativs to work for us and then you must be wit them and at the Same time when we ought to put in our grain it rains So hard that we dare not be out unless exposing our health. Their is no chance for farming in monrovia for it is a Solid body of Stones but they say at Caulwell is achance but Still I find that but few faver it. As it respects Stone masons they can get a good price, three dollars and a half a perch. A pearch is fo[u]r foot high and four foot wide but the Sun is So hot that people from america can not Stand it in the dry Season and in the wet it rains to much. Their has Some come from america that hav learnt the nativs and they hav hierd them to put up a two Story house eighteen by twenty for twenty galens of rum. As it respect Coffe it Sells at 50 Cents per pound. I hav Seen the coffe tree and all So Coffe on them.

Their is but a few treas in their gardens and as it respects that wich grow wild the nativs and monkeys take it. The nativs do bring theirs to town. Loaf Shugar Sells at twenty eight dollars per hundred, brown Shugars at twenty five dollars per hundred, pork twenty five dollars per hundred. We hav a little fresh beef and it Sells at twelve Cents per pound. As it respects the fruit in this Country it is to tedious to mention at this time but new comers dare not eate much of it. I have not Seen enough of the Country to tell you much more at this time but will tell you more when I See more of the place. I want you if you please to write to me by the first oppertunity and let me no on what terms I can come back for I intend coming back as Soon as I can. I must Come to a close. Give my respects to all the family and allso to all inquiering friends. My wife allso and children Sends their respects to you all. Direct your letters to monrovia.   Peyton Skipwith

20 / PEYTON SKIPWITH TO JOHN H. COCKE

Monrovia, March 6th, 1835

Dear Sir: I embrace this oppertunity to write you these few lines to inform you that I am not well with a blindness of nights so that I cannot see. All the information that I can get from the doctors is that [I] must stop laying stone. I have lost my wife. She died on July 2d, 1834. The rest of my family are tolerable well. Sir This is the third letter that I have wrote to you and have received no answer and would be thankful if you would write by the first chance and I do not know of any better chance than to write by Mr. Jos. J. Roberts. I wonce had a notion of coming home and still have a notion but I want to go up to Sirrilione [Sierra Leone] as I am advised by the doctors to quit laying s[t]one for it is injurious to my health & if I get my health by going there I will s[t]ay there. If not will return back to America. Give my respects to your family, also to the people. Let my Mother know that you have received a letter from me. I dont want you to say any thing to [her] about my being blind but let her know that I will return. Dianah send her love to Miss Sally[1] and all of the family and is very desirous of returning back again. She wants you to write her word also by the first oppertunity. Let her know how Miss Nancy Cavil and her family [are]. I have put myself to a gread deal of truble of searching [for]the servent of Mr. Cavil and also that of Mr. Harris but I cant find eather of them. Nothing more but I remain yours truly,   Peyton Skipwith

21 / PEYTON SKIPWITH TO JOHN H. COCKE

Monrovia, Liberia, April 27th, 183[6]

Dear Sir: Yours by Bro. James Byrd came safe to hand. He arrived here after a passage of about thirty six days. When I wrote you by Mr. B. Wilson I truly were in a distress situation. My health at that time was not good, and I expected to become blind as my eyes faild me daily, and the Doctor had advised me to stop work and travel for my health.

The idea of being in a new country with a large family of helpless childrine, who could depend only on me for support, & I being so indisposed as to be of no use to them nor myself having no means and the prospect of their suffering made me feel distressed and greatly so but thanks be to God my health and sight is recovered and that day of awful gloom is gone and I feel satisfied with my present home and desire no other. I write by almost every opportunity but cannot tell how it comes to pass that only two of my letters have [been] received. For sometime passed we have not had a regular School as we have at present. I have two of my children now in school and the others I instruct at home.

I cannot express the comfort it gives me of hearing of your health, of the family and my friends and relations in general and would be [manuscript torn]. . . . I had time to write your at greater [torn]. . . . but this is now in haste as the [torn]. . . . Vessel is expected to sail in a few hours. I am still Single myself and so are my daughters. I received the tracts on temperence, am still an advocate for the cause, and rejoice to say that as to the use of ardent Spirits there never was a more temperate community. It remains now to be put down as an article of trade and the point is gained. The amt of ten Dollars you requested Mr. McPhail to forward never reached me. If you find it convenient to send us such articles as provisions they will be of more use to us than any thing else for there are times that we are obliged to suffer for such things as must be expected in a new country where we are not yet prepared to raise for ourselves enough for support.

Give my love to all the family both white and colored and all my friends in general. I shall end[eavor] to give evry par[ticular] the next time I write. Respectfully Yours in the bonds of Christian affection,

Peyton Skipwith

22 / DIANA SKIPWITH TO SALLY COCKE

Aug. 24, 1837

Dear Miss Sally: I take this opitunity of writing yo theas fue lines to in form yo that I and family are well and hope that theas fue lines may find yo the Saim. I am hapy to in form yo that we are much beter Satisfy with this place than we were the last time we roten to yo awl. We are much helther now than we ever was. Times has bin verry hard for Something to eat but now the natives are foching in rice and it is not So hard now. I think verry hard of you not ritting me a letter but howsoever I Suspose that you had not time. I go to School to Mr. Le[w]is Jhonston and I think that he is one of the bes School masters in the town.[1] He is verry Stud[ious]. My Sister matilda go to Miss ivens.[2] The climet is getting much beter than it was when we caim out hear. My father has got A wound and he can not go upon it so me and my Sister keep house for my father.[3] He has not got married as yet. There are 5 publick School. I hav mention in the first part of leter that me and my Bother Nash goes to Mr. Lewis Johnston and my Sis[t]er matilda and Napolun go to Mis ivens. Martha has got a wound one her foot goin on 6 munts. My father has bought him 2 lots. One of them had a house in which he ar now living in both on groe Stret & his lot what he Draw he has improve it and has got A Deede [to] it and free thinple [fee simple?]. We have got hogs & I have got one but we have kill 3 and the wild Beast has kill 2. The things heare Sell verry dear. Evry yard of cloth Sell for twenty five cts pr yard. Every pare of Stockens Sel for 100 [cents] and dollar and half. The infearest Shoe in the Colony is goan [at] three dollars a pare. Yo cannot get even So much as one fould [fowl] without gaving twenty five cents for it. So thire fore if yo are pleast to Send us Some thing, Some to bacco in perti[c]lar for tobaco Sell twenty five cents a pound. Pleas to Send us out Some flower or anything that yo awl hav to Spar for we Stand in neede of Somthin verry much. Meat is a great nesesity hear. Yo awl must know that we Stand in need of theas things for we awl Like to Starv this Season and I hop that yo will take us in con Sid erration and Send us Some thing. We have got our yard planted in potatoes and cassaders. Pleas to Send us out Some of awl kind of Seeds for we cannot [get] any Seeds to plant. Yo wil be please to Send me out [some] paper for I hav [been] triing two days and could not get any paper but this one Sheet. Tel master and Mistes that I think they treat me with contemp. Gave my best respect to them. I am glad to hear that master in joy his health. I have no good nous to ri[te] yo at this time pressent. We have to gave two dolars for half Bushel of rice. Ther is Some of the Beau[t]ifully bullock hear that I ever Saw and Some of the largest. Gave my best respect to my granmother and au[n]t luvena and to uncle Geoge and tel them that [they] dont think as much of me as to rite me a letter. Pleas to rite me a word if the School is goin now and if Betsy can rit good and tell her that She would of Send her love to me if noth[ing] els. I should like to come Back thire again and we expect of coming back again. Gave my love to ant Lizy and to ant Cissiah and to uncle Ned. Gave my love to awl incuiring friends. This is Some of my one hand riting. Do yo think I improv or not? Tel ned that the children Send thire love to him. No more But remain yours,   D[i]ana Skipwith

23 / PEYTON SKIPWITH TO JOHN H. COCKE

Monrovia, January 30, 1838

Honored Sir: I embrace this opportunity of writing you these few lines to inform you that my health is very bad at present; I have a wound that has lasted me for more than five months, and it is not well yet. I have not been able to do any work for nearly that length of time. The wound is not well, though I believe it is on the mend. My two small boys have wounds, for such are the diseases of a tropical climate. The three girls are in good health, and as these leaves us in as good health as could be expected, we hope that they may find you and your family enjoying of very good health. Your letter dated the 12th of Nov. 1837, was received a few days since, by the arrival of the ship Emperor, and read with much pleasure. Sir, here permit me in a very few words to lay before you, some of the difficulties that I have had to encounter with since my arrival in Africa; As it respects my trade, I can get as much work as I can well attend to when I am in possession of my health and have the use of my feet. Rock work is worth from Two Dollars and fifty cents to Three Dollar per perch; and day work is worth per day $1.50; but the payment which workmen get here for their work is of the most inferior sort, and at the dearest rate; viz: cloth, Tobacco, powder, pipes, &c. all of which are paid to workmen at the highest market price, so that we are unable to trade them off at the least advantage. I have put a stone wall for a school house, 30 feet by 20, for the Ladies Society in Richmond, one story and a half high for $275 [$2.75] per perch, but I have not the money for it yet. I under stand that Rev. J. J. Matthias, Governor to Bassa Cove, is empowered to settle the claim, as he has the money in hand which I presume he will pay shortly, according to what Leut. Gov. A. S. Williams says, being employed by him to put up the wall.[1] By the ship Emperor forty days passage from Norfolk Virginia, I received the hoghead of Tobacco which you sent me, for which you made a demand of $55; but I do not think it prudent in me to send the money by this Brig as she is bound for New York. But the ship Emperor will sail after trading a little on the coast, the[n] I will send you the money. I am very much oblige to you for the Tobacco, indeed, but is rather short, not withstanding it arrived here in good time. The shortness of the tobacco may prevent the quick sale of it, as we use it principally for native trade, though I may be able to sell it in the rains, which is fast approaching. I would be glad if you would appoint an Agent in New York, and write me his name, the street on which he lives, the number &c. so that I may have some person to sent your money to. John is living with me.[2] He arrived here safe and in good health. He has not got the fever yet. He is much pleased with his new home, and bids fair for usefulness in this place, though all new-comers seem well pleased with the place. John is going to school every day to the Methodist Mission School. You says that you wish me to let you know what things I stand in need off, which I will do in another letter. Noth[ing] More at present but Remain your &c Truly,

Peyton Skipwith

24 / DIANA SKIPWITH TO SALLY COCKE

Monrovia, January 30, 1838

Dear Miss Sally [Cocke]:   I rite you theas fue lines to inform you that I and family are well and hope that theas fue lines will find you the saim. This mak the 4 letter I have rote to you and have reseaved one ondly but I hope you will answer these fue lines. Master say that mistress answer my letter but I never get it.

I have not rote a long letter because I have not paper. If you pleas to send me out some paper & tell grandmother that I have not forgot her for I have not any paper. This paper I got it out of my copy book. I am going to send you 4 peases of ginger for youal to plant. The largest peas is for you and you wil give [a] peace to Mistress and a peace to grandmother and [a] peace to Miss Ann Covil. I have sent some seads to you. They go by the naim of sower sap seads. You mus plant them in the hot house. The fruit that grows and the tree is very nice.

I have not say as much as I want to say because opitunity wil not admit, Please to answer this letter. Give my love to all of my inquireing friends to my grandmother [in] particular. Nothing more but remain yours until Death.   Diana Skipwith

25 / DIANA SKIPWITH TO SALLY COCKE

Monrovia, Liberia, May 7, 1838

Dear Miss Salla: I rite you theas fue lines to inform you that I and family are well exsept my father and he is verry unwell with his wound. The last of this month wil make 10 monts Since he has hit a lick for his Self or any person els.

The rest of the family is quit well. John H. Faulcon is going to School and the rest of the family all So. The fever was Quit[e] faverable with him. I think that this Cuntry agrea with him.

I was verry Sorry to hear that my grand father was Ded But one thing give me great consolation. I know that he is gone home to Rest and we have nothing to do but to p[r]epare and meat him.

I have nothing Strange to tell you. Times is verry dul hear in this colony. I rote a fue lines to you by the Brig Susan Elithebeth. I Send a Small Bundle to you with Some Sowersap Seads and Some green ginger for you to plant, I am going to Send you Some more Seeds by Mr. Mils. If you should get them you had better plant them in the hot house. Sowersap is one of best fruit that we have in this cuntry. I am going to Send you one of the Seads which will be the large Sead and it is call the mangrove [mango] plum. It is some what like the plumb peach and verry nice in taste; I am verry glade to hear that the Scholl is Stil going on and that master has bild A church for the people. They had better be thire [than] to be hear Sufferin Enlest they had Some money to Start with. You will be pleas to tell the people that I would rite to them but I have not the paper. Give my love to Mistress Ann Cabble and tell her that I thought She would of rite to me before now. I have never reseave the money that you Send to me yet but I hope that I wil get it in a time for I stand verry much in nead of it. I am verry much ablige to you for it. I wish that I could See your faice for I cannot take rest of nights Dreaming About you. Some times I think I am thire and when I awake I am hear in Liberia & how that dos greave me but I cannot healp my Self. I am verry fraid I shal never See your faice again but if I never Do I hope I Shal meat [you] in the kingdom. Give my best respect to Master and Master John and Master Chas. and Miss Nancy Moldan. I was verry glad to hear that Master Philip was Marred. Rite me word whether you is Marred or not. You wil be pleas to Send me Some paper & Some books. I have nothing Earging to Say. I wil close by Say[ing] I remains yours,

Diana Skipwith

26 / DIANA SKIPWITH TO LOUISA H. COCKE

May the 8, 1838, Monrovia

Dear Mistress Louisana: I reseave your Litter Dated Oct. 27, 1837. I was hapy to hear from you. All the family is well Excepting my father and he is Still down with his wound. If he is Spard to see the last of this month it will make 9 month since he has work any. John Faulcon is quit[e] well. He is still going to school. The fever went quite Light. The money that Master Send to my Father he have not reseave it yet. He says as soon as he get it he wil let him know. I know dout but what he wil Say Something to him upond the subgect. You will tell grandmother that father Talks of comeing back but his wound bother him but I think if his wound ever get wel and if he can get money Enough he wil come for he want to come back as bad as She want him to come. We ware amase to hear that Grand Father was ded but was hapy to hear that he was gone home to rest. We was hapy to hear that our uncle Erasmus is maid his peace with god.[1] All so I was hapy to hear that Master has bild A church for the cullard people. I know that they injoy thereselvs better than they would hear. They things that Grand Mother Send to us we get the hankerchievs and one pare of socks but as to the frocks and socks we never get them. Tell betsy that I reseave the hankerchief. Tel her for me if that was her hand riting She can right wel enough to rite to me for I dos want to get a letter from her verry bad. Tell her that I was verry much ablige to her for it. Tell her school she wil mak a Mishinary before long. I have nothing Strang to tel you. I am going to Send Some Seads by Mr. Mils to you and Miss Salla. The largist sead that I wil send you must take good care of it. It is some of the inglish fruit very nice. The naim of it is mangrove pl[u]mb. It tase some what lik plumb peach. Give my love to all of the friends and tel them that I would of rote to some of them but paper was lacking. Give my love to uncle nedd and his wife to ant Cissiah and tel them that I want to se them very bad. I have nothing more to say at Pressent but I still remain yours,   Diana Skipwith

27 / PEYTON SKIPWITH TO JOHN H. COCKE

John H. Cocks   May 9, 1838, Monrovia

Dear Master: I rite you theas fue lines to inform you that I am verry unwell but the rest of the family are well and I hope that theas fue lines will find you the Saim,

I rite you by the Brig Susan Elithebeth but I dont know whither they come to hand or not. As it respect the Tobaco you Send me I have not Sold it and I will give you my reasen why. If I Sel it at publick Auction it wil fetch verry little and thire have bin So much Fiting with the Natives that they dont Come to town. Thire-fore I thaught best to wait A whil as I knew that you was not in imediant want of it at pressent. I am in hopes in a Short time this war among the natives wil be done; the head man Jinkens have bin at war with the Golar Tribe.[1] Come down to our agence & desiar him to Stop the war and Show him plan what to fall upon that the war might be Stop and the plan that he fall upon was Simply this, that he wil not fite the Golar tribe and if the Golar wil cetch his people he want to know if our governor wil portect him. A commity of 3 men was

Chosen to goe and See what termes would the Golar Stop upon but the Commity has not return yet. I wil now go ond to tel you of a Sertain Death took place by M. D. Logan a gentleman from the City of Richmon. He was a man of wealth and had a great deal of influance amung the heathens but he got whim-Sic-al and thought proper to leave the Cape and to go and Seak a cuntry Seat a bout 9 miles from the Cape. He went on doing bisiness with the natives trading and So forth. After he had bin thire about 5 mounts they came down a large tribe of heathens with Bullocks, Came wood [camwood], & ivry and amoung them thire was Some that was in debt to him and they had a Bullock which he went up and seas and give it to a nother gentleman whome he had as a companion. As Soon as he don that the natives Sirround him and Say that he Should [not] have it. They attemp to tak it & he cill one of the men. Mr. Logan was brot down to stand a trial. He was brote in gilty by the Grand Jurry and the petti Jury Clear him. Mr. Logan was then advised not to go to his cuntry Seat a gain but he say that he would for he and Mr. Harris was not afraid & he return back to his farm and was not thire 3 weaks before thire Came a nother tribe down to him with Came wood and ivry for him to by & whiles he was waing the wood one of them draw of with his Cutlis and Struck him down to the ground & cilled him. [When] Mr Harris saw that, he up with a hatchet & maid the attemp to cill this fellow but he mist it and [when] the others saw this [they] throw thire Spear at him and he being up to thire Capers Caught it and run a way with it and then they Shot him cilled and they took every thing that they wanted out of the house and then put Logan in it and Set it afire.[2]

A nother Sircom Stance, thire was a Mr Grean a Emerican, ho keep factry at little Bassa. His money growed Short and he went in the cuntry and took two natives boys and he told thire fathers that he was going to learn them to Speak inglish. He brote them to his factory and the ver night one of them run a way. He rose up in morning and took the one that [was] lef and carried him to the Slave factory and Sold him. He Sold him for 2 Two Dubble lowns [doubloons] and one peace of cloth cost about 5 Dollars; in short time the news reach Edina which is about 20 miles from little Bassa and they send and had him arest by the natives. They brought him to edina for a trial. He resist against the natives and would not be taking by them but they wounded him verry much. He was tried before the jestos peace and they found that they had no power to try a sienson [citizen] of Monrovia and he was sent up to Monrovia [to] have a trial and he Stud two trial and at last the petti Jury clear him; I dont know what wil become of the Colony.[3]

The richist of the men seam to be failing for they have mogage thire propity to the firroners & I exspect before long thire wil be a great desstress with them. Captain Tailor is hear now, an inglish man, and he has given his agent power to Sue for his rits. One thing what pleas me they have not got no money and they are oblige to go to farming. You may know that this is the fact for thire is two vessel in harber; hats that use to be 5 dollars is orford for 150 cents. Brass that use to be $1 is offerd for fifty cents. Clothes and varias things is orford as cheap durt and thire is not money in the colony to bye. I had the pleasur of seing Mr. Mils last sabbath evening. He hold prairs in my house. This is the second time I have sean him since he hav bin out hear. He is now about to leav for amerrica and by him I rite you. I wil be verry glad if you wil Send me a cag [keg] of Shingles nails and some Riting paper. I wish you to appoint an agent in new york or some person whome you can place confident in. John is got through the fever verry well so far. He is now going to School. You desire me to rite whither my children was going to the Richmon Ladies Sosiety School or not. They never was a School thire for it [is] so much out of the way it is unconvinent for them to go but as Soon the new School house is don I wil send them. Give my respect to all of your family and to Miss Nancy Moldon. Pleas to give my love [to] Mr. and Mistress C. T. Cabble. Give my love to all inquireing friends. I have nothing more to Say at pressent but I Stil Remain yours,

Peyton Skipwith

28 / PEYTON SKIPWITH TO LUCY NICHOLAS SKIPWITH

Lucy Nichels   May 10, Monrovia, Liberia

Dear Mother: I rite you theas fue lines to infom you that I am verry unwell but the rest of the family is quit[e] wel[l] and I hope that these fue lines will find you in good health; I am in hopes that you will not greav after Father because I beleav if he keep the faith he is gone to beter world then this. All that you wil have to do mother is to prepare to meat death for the Lord giveth and the Lor Takeeth and blessed is the nam of the lord. I have not greve after my father for I be leav that he is gone to a better world than this. I was more shock when I heard the death of Cussan Charls be cause you did not rite me whither he maid his peace with god or not. Tell my brother Erasmus [to] deal fair with his self for I know that if the love of god ever was applied to his troubleed con[di]tion he know it. You wish to see me but cant be more disires to see me than I am to see you all. I Calculate to come and see your all this year but this wound have throw me so far back I dont know when I shal be able to come and this mother I hope wil give you consolation: if you never see me no more in this world, I am triing to meat you in a bet ter world than this whare we Shal part no more. Tell Brother George that I hope his faith has not fail. Ask him is he a solder [of the Lord]. Do he mean to fite in the in-dureing of the war? If you dos you go on for I am bound to meat you.

Tell uncle ned that I am verry glad that he is got his family and that he is living well but I am verry much Surprise that he have not rote me a letter Since I have bin hear. Ask brother Gerry do he mean to dy a Sinner or what is calculation. Tel him to write me for I feel consurned bout situation. Tell Lavinia that I Shant say much to her because she told me when I cam from home that nothing Should Seperrate her from the love of god. Tel me by your next letter if all the membres of the temperanse Sosiety that I leav is hold out faith ful. I wil tel you uppon the oner of a man that I have ceep my pleg for I have not baught one gil of Spirrit since I leave emerria [America] nor use it in no way. Give my love [to] Father Primus and his wife and the rest of his family. Tell Charls most that I wish to se him verry much.

It is so teagest [tedious] for me to call all of people naim but give my love to Cissiah and her children to Sam Kello and to all of my inquireing friends fer and near. The children all send thire love to every body. Matilda send her love to ned and aunt Luvina and to the rest of the family. I get the ribbons and hankerchief and one pare of socks. I have not sene mr. minor yet but if my health wil admit I expect to go to Capepalamos for to work nax dries [dry season] and thire I Shal Se him if he dont leve for emmerica before that time.[1] I have nothing more to say.   Peyton Skipwith

29 / DIANA SKIPWITH TO LOUISA COCKE

To Mrs. Louisa Cock   Monrovia, Liberia, May 20, 1839

My Dear Madam: Though i [am] not concious of having any thing to offer for the consolation of your mind yet i canot refrain from imbracing this oppitunity which pressent it self of sending you a line if it serve only to assure you that i reseave your letter in time. You request of me and my Father to come over to Emerrica but i do not excpect ever to come thire a gain not because i will not but becawse i cannot. But i think that my Father will come over before long but it is quite convininent for him to com by this oppitunity know [now] that he have bin wonded So long but are now restore to his health a gain. I could not arange his bisness for to come just now. I Trust that i will see your face a gain but i am affraid that i never will in this world. I am constran to say like the Monach did, my Friends do they now and then send a wish or a thaught after me? Oh tell me i yet have a friend though a friend i am never to see. It is my hart desiar to come but my Father say that he cannot trust the children to any body exsept me. You may judge by this whither i can come or not. I think that he will mention something concurning of his coming in master letters what time he will come. John Falcon is well and harty. He send much love to you. He is a good obident young man. He is now worken at his Traid. He wish you to give his love to his aunt Daphney and all of his inquireing friends. We reseav the Box that came from you all hands. We ware highly gratefide indead and we give thank to you for the things that you sont to us, me in particular giv you thank for them. You will pleas to give my love to Mrs. Ann Cabell. We have got some curiosities to send you all but forfear that you all will not get them i will ceep them untill my Father come and then i will send it. But if he do not come i will send it by some other oppitunity. You said in your letter that you think some young Fellow have bin trying to make me think well of him but there is not a Native that i have see that i think that i could make myself hapy with. Ware you to see them you would think that i am write in my oppinion all though they ar verry ingenious people. They make some Beautiful Bags which I inte[n]d sending you all some by my father. Remember me kindly to master and to Mrs. Nancy Moreland. My Father is not marrid yet and i do not think that he will get marrid a gain without he get one when he come over to emerrica. You will pleas to give my love to Aund Lisa Cellar and to aunt Casiah and to aunt Mary. You will p[l]eas to give my love to them all. You know that it would be Teagious for me to call all of thire naim but give my Respect to all of the people perticular to my uncle ned edward and his wife and children. Sister wish me to say to you that she know not how to return thanks to you all for the things that was sont to us and She wish you to give her love to all of the people perticular to master and miss Nancy Moreland and master John. She wish you to give her love to grandmother and to her aunt Luvinar and all so her thanks for the things that you have told me i have it to come true. But now i must come to an close. You will pleas to Send your pertition to god that i may repair my ways and turn to Christ. I am your Sincear and humble Servant,   Diana Skipwith

[*In same envelope*]

To betsey mors

Dear Miss: It was with pleasur that i reseave your let[ter] and i [am] in hopes that you will not make this the last time. I am quite well at the presst time and i [am] in hopes that theas few lines will find you the same. It [is] with pleasur that i now answer your letter. My Dear Betsey do you ever think that you will se me face to face a gain? I think not in this world but if we repair our wicked wais and turn to Christ we will shorly se one nother face to face but not in this world. All though i would frealy come yet i cannot. I reseave the things that you sont to me, my Dear miss, and i give you thanks for them. You want to know whether i am marrid or not but i am not and i dont know that i ever shall all though win and tide can bring all things to work to geter and god can work when no man can hinder. You are fur before me. The young man that you mention you was going to [be] marrid to but i do not know him. He is quite a stranger to me. Where was this Mr. Wilems live? My Dear Betsey, my hart in a maner of speaking Blead when i think of you all and think that i never shal se your all face a gain. You will give my love to one and all of the people to my grandmother Bety and father Primus and to all of my inquireing friends. I am your Sincear and Affectionate Servant,   Diana Skipwith

30 / PEYTON SKIPWITH TO JOHN H. COCKE

Monrovia, Liberia, May 20th, 1839

Dear Sir: Having receving you letter dated Nov. 10th, 1838, stating about my wound I have it in my power to state to you that they are all well and [I am] once more spared to be getting on handsomely at my trade and am in tolerable good halth together with my children. I had the misfortune to loose my youngest son accasioned by a soar mouth. I certainly must say that you have bestowed a great kindness on me by giveing me the proceeds of the Hogshead [of] Tobaco. My children are getting on very well and are goeing to school every Day, and I have yet to maintain them all. John Faulcon have been Bound to me to learn my trade and appears to get on tolerable well at present and conduct himself very well. I received the packages that you sent and was very glad of them, also the children. Mr. Minor has sent me word concerning the amt you placed in his hands but he it appears do not wish to send it to me. He wishes to give it to me himself, in person. You stated in yours dated the 28th that you wish me to state to [you] some particulars relative to the colony. For my part I am at a loss what to say. There are so many things that I call trifling. Perhaps [it] may be some advantage to you to know & hear that is the colony has made some effort to exonerate herself from hunger by a few of our ablest men turning thire attentions to agriculture but before that we could have hardly thought that we could have existed for our dependence was mostly on the tribes of the country. Gov. [Thomas] Buchanan have arrivd in the ship Seluda and I hope that the Friends of the Society will either support her colony or let us alone. I beg to be excuse for thus addressing you so harsh as respect the Society. But for three years we thought that they had entirely forsaken us and left us to our own resources. We have continual wars amongst the natives arround about us so that trade is very dull and scarcly any thing doing. The fisherman at Grand Bassa Cove like to have taken that settlement and if they had not to have been such coward it would likely [have] been the case which war is not settled as yet.[1] I did hear that the Gov. did make some effort to effect a peace when he was down there but am not able to know on what conditions but did hear that the head fisherman should say that he did not care how it was &c. The natives are very savage when they think they have the advantage. I also wish to remind you that I see daily the Star Spangled Banner unfurled on the cost of Africa as a protection for the slaver to keep the British man of wars from takeing them which we think as a hand full of peaple to that of the United States a disgrace to her Banner. We if we had vessels could defy thim to take our cross & stripes and Hoist them to her mast head for the protection of the slave trade.[2] Please to send me some stone Hammers & trowels by the Revd C. Teage. Yours in due Respect,   Peyton Skipwith

31 / DIANA SKIPWITH TO SALLY COCKE

Monrovia, Liberia, November 7, 1839

To Miss S. F. Cocke: I now find you much on my mind and I have a desire to see you. In this I will endeavour to write to you and let you know that wee all is living and quite well, but one thing I must say to you that wee think verry strange of you all not writing to us as you all had such a faverable oppitunity by the Rev. C. Teague who leave this place on perpos of paying his friend in Richmond a visit. This gentlemen took our letters promising us that he would put them in the ofice; whether you reseave them or not I do not know. This gentleman was verry close to you all. I should of ben happy indead to hear from you all but not a word could I hear. The gentleman Died on his way out hear, therefore wee could not hear whether he see you all or whether he had any letters or not. We thought verry strange of not getting any [letter]. Did I say strange? I did not know what to think as I wrote to you in my last letter that Father did expect to pay you all a visit when the vesel return, but as he never reseave a Letter by her I do not expect that he will come. There was some things that we wish to know, that is conserning of the Laws of the Cuntry. We hear from People that they are verry strick and I wrote you conserning of it but never get any letter. I do not know what he will do about it. I expect that he will write to [you] conserning of the mater his self. I am happy to tell you that wee all are much better satisfide with this place than we was sometime ago, but I would be much better satisfied if I could only see you all once more and then if I was a Child of God I think I would be ready to Die. I am not out of hart yet. I live in hopes. My Father have bin to war and return back with out a hurt [?] or Sine & Father have sont you & Marster some Newspapers. In them you will see all about the War. I have sent you three of the African Luminary and one hearald.[1] One of the Luminary are for you, one for Miss Louisa and one for Miss Ann Cable. The Hearald are for you. Take them and read them and think of me. If we never more see each other in this world let us try to meat in the other whare parting are no more. I think I said in another leter previous to this one something conserning of Father Wound. It is now Well and he is able to work at his traide. Father will tell you after conserning of the money in his Letter. He can inform you more correctly than I can. I mean the money which Mr. Miner had. I feel a Delicacy in writing to you all for anything, knowing that you all have bin so cind to us since we have bin out hear but I [am] in hopes Miss Sally that you will not think hard of it as things hear is so verry Dear and are not to be had at that. You will, Miss, to send me one Bonnet & a umberrela if you pleas. Madam, is Betsey marrid yet or not? Tell her she leav me verry far behind. Miss S. I am verry much afraid that you will think hard of my writing to you for these things but I Humble Beseach you not to think strange of it as I am in want of them. Pleas to give my respect to Mrs. L. Cocks & tell her that I would of wrote but the vesel was all most about to sail before I knew any thing about it. My love to Mrs. Ann and to Miss Nancy Moreland & to all of my inquiring friends.

To Miss S. F. Cocks

[In same envelope]

Mrs. Lucy Nicholas

My Dear Grandmother: I am most happy to inform you that we are all well at the present time and may this also find you all as this leaves us. My dear G[rand]mother Hapy am I to inform you that we are much better satisfide with the place than we was [some]time back. Father is now able to work at his traid. I have nothing strange at all to say to you but I think that you would like to hear from us was my reason for writing to you. And i do want also to hear from you. I [am] in hope that you may reseave theas fue lines with Joy. I wrote to you by Mrs. C. Teage and I thought that as Mrs. Teage was so close to you all sertainly you all must of writen and the letters never reached us, but not with standing that I trust that you all will endeavor to write by the first oppotunity and you will please to write me how do my Grandmother Bety do, also my Grandfather Primus, Aunt Cisah, Aunt Mary, Aunt Lisa Celler & My Uncle George & Uncle Ned. It would be quite Teageous for me to call all of my friends names but I has not forgot them. Please to give my love to all of them and tell them I do want to see them verry bad. Dear Grandmother I am almost a shame to write to you for anything but [things are so difficult] at this [time] I will venture [?] [a request]. You will pleas to send me some cloth to make me one white frock as there is none to be had in the Colony. Those things is not hard for to get, that is, there is a plenty of every thing in the States and there is none hear. Now my Dear Grandm[other] I will close. My love to all inquiring friends. The Children send their love to you all. I am your Affectionate Daug[hter],

Diana Skipwith.

32 / PEYTON SKIPWITH TO JOHN H. COCKE

Monrovia, Nov 11th, 1839

Dear Sir: I did write you by the way of the Ship Saluda when she was home Last voyage and expected to receevd a letter from you and that the Revd Colin Teage should have Brought it to me but he did not reach his home but died in about fourteen days sail of Monrovia which was a great disappointment to me and friend and also not to receive any inteligences from you nor none of the family as I am always anxious to hear from you all and I thought that the Lord had favour us by sending a regular packet to sail to and from said ports so as we might never want for an oppertunity or have any excuse. It has been very sickly here and has occasiond some few death of our respectable citizens but I believe the rest of the settlers are enjoying tolerable good health at present. With my family the children ar still going to school to days & Sunday school that has Lately been establishd in the Baptist Church of the Town of Monrovia. I think that our Laws Lately made by the agent & council are two binding upon the inhabitants. If they can get along with them in the end they may prove a great benifit. I think that they have occasion the Inhabitants of Monrovia to see all ready by not suffering the spanish [slave] trader to come to the colony that they are in better circumstances. As relates to rice, abundance of rice has come in our Market and some of our retail shops are over run but this would not have [been] the case if the slave dealer had to have been allowd to come in our town for he would have bought from them faster than they could have obtain it. I have sent you the Liberia Herald and Diannah the Luminary which will explain to you what Laws [have been enacted], &c and what we about here [are doing]. I no you all are desireous to see me but it is imposible to come home at this time. I am building a house and the rock and wood has to be carried by the hand of men so you must no that I can make but little progress in Building [and that] is my reason that I cannot come at this time but perhaps as soon if the Lord Blesses me with health and strenght to finish it then I will make some preperations if a live to visit you once more. John has been bound to me and keeps quite steady and Learn very fast and is glad that he undertook to learn the trade.

A Slave dealer for sometime had a slave factory at Little Bassa and Gov. Buchanan after he came out orderd him away and said to him that he had no right to deal in slaves in that teritory and that he must remove in so many days. It appears that he agreed to it and that he would not buy no more until he did remove the said factory but the gov., hearing that he did but contrary to his agreement, warn him again if he did not leave the place that he should destroy the establishment and all the property that it containd should be confiscated. He would not believe but still remaind and we went down and broke up the factory and brought away all the effects say in goods and destroyd about fifty puncheons [of] Rum which was turn loose on the ground say the effect in goods &c to the amt of ten thousand Dollars. After we had taken the goods or a part we had to contend with the natives which fought us two days very hard but we got the victory and form a treaty before we left with one of the chiefs but not with the other and only got four slaves so we cannot say that we concluded a final peace without the other partys consent. We were gone fifteen day and only Lost one man in the Battle and he was a crooman. Two or three of our men got wounded but not dangerously but we killed a great many of tribes on both of the parties say of Bargays & Princes as they were the prinpal head men.

NB: You will be informd that we did not go from home to interfere with the natives atall and would not have done it if they had not began it themselves.

You will give my best respects too all your family and my mother. Nothing Moore at Present But Remains Your affectionate Friend & well wisher,   Peyton Skipwith

33 / PEYTON SKIPWITH TO JOHN H. COCKE

Monrovia, April 22, 1840

Dear Sir: I receivd your letter and was very glad to hear from you and was very sorry that you did not see Mr. Teage when he was in the states but he is no more. He never lived to reach home. I also receivd the letter from Mother and was very glad to her from her indeed. Dianna receivd her letter also from Miss Sally. I am very glad that I can say that my health has been so good that I took my Rifle in hand to go to fight a savage King [Gatumbe] about three days travel through the forest. Slept one night in the bush and took his Town the next day about 6 o'Clock with my Capt Mortally wounded and [an]other man, and two others with flesh wounds. There we encamped that night and on Sunday and Monday we set fire to the Town and took our line of March for home, and was two days in the wild bush. But [it is] a pretty country well waterd and timberd.[1] I have as much work as I can well attend to at present with my apprentices and others. You mention in your letter that you would like to no the prices of stone masons pr day Carpenters &c. The wages of stone Mason can get when work is to be had [is] about $1.50 pr day, Carpenter from 75 cts to $1.00 to $1.25.

My daughters have a good time to improve themselves in education for they have nothing else to do much but to go [to] school and I think they will improve. Dianna keeps up her night school as yet and also is a teacher in the sunday school of the Baptist Church. It would be well if we had some advantage in getting things cheap to this market for every thing that we get is at least from 100 to 200 per cent above cost which will forever keep the inhabitants poor. If the Steam packets were sent and would sell there things cheap we would like to have them and to increase our population. It is something strange to think that these people of Africa are calld our ancestors. In my present thinking if we have any ancestors they could not have been like these hostile tribes in this part of Africa for you may try and distill that principle and belief in them and do all you can for them and they still will be your enemy. It is a fact that agriculture has been carried on very rapidly but we must say a little on the retrog[r]ade. The gardens are tolerably well furnished with vegetable matter and pretty well supplies the market. I saw Mr. [Lancelot B.] Minor. He come out in the ship Saluda this time and settled with me in full. Apprentice Labour is worth from 50 to 75 cts pr day. We have Blacksmith one or two and they have as much work as they can do and more. I think a blacksmith that would follow his trade might make a Handsom living in this country. The Blacksmiths say they make from two to three dollars per day. I have no work cattle, mules, nor Horses but there are two or three Jacks on the cape and three Horses. Cows are worth 18 to 20$ and ox the same again. I must say that the greatet war that ever was fought by man was fought at Headington, a Missionary establishment about five miles from Millsburg.[2] It was said that a savage host of this man that we took occassion to [go] against sent about four Hundred men to attack this place about day Break. There was in that Town three Americans and they took there stand in the House and whipt the whole enemy. They killd on the feeld above 20 dead, and god he only knows how many was wounded and carread away. It has been said that a great number died, but how many I do not no, with the lost of one Native man mortally wounded. They then persued them and found the General's [Gotora's] body slightly intomed about twenty miles from the feeld of Battle. His head was taken from his body and now made an ornament in the Hands of the Governor Buchanan. The Battle lasted about one Hour fifteen minutes. How this was done they had and over quanty [i.e., a surplus] of musket loded and had nothing to do but take them up and poor the Bullets in thire flesh and they would fall takeeng fingers and tearing the flesh assunder. Our selves, we have made a com-

pany of rifle men and I hold an office in that compan[y]. The Churches is
somewhat in prosperous sta[te]. Food appear to thrive. I send you the
Liber[ia H]erald so you can acquaint yourself of the particulars about
our goeing to Gaboombah, and what I fail writing you can correct yourself in that. I try to write you every thing that I can think of. There is a
man in jail to be hung, a crooman, for killing an american boy the 2d friday in May at ten o Clokk. This boy was shockenly murderd by this fellow. He broke his legs, his arms and stabd him in several places and the
next [day] absconded to Junk about sixty miles and there he was detected
and brought back to Monrovia an he had his trial in our seperior court at
his first setting with two the abliest judgest our town could afferd, Judge
Benedet [Samuel Benedict] & Gov. Buchanan.[3] Nothing More at Present,
Yours,   Peyton Skipwith

34 / PEYTON SKIPWITH TO JOHN H. COCKE

Monrovia, Dec. 29th, 1840

Dear Sir: The time has arrived again for me to write you by way of
the Bark Hobert hopeing that you are well and the family. I am sorry to
say that we have had a great confusion in our Colony by the instigation
of the Missionare of the Methodest Espescopal Church respecting a duty
which they owed to our commonwealth.[1] The collection waited on the
superintendent of the Mission for six Months at most or at least untill the
Govr had written to the Board of directors [of the American Colonization Society] for an explanation of the Law and the Board in there opinion considered that the duties was lawfull to be paid when the superintendent considred that he had no right to pay them for the Board had no
more right to make the Mission pay duties than the Mission had to make
the Board pay duties and that he would not pay it for five hundred Doll
and that he wish the Collector to sue him which the collector did after the
Govr could not prevail on him to pay them. The suit was enterd against
the superintendent in the supreme court where the Gov. [p]resided. A
Jury [was] impanneled on the case and the trial commenced after many
hissings &c from the Mission Coleauges of the Govr peceedings but he
discoverd it and put an end to it. But through much confusion by the citizens takeing sides with them the missioners after many witnesses were
examined to prove that the Superintendent did trade in so much as he
paid goods for Labour and that other citizens did purchase from him for
money was out of the question [i.e., beyond questioning]. He the superintendent considered that it was not trade and he had no right to pay
duties. The Jury retired and found no Bill. The Govr dismissed the case,
and on the whole the same like to have caused a serious time in our Col-

You will observe that it is very yellow but the way that we dos it hear is to put it on the fire in a Spider or pan or any thing of the kind & let it Burn white then it looks like thin lard but in burning it we find it very dangerous. Some times it catches a fire & so is very difercult to put it out. Several houses have been burnt down by it but as soon as it cetches afire, Clap a top on it and let stay for the space of three or four minutes and it is out at once. It is a capital thing for greasing the hare; it makes it grow first rate, that is after it is burnt. You will also find in the Box a pocket that was maid by the natives. You mus[t] not give it a way but keep it as it come from me. A few other articles you will find in the Box for your self & others. You will also find some Newspapers in the Box which likely you will find very interresting. Theas papers are printed by my husband brother & my husband ocupation are Captain of Vessel. My letter do not contain much about my self & family. If any thing that you wish to know about me are not in heare you will inquire of the Gentleman that is Just from heare & he will tell you all about me. The young man is name Feny Smithy. I have told him that I expect you all would be down to see him & that he mus make him self known. My Father is not home. He have bin employed by Doc Day to go to Setra Croo to do a job of work.[2] I do not look for him back under two or three months. Therefore I shal write your Par a letter. Had I of known that Mr. Smithy was going to leave this place for America or had my Father of bin home I should of bin beter prepared but so as it is I am in hopes that what I do send will [be] excepted as from the hands of a friend. Pleas write to me by the first Oppitunity. I am very anxious to hear from you all. Remember me kindly to Mrs. Ann Cable & husband, Master John and Mrs. Nancy Moreland, Master Charles & to all of [my] inquiring friends. I shal write as often as I can.

Diana James

Pleas excuse the Blots & misstakes.

38 / DIANA SKIPWITH JAMES TO JOHN H. COCKE

Master J H Cock Senior   Monrovia, L[iberia], March 7, 1843

Sir: For the first time I now address you a few lines which will inform you that we are all well at the present time hoping you and your family are injoying the same blesing of god. Though I have express a great dissatisfaction with regard to this place since I have bin out heare, but now I can truly say that I thank god & you too that I am heare. My mind are perfecly at ease & I wish to make Africa my home the longest day that I live. Yet I do not pretend to say that I do not want to come back and see you all. This is the place for collard people if they come out with the exspectation of working for unles this is done ther is no living out. In my

ony. For myself I thought that we would have to take arms one against the other, to name them, one of Seys party & the other for the Govr. I believe it has nearly coold down but I believe it to be very rancorous in some of the leaders on the Mission side. Perhaps you may get a paper or two and there you will see all the trial and what was particola on both side [in] the Govr nutrial. Haveing got through the above in a broken way in trying to explain to you our situation you can judge for yourself and make the best of it you can. But shall I aquaint you that within the last month that the Large [slave trading] Establishment of [Pedro] Blanco has been destroyed by one of his Majesties ships of war.[2] It is said that they took one thousand slaves from that factory and destroyed and taken to the amount of one hundred thousand Dollars. Kennet [Canot's] factory, under the same firm, has been given up by him to one of the cruisers with one Hundred slave and put himself under the protection of the English.[3] He has been since that to the Town of Monrovia and was admitted to come on shore and he has proceeded to see the ruins of that splendid slave factory at Galenas that was belong [to] that rich man Blanco. Sir I am more than happy to inform you that Both of my daughters have been I trust converted to God and has been Baptised and are now members of the Baptist Church. You stated in your last letter that you intended to send some one out. I have not forgotten it. I have been making preparation for them and the sooner you send them the better. Nothing More at Present But Remain yours &c.,   Peyton Skipwith

35 / PEYTON SKIPWITH TO JOHN H. COCKE

Monrovia, April 27th, 1841

Honr'd Sir: I have taken the present chance of conveyance by the Brig. R. Groning now about to leave our port for the U.S. to acquaint [you concerning] my health and my family. I am happy to say that we [are] all well, and that my children are improving as also my apprentice John who is learning his trade finely and I must say upon the whole is a very fine boy, and suits me very well, and I think will (if he continues thus) make a useful man. The colony is not now as flourishing as it was not long since. Trade is dull and country produce for subsistance scarce, as the past season was very unfavourable to the growth of rice, our main staff of life. The wars round about us is subsiding & the natives are about turning their attention to agricultural persuits as [are] also many of Settlers, and [there is] a bright prospect of a good crop the ensuing season. You did not send those people of whom you spake. Should you make up your mind to send them I should be glad to see them, and do all I can for their advantage. If they are well provided for they will not suffer much.

Cattle sell here from 15 to 20 Dollars ea[ch], Sheep from 2 to 3 dols., Goats 150 to 2.50, Hogs of different prices according to sizes fro[m] 1 to 16 Dolls, Fowls Three dols pr Doz. &c Duck 1 doll ea. You will learn the state of the colony much better than I can express as there will leave here about 20 pasengers from some of whom you will likely obtain information. But if you take the papers you will learn all particulars about political affairs Please give my love to my mother and relations and friends in general and recieve the same for yourself and family from Sir, Your Obt. Hum. Servant, Peyton Skipwith

36 / ERASMUS NICHOLAS TO LUCY NICHOLAS SKIPWITH

West Africa, Monrovia, March 5, 1843

My Dear Mother: Theas few lines will inform you of my health and also of my safe arrival on the shors of Liberia. We arrived to this place last August 16, 1842 & are happy to say that I am well Pleased with the Country so far. But as to my health it have been bad for Every person that come to this Country naturally must go through a course of sickness before they can Expect to Enjoy health. Such have been my case, but are now gaining ground Every Day. On my first sight of this part of the world being so Differrent to the part where I was born that it appeared to me as though I was in a new world. But since I have gotten nearly over the African fever I like the place better & Better for I find it is the only Place for the man of Colour. I would have written to you before but as I had written to Mr. Cocke & stated in his letter all I thought was necessary to be mentioned is the Reason I have not wrote you. Therefore I shall consider you both in debt to me & shall not write until I get an answer from both of you. I want to hear from you by the first opportunity & let me know all the late occurrences since my Departure. Brother Peyton is in good health but he is gone down to Settra Kroo to do some work but will be back in a month or two. He sends his best Respects to you & all the friends. He says His health is much better in this Country than it were in America. Diania's husband is a smart, intelligent young man. He is Captain of one of the Colonial Vessels and he is doing well. Diania seems to Enjoy the married life in a very Respectable way. The young man that was Engaged to Matilda got Drowned some months before I arrived here. Consequently she is not Married. Matilda is the very sponde [?] [image] of her mother & Diania takes hers after her father. I cannot say much to you about farming nore the General state of things in this Colony at Present as I have not seen Enough so as to write fully but hope to Do so the next time I write.

My best Respects to Bro. Ned Edwards and Sister Lavenia and all enquiring friends. I must beg you to Excuse me at this time for not writing more but when I hear from you again I hope then to be able to write more fully. My Respects to all the white friends.
    Respectfully I am your Dear Son,   Erasmus Nicholas[1]

Bro. Peyton is Doing well. He have Built himself [a] large 2 Storey Rock House. It is not fully completed. He says he shall come over to see you all.

37 / DIANA SKIPWITH JAMES TO SALLY COCKE

Miss S. F. Cock   Monrovia, L[iberi]a, March 6, 1843

Dear Miss: I am truly hapy to write you again & I am no doubt but what you will be hapy of reseaveing one from your long and absent friend. I [have] no doubt but what you have got the letter that I last wrote you & if so you have long since learn all about me and all about my present sercomstance. I have nothing strange nor interesting to acquaint you of only to tell you of the comet that was seen here the 4 inst and it was said to be the largest one that ever was discovered.[1] Many of the Monrovians were very much frighten thinking that It was Judgment or that Judgment had come but I was not the least frighten. After I saw the Star at the end of it I concluded at once that it was a comet. I wrote you a long catalogue about the Natives customs which I am in hopes that you have found very amusing. In conversing with one of them I ask him how was it that the[y] could not read & write like white man (they call us all white man) & had not as much Sence as the white man & he said that it was thire own fault; that God give them the Choice either to learn book proper as they says or make Rice & they told god they had rather make rice. I labored with him & told him that it was a misstaken Idear altogether. I farther told him that God had bless them with as many Sences as the white man and if they ware to only put them in exersise that he would be the same as white man. After talking with him some time he said in answer you tell true too much. I think by theas means we will be able to get them out of their Supisticious Idears & at last they will become Siverlise for we have every reason to think so from two or three sercomstances which hapen in 1842, namely Marriages. They have pertition for lisons and have been Marrid in regular matrimonial form. Let this Surfice on the present ocasion as there will be a weding soon & I may not be ready for it or may not get there in time. By this oppitunity I have thought proper to send a small box over with a few articles for my beloved friends & in that Box you will find a Small Phial of the Palm oil.

last let[ter] to Miss S I told her all about my self & sercomstance which I think you have heard. Thirefore I think it needless to say any thing about it again. There was a temperanse meeting got up heare this yeare of which my Sister Matilda & my self have become a member, July Nicholas also. By this sir you will see that we have not forgot the things that you use to instil in our Brest nor have we departed from, nor I trust never will as long as we have our right Sences. All of our family—I mean those that was sot free by Mrs. [Sarah] Falcon—are well.[1] They have got out of the fevers; not one of them is dead. We took them all and nurse them. They ware very poorly attend by the Publick. The privision that ware given then weekly would not last them more than half of the week. As to bread Kind they were ondly alowed three lbs flour [and] 2 lbs me[a]t. Had it not bin for us they must of had suffered.

My Father is not home at the present. He have bin employed by Doc Day to do a Job of work down on the cors of this place, thiefor you will not get aletter from him this time.

I have sont abox with a few articles for the friends & you will find tuo cuntry whips or natives whipes for your Self and a nother Bag mad of Skin that Mr. James send it to you, but the whips I Send you. They are not much but prehaps they will be a curiosity. One of them the handle is coverd in part with aligator Skin. My sister is not marid yet. The young man that will be the Barre[r] of theas things if you will see him & talk to him he will tell you all about us. His Name is Feny Smithy. Will you if pleas Sir be good enough as to send me out a little Tobaco & Some provision. If you Should Send it pleas Sir Send Some that is long. I mean Tobaco that is short will not trade hear. I know that you have bin very kind indead in Sending us thing & I feel like I am intruding on good nature but rearly Sir I am in hopes you will not think so. Sister & Couzen Judy send thir Kindest respect to you. Mr. James all so. I have sont you Some news papers. Your humble Servt,   Diana James

P.S. Pleas Sir remember me to Mrs. Louisa & tell her that I have bin researving Some mats for her & intended to send them by the first oppitunity but I find that I cannot Send them. The Box is not long enough to hold them.   Diana

39 / PEYTON SKIPWITH TO JOHN H. COCKE

Monrovia, Liberia, Western Coast of Africa, Sept 29th, 1844

Dear Sir: Having reseived yours pr. American Ship Virginia, and was truly happy to hear from you indeed. Being as an oppertunity now affourds itself, I hasten to write you a short letter, which I Sincerely hope will find you and all in good states of Salubriety. I was very sory to hear that the letters I wrote you by Govr. Roberts did not reach safe to you.

Sir You requist to know how Peter [Jones] is getting along with our African climate. He is quite well and has a School in charge, which I believe he is Computant of teaching and I am in hopes he will be enable to make a living by it. He is not able to walk as yet & it appears as if he will never recover his strength in the legs again so long as he lives.

Dear Master, I am sorry to say that Erasmus is displeased with the Country because he is of no trade, & therefore he sees no way to make a living. I wanted him to come in and learn the Mason's trade, but I could not prevale on him enough to get his consent. It was so ordained by the Lord that Mr. [Beverly] Randolph, the son of Mrs. Jane Randolph, came on shore here, from on board of the U.S. Brig Porpoise, and being acquainted with him gave him a recommendation to the officers of the Ward-room & he theire became a steward and all the officers being much pleased with him advised him to go on to the states with them and he after consulting of me Complied with theire request. The first Lieut. Mr Wadkins from Gooseland County came on Shore, and advised me to get his Passport, and said he would do all he could for him. Dear Master, as to myself, I am as well satisfied as I can be in this little Community, & I must thank you sir for the care you had over me while I was young, for when I was young & Knew Nothing, you studied my interest. I am blessed with a trade, for you has sont me to this country where I can speak for myself like a man & show myself to be a man, so fair as my ability allows me.

You are quite desireous to know the situation of our little Colony, which I think is in a prosperous situation. The farmers is following their trade rapidly. They are very extensive in theire farms this Year, more so than I has seen them for some past Years. Theire produce are as followes: Rice, Potatoes, Plantains, Corn, & Cassadoes. All the time I have been here I have seen no want for a mill, 'till this Year. I would be glad if you would Sende me on one, by the first affoarding oppertunity. Peace and harmony exists among us, with our Savage natives. The U.S. Fleet has done great good on the Coast of Africa. They has in a measure dispursed the slave trade, & also subdeud the Natives & brought them to Know theire place, more so than they did before the arrival of said fleet.[1] Since I has been here, the ministers of the "Gosple" were only allowed to preach the "Gosple" around about the Colony, but now they can go as fair as a hundred Miles in the interior.

Though our Ministers are out in the interior yet we has to keep an Eye single towards them. If you should see Mr. Randolph who has left for Some time for the States, he can give you a true statement about me, for every time he was in our Harbour he would come on shore to see me. Please present my respects to all of my acquaintences both great and

small, Particularly Master Phillip. I now beg to Come to a close by saying I Remains Truly Yours,   Peyton Skipwith

40 / RICHARD CANNON TO JOHN H. COCKE

To Genl Cocks   Monrovia, Liberia, Western Coast of Africa,
                                                September 29th, 1844

Dear Master: This being the second time I have attempted to address
you mearely to inform you that we are all well and has not forgotten
you, though you have said that we have forgotton you. I can assure you
that you[r] name are as frish to our memory now as ever it were & I hope
you do not think because we are out of your reach that you are forgotten
by us. May heaven forbid that such ever should be the case, so long as I
have breath in the boddy.

Brother Peter are a School Teacher and resides in the same House that
I do, and he is as well as we can expect him to be. Brother James Could
not Contente himself here & lift Some months ago for Kingston, Jamaca
& I has never been enable to heare from him Since theire he has been.
Please Remember my love to my Brother & Sister. Tell them I am well
and hope they are the same.

I am under ten thousand obligations to you for some Tobacco &
Cloth. I am no ways choisy what Kind it Consist of. Sister Julia are as
well as She Can be & is expected to be married in Short to a Gentleman
by the name of Jonas Carey a Commission Merchant. I are married & has
been for some space of time. Little Dianna Sterdivant sends a great deal
of love to you all & says you will be please to send here something. I now
beg to close by saying I remain Yours with due Respects,

                                                       Richard Canon[1]

41 / MATILDA SKIPWITH TO SALLY COCKE

                                  Monrovia, Liberia, October 23rd, 44

Miss: I embrace the Oppertunity of writing You these few Lines
hopeing they may find you in good Health as they Leaves me enjoy[ing]
that Part of Gods Blessing. I was much Disappointed when the Govr of
Liberia arrived not Receiving a Letter from You, I have nothing of Great
Importance to Write. You Requested me to State to You how my sister
[Diana] Departed this Life. I Can just say that Her End was Peace and
from the Time of her Conversation [conversion] her Life was that as a
Christian. I am trying to Live in that way as to meet her at the Right hand

of God. I must say to you that I am Completely Left alone [with] only Nash my Brother Since my Sisters Death. Do tell my Dear Grand-Mother that I am yet alive and yet Expects to See her in this life. Do write me about Uncle George Skipwith. I have not heard of him Since I have Been in Liberia, or Aunt Luvine, Uncle Ned, his Aunt Falitia, Primous. I was very sorry to hear of the deaths of Aunt Luvenia two children. Erasmus has Left us and gone to Philadelphia. I Believe I sent five Letters By him. I hope you all will Receive them. Write me word if any of you all is Comeing out. Father is well and sends his Best Love to his Mother, Sister, and all enquiring Friends. In a month or two from this I Expects to change my life. All of you must send me something. Nash sends his Love to his Cousin Ned. Govr. Roberts Says that he saw the ginrl [John H. Cocke] and he Said he intended to write. But we did not Receive any Letters from Him. We was very sorry. I Remains Yours in Much Love,

Matildia R. Skipwith

42 / ROBERT LEANDER STERDIVANT TO JOHN H. COCKE

Liberia, June 11, 1846

Dear friend: You may know bey this that my self and children ar well and all of my friends who came out with me.[1] James I have not seen for a lon[g] time. He hav left this plac and we know not wheare he is but I am contented with this plac. I am sorry to find that you hav not recived the letters that I sent you a long time ago but I find in your letter that we hav gust Recived that you hav not Recived them. I deem it a geat blessing from god that he has sent me to this plac. I hav bin [in] the cuntry for 3 years in the pamoil [palm oil] traid for Mr. James B. McGill. Dianner is with me, Rose with her ant, and Leander my son I hav put him to a traid with a friend of mine. We are all well god be thank. We hav not Receivd the letters or anney things bey governer Robert[s]. I must ask you sir to giv my best lov to all of your family. I hav not time to call them bey name, and giv my lov to all of my Relations and tell them that tha must wright to me. All so my dear sir I hop that you will pleas send me some as sis tanc [assistance] if you please sir. I hav sent you 4 letters at diferat times but i hop that this may come to hand. I hop that you will send me some little might [mite] which may serv to help me and my children. Sir you no that we that hav latly came heare have hard trials to get on. I hop that you will send me some books as you will see by this that I am trying to make some thin of myself. I hop sir that you will help me. As my friend is gone I must look up to you.[2] I no if she was alive I should not suffer but she have left me and I come to you for help and I hop that God may bless and sav you from all the trials of this world and sav you as he have savd our friend. I hop that God may feed your sold with the bread of life and when we come to die ma we meet at the gat of heavin the Kingdom of everlastingness. Theare we [shall] sing the prayes of moses and the lamd. I hop that we may hold out and proov faithful evin to the end. I am happy to say to you that I have Obeyed your word in and hav don all in my power to instruct the natives. I [think] tha hav becom much fond of me and oftin ask me to Read the Bible to them and tell them what god ment bey this larg fire of which the bible speake. I hop that you will pardon these Lines. I gust got home last sunday and [am] verry Buyssy but this is my hand an pen, it will be good, but god knos when. If you should send me any things you will pleas direct it to Mr. James B. McGill of this place. If aney things goes to the publick s[t]ore it is never seen bey the oner that is a [two words illegible]. I hop that you will not think hard of what I said but it is so but I am sorry to say that of my fellow men but I tell you the truth.

Peter Jones has goten much better and is at one of the settlements. He keeps a school. He makes him self as yousefool as he can. I hop that you will let me hear from you as soon as you can. All send thar best lov to you. I think that [I] shall be home untill september and then I shall go back again.

May god bless you and sav you and hold you in the hollow of his hands is my prayer of your friend and beloved.   Robert L. Sterdivant

43 / PEYTON SKIPWITH TO JOHN H. COCKE

Monrovia, June 25th, 1846

Dear Genl.:   I write you a few hasty lines, by a vessel now about to leave this place for the states.

You earnestly request me to give you the particulars of our Colony. Since the Authorities has thought it proper to declare theire independence I Canot with Confidince say much about the present Situation of the Colony. It is not yet determined with the Colonists whether to receive the Constitution Sent on by the Board or not.[1] The majority of this place is much in favour of independence & those at Edina, the Leeward Settlement, are against it & that bitterly. The Counsil has not conveined to deliver the Constitution to the people as yet. It is thought that It will be done in July. It is my belief that the Majority of this place will gain the effections of those of Edina & Bassa Cove and cause them to Join heart & hand with them; this is my expectation about the affair. We must be a people recognised by foreign Nations, or Else come under the Eye of some [one] that will protect us when called upon. You have I no doubt seen that there must be something of the Kind done before we can enforce our "Laws;" for it has been already said by the British that we have no right to demand Anchorage Duties &c of them. If we are to remain in the state we are now in, it is deplorable. Sir, I am in hopes that when the Constitution are presented that the Eyes of the blind will become opened. Though our love for the society is great we canot return her that gratitude of thanks that we [are] due to her. Sir You wishes me to give You some information of the different productions. I myself do not farm it at all. I have my lot, only, planted down since here In Africa. I have been [cultivating my lot] & it is all the farming I does. At the present time I feels an inclination to lay a side my trade and go in to Farming of it. We have had rather a sever season of it for bread kind. Those who turned theire attention to farming some time past caused us to weep almost at the Idea of paying theire Exorbitant prices for produce. We pay at this place for Potatoes 1.50$ Cents per. Bushel, Corn 25 Cents pr. dozen, Rice at this tim brings 3$ per Bushel. Cassado at the present time is 50 cts. per Bushel and that in specie.

We are blessed with a good soil for raising Corn &c. We raises corn from 12 to 13 inches in lingth and that good and full. Cotton can be abundently raised here but no person seems to turn theire attention to it. Coffee grows wild in the woods and can be raised abundantly, if it was attended to. Thire are only a few individuals who raises said article and theirs is as promising as Ever I saw coff[ee] in the States. You wishes that I should say something about Miss Sally's people: I have and can do so a gain. Leander is here and is well and all the people that came out with him is here excepting James Nicholas. He left this place for *Jamaca* & I have not been enable to hear from him since. Richard is now on board of one the U.S. Ships of War Cruising on this Coast. Cousin Peter is at Mashall. He went theire to see if it would not be an addition to his health. I am very sorry that I did not turn my attention to farming when I first arrived to this Country, but It was Entirely out of my power as I was alone in a Manner & had no male kind to render me assistence. Now I Am very well Situated and has several apprentices with me Exclusive of some of the Barque Pons cargo of Congoes.[2]

You desired to know whither we stood in kneed of Bibles; this we do not kneed so much as we do other Books. We have a plenty of bibles here, more than are used. If you deem it necessary you can send on some Valuable Books for my family such as Historys &c &c. Please send me on some writing paper, quills, & wafers and you will be confuring quite a favour on me. As the Revd A. D. Williams will be in the states you will be please to send me on some Flour & Pork and any other necessary article you may think will be of service to me.

You promised me in your letter that you was going to send my Bro.

George on to this place at the Expiration of three years & I would be happy indeed to see him and all the people that you have promised to send on. My love to all the family & inquiring friends. I beg to close by subscribing myself to be sincerely Yours,   Peyton Skipwith

NB: Please remember my love to Master John, Charles, Phillip, & Merret also Mrs Nancy Cavel & Family, Miss Sally also and Miss Coatny.[3] Tell them I am well.

44 / PEYTON SKIPWITH TO LUCY NICHOLAS SKIPWITH

Monrovia, June 27th, 1846

Effectunate & Dear Mother: I embrace this favourable oppertunity of writting you a few lines to inform you of my health which is very good at present and I hope this may finde you and all the same.

Dear Mother It has been for some Considerable time since I have recd a letter from you. I only heard from you through the Genls letter to me bearing date 28 oct./45 to which I was very much pleased indeed to learn that you were in good health. In your last to me you expressed an anxiety for me to come over, but I am affraid that I shall never be enabled to cross the Atlantice again though I would like much to see you once more in the flesh. Errasmus has not returned since he left here for the states & it appears as if I cannot receive eny intelligence from him. I would like much to hear something of him if he is in the States. You will please to write me by Mr. Williams and let me know whether you have heard any thing of him or no.

Should I never be blessed to cross the ocien again the Genl has given me his faithful word that he would send Bro. George on whom I would be happy to see if it is the will of the Master.

Dear Mother I find that the people are affraid to come to this country. I can assure you that any person can live here if they has a little money. All persons having any expectations to go to Monrovia should endeavour to accumulate some money if they possibly can and that is no hard matter to accumulate in the States. In regard to the Fever that need not be much dreaded as we feel our selves pretty much Skilled in regard to that part. Every family more or less that has been here any time knows what to do in regard to the fever. Through and by the assistence of the Almighty we carried Miss Sally's People through without a death. Cousin Peter who was likely to have Di[e]d is yet alive and enjoying good health. I wishes to see some of the people from the very place I went from & that very much indeed. I think the people would go over if they were not affraid of the fever. That should not be an obsticle to any of them that knew me before I left the states. I have now been out theire nearly 13 years and Am ase well acquainted with the climate of the country. My efforts have been Crowned with Success from on high ever since theire I have been & I canot thank him enough for his kind blessings that he has bestowed upon me since I left you all in the states.

And I still feels as if the Lord will bless me in all my undertakings if I put my trust in him. Mother my confidence in the *Lord* is as bright now as ever it was when I first left—if any thing more so. When I went to Liberia I had no one that I was acquainted with. After a length of time a man came from Richmond in whom I was intimitly acquainted with & that revived my spirits. After a few Years the Lord brot it about so that Miss Sally sent on her People to Africa, which has been a consolation to me from that day to the present time. I still feeled buoyed up as Master has Promised to send on my Bro. Geo. & his family. I believe I shall have more help in this dark benighted land, to try and civilize the heathens and bring them to know life and life eternal. I now wish to close by subscribing myself to be your most Humble and obedient Son,

Peyton Skipwith

NB: Please say to Uncle Ned that I hope he still has Jesus in his Soul and Heaven in his View. If so Uncle I shall meet you where we shall be blessed for ever through Endless days. Please give my love to aunt Phalitia. Tell sister Levina that I wants to see her very bad but if I should neve see her in this life I will try to meet you [where] We shall part no more. My love to all inquireing friends. Tell them I am well & my confidinc is still anchord in the Lord.

45 / MATILDA SKIPWITH LOMAX TO SALLY COCKE

To Miss S[ally] F. Cocks   Monrovia, July 4th, 1848

Dear Miss: I now avale myself of the favourable oppertunity of addressing you with a fiew lines to inform you that I am well, and hope this may finde you and all the family in the enjoyment of the same.

Dear Miss, I hope that from our long Silence you have not been induced to think that we have withdrawn our Communications from you. If such have been your thoughts let me beseech you to do away with it as I am aware that I have not written you as often as I ought, but such shall not be the case again, that is whenever an oppertunity affords. I hope you will not fail to write me by the first affording oppertunity as I am very desireous to hear something from you all.

You requested of me in your last to say something about my marriage. I was wedlocked to a Young man by the name of Samuel B. Lomax.[1] He is a Young man who masters one or two trades, firstly a Cooper, 2dly

Printer, 3dly Sea Captain and Clerk. The latter he now turns his attention to principly as his health has been quite bad for the past Six or Seven
months, and Liberia is a Country where it behooves every man to be up
and doing something for his future prosperity.

I suppose you have long since heard of the Congoes that was landed in
Monrovia from on board of the Am. Barque "Pons." Numbers of them
died from the fatigue of the Cruel Imprisenment on board of the ship before Captured. The surviveing ons are as healthy a set of people as ever a
person would wish to see. Several of which has embraced the religion of
our Saviour and making rapid improvements in Education, Tho I must
say of a truth that they are the most Savage, & blud thirsty people I ever
saw or ever wishes to see.[2] My Father's love to your father and You. He
would of written but is not in Town. He desires that you[r] fathe[r]
would be so kind as to send his Bro. on, also that he would send him a
Set of Mason's Tools. Please send me on something for my Children as I
have been the mother of 3 since my Marriage one of which I have lost.
The other two which is girls yet servives. Theire names are as Foulers:
Eliza Adala & Lydia Ann Lomax. I must now close as I wishes by indul-
gence from You to say afiu words at the bottom to my dear Grd Mother.
I am with Respects Yours,   Matilda R. Lomax

[*On same sheet*]

Dear Grand Mother [Lucy Nicholas Skipwith]:   I suppose you have
thought from our long silence that we had forgotten you. May the Lord
of heaven forbid that such ever should be the case & I hope from this day
henceforward to write you by evy oppertunity. I have writen you several
times & received no answer. Consequently I had almost come to the
Conclusion that I never should hear from you again which I hope I shall
do by the next oppertunity after this reaches you. We are all well and enjoying the blessings of our heavenly father & it is our sincere wish that
this may finde you in the enjoyment of the same. Please write us word
about uncle George. Your dear son Peyton is well & would of written
you but is out of Town. He Joins me in ascribing all manner of love to
You and all the family. His love also to his Sister Levinia & Uncle Nid.
Nash my Bro. sends his love to you and also request that you should attend the same to Ned Washington and request that Ned should send him
a present & he will endeavor to return the same Complements. My love
to my Grand Mother Betsey & Grandfather Primus and all enquireing
friends. My Husband Joins me in love to you all tho' a stranger to you.

I now close my dear Grd. Mother by subscribing myself to be your
Grand daughter &c &c,   Matilda R. Lomax

NB: Uncle Erasmus has been out to Liberia since you requested that we
should give you some account of him. He is now on his way to the States
& will leave for Africa again by the return of the "Liberia Packet."

Please excuse all Errors as my husband was quite unwell when he wrote this. It was done lying on his bed.

46 / NASH SKIPWITH TO JOHN H. COCKE

Nov. the 2, 1849

Dear Sir: I take this oppotunity of wrighting you theas few lines to in form you of my helth which is at this time verry well andihope that theas few lines may find you in the best of helths and all the family. And this is the first time that I ever rote to you andihope and trust it will not be the Last time. My reason for not wrighting is becase I was so small when I come from thir and I did not know Enny one thir when I come from thire and I has to give my best respects to all my Kindred and tell them all Pleas to try and send me something as iam in the want of it.

[*On same sheet*]

Mrs. Genrel Cocks

Dear Sir: If you can make it convenent as to send me a soote of Black Brod Cloth as ihave Lost my Father and have now my silf to find and besides 3 Children and my father wife and have to worke very hard and sometime ihave but 1 dollar and sometimes non and iam sorrow to say to my uncle Gorge this. I should hear that he should [two lines illegible] My Father died in Oct. the 29, 1849. Will you pleas to send me a stoomstone for him. I [have] no more to say at Present. Yours Respeteful,

Nash P. Skipwith

47 / JOHN H. FAULCON TO JOHN H. COCKE

Monrovia, Liberia, West Africa, November the 22, 1849

Dear Sir: By this you May Learn that I am well and I hope these Lines May find you and family the Same. In your Last letter to Mr. Skipwith I was informed that you wantted to See my hand writeing and composietion. This you May take for granted to be my own writeing. I have not Spent six mounth at School Since here I have been. What I have Learnt was by hard night work. I have joined the Clasical School under Revd. Mr. H. W. Elles.[1] Also I am a member of the Junior debateing Socity. Last Febuary I delived an adress on chimesty. You can make an inquiey from som of your white friends. Doc. J. W. L. is a friend of mine. Dont under stand me to say that we cept compeney to gether. Mr. Skipwith died soon after you Letter came to hand. I Just Baught a Lot few

weeks ago. Now I am about to put me up a Small house if the Lord
Spares me Longenugh. You Must Excuse My bad composed letter as I
have two letter to write one for you and one for Mr. Maxwell. Nothing
More at present, yours,   John H. Faulcon

NB My Love to Mother Sisters Brother aunts and uncles friends also
[e]very Body on your plntation.
    I was wateing for you to write.

48 / MATILDA SKIPWITH LOMAX TO JOHN H. COCKE

Monrovia, R. P. [Republic] Liberia, November 23d, 49

Dear General J. F. C——:   As the Liberia Packet sails from this Port
for the U S on the 24th Inst I hasten with a heart over burdened with grief
to write you a letter in answer to the one by the packet to my Father,
which was duly received, affoarding us all much pleasure in hearing from
you and all. I shall now give you the sad and mellancholly news of the
death of Father who parted this life October 14th. His end was peace. He
did not live more than two weeks after the arrival of the "Packet." His
complaint was that of the head and breast. He was taken sick on wednesday and expired on Sunday; he was perfectly sencible of his death. Mr.
[Hilary] Teage[1] visited him regularly during his illness and questioned
him from time to time concerning of his Sole's Salvation, whether his
way was clear from earth to glory or not, which he would always answer
in words like these if not the same: death is no dread to me, my hope is
anchored in Christ Jesus. A fiew days previous to his being taken Sick, he
was remarking to us what a Kind and Effectunate letter he intended writing you and his mother, but before the "Packet" returned from Cape
Palmas he fell to sleep in Jesus' Arms never more to have earthly communication with you all, but trusting to strike hands with you all in the
Fathers Kingdom where parting shall be no more, and where we do all
trust to drink of that stream that maketh glad the City of the New Juru-
salem. You requested in your last to Know of Father to whome he was
married to, also whether his wife belonged to any denomination or no.
She was a widdow before he married her, with two Children, also a
Member of the M. E. Church in Monrovia. As regards his yearly income
that I can give no statement of. I can mearly say that it was derived entirely from his trade during his life. Jack Faulcon I shall say nothing
about as he has written you himself. Bro. Nash has also written to you.
He is not married and still carries on the Masons trade. He is capable of
taking under his charge fathers apprentice boys and carry on the same as
when father was liveing. Cousin Leander is not home. He has joind the

[United] States Navy as Stewart. Consequently I can not give you a correct accout of his health, tho he was well when last I saw him. His Children are all well. Cousin Julia and Peter is both dead, and has been for more than two years. Father had acquired ten acres of farm land & five town lots. He had just entered in a good way of farming before his death. We in generally raised on our Farms Corn, Potatoes, Cassado & rice. Of the latter father had not entered or commenced its cultivation befor his death.

Labourers can be hired in Liberia for 25 cents per day and at the out-side from 3 to 4$ per month. A person may hire good common labourers to work the ground to make it productive as that in the States com-paritively speaking. My husband Mr. Saml B. Lomax who writes this begs that you would receive his kindest regard and attends his respects to you and all the family trusting that you would keep up a regular corris-pondance as ever, which he shall endeavour to give you every particular relating to Public as well as private affairs, taking great delight in so do-ing. I now close by begging of you to pardon all Grammatical and other errors &c &c. Yours with much Esteem,   Matilda R. Lomax

NB Should it meet your approbation to send us on any thing please direct to Care Rev H. Teage.

49 / NASH SKIPWITH TO JOHN H. COCKE

Monrovia, Liberia, November 24th, 49

Dear General: I drop you this to inform you that I would like to come over and spend a fiew months with you all as my father is dead, provideing you would arrange it so that I might come over in the next packet. Should you make this arrangement I shall certainly come, if life are speared and Sickness do not take place.

Should you write for me, please arrange it so as I may be sent direct on to you as soon as I arrive in the States. Please send me a fiew things to as-sist in prepareing me for the Voyage.

My Brother in law request that I should beg of you to send him on some books, such as you may deem proper, as he canot get any valuable Books there unless he order a regular *Libary*. I am most Respectfully your Obedient Servant,   Nash Skipwith

NB Sister request that you would so kind as to w[r]ite her concerning of her [and] my Grand Father Primus & Grand Mother Betsey.

Skipwith

50 / RICHARD CANNON TO JOHN H. COCKE

Monrovia, Sept 30/50

Dear Mr. Cocks: By this you may learn that I am well & all the family & hopes that these may find you & your Family the same.

Mr. John H. Cock: Sir may this meet your approbations & please to send me by the first opportunity one hundred pounds of twine. If you please to sends me some pervissions & some Clothes. Please to excuse my letter. I had not time to write it correct. I did [not] full it [fill the sheet] as I intended to do. P[e]r a servant of Salley forcan [Faulcon]. Yours obedient servant,   Richard Cannons

51 / MATILDA SKIPWITH LOMAX TO JOHN H. COCKE

To Honorable John H. Cocke   Monrovia, Sept. 30th, 1850

Dear Sir: I lift my Pen to Embrace this opportunity to inform you that I am well, and Hope that These few lines may find you and all the families well as they leaves me and mine. This letter will inform you of the sad, the Heart broken intelligence of the death of my Dear Husband. He was Drowned about 90 miles from this Place, attempting to go on shore, when the Seas was runing mountain High. This took Place on the 23 of July Last, leaving me with three small children to provid for, in this New Country Where Every thinge is hard for a widow without sufficient means to take care of them. The Youngest child is at the Breast. I Hope that you will give me some little aid by the next vessel coming to Liberia, for if I Ever in all my life needed Help, it is now. For my father who, were he a live, I might make out beter, but he is also gone the Way of the Earth leaving behind small children who are Depending upon me to provid for them. Also, my youngest and only bro., Nash, sends his love to you. Leander is in the U.S.S. Yorktown, and has been for the Last 10 or 12 months. All of his Children is well. You will be [so] Kind as to write to my Uncle and inform him of the death of his Brother. Tell him he Departed this life on October Last—I mean his Brother George. I now write these few lines to Miss Salley F. Cocke. Tell her I Received her letter by the Packet before this, but did not get the things her agent sent. I heard from them, and that was all. If She Should here after send me any Thing Please Tell her to Direct them to the Care of Col. Jas B. McGill, Monrovia, and I will be Sure to get them. Please Remember me very kindly to my Dear Old Grand Mother. Tell her I am well in Body, but are Buried in sorrow in consequence of my Great losses, of Husband and father. Also Give my love to my other Grand Mother, Betsey, and all of my relations & friends Both White & Colored. I have nothing more to say at Present, only Remain yours &c.,   Matilda Lomax

52 / NASH SKIPWITH TO JOHN H. COCKE

Monrovia, May 15, 1851

Dear Sir: Your letter Came Safte to hand and I ware happy to Receave It and Ware Glad To hire from you and your family and to hire that you ware Enjoying Good helth. You Wished to Know Wither I am a man of Bisiness. I am not yet. I have no more to Tend to than Working at my traid. And a Nother Thing, You Wished to know about Fathers Estate and What did he Leaven his family. He left them Nothing. And you wished to know Wether father had enny Children by his Last Wife. He had non by her and, as for property, She had non when She Marred him. I am not married. I am Still Working at my traid. You Wanted to know how much do I get per day. I will Tell you. It is but Verey Little, 50 Cents and Some times 75 Cents pr. day. You wished to Learn from me how much Propity have I Earn by my o[w]n Industry—about $75 worth or more.

You wanted to know What did I get of father Estate. All I got of father Estate Ware one Rifel and I would not got that if he had not give It to me before he died. His Houce and his Lots will be Sold and we will not Get Ennything.

Dear Sir will you Pleas to Send me Some Trowells and hamers. They are So hard to get hire that I thought it would be best to Write to you and beg you to Send me Some.

And I would oblige you much if you ware to have murcy on me and try an help me along alittle and Send me a barrel of Flower and Pork and Some other Artickles which you think you Could Spare to help the family along.

Dear Sir I would not of ask you for nothing but Some Books if I had no one to find but my Self, but I have all fathers Children and Sisters Matilda too. [I] am working Evey day of my Life To feed and Cloth all theas Children and I beg you for God Sake Pleas to have mursey on me and the family and Send us theas things. And another thing Dear Sir I would Like for you to Send me about 12 Books which I will menchun after while and allso Some Writting Paper and Some Steel Pens and Some In Velups with Gilted Edges. I will Call the names of the Twelve Books which I want you Send me:

1 Large Dictionary, Webster; first and 2d, 3d, 4 Volum of Alison History and other such Valubil Books as you think will soote my Studdy.[1] I

would Rather have this book and to have the other things for my Convientcy but I hope you will Send them all, for god Sacke. Yours,

Nash Skipwith

53 / MATILDA SKIPWITH LOMAX TO JOHN H. COCKE

To Genl. John H. Cocke   Monrovia, October 18, 1851

Dear Sir: I take this oppurtunity of writing to you hoping this letter may reach you. Some of the immigrants by the last trip of the Packet come direct from Lynchburg & I hoped to hear from you but did not. I am afraid my last letters did not reach you. You desired to know how I get along since the death of my husband & father. I am not disposed to complain & I feel great gratitude in being enabled to say that although I am now husbandless & fatherless, & have three small children to provide for in a strange land, yet the Lord hath not left me to want bread nor a place to shelter me. Yet I have to work hard, which together with the benevolent attention of some friends has furnished me with necessaries of life. Still, if you or any of your kind family, to whom I and all my connexions out here are already under so many obligations, shall please to send any thing for me it will not be a misplaced charity. Please give my love to my grandmother Lucy; to Mother Betsy Randal & to all inquiring friends. Please say to Miss Sally that I have written to her once, and will write again; & I trust it will not be considered an attempt to finger, [flatter?] if I assure her that nothing could afford me more pleasure than to visit again the scenes of childhood or look upon those faces which were once familiar to me. But the hope of this is forbidden by circumstances over which I have no control. My Brother is not married. He lives in my father's house. My father married an American Woman. Mrs. Falcon's people are generally well. R. Cannon is at this moment very ill, hopelessly so, with the dropsy. Should you send any thing for me please direct it, as also all letters for me, to the care of Mr. H. Teage, Monrovia. Your Obdt Servant,   Matilda Lomax

54 / MATILDA SKIPWITH LOMAX TO JOHN H. COCKE

John H. Cocke, Esq.   Monrovia, Jany 27, 1852

Dear Sir: I am again called to be the messenger of melancholy intelligence. My brother [Nash Skipwith] to whom you addressed a letter from Philadelphia on the 27 Oct last departed this life a few weeks after he received it. His illness was severe and of only three days' duration when it terminated fatally. It was occasioned by a strain in lifting a rock. I am thus bereft of my last near relative excepting only my three small children of an age to be of no service to me as yet. In Nash's letter you said Miss Sally would probably write to me but she probably did not find it convenient to do so, as I did not hear from her.

You stated in John Falcon's letter that you sent me some things in the Packet, but I did not receive them. The last articles I received from any of the family were brought to me from Baltimore by Mr. H. Teage in 1849.

I am doing as well as a lone woman situated as I am could expect to do. By hard labor & the assistance of some friends I and my Children are kept from suffering. I can not therefore complain; but endeavour to [be] content with such things as I can conveniently get. If Miss Sally should send a letter or any thing else for me you will do me a favor to ask her to direct to the "Care of Mr. H. Teage for Matilda Lomax, Monrovia, Liberia."

Our people has just returned from a campaign [against Chief Grando] at Trade town.[1] Perhaps they had harder fighting than has occurred since the formation of the Colony. The loss on our part was greater than in any former battle, being 6 killed & 25 to 30 wounded. The strongest & most populous native town on this part of the Coast was taken, burned & the natives completely routed. The natives force is said to have amounted to 1500 men well armed & equipped. The war is supposed to have been excited by british traders on the Coast. Leander is in the United States service on board the Dale. Dianah is here. Your Obdt. Servant,   Matilda Lomax

Genl J. H. Cocke

55 / JOHN H. FAULCON TO JOHN H. COCKE

Monrovia, Liberia, May 12th, 1852

Dear Sir: I recived your letters in February one ritten by the Liberia packet and the other by the Morgandick which vessel arived at the time I was at Bassa as a Volentear in the Servis of the Republic as a gard. There I stad until the trups came down. Then I continued on with them to war. We riturned in February [at] which time your two Letters came to hand. I was absent two Mounth and Seven days. I wanted to write by the Morgandick but I was too Slow. Therefore I take this oppertunity to answer yours. There is nothing Strange Just now to relate more than the war that you can See in the papers or perhaps have seen. Nash Died wile i was absent. Matilda is here and her children. Mr. Leander Sturdivant and his children also. They will write to you i think by this packet. I saw in your letter a chance of Seeng My Mother and Sisters. That will be good for me, very good. H[o]wever you are aware of what kind of feeling of Grattification it would be. Also the fifty dollars whch you says they will have to help them in this new and hard cuntry. Hard as it is the harder times get it appears i love it better. However I would not like to change it in good times nor in bad. I [have] not done one Stroke of Work for the Space of Eigt Mounth except planting Casaders and potaters. If I had not planted them last august I [should] not [have] had any thing. I could Neither Sell nor Eat as Mason work took Such a Suden Stop on account of the war. Mechants could not prosper therefore Labours [ceased]. You has to Stop until times becomes good. I See in the colonization Journal your name stiled as vice president. Makes me feel like our folks has doings with all and every good thing. I hope through your influance I may get a Situation. Send my relations out as soon as [you] like or can, in the next packet if possible. Tell My Mother to try and get me a good Sunday Coat and pants. When you write to me, pleas to let me kow how Mr. Maxwell is. Evry time i write to you i write him and no answer.

Nothing More but hoping these may find you and family both Whte and Cullard in good health. Yours,   John H Faulcon

56 / MATILDA SKIPWITH LOMAX TO JOHN H. COCKE

Monrovia, May 19th, 1852

Mr. J. H. Cocks: I take my Pen in hand to inform you of my health. I am well at Present and hope you are the same sir. I Received Nashes Leter a[nd] Red it with the greatis Pleasure. I Riting [wrote] the answer to it and signed it ti [to] Mr. Piney and i hope you have Receved it.[1] The Leter you sent Nash he Received it and Did not Live but 3 weeks after he Received it, And was not sick but 3 days. I have seen Mr. Eli Ball and have Converse with him.[2] I have seen a great Deal of trouble since the Death of my People and all my hold hart is on the Lord. This is avery hard Country for a poor widow to get along and i have to Work one Day for alone 25 cts and men get $1.50 cts per Day, Masons. I would be very glad if you could send me some things for me and my Children, Some Provisions and clothings. Sturdiv[ant] is well and Jack faulkin is well and sens his Love to you. I have a great Deal to say but time will not atnit [permit]. Give my love to all inquirung friend. No more to say at Present, But Remain yours in Love,   Matilda R Lomax

If you Send any thing Please gave it to Mr. yates from Monrovia a membr of the Baptist Church. Yours,   Matilda Lomax

57 / SUCKY FAULCON TO JOHN H. COCKE

J. H. Cocks   Monrovia, April 20th, 1853

Dear Sir: I brace you this oppetunity to iform you that I am well &
hoping that it will find you and all well. In coming out my loss was
great.[1] Loss my daughter and I could [feel] great, If I could rid of my
great loss I would field happy, otherwise I will be cass down. While
coming out I was so fortunate as to go in via Sevanah & grab a Doctor to
tend to george Which release him instantly. We was so unfortunate to
come out in a vessel whose sailor was fond of intoxicating drinks & during my child illnes shee cried out that she was going a way from here,
that she was going a way from here, and I aske her whats matter & She
told me not to Confuse her, that shee was going away & told evry body
farewell. As for the [country of Liberia] sofare as I have seend of the
Country I thinke it is Consideable place as now wher you can get along
without work. Please to give my [regards] to Richard Schipher[?]. This is
a find Country for her becais She can use her nedle & pen. Please to tell
Frank Randle that this is a find Country, fruit in a bundenc. Please to tell
Cater Morris that george which [wishes] him to reconcile his mind &
come out, that he will know nothing of this country not unttill he comes
out. I hope that I will have something more to say nex time [I write]. Tell
Chater [?] make up his mind to come, that this plaisce is a Remarkable
place and he must come out. Please to tell Frank Randle that they dont
use cornbread out here, nothing but Rice, & if eny body should Come
out here to send them seeds of all descripsins. Send them in a bottle for
all of mind get loss, & pleas too send me word how many has dead since I
left & do not flatter me. Rite me as soon as posible & please to tell Uncle
Frank that his neece which [wishes] to see him & kiss him. Yours,

                                                  An Sucky Faulkin

58 / MATILDA SKIPWITH LOMAX TO SALLY COCKE

                                               Monrovia, April 20, 1853

Dear Miss Sally: I allso embrace you these few lines hoping you are
well to informe you that I am well & hoping that these few lines may find
you the same. I am very glad to her that you are well. It have been a
good while Since I heard from You. I hope you are well. I have recieved
You[r] Present & am extremly oblige to You. Seem that [God] have seen
my suffering & cause you to Send it. I have some present to send to you
but I cant make it convenient to send it to you. I fear If I send it you want
get it unless you send me word how to directed it. I recieved the letter

from you by the Ralf Cross & them present before shee got loss at Cap Palmmas. I was extremly thankfull for them. I would have sant it than but I was convenent & You mus give my love to all inquiring friend fare & nere. I think that it is a hight time for you to be looking out for a beau. I think I mus pount one out for you & it is my desire to see tham all once more. If I dont see them I shall [hope] to see them all in heaven, and please send me some garden seed of all description and if you send them [pack them] so salt air want get to them & I hea[r]d that You father where going to send fifty people by Mr. Peices in Columbia & If it is so I am very glad. May bee some [of] my kin may be with them, & Please to give my love to My Aunt Luvenia. I have a great many thing to say but time will not abmitte. I will ritie to you as long as I can find a peece of paper. I hope this nex time I have time & opetunity. Your affectunate

Matilda R. Lomax

59 / MATILDA SKIPWITH LOMAX TO JOHN H. COCKE

Mr. J. H. Cokes   Monrovia, April 20th, 1853

Dear Sir: I brace you these few lines hoping to find you & your Children are in good helth. I thank god that I am spared throug[h] life and still living in hopes. It is true this country is quite hard yet I lives. It is true I am the only one living and sees a great deil of truble. My Brother is dead & has been dead for a year & six months and he died very sudden only three days dying and he was dying preparing to go to war & since the deathe of him I sufferd severe hardship. I am a glad to hear from you all. Ann Sucky Faulkin have [arrived] lately & has good helth thoug[h] her voyage was unfourtunate. She loss her daughter. Dear sir I think this Country is improveing evry day the more & more & I think affter an alapse of years it will be a find couty. I am now sending my children at [s]chool and I try to teach them with the best of my knowledge & ability. I will now relate to you what took place in the Vey Country.[1] A stratagem of war. Bombo & Dwahling-bey the former a cheif of the gholah tribes the lat[t]er Vey. They have been intruding upon the Republick and is fond of abatrary authority in stoping the mart from coming in & that rouse the citizen & at last cause the offercers in chiefs to make a positive Conclusion and they went to war hoping or expecting to have some fight. But Bombo who have been domerneering over Dwhalabey Came under submission & several times attempted to run a way but through no excess he was erested took & Brought him up to Monrovia & waiting for a proper decision whether he shall be punesh or noe. [this] is all at pressent. I have a great deel to Sey but time will not abmitt. Yours Affectunalee,

Matilda R. Lomax

Monrovia, Liberia, Sept 26th, 1853

Dear Sir: I now Embrace this favourable oppotunity of writing you
theas fiew lines to inform you of my Helth which is now Very well and I
hope that theas fiew lines may find you Enjoying the Best of Helth. I
Received your Doughters letter and it afford me the greatis pleasure to
Read it and [I] was Glad to heare from you all and Pleas to give my Best
Respects to all the family. And now I will Indevr to tell them the state of
my mind now I am left a lone in this Lonsum Cuntry, Now [no] one to
look up to. My Brother has bin Dead for this 2 Years and I have bin
suffering for to find my Self and three [children] evry since his death and
I have to work so hard evry Day and dont get but 25 cents pr Day and
you Know that is too hard for a poor widder to get a long at that Rate
and have three Children to find Vitels and Cloths. And I was Very Glad
to Received the preset from Miss Sally. And this Year it was hard to get
Provisions and I beg that you will have the pit[y] on me and send me
some Provisions out by the first oppotunity and if you do send it Pleas to
Derect it to Henry W. Dennis and write him that you have sent it out for
Mrs. Lomax.[1] There is so much dificulty to get things when there are sent
out to us unless we have som one to get them when they are landing.
Now I am trying to send my Children to School and trying to bring them
up in the fear of the Lord. I now will tell you about Aunt [Sucky]
Faulkin. [She] is now over the feavours and george all so and he is gon up
the river to farming. Jack falkin is quite well and still Remain at his traid.
And pleas to send me some seeds and nail them up in a little Box so that
the Sault are [air] will not get to them. If the Sault are get to them they
will not Come up. And some times I live in hopes to see you all again and
then again it seemes that the way looks so gloomy and if I ar not see you
now more in this world I expect to meet you in hevin. I have a great deal
more to say but time will not admit. I remain,   Matilda R. Lomax

[*On same sheet*]

Dear Aunt Lavinia: Will you pleas to send me one ribbin and a siftr
to Remember you as I never Expect to see you all in this world but I expect to meet you in hvin wen parte will bee no more. Yours,

Matilda Lomax

61 / SUCKY FAULCON TO JOHN H. COCKE

Monrovia, Sept. 27th, 1853

My deare Friend: Having a favorable opportunity of writing you by
the departure of the barque "Shirley" which leaves this port in a few days

I concluded to write, being assured that you would be pleased to hear from me. I have written one letter to you since I have been to this country; but I am not confident whether you have received it. You no doubt have ere this hour been properly apprised of the serious mortality that took place among the passengers of the brig Zebra in which I immigrated, occasioned by the very bad water that we were obliged to use, which [pro]duced a malady that threa[tened] our entire [num]ber with death; but happily it occuring so soon after our leaving New Orleans, we were enable to reach Savannah, & Providentially the contagion was arrested, and those who, no doubt, would have died had the former voyage been pursued, their lives were preserved. In the first stage of the disease, My daughter Aggy fell under its baneful influence, George was also quite ill with it, in fact he suffered upwards of a month from the effects of the disease. Truely it was a time of great distress until, in fact, many of those who having been spared from any effects of the disease seeing so many dead at once—others dying—that they appeared to loose in a great degree that sense of humanity that belong to a Christian people. Truely the Lord was merciful to us in this Sad hour of deep affliction that while he sees fit to call Some home, he in His Almighty wisdom spares the lives of others. How thankful then should we be under all circumstances. I am glad that I can say that I love this country more than I did at first. I think that we are at all events through the acclimating process. I feel under a thousand obligations to you for the benevolence you exercised in putting up a box of goods for my benefit after I reached this country. Indeed they have been of great service to me. I found my Son John well, and doing as well as could be expected.

I will be happy to hear from you at any time when there is an opportunity—and also to know how all the friends and acquaintances are in Virginia and Al[abama] and furthermore whether any of them [ex]pected to be sent out in [word illegible]. [Let] me here from all of you, and about home [particu]larly, for it will be interesting to me. The seasons here are quite different from those at my old home & county, yet the wether has been very cool ever since I have been to the county. Gorge & John joins me in love to you all. Give my love to Charles Moss & family. I should be very happy to see him out here. I think this country will suit him and Frank very well and I think they would be of much service here; also I could be of great service to them should they have the fever. Give my love to Leander & Archy Creasy. I should be glad to see them here also; my love to Spencer Kelly and Anthony Creasy. Geo. gives his love to Carter Moore and says tell him that he has obtained his lot & had it cut of & expects to burn it off in short and is quite anxious to know whether he expects to come out. Also he gives love to Lucy Skipwith and her brother, Howard, Etta Skipwith, and Polly Brown, and whether Howard Skipwith and Polly Brown has made up the Match or not. Give my love to Thomas Skipwith and all the friends for they are more than I can just at this time mention. This Country will be a fine place after awhile. If any one comes send me a hoe and Ax. I remain Yours obdt,

Susan [Sucky] Faulcon[1]

62 / JOHN H. FAULCON TO JOHN H. COCKE

Monrovia, Liberia, Sep 30th, 1853

Dear Sir: I hope these few lines will find you well and all of your family also. Doctor Maxwell I recived your Letters. [I] did not answer them as full as I wanted to do but I shall try to give you [more news] in the next vessel Leaveing this place for the united States. In it I will write a full Statement of my Self. Mother and George has gotten over the fever and Likes africa if they Like me for he or She that hate Liberia dont Like John H. Faulcon. I had Some thing to Send you and Doctor Maxwell, a kind of choice wood to make walking Sticks. I will Send the article by the next opportunity. Please to consider this Letter for you and Mr Maxwel, as time is Short. The next I write will be two, one for Each of you.

My Love to all friends White and Black. I whish all could write to me that has the Least acquantance Ship with me. Yours in respect truly,

John H. Faulcon

63 / MATILDA SKIPWITH LOMAX TO SALLY COCKE

Fluvania, Virginia   Monrovia, December 10th, 1853

Miss Sarah Cox: I take my pen to inform you that I am enjoying good health at present, Hoping this may find you the same. I recd your letter and was extremely glad to hear of your good health and also the rest of the family. I written to you by the Shirley and sent you some seeds, Coffee & sour sop & Faveres. The largest seed were mangroes. The people that your father sent out are all well. They have went through the fever and now are doing well. I heard that your father intends to send out some more & I sincerely hope that he will send out some of my relation as I am alone now and would like to see some of them very much indeed. I suppose you have heard of the death of Mr. [Hilary] Teage. He has been dead going on 7 months. You will gratify me much by giving my love to all my Relatives, my aunt etc. You will please send me out something by the next opportunity. My children are doing quite well as they are going to school and are making considerable progress. I would like you to send me out some good Books for them. The Articles which you sent out by Mrs. Falkland I received two pieces. Studenfant is well & his family and he is still going in the man of war. I have such a Short notice of the opportunity of sending you this letter that I will close it hoping the next will be more. Your Most Obdt,   Matilda R. Lomax

64 / MATILDA SKIPWITH RICHARDSON TO JOHN H. COCKE

Monrovia, June 20th, 1854

Mr. John Cocks, Dear Sir: This will inform you of my health which is good at Present and hope you are the same. For the Last 2 month I have Bin Sick But I am now getting Better and am Permited to write once more. I have writen 3 or 4 Letters and havnot Receeve any answer from them. I wrote By the Shirley and Sont you Some seeds By Mr Sims. The country is improving verry well. The fever is not as Bad now as it was some years Back. Mrs. falkon is through with the fever & George is now [a] farmer. They are Doing well at Present. Now my three Daughters is going To School. Will you Please send me some Books for them. If you Please send me some Provision Say 1/2 Barrel flour & Pork. This Rains has Bin verry hard times for Pervision.

Sir I would Be Verry happy To see Some of my Relation. I am Now Prepared To Received them. I have great Deal to write But time will not admit. Yours in Christ,   Matilda R. Lomax

[*On same sheet*]

Miss Sarah [Sally Cocke]

Dear miss: This will inform you of my health which is good at Present and hope you are the same. I have writn ofton But no answer have I Receive. But am Determin To write until I Do Receve one. Will you Please Send me some garden seeds By the First opportunity. Give my Love To all your Brothers and To my aunt. I Dont expect To see you no more in Life But Trust will See you in Glory. You must excews my Bad writen. No more at Present. You must send me somethn, But Remain Yours,   Matilda R. Richardson

I am now married and have change my Name.

65 / MARY DIANA STERDIVANT TO JOHN H. COCKE

Fluvana Countie, Virginnia   Monrovia, Liberia, August the 16, 1854

Mr. John H. Cocks, Sir: I write you to in form you that I am well and hopin that thease lines may find you and family well. I have hurd from you onlie by the leter whitch you sent George and that you wish to hear from father and the children. Father is yett [a]Board the man of war. Leander is at his traide and has be come a member of the baptist church and Rose is maried. And you wish to know what we are adoing for a living. Rose husbon goest to see [sea] and I am not maried yett. The cunty is hard and our wants have bin very greate. I have to worke very hard and get onley too dollars per month. We will be glad if you will Send us Somthing to help us. Cusin Paten Skipwith has three suns here, William and Edward and Paten and they send there best Respeck and beg that you would send them sum thing. They are very Small and are not abel to work. The Reason that I write aboute thmen is because I dont know whether you have herd any thing a Boute them.

Please to Give my love to aunt Sukey and my Relations an friends and tel them that I wish to here from then very much. This is a hard cunty and I hav nothing to send them. I ofton think of them. I hope if we never meet in this world a gain to mee[t] you all in heaven. Dear Sir you must Excuese my Bad writen for I had not time to write. Nothing more I Remaine yours,   Mary Diana Studivant[1]

66 / JAMES P. SKIPWITH TO JOHN H. COCKE

Mobile, August 13, 1856

Dear Sir: I know take my seat to write you A fue lines. Thes leave me enjoyin Good helth and I hope that thes may fine you the same. I have not herd from the Plantation for sum time. Mr. John Cocke ware in town yeterday.[1] He left for Green County this morning on the Car. It is very Warme and dul in Mobile at Present. We all think thir will Be A great deal of Sickness in town this Summer. [A] Great menny of the Citizens of Mobile is Gorn north. Well I surpose the time is neare at hand for the Ship to Sail for Africa and as I am detornet thru you to make Africa my Home and my Earn[est] Prays is that God Will Prived Evry thing for the Junney. I hope that your mind is the Same as when I toulk with you in Montgomery and if so I hope I will Be Ready for the Junney. Thir is But one thing that I hate that is I Cant Carry my Wife and Childreans, yet I Belive that God in his Provenedence Will Remember the Poor in Sperite and the Pure in Hart. I Will like to hear from you and at what time I must leave for Virginia as I think that time is near at hand.[2] Nothing more But Reamaine your humbel Servent untel Death, James Skipwith

67 / ROBERT LEANDER STERDIVANT TO JOHN H. COCKE

Monrovia, Liberia, Africa, August 13, 1857

Dear Genl Sir, I write these few lines to inform you that I am still alive & am doing as well as can be expected considering the hardness of the times, hoping at the same time they may find you enjoying good health. I have written you several times, but not knowing where to direct my letters I suppose they have been miscarried; & now I have received your address by Solomon Creacy. I am glad to think that my letter may perhaps reach you safe. On account of the late War here it has caused a great scarcity; provisions has been hard to buy even with money when we had it, & I have stood much in need, & still the hard times has not as yet subsided.[1] So sir I hop to heare from yo. I could never hear from you, therefore I supposed you was no more & was very happy to hear from you by Solmam Cr[e]sa.

I send my best respects to all enquireing friends & tell them I am still in the land of the living. You will please send me a few provisions to assist in finishing my House as the times is very hard for me to do it without some assistance & as I am much in need. [Send me items] Such as Flour, Pork, Fish, Tobacco, & cotton cloths, Calicoes &c. I would wish to come over to America where you are if you think it adviseable, to see all the people but not until I hear your advice on the subject. We have a good country. All [that] is wanting is men of money & Education to make it like other countries. We raise sweet Potatoes, Cassavas, Rice, Sagur Cane, Corn, (a little), & a good deal of Syrup some times, but very lately our greatest Sugar grower has died, & soon after his Death his Sugar Mill worth $3000.00 arri[v]ed from the States. I forget to mention to you to send me a little brown Sugar & a small assortment of Garden Seed. My Self and 3 children are well. Diana and Rose are marrid. The Rest that came out with me are all dead but James. He went back. I Close yours,

Leander Sterdivant[2]

68 / ROBERT LEANDER STERDIVANT
TO SALLY COCKE BRENT

Monrovia, Libria, August 14, 1857

Mrs brent: I am glad of this chance to drop you these few Lines to in form you that my self and 3 children are in good helth and we do hop that these lines may find you all in good helth. All so I was much Pleas to heare from you by Soloman for I had given out all idea of hearing from you any more for it seems that you all had for goten me. We hav had a hard time of wars and famin for 3 years but thank God that we hav no wars at this time but the famin is still in the Land.[1] Diana and Rose are marrid. Tha both hav husbanz of good standing and Leander my son is an grone [man]. I hav put him to the carpinters trad and he hav Provd well and I will say that my children are kind to me and do all tha can for my comforts. You will be Pleas to give my Best Lov to all your servants and tell them that I am in the Land of the Living for God hav taken care of me and my children. My sone hav bin to 2 wars and came back to me saft a gain. I hop that you will consider the hardness of the times and think of what your ant wood do for me if she was aliv for I am in need of help from those that she Left behind. I am Please to heare that you are marrid and I hop that God will prosper the works of your hands. Present my Regard to your gentilman till he have seen me. I hop to heare from you by this vessil. I close by saying,   Leander Sterdivant

69 / MATILDA SKIPWITH RICHARDSON
TO SALLY COCKE BRENT

Monrovia, August 19th, 1857

Dear Madam: I was very glad to hear about you through a friend of mine. I was also glad to hear that you were married and I hope are doing well. I have written to your father and I thought I would just send you a few lines to let you know that I am well. I have writen you several times and have never received one from you. I wish I could hear from you. Please give my love to your brother Charles and I would be glad if you would send me some thing for myself and three children. Please do not think hard, my asking you for some thing. I would not do it but really the times are so hard out here. Please to ask Aunt Lervenia to send me some dryed peaches and to send my children some nuts & some dryed apples. Give my love also to Uncle Nedd and his wife and to all inquiring friends far and near.

As I have such short time to write and have told you all the news in your fathers letter you must get that and read it. I[f] you do send me anything please send to Mr. William Johnson, C. C. Monrovia, and he will give them to me and if I should die before they gets here he will give them to my children.[1] The person that send you these letters is the daughter of Peyton Skipwith, now Matilda Richardson. I hope to hear from you before long. Much love to yourself. You must tell me how many children you have when you write. Believe me to remain Your affectionate friend.   Matilda Richardson

70 / SOLOMON CREECY TO JOHN H. COCKE

Monrovia, Liberia, August 19, 1857

Sir: You will see by this that I am well at this time and hope that these few lines may find you and family the same.[1] I arrived heare saft and I am Please with the cuntry so far as I have seen as yet but it wants men of money to make it a Land of Plenty. I hav seen Leander and his 3 children; thare all well. He told me that Peter, Judy, and Rithard are dead. Diana and Rose are marid and send thar best Lov to you. AllSo I hav seen John and his mother. Tha are well and send thar Lov. George I hav not seen. He is at Cap[e] Mount. Sir you will Pleas send me a small corn mill. I find that the times are hard owing to the Lat wars and famin that hav bin heare. So I beg you to send me a Barrel of flour, if you Please. I have begun to farm as my trad hav not com in play as yet. Sir you will Pleas Giv my best Lov to all of your family and your servants and my brothers. I hop that you send isom and his family out as we are maits.   Soloman

[*In same envelope*]   Monrovia Liberia August 19 1857

To master charles:[2]   Sir you will see by this that I am in good helth at this time and I hoP that these few lines may find you and your family the same. Sir I arived heare saft and we had a fine Passag. I am much Pleis with this cuntry more then [I expected]. Tha hav a bad time with famin and wars for 3 years so it hav made Provisions very high so I hop sir that you will try and send me some thin in the way of Provisions. I cant work at my traid as yet so I am at work on my farm. The wars are all over but famin is not as yet but hav maid it hard for the hold cuntry.   Soloman

71 / SUCKY FAULCON TO JOHN H. COCKE

Monrovia, Aug 21/57

My Dear Old Master,   I take this my peen in hand to inform you of my present state of health. I must say thank god that I am yet a live tho my health is not very good but it is beter than it have been in girnal and hope that thes lines may find you in joying the Blessing of good health. I am glad to See Solomon out here With me. My Son is quit[e] Well. He is away from me. I have not Seen him for 3 mo. He is at Cerelone [Sierra Leone] im ployed to keep facttry for trayding. I hope that he will do Well there. Please to Write me more for I would like to here from you all [more] oftin than i do. Please to tell me how my Sister is When you Write me. I herd about the death of my Sister, haner taler. I was sory to her it but the Lord Will must Bee don. It be coumes us to be reckinsile to the Will of the Lord. I Would like to See you all on[c]e more in life but it Semes not to bee So. If We never meet in this World I hope that We may meet in heven. May god bless you all. I have my land and A house on it but I have know one to till the Sould [soil] for me. I has to Work out for my living and I am glad that I can Work for it. God give me health and streanth. I Will Write you and till I can get a Letter from you, tell all my inquiering friend houdy for me. No more to Say. I remane yours,

Suckey forking

72 / MATILDA SKIPWITH RICHARDSON TO JOHN H. COCKE

Monrovia, August, 1857

Dear Sir: I am most happy to hear from you through a friend, and glad to find you are still well and that Sally is married at last. I have writen you several times and never received an answer to one. I do not know how it is unless I did not address right. Solomon arrived safe to Monrovia on the 10th of July. He has had but one slight attact of fever— excepting that, he has been well. He Seems to like the place very much, he said better than he thought he would. I think he will do very well out here. Sucky Faulcon is doing very well. She is staying at a boarding house. As for her son George he is at Cape Mount. As for Sturvent he is doing very well, and for Jack Faulcon, he is doing very well at his old trade.

And now about myself: Thank the Lord I am Still Spared to be able to write to you once more. Since the death of my people I some times feel almost broken up and then when I look and think I see that the Lord has not put on me no more than I can bare. I have been in the Baptist Church as a member for eighteen years, and I have [been a] member of Daughters of Temperance for four years [and] Sisters of friendship for five years. I hear there are some of my people are coming out here. Is it so or not? I would be most happy to see some out here before my eyes be closed in death. As for my Uncle George I wish you would try and do all you can in prevailing on him to come out here. My father before he died talked a great deal about his brother and wished he would come out here.

Please give my love to Aunt L. Tell [her] I was sorry to hear of the death of her son nedd. Tell her for me that she must remember "that the Lord Giveth and the Lord taketh away." The fever is not so bad now as it used to be. The older the place gets and the more it is cultivated the better the fever is.

Mason's work is a $1 a day, head workman $3 a day, Carpenters $1 do. Monrovia is looking very finely now. We are improving in most everything. When shall I hear from you? I long to have a letter from you. This year has very hard and I am afraid it will be still more so next in consequence of our people having to go to war so much with the natives and not having much rain this season. The sun has parched up mostly all the rice [in] the fields so if you would be so kind as to send me out something for myself and three children I would feel much obliged, any thing I do not mind what it is.[1] I wrote to you last June but it was only a short one just to let you [know] I am living. Please give my love to your daughter Sally. I intend to write to her by this same vessel. Please give my love to all my friends and Believe me to remain your affectionate friend, Matilda Richardson

[*On same sheet*]

Dear Philip:[2]   I thought I would not let your father's letter go without sending you a few lines to say I am well and I hope you are the same. I thought you would have written me to let me know how your family are. I was glad to hear from you by Solomon. Please give my love to all my people and friends. I would be obliged if you would be so kind as to send me some flour. You must excuse this short letter. Good bye,

Matilda Richardson

73 / SOLOMON CREECY TO JOHN H. COCKE

Liberia, Africa, January 29th, 1858

Dear Sir: I take the pleasure of writing you a few words with a great Satisfaction. I am well as can be expected and my health has permited me to Draw my land and cuted a farm upon it and I am abuilding my [house] at present. James has come out and I Receved the present you Sent me and I thank you so very much for your kinderness.[1] I wood be varry that thankful if you would please to send me Some garden Seeds and a few cherrykee ro[s]es and a few of your best cotten Seede.

James Skip[with], I was Down to See him the other Day from my farm and he had and attack of the fever and I think he is getting Some what over the fever. I [am] very Glad to Say that I am Still yet aholding to my tem[p]eranc[e] Doctrines & I think it is the greatest thing I Ever Done. Thos[e] tha[t] hold to thare temerance Doctrine [two words illegible] whear it is great if improvement to the country and I am vary glad of it to see Such a Doctrine. And I hope that thees few words m[a]y find you well and familey and give my respects to all of you familey and also to the poeple of cullar. I Remains Your Obt Svt,   Solmon Cree[cy]

Dear Master: I Wish you would Be Please to Write to the Baptis church in Alabama. I forgot to get my Pappers from the church. Please

to get them an send them By the Returne of the Ship if you Please. Yours
until death.   Solmon Cresea

74 / MOLLY HAYNES TO JOHN H. COCKE

Monrovia, Liberia. Jany 30th, 1858.

Dear Sir: We received yours of the 2nd of November 1857, and certainly we wer very thankful having recived your letter. But we must say that it was no ways encourageing to us. Farther is not at home now, but on Board of the United States Ship Cumberland, now on this Station. We take this opportunity to write because Father is not home. Therefore, Dear Sir you will allow us to say that we have not at anytime written you. Give my love to Mrs. Brent & tell her that I received the things she sent, and was very thankful for the same, and to all my relations and tell them that I am well & hope they are the same. You sent to know who of us is living—they are as follows: My Farther, Leander, Rose and myself (Molly). Julia, Richard, & Peter is dead; James he went to Philadelphia. I close by saying I am yours.   Molly Haynes[1]

75 / MATILDA SKIPWITH RICHARDSON TO JOHN H. COCKE

Monrovia, Febry 1st, 1858

Dear Sir: I am truly glad to be able once more to send you a few lines and to thank you for the kind letter I received from you by my Cousin James. He arrived here on the 25th December and he seems to like the place very well. He has had but little fever. I have three children, one thirteen the next eight and the other one 7. They go to School every day. Please give my love to Mrs. S. Brent and tell her that I am much obliged to her for what she sent me. Please give my love to my Aunt L. and to all my friends. I expect most all the rest of the people will write to you.

I am happy to be able to tell you that Solomon is doing very well at farming. I must now close my letter as I have told you all the news. I remain Your friend,   Matilda Richardson

76 / MATILDA SKIPWITH RICHARDSON
TO SALLY COCKE BRENT

Monrovia, Febry 1st, 1858

Dear Miss Sally: I have just closed a letter to your father and I thought I would send you a few lines with his. I was sorry not to hear from you. Your father told me in his letter that you were not at home. I hope you will not think any thing about these few lines as I have no news to tell you. As time is so short I hope you will excuse me as this packet will leave tomorrow morning. I must now say good bye as I have nothing more to tell you. Hoping you are well and I hope it will not be long before I hear from you. I remain Your affectionate friend,

Matilda Richardson

77 / JOHN H. FAULCON TO JOHN H. COCKE

Monrovia, Liberia, West Africa, Feb 1st, 1858

Dear General and friend: You have thought hard of my not writing to you so often. Since the arivel of Mother and George I have writen one time and would have wrote oftener but there arivel gave me chance to go away to work. Times was dull here and where ever I could See a chance to make bread I had to do so. The places I have bin going to was Nanna Kroo which is between Sinue and Cape palmir where there is little chance to write to Monrovia much more America. Since Mother and George arived here I have bin away Six times [during] which oppertunities to write to the United States was seldom. God nose I feal it my duty to write you. I was a Slave. How did I get out here? Was it not by your good will? And [did] I Stop writeing because Mother and George was clear of Slavery? Not so. Oppertunity and health has cause this. When Soloman arived here I was Sick [and] could not write. Any of the other people could have Said So in there letters. I would have don So for them. I am now Sick and have bin under the doctor ever Since October—first, Doc Mc Gill and Last Doc Smith from Bassa.[1] I am now bad off but can not employ a doctor no longer because what meanes I had are out. Had I not strove hard through raine and dry whether the beging List would have had me before now. I hope these few Lines may find you and family well. My Best respects to all. I remane your obedent Servant,

John H Faulcon

78 / JAMES P. SKIPWITH TO JOHN H. COCKE

Monrovia. Liberia. Africa. July 17. 1858

Dear Sir: I Now embrace this opportunity of writing to you as the Packet will leave heir in a few days for the states. I resive your letter By the Packet & ware Glad to heir from you & my Friends. Thees lines leave me in as Good health as I can expect & I hope thees will find you well & enjoyen Good health. I am Glad that I can say that I am BetterPlease with Africa now then I ware when I wrote to you By the Packet Before. Now I see that I did not know any thing about this Country. But now I am Better Please with Africa then I thought I ever would Be. I now belive that this [is] the Country for all of my Race & God Grant that I may live to see the day when I will strike hand with meny of my Freinds in Liberia for with a little help we can live heir as well as we can in America. But I tell you that the African fever is somthing that lay as a ded wate on the minds of the Best men in Africa. I am told By the Dr. that I had it very light. In dead I ware more Frighten then I ware hurt. It is true that any one from the South do not suffer like one from the north. Thir is But little diffrencein this Climant an South Ala. Thir is nothing new in Africa, now the Wars is all over for a while. But it very dul times Just now. Oen to the late War in the Country the Govement has Become much embrance [embarrassed] But we hope that in a few years She will recover & hope that we will have a Country at last. I have Converce with the leading & Furst Men of this Republice sutch as President Benson & President Robits which have enlight me & encorge me a gredeal as to getting a living in Africa & I have not the smals dout if I keep my health I can make a living in this Country.[1] I cant Say mutch about my Farm now But when I write to you agane I hope to Be Abel to tell you if thir is any verger [virtue] in tilling the lands in Africa. The most of our Richs & independent Men of this Country is Farmes. You wish to her from thous People that went to the upper County. The People at Carysburg do not suffer as the People that Stop about Monrovia & on the Sea Board.[2] But it is Better for any one to have the fever at once. Tha Stande much better. Matilda and her children are well. John an his Mother is well. As for George, tha do not know what has Be Come of him. Leander children are well. Leander is on boarde of a man of war. I have not seen him Sence I arive hirr. Solman is well an has Compleated his house an [is] living on his Farm. My Respect to all the Servents. Yours in the Bonds of Christian love,

James Skipwith

79 / MATILDA SKIPWITH RICHARDSON TO SALLY COCKE BRENT

Monrovia, Africa, July the 24, 1858

Mrs. Sally F. Brent: I am glad that an opportunity is afforded to hand you a few lines which leave me and mine in good health and I hope may find you enjoying the Blessings of a favorable Providence. I were glad to here from you and the servents By Solmon letter for I ashore you that I am glad to here from you at any time and Beg that you would write to me By evry opportunity as it is a great treat to me to resive a letter from your hands. I am getteing on as well as I can expect But not as well as I should like to do. But I still look forde for a Better times and hope that time is not far of. I hope to live to see the day when Africa this our dark Country shall rise Bud and Blossom as the rose of the Garden of life. Thir is nothing New at this time that is worth writing. My 3 children are well and gose to school and are lurning very fast to Read and write. Leander children are well and send love to you and all the Family. Leander is not heir. He is on Board of a manofwar with Mr. John Barroad. We look for them every day. Cousin James is living with me. He is over the fever an is well please with Liberia an wish to be Rememberd to white and colored. Solmon wish to Be Remberd also to all the Friends. Jack and his Mother are well and send love to all the Freinds. This is the rany seons [season] with us now and it is very dull at this time with us in Africa. It is true that I have Been to this Country 20 years an is true I have not got a Brick House. But what is the case if my father Esate [Estate] had not Been robed, I chould have had a Plenty to live no [on] an to live well all my days. But after my Father death I had no one to see to his Estate thirfore I got nothing from his Esate But 3 or 4 lots in town which is not worth nothing if tha ware sould. Please to Remember me to all the Family. Tell aunt Lavinia that I often think of her and tell her that she must write to me By the returne of the Packet. And if we never meet in this world agane I hope to meet you on the other side of Jordan where we shall Be ever Present with the Lord and ware we shall pluck new lives from the tree of life and where Congregations never Break up and sabbaths have no end. I would like to say agreadel more But time will not atmit Just now. I must now come to a close. Yours in the Bounds of Christen love. Please to give my love [to] evry Body.

Matilda Richardson

80 / JAMES P. SKIPWITH TO JOHN H. COCKE

Gen Cocke   Monrovia. Liberia. Nov. the 12. 1858

Dear Sir: It is with delight that I embrace this opportunity by the United States Sloop of War which arive hirr 4 days ag[o] with the recoved Africans from Charlston and will leave heir to morrow.[1] So I Could not let this opportunety Past. Thees lines leave me well and I truly hope thee may fine you the same and all the Friends. I have Be Come Well Please with this country and is more and more incouage every day. I Belive thir is no Betty Cuntry Below the sun for any race Notwithstanding it is Very dul time heir and Very little cand Be made heir. But we still hope for Better things and as thir is no Wars in the Country now and a Plenty of pervasion [provision] But Very little Cash. The President says

that the Goverment will in a few mounts Be out of det and at which time
we hope to Be a happy Nathinon. I hope to resive severl lettrs By the
Packet which we look for about one mont from this time. All my freinds
wish to Be Remeard to you. Solomon is well an send his love to you. Heis
formind [he is farming] and is very well and wish to Be Remembeard to
all his frends. I am dooing as well as I can expect as times is Very dull and
Very little to Bemade. I am keeping A Bake Shop and I take in about one
dollar a day. I hope that I will Be Able to take in 2 A day if I keep my
helth. You must excuse Bad writing as it is late, so I must Close.

James P. Skipwith

81 / JAMES P. SKIPWITH TO JOHN H. COCKE

Monrovia, Liberia, Africa, Feb. the 11, 1859

Dear Sir: I am Glad an opportunity is afforded to hand you a few
lines which leave me and mine in Good health and I hope may find you
enjoying the Blessings of a favorable Providence. I have not much But
still something I think worth Communicating. Since I wrote you last the
Lord has Blesst us with Good health which I hope will Continner. We are
under the empression that we shall hav to Carry War with the Natives
tribe at Grand Cape Mount. But I hope that we shall be able to Com-
plemise with the kings for this is a Bad time with us to Fight War with
enny Country for this Government is much in need of funds at Present. I
hope nothing will take Place to Pervent her Progress. I am still trying to
Farm But cannot see But little Progress as yet. It is true that I have But little means and cannot get surfishon tools. I have 10 acres of Land for
which I Pade $6 an Acre. I am not disincorrige. I belive that I shall make
my Bread. It is well to Plant Coffee trees and it is well to Plant Cotton
But it will Be several years Before it will Pay. Sugar Cane and Pottaters,
Ground nuts an Foulds [fruits?] of driffrent kinds is Best. Natives Laber
Can Be Obtane for $3 Per Mount [month]. You can Buy Publice Lands
for Fifty Cents acres. The Land that I Bought is front Land on the St.
Paul River. No Better Land has ever Ben found on James River. I hope
that in a few years that cotton will Pay us for making it in this Country
But it will not do it now. We are too Poor to trust alone on cotton until
each Farmer can make from 2 to 3 Bales of Cotton. No one will Care to
take it By the small [amount]. Solomon is well. He will write you By this
opportunity. All of my Freinds is well and wish to Be Rememberd to you
and all. Jack is Marride and has one dorter to Comence with. Solomon is
not Marrade But will Be in short I think. I hope that Before menny years I
shall see some of my freeinds from Alabama in Africa. If you shuld send
them to Africa impress it aporn them to Bring with them tools for tha are

few an very dear in this Country. It makes no driffrence about the kind. All kinds will Come in Play. My self an Solomon Both resive our Letters from the Church in Ala. I thank [you] for your kinnest. Farewell. Very Respectfully yours in the Bond of Christian affection,   J. Skipwith

82 / WILLIAM LEANDER STERDIVANT TO JOHN H. COCKE

Monrovia, Augus th 12, A D 1859

Dear sir: By this you may see that I and all is well and we hope that you is the sam. I am indeed happy that I have this opportunity of writen you these fue lines. I mus say it is by the mursey of God. When I leave thair I was quite A BaBe. I did not no any one that I leave behind me but sence I have bin hir I have hird something about them wich my father told me. He told me about you and how kind you Sister was to him. For that cause I was or felt it my duty to write. I hope that you can Read this leter. I have not Bin to school long. I have Bin to my tread [trade], the carpinter tread, and now I am with my father. My Sister Dinah is well and Sister Rose also. Tha are Both married now. I have Bin to too wars and come out victorersly. I recive one shot in my leg But non to hirt. This is hard cuntry indeed so Dear Sir I hope you will not fail to send me some thing. I would be very glad of it indeed.

P S. My father is well. Mr. Robert L. Sterdivant he goes to se[a] now. I love my contry much. I has no other I prefer bean hir. It is true Provisions is very hie, tobaco, cloth, and so forth. But I hope that they will be cheaper after wile. Those things [that we requested] I hope that you will not fail to send us if you pleas. We will be very happy to Recive then from you. I think I mus close for the PResant,

William Leander Sterdivant[1]

This is my one hand writing. I hope you will not fail to ancer me.

83 / JAMES P. SKIPWITH TO JOHN H. COCKE

Monrovia, Liberia, Aug. the 20. 1859

Dear Sir: I resive yours By the returne of the Packet from american & ware much Please to heair from you & my freinds. I am glad that an opportunity is afforded to hand you a few linaes which leave me & my friends in good health & I hope may find you enjoying the Blessings of a favorable Providence. I have not much (But still something I think) worth communicating. Since I wrote you last the Lord has in mercy

visited the settlement & I have had the Pleasure of seen 31 hopeful converts Reside with Christ in Baptism. Besides a number have Joined the
Methodists. The natives are more & more friendly. Their confidence be-
gins to awaken. They see that it is our wish to do them good & hostilities
have ceased with them. We have daily applications to receive their children in to our church & Sabath school. 4 of the converts are natives of
this country and are fild with the holy Goast. We have great write to
look Back on the few mounts that Pass and thank God for the Menny
Blessing that he has Bestore aporne Liberia. For when I look at menny
things and the goodnis of God to this nathion I think that the time is near
at hand when Ethiopia is to Stretch its hands in Prayer and Praise to
God. I have the Pleasuer of Returne you our thanks for the hansom
Preasent of Sabbath School Books which we resive By the Packet. As I
am one of the Teachers of the Sabbath I returne my thanks also and hope
that the Lord will Bless you for the Good feelings that you have for
Liberia.

Sir you wish me to say what I think of the little one becomeing a
Thousand. Hard hard indeed was the contest for fredom & the str[u]ggle
for independence. The Golden sun of liberty had nearly set in the Gloom
of an Eternal night. But sir all dangers is not death. Our country stands at
the Present time on Commanding Ground. Older nations with drifferent
systems of Government may Be somewhat slow to acknowledge all that
Justly Belongs to us. But we may feel without vanity that Liberia is doing
her Part in the Great Work of improving human affairs. There are two
principles gentlemen strictly and purely Liberian which are more likely to
overrun the civilized world, which are S. A. Benson & J. J. Roberts. Thee
light that led them this far was light from heaven. I Belive that Liberia
will yet stand with the eather Parts of the Civilized world. O praise the
Lord all ye nations! Praise him all ye people for his merciful kindness is
Great toward us and the truth of the Lord endureth for ever! [P]raise the
Lord!

Sir you wish me to say somthing about the high lands of the intur
[interior] about Carysburgh. I have heard a greadeal But have seen very
little. It is sa[i]d to Be very helthy & also that the land is fine table land.
Carysburgh is improving very Rappit and in a few years will become the
seat of Government. I intend taking a small excursion in the country But
cannot Promist when that will be as the rains has set in and I am desirous
to get on with my fairm. I find that time is like gold dust with me. Just
now I am now devideing my time. I Go to Days Hope High School & the
Ballance of my time to my Plantation. I have found that a man must
have an Ed[u]cation to be aman in enny county. I now regreat that I did
not enprove my tallent when I warse young. I now see that what you
tould me ware for my own Good. Please to tell my friends that think of
coming to Africa [to] try an master thir Book. I am truly sorry that I did

not take your advice when I ware young. But I have one hope. What man has don man cando. I am Studing for the Ministry. I belive that is the Work that the Lord has apoint [me] for in Africa. Solmon is quit Sick and has Ben for sum time. He is a little Better now. He expose him self & taken Could. Matildas Husband is unwell & has Ben for sumtime. The rest of my friends is well. Jack will write to you [about] the tools for farming. We use all the tools But the Plough—enny that you wish to send. Yours truly,   James P. Skipwith

P S I have enjoyed som of the Pri[v]alige of a free man. I have surve my Curntery as Grand Juery and as Pettet Jurry and also as voting, somthing strong [strange?] to me. One thing more that I must Say. Thir is one thing that I am fraid will Prove as a Curst on Liberia. Mr. Cooper the oner of the Sugar mill is about to still Rum. I am fraid it will curst to Liberia.   J. P. S.

84 / JAMES P. SKIPWITH TO BERTHIER EDWARDS

Monrovia, Liberia, May the 31. 1860

Dear Bertheer Edwards,[1] Dear Sir: The arrival of the Bark Page Gives me an opportunity to hand you a few lines which I hope may find you in good health. Nothing very interesting has taken place since I wrote you last only that among the last Emigrants that came out there has been some Considerable Sickness But only two death. I know you wish me to write you a Great deal But I must Plead the old Excuse, Want of time, for I find that a man must work Both head & hands to make a living in this country. Our work is almost like Building the walls of Jerusalem. We have to carry our tools all day in our hands & our Bibles at Night. Yet Notwithstanding it is the Best Country for the Black man that is to Be found on the face of the Earth. God intended Africa for the Black Race.

Please Give my love to Patesy & Children.[2] Tell her that I did not write to her By this opportunity. I writen to her a few monts ago By the Bark Benson & will write again By the Packet if nothing hapens. Tell her to write to me By the first opportunity. I have not heard from ala. for along time. Whin you write againe tell me sumthing about them. I wish to write to them But do not now how to derit [direct] my letter to. Please give me de rection.

I must now come to a close as it is now late. My respect to Both White & Colored. Farewell, very respectfully your,   James P. Skipwith

P O By the first opportunity send us some of your Gardin seeds as we cannot Get them heair. Cabage seeds, Beens Snaps & as meny other kind as you like and do not fail to write Soon.   J. P. Skipwith

H. W. Dennis Esqr,   Monrovia, June 25, 1860
Agt A.C.S. Monrovia

Sir: In december last you was kind enough as to inform me that a
box to my address had been landed from the M. C. Stevens at the Colonial Warehouse. On calling for it, it could not be found, nor have I recieved it up to this time. I am not informed of its Value, Not having recieved any information as to what the box contained, nor was there any
bill of Lading for it sent me. As you seem to be certain that it was Landed
for me & as I have not recieved it, I think the loss should be made good to
me, and I do hereby claim and demand thirty dollars of you for it, which
I hope you will be good enough as to settle without futher delay. I am
Sir, Respectfully Yours,   James P. Skipwith

Recd payment June 25 1860

86 / JAMES P. SKIPWITH TO JOHN H. COCKE

                                            Monrovia, July the 10. 1860

Hon & dear Sir: I received your letter of the 16 of April 1860 & read
its contents with much interest by the arrival of the Packet. I am Glad to
heare that your health is much Beter now then it ware last winter. Thees
leave me & freinds in as good health as can be expect as the rains is now
Very heavy & the health in Genreal is not Very Good. I am Prode to hare
of the Great revial that has taken Place amoung your Servints. God
Grant that it may not Stop thir But it may cover the hold of america like
the Water cover the chanil of the Great deep till all shall know the Lord
whome to know is life eternel & may the grace of our Lord Jesus Christ
may be with you, with your families, & with all you have to do with.
Tell the Breathen to Be Strong in the Lord & in his mightey Power for as
much as we know that thir is a rest remaine for the People of God, a
House not made with hands But eternel in the Heaven. Since I writen to
you last I have Vissit Carysburg also Grand Cape Mount. It is a good
healthy Place & thir farm lands can be obtain about ten miles from the
Cape up the river. Thir are 3 drifent rivers. Each have Good table lands
for farmes. The People of Cape mount has now Cormence to turne thir
minds to till the Earth. Thir is no Better farm land in Liberia but your
People must have sum thing to make a start or thay will not do well in no
Part of Africa.

      The Settlement of Carysburg it may sute sum But it donot Suite me. It
is a healthy Place, I belive. It is an out of the way place in the first Place.

If the People makes more then they want for them selves thir is no way to convate it to market which is monrovia. Thir is no other Place for them to sell such things as thay make for market. But to live in Carysburg & to have sutch things as you may wish to sell, to have them Brought 20 miles to the river & 20 miles down to Monrovia which is 40 miles, the Prophes [profits] that is made is nothings, so you see that the People comes to this Country Poor & thay remaine Poor. Carysburg is not what it is Crackup to be. At last dear sir you wish to have my advice about the Best Place for your People. My dear sir do not Give Your Servents all to girther to the [colonization] society. Do a little Sumthing for them your self. When your six mounts is up, sick or well, you must come out of that house. Evry man that comes to this Country do not Get over the fever in six mounts nor twelve mounts. I must say as I think if you can make sutch arangements which I no dout that you can that is to Settle your People on the road leading from the St Paule river to Carysburg. It is good table land and good water and they can settle from 2 miles to 5 miles on this road. This is the Best Place for them. This land can be bought for 50 cents per acre. Idonot know of eny thing that could make me Happyer then to See your People up by the side of eny People that has come to Liberia. I ware in hopes of seen sum of your People & my freinds on Board of the Packet this trip. I ware sadly disorpiented but I Hopes to see them in Shorte. Now is the time if you wish to send your People to this Country. I know that it would be a Great Pleasure to you to heare that your servents ware doing well in this Country. Now settle your People on that road & you will have Pleasure with little Expence. I am Glad to hear in your letter that they are doing Better then Ever as thay has now come up to the mark that you wish them to come to. Send them that thay may do sum thing for them selves. The road to Carysburg is not compleat, no Bridges on this road. Mrs. Faulcons People is heair & doing well as can expect. Leander, the Old man, I have not see him as yet. He is on Board of the man of war. His 3 Children is hear in Monrovia. The 2 Girls is marread. The Boy is working at the Carpners strade. Jack & his Mother is heair. I will not say much about them, you can Judge the Balence. No Cats & no Gogs [dogs] live worse. [They are] a disgrace to our famely. I do not ond [own] them. They ought to be in the Back side of your cotton farm. Mr. Teirls Peopls is in Carysburg.[1] I converse with Sum of them when I vissit that Place. They told me of the Great disavange in which they labirs under. Matilda wish to be rememberd to you & freinds and says you have for Goten her. You have not writen to her nor say eny thing in your letter about her. She will Be Glad to resive sumthing from you By the returne of the Packet. I will write to you again in Short at which time I will let you know sumthing about my farm & my prospect as for the Preaching of the Gospel. You must excuse this Bad writen letter as I am very nervis since I cormence this. Now unto him that is able to keep me from falling and to present me before the presence of His Glory with Exceeding Joy Be Glory and majesty dominion and Power forever and ever aman.   J. P. Skipwith

87 / MATILDA SKIPWITH RICHARDSON
TO RICHARD SKIPWITH

Monrovia, Liberia, Febry 22nd, 1861

My dear Cousin: I am sure you will be sorry to hear that Cousin James [Skipwith] is dead. He went to Bassa last year and going all in the wet he got cold and gave him diarrhia and he had the Doctor to him but could do him no good. It lasted on him until January last. When he received your letter he was sick in bed and it made him worst instead of better for he was expecting you. He wanted to see you but as you did not come you will not see him any more in this world. But he said he was going to rest and hope that you all will meet him in heaven. He said that he hope that you will take good care of his children and bring them up in the fear of the Lord. When he came out here he came to my house and staid with me until he died and I done all that I could for his comfort and happyness. But you must try and not let it go hard with you for the Lord givinth and the Lord taketh. You must try and look to the Lord and he will help you through all you troubles.

I hope it may not be long before I will see you out here. I must now come to a close as I have told you all the news. My husband died a year before James. Hoping that you are all well—I remain Your affectionate Cousin,   Matilda Richardson

[On same sheet]

My dear Cousin William: I thought I would just send you a few lines to let you know that your Brother is dead. He was sick in bed when he received your letter. He talked a great deal about you all. He said that he hope you all will try and meet him in heaven for he said that he was going to rest in Jesus.

Please give my love to Berther Edwards and tell him that I can not write this time but will do so another. I hope he is well. You can tell him that his Cousin received his letter also and was glad to hear from him. I must close as I have nothing more to say. There are a great many of our people gone to war. I want you to give my love to all the friends. I must say good bye—Your affectionate Cousin,   Matilda Richardson

Monrovia, Febry 23rd, 1861

Dear Sir: I thought as my Cousin was dead I would send you a few
lines to tell you all about him. He went to Bassa year before last and took
cold and it lasted on him until the middle of January. He spoke about
you all. When he received your letter he was down in his bed very sick.
He was hopping to see his wife and as she did not come it made him
worse. But he spoke very cheerful about dieing. He said he was going to
rest in Jesus and he hope that he may see you all there.

As for his prospects in life he did as well as could be expected in Africa
and as about his Church affair he done well and perhaps he would have
been a preacher if he had been spared. But as the Lord knew best he took
him to himself. As for his mother and Father he talk a great deal about
them.

As for Aunt Sucky she has been very sick but I think she is on the
mend. As for all the rest of us we are well. There are right smart of our
people gon to palmas to war. Them have been gon 3 weeks and have not
heard from them but are expecting them the end of this week.[1] There was
only a year and 3 weeks between my Husband and Cousin Jameses
death.

Please give my love to Mrs. Brent. I have writen to her but have not received an answer. Tell her that since I wrote to her I have seen a great
deal of trouble and am now left all in the hands of the Lord. Please give
my love to all my friends. Tell them that I am still living and well. Please
give my love to Aunt Levinia. Will you be so kind as to send me some
seeds and let there be some hard head cabbage.

I must now come to aclose as I have nothing more to say. I remain
Yours Respectfully,   Matilda Ritchardson

3/LETTERS OF THE PAGE–ANDREWS NEGROES

Mrs. Anne Randolph Page was one of many members of the planter aristocracy of late eighteenth- and early nineteenth-century Virginia who viewed slavery as an evil and earnestly desired its elimination. Establishment of the American Colonization Society in 1817 offered solution of the troublesome problem of disposing of emancipated blacks in a way that promised to benefit both servants and masters and at the same time promote the cause of Christianity in Africa. Mrs. Page, a deeply religious woman, was an early and enthusiastic supporter of the society and its work. The death of her husband, Matthew Page, in 1826 required the sale of more than 100 of his slaves to settle debts owed by the estate. After witnessing this sad event, Mrs. Page applied herself with renewed zeal to the task of preparing for freedom in Africa the slaves remaining under her control. Like John Hartwell Cocke, she considered intensive religious training to be an essential part of the preparation. To this end she scheduled daily worship services at which she or a minister expounded the scriptures to the blacks, led them in prayer, and urged them to pattern their lives in accordance with Christian principles. She warned them of the hardships that they would experience in Africa and encouraged them to develop qualities and skills that would enable them to achieve success and happiness in their new homes.

She sent the first group of servants to Liberia in 1832 and before her death in 1838, two more parties were dispatched. The total number sent may have been twenty-three, of whom a substantial portion were mechanics and artisans. She furnished the émigrés with implements and tools that they would need in Liberia along with a year's supply of provisions and other useful articles.[1]

After Mrs. Page's death, her daughter Sarah and Sarah's husband, the Reverend Charles W. Andrews, an Episcopal minister, sent some of their blacks to Liberia. Sarah and Charles Andrews kept in close touch with Mrs. Page's former slaves as well as with their own.[2]

The experiences of the Page-Andrews blacks were similar to those of Negroes sent to Liberia by other planters. Adjusting to the strange land and earning a livelihood involved many difficulties. Those who were able to combine farming with some other activity such as blacksmithing or trading usually got along better than those who were restricted to agricultural pursuits. Vegetables, including rice, potatoes, and cassadas, were the principal crops.[3] One of the blacks grew coffee and sent a sample to Reverend Andrews, but he had difficulty finding a market for this product in Liberia. These colonists, like most others, plied their white correspondents with requests for many articles needed for their sustenance and comfort or for use in trade. But requests were made in a dignified manner, without begging or fawning. Books had high rating among items requested, and next to livelihood, health, and religion, learning seems to have been their greatest concern.

Some of the correspondents expressed great pride in the progress of their adopted country, and at least three of them participated in military operations conducted by Liberian authorities. Two of the most interesting letters tell of a successful expedition against a Spanish slave-trading establishment and the release of some of the black captives intended for the slave traffic.

The letters indicate a deep and enduring affection of the colonists for their white connections in Virginia. More impressive is what they reveal of the closeness of family ties among the blacks. A typical passage is that contained in Robert M. Page's letter to the Reverend and Mrs. Andrews, May 6, 1839: "Please give my love to my dear mother and all my dear friends in America. If I should not see them again in this world I hope to meet them all in heaven." Residence in Liberia as freedmen seemed to strengthen pride in family, in individual identity, and in a sense of obligation to near relatives, especially those who shared the Liberian experience. Solomon S. Page in one of his letters requested Andrews to "let me know what S stand for in my name," and Robert M. Page wrote: "I would be glad to learn our true ages as somehow we have lost the acct." Thomas M. Page closes his letter of May 1849 with a tribute to his second wife, noting particularly that she was good to her stepchildren, "quite an industrious woman . . . makes all the clothes . . . and . . . is a good Christian too belonging to the same church that I belong to viz. the Baptist church."

Most of the correspondents were kinfolk and while precise relationships are sometimes difficult to determine, it seems clear that Robert M. Page, John M. Page, Sr., and Thomas M. Page were brothers. Solomon S. Page was the son of Thomas M. Page. Another John M. Page, who once signed himself John junior Page, was the son of Robert M. Page; he took great pride in serving as his father's amanuensis.

Nine of the eleven extant letters were edited by Mary F. Goodwin and published as "A Liberian Packet" in the *Virginia Magazine of History and Biography* 59 (1951): 72-88. The originals of eight of these letters are in the library of the Virginia Historical Society. Although I found Miss Goodwin's transcriptions to be remarkably accurate, I used the manuscripts in preparing this chapter. Since I could not locate the original of the letter of Thomas M. Page to Charles W. Andrews dated May 1849, I used the printed version as it appears in Miss Goodwin's article. The letter of Robert M. Page to Andrews written May 6, 1839, and that of John M. Page to Andrews bearing no date but obviously written in 1840, have not previously been published; for these I used the original manuscripts from the Charles W. Andrews Papers at Duke University.

89 / ROBERT M. PAGE TO CHARLES W. AND SARAH P. ANDREWS

Edina, May 6th, 1839

My very dear friends,   Your very kind letter of the 5 of Janary was duely received and read with much satisfaction, I was glad to hear that you were well and that you continue to feel interested in my welfar. The Lord is still blessing me with health and comfort. Though Africa is a new country with some inconveniences, yet we enjoy many blessed privileges. We have to work ha[r]d but we get a tolerable comfortable support. We live in a village where we have good opportunities of hearing the gospel and of schooling our children. We have a small Baptist Church where we have preaching every Sabbath. Three of our boys, Afred, John and Robert go to school constantly. John attends the Mission school and has made very good improvement. He can read well in the Bible and write intelligleby. He is also studying Arithmetic and geography. My principal business is farming and working in the black smith shop. Last year I raised on my farm some Rice Cassada, Potatos and several other vegetables. This year I have a larger farm and hope by the assistance of the Lord that I shall get a better crop. I have been more unfortunate in my blacksmith business. Nearly one year ago my shop was burned down and I lost my bellows and some other tools. I have built another shop and got another bellows; by so doing I am some in debt. Now my dear friends although an industrious man who is free from debt can live tolerably comfortable, yet when a man is involved in debt he finds it hard to pay his debts and often suffers much from this circumstance. My dear friends if you can help me a little, by the blessing of god I shall soon be able to move on much easier and more comfortable. A little aid from you at this time would do me much good. "Giving doth not impoverish," "Cast thy bread upon the water and thou shalt find it after many days." Though cotton is raised in this country and we hope soon to be able to manufacture our own clothes, yet at present we have not got so as to make them. We have them to buy and to pay very high for them too, If you could send me some strong cloth to make me and our boys some shirts, pantaloons and other clothes I should be able to devote the more of the avail of my labor to the liquidation of my little debt. I cannot feel easy while I am debt, I have five children. The oldest child of my present wife will be tw[o] years old the 29 of July, her youngest is four days old. The oldest child of my second wife is a girly and the other a boy. My children are strong and healthy. On the whole I am well contented. I would be very glad to see you and all my dear friends in America but I have no desire to go there to live. Please give my love to my dear mother and all my dear friends in America. If I should not see them again in this world I hope to meet them all in heaven and to dwell with them fore[ver] . O blessed hope to meet where there will be no more trouble, no more parting, but to sing the praises of God and the Lamb forever and ever! I find the religion of Christ to be my greatest comfort in this dark world, but oh! the bright and everlasting glories of that better world where I hope to meet my dear friends.

Brother Thomas made a profession of religion about a year ago. He has united with the Baptist Church and led a christian life since. He is now on board Dr. Hall's vessel, who is trading on the coast. His business on board is coopering up his oil casks. He will probable be back in a few weaks. He left his children in my care.

I need a gun screw plate very much but can not obtain one in this country. You gave me when I left America a piece of steel and some iron which did me much good. If you could without too much trouble send me these articles you would confer a great favor on me. Also a little tobacco would be very acceptable, as we are obliged to have this article to purchase small things of the natives which we need. Leather is very scarce in this country. We some times buy shoes which are imported from America but they are usually very inferior in quality. I also need some borax but cannot get it in this country. Again remember my love to you all. The children send their love to you. Do wrte me another good letter soon.   Robert M. Page.

90 / JOHN M. PAGE, SR., TO CHARLES W. ANDREWS

Rev. C. W. Anders   [n. d. but probably 1840]

Dear Sir;   I again attempt to drop you a few lines 'tho I looked for answers to my two letters to you. I hope the old saying is not verrified "out of sight out of mind." However I hope these few lines will find you & family in good health, as they leave me and my family. I have made up my mind to see you & family if mony will cary me, that is if I can accumulate sufficient mony. But mony has been & is now the impediment. Some Captains will take me to Baltimor for forty & some for fifty dollars, and different prices. I have made several attempts but evry time the vessel is ready I cant gather sufficient means. Soon as I can hear from you I will make another attempt if God spares my life and I am well. My regards to your wife and family & your Son Matthew particular. Tell him I say he must be studious as well as assiduous in a point of literature. I have much to say but time will not admit, but I will close by saying tell Matthew to write me by the first opportunity.

No more at present but remain, Yrs truly,   John M Page

[On same sheet; part of letter missing; these lines are to John Page's mother]

. . . and particular my older brother Solomon write me how they are getting along.

I am sorry to inform you of the death of Cousin Sarah William's sister. She died triumphing in the faith and left a good testimony with us all. When she was asked "How stands it between thee and thy God"? her answer was "All is clear. I am willing to go." Yes, these was her words ten days before her death. Now Mother please tell me about my Uncle Joseph. Write me if he is dead or alive, and if dead, let me know his testimony, & if living, tell him I hope to meet him in Heaven. Since I been here I have been to three wars but the last was indeed the hardest, for it was to a country (Kingstown) about 35 miles from Edina. We were in combat three hours before we could take the barricade. His name was King Bucah of tradetown.[1] Now dear Mother I must now come to a close hoping that God will bless and take care of you and at last receive us all in Heaven. No more at present but remain yr affectionate son,

John M. Page

91 / PEGGY POTTER TO CHARLES W. ANDREWS

Monrovia, Liberia, December 29th, 1847

My dear sir: By these few lines you may know that I am well and the Family and I do hope that these few lines may find you and the family the same. You wrote in the last that When we write we must write a full account of the Colony and of us in particular. As to the regard of this Colony, any man can live heare that will Work, and if a man is got money he can live. All the Fault I find in this Place [is] the things is so deare that I has to work to get something for me and my children to Eat, and as fast as I can get a little money I have to take it all to Buey some Cloths for my Children to ware. 'Tis not me [who is] well married; 'tis my sister, Winey; she is married to a man call Mr. P. Reid. All that did use to give me anything is Dead, that is my Brother Daniel, he is Dead and left 3 children Behind, 2 girls and 1 Boy. I suppose you know my son Daniel; he is living with Mr. Reid, the man that married my sister. But I beg you if you Please to send my money. Please to take the money and Buey some goods for me and put them in a Box and send them to me if you Please, Mrs. Saley, if you Please, for I am in want of it to get me a house Built. I am living in a Tach [thatch] Hut for the want of money to get a House made for me and my mother to live in. Please to send the money or goods as the Fowlings [following] articles: Tobacco, Cloth & Flower & meat, Powder & gune and nail. Yours obed'nt servent,

Peggue Potter[1]

[*On same sheet*]

Mrs. Sarrah Andrews: I nearly [merely] write you these few lines to let you know that I am going to school. I wrote this letter for my mother. Miss Sarrah I Beg you if you Please madm to send me some Books: smiths geography, smiths Arithmatic [and] smiths grammar and some slate Pencils and a slate and some Pens and paper and Ink. Please to send me some Books of all Kinds if you Please. Mrs. Sarrah I Beg you, if you Please, to send me a set of shoemakers toules if you please madm Mrs. Sarrah I beg you if you please madm to send me some Cloths such as you Please. Please to send me some leather. I want to help my mother and grand mother all I can. Please madm to send the Toules if nothing Else. Give my Respects to Mr. Andrews and the children and to you my Respects. Give my Respects to all White & Black. Yours obeent servent,

Daniel W. Nelson, the son of Peggue Potter

Mrs. S. Andrews this is my own writing.

92 / SOLOMON S. PAGE TO CHARLES W. ANDREWS

Edina, April 22, 1849

Be Dearest friend: Another opportunity faces me and I must with anxiety make good use of the same, as it is not always that we meet with opportunity to write to you. Sir I hope these few lines shall find you and family in no other but a good state and enjoyment of health. All of us are well but uncle John's wife is not long since delivered of a child; she is poorly. We are well today, but we do not know what younger [yonder] days may bring us. I received your letter that came with uncle John's, and was glad to hear from you in so long a time. We also received the books which you sent, Thos that were in the box & a packet of some very interesting readers. The books contained, those that were in the packet, are of different kinds, therefore it would take no small space of time to write their different names down. They were Divided, as you requested uncle John to do, in the letter you wrote him, and we do severally and jointly send our thanks to you for your bountiful kindness to us all. Uncle Robert, father, uncle John, Peter & myself were all Present when the books were distributed. John Page, Junior, uncle Robert's eldest son of those he has now (I.E. by his second wife) & Thomas Parker, my youngest brother of Mother's Children, were not present when the books were divided but they all got books. As regards Alfred, uncle R.'s eldest son, I suppose you know that he died long since. In your letter you mention'd something of Peter; he is yet alive & is a member of the Baptist Church. He wrote you last year long before I did by Mr. Clarke, a missionary with whom I lived and of whom I obtained the little education I have, but I suppose it was transmitted into different hands and you did not get it, as it will happen sometimes. But before I close my letter I beg your patience a little while. After the President's arival from France &c, or before his departure, he determined to stop the slave dealers from cruising our coasts. After his return we were all commanded to get ourselves in order for the war, as we had to contend against an african tribe, called the New Cesters' tribe.[1] The war was declared in march, and on the 5th of march we shipped on board a vessel from Monrovia that came for us. The next morning viz. wednesday morning, which was the 6th of march, the frenchs' steamer hove in sight. This was sent to our asstance. We took our departure for young Cess (as the place where the spaniards resided is called). We reached there the same day evening. On the 7th, our war, as I may attempt to call it, commenced. The natives, seeing that we were about to land soon began to burn their towns along the sea side, for fear that we might get shelter during the war. But all this did not discourage us, for we intended to land & fight. But to cut the history short, a bumb shell was fired from board the steamer amongst the savages. I am not able to tell you how many were killed of the savages, but while landing they fired on us [and] one or two of our people were wounded but not fatally. They soon recovered. One of the natives was shot dead by one of our riflemen. I am sorry I have not room to give you the whole history of our war. After remaining here where we landed at first it became necessary for us to go to the spaniard's residence. But in order to get there we must cross a river on the oposite side of which is a very steep hill covered with a dense forest. On this hill there one of the spaniards by some means had conveyed an old canon, which he intended to fire in the midst of us while crossing the river. But a day before we crossed, a Frenchman on board the steamer had visited the place where we camped, which enabled him to view this place on the oposite side where they were accustomed to apear in great flocks, I may say. He goes on board, measures the distance, and hurled a bumb shell in the crowd. This threw a dread on them, something they never saw or heard of before, which they deemed supernatural, and with dread they fled. Time would fail me to give you a complete History, therefore, I stop here. 5 murderers [were hung] & one of our own citizens for shooting another. At about 7 o'clock P.M. 4 natives of africa were hung for killing an american on an Island up the St. John river, commonly called the Factory Island. For fear of wearying you with my ingrammatical speaking, I must cease here. Sir with Respect, I have the honor to remain your humble & Ob't. servant,   Solomon S. Page, Edina

Please let me know what S stand for in my name. The number that was killed by the bumb shell I am not able to tell you now.

93 / SOLOMON S. PAGE TO CHARLES W. ANDREWS

[Edina, 1849]

D[ea]r Mr. Andrews, Dear Sir,   I have not very much more to say relative to the short war at New Cess. After our arrival at trade town, according to the Promise before made by the King of trade town, he fulfilled his Promise by sending the slaves. They were all chained around their necks; they came marching in trade town in a long row; all had chains around their necks. They were shipped on board the vessel, but they were unchained & it appeared that they were very glad that they were Providentialy relieved from the slaver's tyranny. We shipped on board and came toward home in order that we might get to this Wei's town (the same fellow that arrested the new cess spaniard out the hands of Joseph West). We came & took up the line of march to this wei's town. We did not reach his town the same day we started, but slept at a town whose king's name (was) is Duaga (the two letters a in this man's name are sounded as a in father, g hard). He went to this king telling him we demand the Spaniard; but the Saucy fellow would not listen to this king's counsel, put a great many of his warriors in ambush to wait our coming, the which we were informed of. But we were well prepared for any attack. The next day we took up the line of march to this fellow's town. We were attacked not far from his town by some of his troops, but though in very thick bushes we rallied up as brave Soldiers, soon took Possession of his town. But oh! I have not told you the funnyest of it yet: It appears that satan will find mischief for idle hands to do. Some meddle Some person, it appears, was oblige to trouble a bee hive that was in the Toun we were guarding. While the general & captains were holding a council to determin what to do, when suddenly there come out a person (one of our

Soldiers) brushing his head, face & neck, blowing for life. The bees soon found us out & come to us in swarms, in our faces, heads & the whole of our bodies. We paid the greatest reverence to those bees that day, for they made us bow, while some were Praying, others hollowing for their Captains, to come & deliver them from the hand of the enemy, viz. the bees.[1] After Council was over we set the town on fire and we took up the line of March. The fellows did attempt to fight us while coming back, and they fired on us, but we could not get to take a deadly aim at one of them. But none of us got shot, save a Congo* man.[2] We came safely to Duaga's town. Ere we came in town before the same fellow (we had) who had fought us sent a white color as an emblem of submission, acknowledging himself conquered and [promising] that he would send the Spaniard the next day, which he done accordingly. The next day we took up the Line of march for home. About the 25th or 26th we were dismissed. Thus ends our war, which lasted nearly one month. Sir, your Most Ob'd. Servant,
Solomon S. Page

*The Congo was shot while going to the town.

Father, uncle John, Peter, & myself went to the war but none of us got shot. We were successful during the war, something which I did not expect or anticipat before we went. Truly it would have been a dreadful time on our behalf had the enemy come on us during the time of the bees, for our attention was called from watching for the enemy and directed to the bees. I lay prostrate on the ground; I did not fight them neither did they trouble me much. Sir, if my words and sentences in any parts of my letters are erroneous, you must really make some allowances for me, as I am semi-educated and hardly so. Yours Respectfully,
Solomon S. Page

94 / ROBERT M. PAGE TO CHARLES W. ANDREWS

Edina, Grand Bassa County, Republic of Liberia, May the 5th, 1849

Dear Sir: As an opportunity favorable to writing you presents itself, I embrace it in addressing you with a few lines. As it regards the health of my family and myself, I have not much cause to complain. We are, as far as can be reasonably expected, getting on very well. As it regards our occupation in life, it is as follows. I keep my blacksmith's tools in occupation so far as I have a run of work; at the same time I endeavour to keep up a small farm. As it regards the farming part of my occupation, I might perhaps carry it on more extensively had I capitol to carry it into effect.

I send you by the *Liberia Packet* one box containing seventy three pounds of Liberia coffee, Marked with the initials of your name, Charles W. Andrews. The coffee I send is altogether of my own raising. I would be happy if you could contrive to send my mother say about four pounds of coffee wish [which] I would like her to have more especially as it is of my own raising.

I would be very happy, should you find it convenient so to do, though i must confess I am some what delicate in making such proposal—however, I proceed—You are aware that in this country we do not raise anything like wheat, consequently such articles must always be imported here. Therefore if you can as I mentioned above make it convenience, I would be glad if you send me by the return of the Packet a little flour, some Molasses, a small flitch of Bacon and such other little trifles as you may find convenient to send. In asking this favour of you, it is not in return for the coffee; but the fact is I would be glad receive the articles I mentioned and if coffee & arrowroot are receivable, I would endeavor to make some returns to you in that line.

And, provided I do not tax your patience, I would be glad if you would send me a few yards of Alipacaca for Ladies dress; and as I am now commencing a new building, you will please to send me a half keg of 10d nails and a half keg of 4d nails and I will endeavour to make some returns.

I would be glad to learn our true ages as somehow we have lost the acct; please send us the acct.

But for the spiritual part, residing out here as we do we have every means of worshipping god after the dictates of our own consciences, for which we thank the great creator of all good. I trust you are still pressing onward in the good old way. It is my endeavor so to live as I shall be enabled to rise glorious in the coming day.

My family are all in a thriving state. My wife whom I married in this County enjoys her health. We have five Children, one of them a fine boy. Three of them attends school regularly, two of them can read passages in the Bible. Now in closing, Receive my best respects together with those of my family. The children all join me in love to their Grandmother whom they have never seen. Give our love and respects to your family and all enquiring friends. Hoping you enjoy your health, I Remain yr's in Christ,   Robert M. Page

To Mr. Chas. W. Andrews

Bassa Cove, May the 7, 1849

Dear Sir: By this you may learn that I am well hoping these may find you enjoying the same, as it leaves me and all of my fathers family. Dear Sir, their is none of my father family alive that came to Liberia, except it is me. I am the only one that is alive of Mr. Roberts Page family, or only one of my fathers children alive. I would have written before now but I did not know where to direct my letters to, but as I have seen letters frequently that came from where you was at, their fore this is my entention for trying to write you a few lines. Father carries on his farming business as usual and also his blacksmith trade but [it is] very hard getting on sometimes. He has a great large coffee farm which he can scarcily sell his produce which he raises on his farm. If he could only contrive away to send it to you he would be very glad, which I expect he will send you a bushel of coffee or so now. Their might be a great deal raised on his farm if he only had a little encouragement or a little money such as common trade goods which I expect he will write for in his letter. I would be glad to plague you a little myself to see if you woulden send me out some trade goods, so I can buy just what you would wish. If coffee, ginger, arriroot and dried peper would answer, or palm oil either, Just what you wish. I am partly doing business now for myself. At the present time I will name such goods as will sell well in liberia, such as good tobacco and calico and good prints and pantaloons stuff and white shirting, shoes, stocking and a good many other articles as I could mention. I am following doing business in stores part of my time and the other time I am working in the farm, when I have no business to do. If you should send me an anything you must direct it to a place called Bassa Cove. This [is] where I does my business at. But my father he lives at a place called Edina which is about a quarter of a mile apart, all one county. I wish you would tell grandmother howdy for me and all of my relation. Them as I don't know, tell them I wish they would send me something as a token from them and I will do the same when convieniet. I hope to hear from them all. When the L[iberi]a Packet return for Liberia again I hope you will not fail in sending me what I request of me. I left out some main article, flour, pork, mackrells and all other provisions, sugar, molasses, good prints calico, Tobacco, [clothing] such as men ware and good finery for woman; & also do I besseech and beg you kindly please to send these articles that are mention in my letter. If you do I will be a thousand times thankfull to you about them. Father is married and has five children. I would mention a great deal more but time will not admit. I wish you would send me some good books to read and if you send anything please to distinguish our names from one another. If you write to him (uncle John) please put Scenier in his name and in my name, junior. You will please to answer my letter, if you don't send anything, so I may hear from you all. I am Mr. Robert Page, son John M. Page, that written this letter. This is some of my hand writting; it is not so good but will answer I suppose so as to let you all know that I am yet alive. I must Now come to a Close by saying I am your dear affectionate friend,

John M. Page

96 / THOMAS M. PAGE TO CHARLES W. ANDREWS

Edina, My - 1849

Revd Mr. Andrews; dear sir,   as this letter leaves me not in a good state of health, I hope it will find you in a better state, both you and your family. Excepting me my family is enjoying good health. Sir the books you sent us came safely to hand, so each one of us have our respective number. Among them are some very valuable readers. I do sincerely thank you for your kindness to us. I suppose you have heard of the number of children I have by my second wife; they are three in number, two boys and a girl. Sir I am very sorry I have no curiosities to send you. My Present occupation for a livelihood is farming, on which I raise many Potatoes and casavaos &c. have found it to be the shoest [surest] foundation for support. Peter and Solomon does not stay with me alto-gether now but are employed as assistant school teachers in children Schools, but help me along. Peter belongs to the Baptist Church. I hope I shall be able to send you something by the next Packet, the which I have not ready to send now. Sir Previous to my arrival in Liberia, I was in church when suddenly the thieves came and broke on me, took nearly all I owned. My children were then very small and could do but little to help. Without doubt methinks I can anticipate your idea that I have been in Liberia so long a time and just thought to mention about this. If so to this I will respond that I have written to you several times but received no answer. Whether you received them or not I cannot tell, you knows best. As I have said, I Prefere farming to any other occupation but from my Present anticipation of health methinks I shall not be able to follow it regulorly, as health is decling & I have a complaint in the hyp which I had before I left America in consequence of being thrown from a horse. But all this I think is my farther's good will. For though after many tribulations here below I expect to reign in heaven with Christ my ad-vocate on high. Therefore if we should not be premitted to see each other in this mortal fleash, Pray that we will above where Parting shall be no more. Remember me to Mrs. Andrews. Tell her to Pray for me that we all may meet above. As regards my Present wife, I have the honor to say that she has faithfully discharged the ofic [of] Mother to my first wife's children. They all live peacefully together as children ought to live and she does act a good part to them. Now that she is quite an industrious woman she Performs all the duties relative to house keeping—makes all the clothes in the family required of her and I am in hopis a good Christian too belonging to the same church that I belong to viz. the Baptist church. Cousin Sarah is now a widow with two children of her first husband. She was Married a second time, had a daughter by her second husband [and she] not being three years old, was taken with a disease and soon died, the Father not long surviving his Daughter died also— died in April 1849, leaving cousin Sarah behind. Friend with these lines I close by bidding you fare well. Yours Truly,   Thomas M. Page

Remember me to Mrs. Christian Black Bond, as I have lately heard from her.

97 / ROBERT M. PAGE TO CHARLES W. ANDREWS

Edina, Grand Bassa County, October 28, 1849

Dear Sir: By this you may learn that I am well and all my family, except my son John; he is not as well as can be expected, hopeing you and yours are quite well. I receive your letter By the Packet and was very glad to hear from you all, especially my mother and my other acquaintances who lived at annfield. My occupation is farming and tending to my Blacksmith trade. I have now growing and bearing one thousand coffee trees and arriroot also. We have not got any to send by this Packet this time but will have some ready against her return. As one of our citizens expect to come in the next packet, I shall send my produce by him and shall communicate to you at the same time. Dear Sir you will be please to try and obtain me a family Medical Book on tom soiugn.[1] Please to put my name in it. Dr. sir if you should send us anything again, please to put it on the bile [bill] of Laden. I mention this Because the nails you sent me I did not obtain them, neither the carpenter tools you sent. Bro. John, we got the Books and was very thankfull to you for them for the Life of Revd. John Newton Doddridge Rise and Progress, Life of solomon, City couson, and, indeed they all are good Books. You cannot intrude on us by sending us Books. Give my Love to all the enquiring friends, espesally your wife and all her children. My love particular to my dear mother and all my Brothers and sisters also. You must excuse the bad writting. My son John wrote it; he is not so well at the Present time But acquire of you to send him some good Books such as an Family medical Book on Tom sowign as it seem to be more usefull than real doctor medicine. I written to you Before By the Packet, and send all of the Books that are concern in the Tom Sowign; I wishes to make it my Practical study. Please to put my name in them; this is the way you must write my name in them, John junior Page Yours Trully Frend,

Robert M. Page

98 / JOHN M. PAGE, SR., TO CHARLES W. ANDREWS

Rev. Charles W. Andrews   Edina, July 27th, 1854

Sir: As the opportunity affords Itself, I embrace it by tendering to You these few lines wich I hope will find you and family in a perfic state of Celubrity as they leaves me and family. I am truely and heartily Glad to have the privelige of Receaving a Letter from you, one who I know to be my friend. It affords me unspeakable joy to hear from your family wich I hope soon to see. I Received your kind and affecting letter which was surtainly a treet to me and my family. Your proposals were red and under mature deliberation I have concluded to except your proposals, and if the lord Spares my life to behold next year the year of our Lord 1855, I will See Your face and the face of my beloved mother and, after wich, I beleave I can say, as Simeon of old, Lord they Servant has behold thy salvation, now lettest thou thy Servant depart in peace. I will try to arrange my business so as to leave for the U.S. in May if I am bound to make Some Sacrifice, for I would like to spend the whole summer with you, If my life is spared. No more at present but I remain Yours till Death.   John M. Page, Senr.

[On same sheet]

Mrs. S. W. Andrews

Dear Madam: I am allmost at a loss to find words of language to express my gratification for Receiveing a few lines from you one who I must ever hold in remembrance not only for kindness manifested but the intrus and care the councels gavin me from you in your Dining room at Anfield. I am deturmin to see your face next Year if the lord Spares my life and I am in good health for such is my angziety to see you and my mother, that my deturmination is to see you in June or July next. My wife joins in regard to you whose name is Malinda Page. Your son mathew is as fresh in my mine as he were when he ware a very small lad when I used to nurce Him. Now a few words to my dear beloved mother,

Dear mother,   Your advice is in my breast as fresh as they were when gavin to me. I am Happy to hear from you and pray that God will spare you to behold my face once more. Mother I Beleave if I follow Your advice during the days of my life, in death it will be well with me.

Brother Thomas is not well But his family is quite well. Peter and

Solomon is quite well when I heard from them last. Brother Robert and family is quite well. Yesterday I enjoid myself quite well celebrating the anniversary of Liberia's Independence. No more at present But I remain Yours most Respectfully,   John M. Page, Senr.

99 / JOHN M. PAGE, SR., TO CHARLES W. ANDREWS

Edina, Grand Bassa County, Liberia, April 1st, 1855

Mr. C. W. Andrews: Your polite interesting and much esteemed favior of March 10th 1854 was duly recieved, and you may rest assured that a letter from one whom I so highy esteemed was perused with peculiar pleasure. I highly appreciate the liberal proposal of refunding my passage expensis after my arrival in the United States, which amount total must Cost some $60.00 dollars. But as my intention and desire is to carry with me a few of our african productions, some for your amusement & some for your consummation [consumption] which when purchased I am aware, would consume the money which I necessaryly am compelled to devote to passage expensis &c.

I beg to request that you will, either verbally or by written Communication with Mr. George Hall or father, effect a understanding in my favor, in order that I might be privileged from liquidating said expensis untill my arrival in the U. States. As regards our family generally, they are tolerable, notwithstanding we as a family enjoy blessings innumerable from our Heavenly father, yet we are, like all other human creatures, subject to a higher Authority & as a family we have been greatly afflicted, yes bereaved of a friend, a christian, a husband, and to me a affectunate bro., namely, bro. Thomas, who with christianlike resignation gave his spirit to the god who infused it. Please Remember my compliments to my dear Mother and I hope she is well. Also remember me kindly to Uncle Joseph and my brothers and my sister, Nancy & Margarett and their children. Feeling desirous to say a few words to Mrs. Andrews in this your letter, permit me to close by saying I am yours with enduring respect,   Jno. M. Page.

[On same sheet]

Mrs. S. W. Andrews

Dear Madam: The few but interesting lines addressed to me in Mr. Andrews letter was of course received & read with delegent attention. I am glad that you cunce [conceived?] so kind a feeling of interest for our prosperity in this & in the world to come, & I am also glad that the desires of your dear mother have so mysteriously been accomplished. I hope your son Matthew will improve himself, take hold of golden minutes as they fly, and thereby prepare himself for future usefullness in this world, and dying leave abundant testimony that he has not be reared in a christian Country for naught, but have so improved the talents granted him that he can enter into a world of rest. Please remember me kindly to little Coatney bird & her sister. As I have written to Mr. Andrews fully in refference to my coming to America, I cannot write you anything much untell I recieve his answer. My wife and little daughter, who is now nearly 5 years old, joins in respect to you.

Liberia, Our glorious asylum, is still under the wise and judicious protection of a god, moving slowly, yet surely, in wealth & prosperity. May the god who promises to be a god of nations, provided the[y] obey and serve him, weave and continually retain around us his strong & impregnable shield is my prayer. The Episcopal Church, or Missi[on], has erected a school in our County under the Superintending care of Rev. J. Rambo, who has lately come from Palmas.[1] I am dear madam with enduring respects your friend, &c.,   Jno. M. Page

4/LETTERS OF THE JOHN McDONOGH NEGROES

John McDonogh, an eccentric merchant, planter, and philanthropist, was born in Baltimore, Maryland, December 29, 1779. During his boyhood he served an apprenticeship in the mercantile firm of William Taylor, and at twenty-one he was sent to New Orleans to act as Taylor's agent in that city. After representing Taylor for several years, McDonogh established his own mercantile business in New Orleans. Following a period of outstanding success during which he invested heavily in Louisiana land, McDonogh retired from the mercantile business in 1806 and devoted most of his time to planting. Before his death on October 26, 1850, he had acquired several plantations, a large brickyard, and numerous slaves.

In 1822 McDonogh initiated a plan that allowed his slaves to earn money for their own use by working Saturday afternoons. Success in this experiment, along with an increasing belief in gradual emancipation, led McDonogh in 1825 to make an agreement with his slaves permitting them to buy their freedom on an installment plan over a period of about fifteen years. With him acting as banker for their earnings at the rate of 62 1/2 cents per day for men and 50 cents for women, the slaves were to start the emancipation process by applying money earned on Saturday afternoons (already theirs) to the purchase of freedom for Saturday mornings. This would require seven years. Then, with money earned on their free Saturdays, they would in four more years purchase Fridays; wages for Fridays and Saturdays would in two years more buy Thursdays; by continuation of this procedure they would in one and one-half more years buy the fourth day, in one more year obtain the fifth, and in six more months purchase the sixth and thus become completely free. Then, as free persons, they could complete the purchase of their children who, by working at proportionately lower wages, had already earned a substantial portion of their freedom.

McDonogh laid down a strict code of conduct for those subscribing to his proposal, and slaves who failed to live up to the code, either through slothfulness or moral delinquency, were to be denied all or a part of their compensation.[1]

The scheme worked well. After its implementation, according to

McDonogh, "the blacks were no longer apparently the same people; a sedateness, a care, an economy and industry took possession of them. . . . They became temperate, moral, religious."[2]

Within fifteen years seventy-nine of McDonogh's slaves earned their freedom. In 1842 these blacks were turned over to the American Colonization Society, to which McDonogh was a regular and a generous contributor, for their passage to Liberia. They left New Orleans June 9, 1842, on the *Mariposa*, stopped briefly at Norfolk, where another McDonogh freedman, Washington Watts McDonogh, one of three blacks sent by the master to Lafayette College for advanced schooling, joined them. Twenty-eight days later they arrived at Monrovia.[3]

McDonogh shared the view held by many other colonizationists that free blacks and whites could not dwell peacefully together in America and that emigration of Negroes must be a condition of their emancipation. He tried hard to prepare his Negroes for freedom in Africa, by teaching many of them to read and write and training them as agriculturists, mechanics, carpenters, blacksmiths, spinners, and masons.

In 1859, nine years after McDonogh's death, forty-two more of his Negroes were emancipated and sent to Liberia in accordance with provisions of his will. No letters written by members of this group have been found and nothing is known of their experiences in Africa.

Thirty-eight letters written by the first group and addressed to McDonogh have been preserved. Twenty-nine of them are filed with the John McDonogh Papers at Tulane University and nine are from the *African Repository and Colonial Journal*. These letters indicate an unusually affectionate relationship between the writers and their former master. The black correspondents saluted McDonogh variously as "Dear Father," "Honored Parent," "Dear Beloved Benefactor," "Dear friend & benefactor," "Dear Beloved Sir," "Dear master and friend," and "Dear Sir." These expressions of affection may have been prompted in part by a hope of moving the recipient to generosity in meeting requests for assistance. But it seems reasonable to concede some sincerity to those who expressed warm regard for the unusual man who had made possible their release from bondage and their settlement in Africa.

McDonogh told his Negroes and the agents of the American Colonization Society to whom they were entrusted that he wanted the blacks to settle at the mouth of the Sinoe (also spelled Sinou) River 130 miles below Monrovia; this area had been acquired for colonists from Louisiana. But on their arrival at Monrovia they were alarmed by reports that Sinoe was an unhealthy site vulnerable to attack by hostile natives. With the assent of the governor of Liberia the McDonogh Negroes, with one exception, took up residence at Monrovia and at Caldwell, a community located on the Saint Paul's River about ten miles above Monrovia. Later some of them moved farther inland to a settlement that they called Louisiana. On McDonogh's persistent urging one or two families eventually moved from the Saint Paul's River to Sinoe.

Wherever they settled, the McDonogh colonists experienced considerable hardship in the form of sickness, depredations of wild animals, shortage of farming tools and other equipment, and inadequacy of shelter. Death took a heavy toll, especially during the rainy season. Most of the settlers were sustained in their troubles by a firm reliance on Divine Providence. Since they regarded their former owner very much as a father, they did not hesitate to call on him frequently for money, clothing, tools, tobacco, food, and other items that would contribute to their sustenance and comfort. After expiration of the six-months maintenance provided by the American Colonization Society, most of them acquired plots of land ranging in size from five to fifty acres and devoted themselves to farming. Some raised a wide variety of crops and a few appear to have prospered. On March 25, 1847, one of the more successful farmers wrote his former master that "our people are doing tolerably well" and this seems to have been a fair judgment when applied to the McDonogh Negroes as a group.

Perhaps the most remarkable of the blacks sent by McDonogh to Liberia, and the one who wrote him the most letters, was Washington Watts McDonogh. This Negro was reared in the McDonogh home and the term "father" that he so often applied to his former master reflected the closeness of their relationship. McDonogh sent Washington to Lafayette College to prepare him for a missionary career in Africa. He was the only one of the migrants who refused on arrival in Africa to settle at Monrovia; instead he proceeded more than one hundred miles beyond to Settra Kroo where he became a teacher in a mission school maintained primarily for native Africans. He found the natives "very ignorant and superstitious" and their language difficult, but he labored diligently "to teach them the ways of God." Despite discouragement because of the slow progress of his pupils, his poor health, and the loss of his mother and other near relatives, he remained steadfast in his religious faith and in his effort to enlighten and Christianize the natives. In his last letter he stated that he had not heard from his former master for three years and that he had "almost come to the conclusion that you have repudiated me." But he told of his recent marriage "to one of the best in Africa for she is a Christian" and indicated that with his wife's help he intended to continue his work as a missionary-teacher. In 1873 he became a member of the lower house of the Liberian legislature.[4] One of Washington's brothers, David, whom McDonogh also sent to Lafayette College for training as a missionary, never went to Liberia, much to McDonogh's disappointment. Instead he attended medical school and became a successful surgeon in New York City. Another brother, George R. Ellis McDonogh, who apparently did not have the benefit of college training, went to Liberia with the other McDonogh settlers in 1842. His letters, nine of which have been preserved, are as interesting and as informative as those written by his missionary brother. In April 1844 George wrote McDonogh: "I look up to you as a Son to a kind Father and shall ever expect assistance from you." He lived up to his pledge but his frequent requests for aid were never suppliant. In a letter dated March 25, 1847, he boldly stated: "I will certainly look for something by the first Vessel from there as the amount of three or five hundred Dollars would be of no consequence to a man of Your wealth and as I find myself so much in need in this hard Country and feeling assured that while I was with You I acted upright and just towards You and believing You know the same is my reason for making this request of you." This was not the statement of one who had been cowed into childlike submissiveness or dehumanized by brutalizing bondage, but rather was the remark of a man who took pride in the independence he had been permitted to earn by his own exertion. Little wonder that he achieved notable success as a farmer in Liberia.

In his last letter to his former master, November 24, 1849, George told of his pleasant association with Ralph Gurley, on the occasion of that agent's recent trip to Liberia. On March 6, 1850, after his return to Washington, D.C., Gurley wrote a long letter to McDonogh in which he gave a favorable report on the McDonogh settlers in Africa. Concerning George he stated: "Mr. GR Ellis is one of the most intelligent & respectable citizens of Monrovia, living in a very substantial, well-furnished house, while he has a flourishing plantation some seventeen miles up the St. [Paul's] River. I visited him frequently. He has for his wife one of the best educated women in the Republic & is himself a man of great activity and enterprise."[5] Perhaps this glowing tribute enabled McDonogh to forgive George for his failure to settle in Sinoe and to conclude that in at least one instance, his venture in colonization was an outstanding success. Apparently George was as superior as a freeman in Africa as McDonogh was as a master in America.

Seven of the thirty-eight letters reproduced in this chapter were published in 1974 in Robert S. Starobin, ed., *Blacks in Bondage: Letters of American Slaves* (New York: New Viewpoints, 1974), pp. 173-88. These contain some errors of transcription and the letter of November 17, 1843, is mistakenly dated November 17, 1845.

100 / GALLOWAY SMITH McDONOGH TO JOHN McDONOGH

Norfolk, Va., June [July] the first, 1842

Dear Sir,   I am very happy to inform you of our safe arrival and properous passage to this place. We were only 11 days and favoured with fine weather. We are all well with the exception of Sam and his Grandmother Bridget. They were all Sea Sick except myself. I heard a sermon from the Rev. Mr. Gurley last Sabbath in the forenoon and also in the evening on board of the ship. Ther is about 180 [140?] to come on board here. We are likely to Sail in about 3 or 4 days. Washington has not arrived yet although he is dayly expected. We are all pretty much unwell at present by drinking the canal water which has been put on board of the Ship. I have no more to say about myself or the people which can be interesting to you. So farewell dear Sir and receive the kindest wishes of humble servant. I have only to say that I wish you to give my best respects to Fanny. I did not tell you of my partiality to her but after she received your permission to marry I put my addresses to her and am true to her yet and expect to be till I die, I wish you if you ever have a chance to do so to send her out to Liberia. By doing so you will confer a lasting favour and will deserve the warmest grattitude and kindest thanks of your humble servant. I wish you to be so kind as to remember my best resptes [respects] to James Thornton and George Carpenter, Noel [?] and all enquireing freinds whoever they may be, and believe me to be your humble Obedient Servant,   Galloway Smith[1]

P S Honoured Sir: May God bless and preserve you. May your last hours be as happy as your good works deserve and if we never meet again in this world I hope and trust we shall meet hereafter in that world of joy beyond the grave. "Where the wicked cease from troubling and the weary are at rest." Farewell. I can say no more. I can wish for no higher or purer happiness than that.

101 / GEORGE R. ELLIS McDONOGH TO JOHN McDONOGH

Norfolk, July 5th, 1842

My Dear Master,   I have been disappointed in not hearing from my Brother as I expected to do when I came here. You must not blame me for not having written, as I have been busy since the ship arrived. All of us are well. We had a pleasant voyage & expect to sail tomorrow. We have got along very comfortably, & although we take a good many on board here, I trust we shall all do well. I think we are to have a good Captain, Captain Shute, who has been many times on the coast taking the place of Captain Chase, who treated us very kindly on the way. I have attended worship here two Sabbaths & found the people very friendly. We all pray God Almightly to bless you, & beg you to write to us, as we will write as soon as we get to Liberia to you. Ever Dear Master With greatest respect gratitude & affection Your faithful Servant,

George Ellis McDonogh[1]

John M'Donogh, Esquire

Mr. Gurley tells me that he has written to Mr. Lowry & hopes to hear from my brother before we sail.

102 / WASHINGTON W. McDONOGH TO JOHN McDONOGH

Setter Croo, September the 5th, 1842

Dear Father: I resived your Kind letter dated 15 of April and I would have answered it befor I left Eaton but as I res [received] one from Mr. Lowrie at the same time saying that I should get my things to come on to N.Y and still persue my studies, I had not time to write you. But thank God that I am still a live and have the pleasure of writing to you from a far and distant land. I left the College on the 11 June. I still persued my Studys untill [June] 10. [I left] for N.Y. on a Saterdy, [stayed there] Sunday, & on Monday I started for Philadelphia. I sailed from there on the 16 of June and on the 19th we left the Cape Henlopen. And on 16 of July we arived at Cape Verd on the Coast, and on the 18th we Cast anchor about 5 miles below a little town on the gambier River. We stoped here one day & I went on shore with Captin to look around. It is a butiful town settel by English. The next day we sailed [for] Sierra Leone another town Settled by the same nation. It is the nices & larges Settlement on the coast. It contains, I was told by the Captain, 60,000 inhabitanc. Here we arived on the 28 of July and discharged Cargo untill the 13 of August and at which time we saild for Monroviar. I was astonish to see the grass and bushes that grws in the s[t]reets. It is the worse plac on the coast for an old settelemnt lik that. We left there on the 25. The ship arived safe in Monrovia with the Emigrants after 44 days passage. They arived on a Sunday morning August 21. I had 28 days and they 44. They were all well except old Maria and big Nancy. Mother says that Nancy has been unwell every since they left Norfolk and Maria has lost here old dest Daughter Lusy on sea and she has been in bed every since. She was very bad when I left. Sarh lost here son also. Lucy died on 19 of July and Sarh's boy on the 18. The rest are all well and had a pleasant passag other way. The plac where I am at present is a fine and healthy part of the cuntry but I am told that snow [Sinoe] is a better place then this. It is true that it is very hot here middle of the [summer] but if a man is industrious after he becoms aclimated [he may] get a long very well but the most of the people that comes out here by the time they get over the fever they becoms some thing like the natives and wont work if they find that they can get along by stealing. I have seen numbers of them in cans [jails] for the like since I have been here. Africa is afine place for to live in. Thank God I have been spared to reach here in good health and do still enjoy it by his devine permission. I have been told sir that David [McDonogh] said to you that he had to spend one hour every day in teaching me. It is true that he use to teach me but he never spent one hold hour with me the hold winter at a time. I do not wish to telle you how he treated me whilse I was at College with him, nether do I wish to say any thing to him now, but I know if I had have writen to you about it whilse I was there he would have treated me worse. I understand that he wrot to you that I was well provided with every thing whereas I have not a book that I wanted. I came out here without a cent far a way from home. I am really asstonish at Mr. Lowrie for not given me a little of the money which you sent him. I will be much oblige to you if you will send me a [little] money for without it a man cant get [along] here with the natives for he must eather have money or tobaco. I entend to Stop here untill the ship arives with the people which I hope will be in a few days. They all desire me to give their best respects to you and all their frinds. Your most obbedient servant, Washington W. Mc Donogh

P S Pleas to send us a corn mill such as we left home if you has not given them one for without it they cant get along here. I hope sir when I write to you again I will be able to give a more full account of the place. It is my brotherses wish that you will be so kind as to send this letter in to Mr John Gato your next door nabour.

103 / WASHINGTON W. McDONOGH TO JOHN McDONOGH

Monroviar, October the 19, 1842

Dear Sir: I now take up my pen to write a few lines to you concerning the people. They arrived here on the 21th of August and I stayed with them untill the 25. I then left them for Setter Kroo. There I stayed untill the 12 day. I was teaching school for the Rev. Mr. Sawyer. After being there so long and finding that [they] had not come down to Snow [Sinoe] I thought it my duty [to] come up to see about them and on arriveing here I found all ashore and woundring all over town. My Brother says that Mac George and Galoway was the cause of the whole. They came ashore here with the captain and got persuaded by the settlers here to stop here and not to go to Snow, just as you told them before they left home. Mack George and the other then went on board, told the rest what they had heard, and from that they all agreed to Stop here except our family. He then came a Shore to see the govenor and he told him, that is my brother, to go on board and consult other and on consulting he found they all willing to stop here except himself and famly and after finding that they were all willing and that there was such heavy theaths [threats] made finely agreed to stop there. Galoway and his nephew John said that George was to go to Snow and the natives was to take up arms again them that he would healp to kill him. So they are here geting drunking and laying about and doing nothing. So you see that there is no dependance to be placed on them. They are going through the fever very fast. My oldes Sister has had the fever very bad & She is now geting better. July Ann and husban is getten better. George has not had the fever yett nether mother nor Mr. Gray. I have not seen any of the rest of the people. They are woundring about here. Bridget is liveing with mother. She has had the [fever] and is getting better. George says he is very sorry that things has turned out so. He says that they are here now and cant go to snow without paying there passage down there and that the govenor Says that he will give them the same land here up the River Sin [Saint] Pauls. George says that he has been up and seen the place, nothing more. Mariah is gone home to rest. She died a Short time after she arrived here on Shore. Mary lost here child here also and my younges sister lost here child. She fell and haert hereself on board the vessell. George told me to ask you if you would be so kind as to send two drum heads. He says that he gave it to the captain to tak care of but it got wett and the mice mad a hold in it. Nothing more at present. Mother send her love to you & says that she injoys better health at present then she have for along time. Bridget send her love [to] you also. She has been very sick but is now getten better. Her daughter Sarah has not been sick yett. George has not had the fever eather. They desierd there love all ther friends.

Washington W. McDo[nogh]

104 / WASHINGTON W. McDONOGH TO JOHN McDONOGH

Settra Kroo, August 3, 1843

Dear Father: I Know embrace the present oppertunity of writing a few lines to you hoping that these will find you well. I am very well at present and all the family like wise. My Sister died wit the fever, my oldest Sister. Bridgard's daughter Sarah died also with the dysintary. The rest are all well and gone up the riv[r] to farming. They have disgraced their names for ever, Sume of them. I am still at Settra Kroo teaching school. I have had the fever and I am now enjoying good health and I hope that these few lines will find you the Same. I exspect to remain here untill I heare from you. I like the place very well. It is very health[y], a great deal mor health[y] then monrovia. I received a letter from Mr. Lowrie dated April 15 Stating that he would not Send me a book untill he heard whether the people were goin to remain at St. Paul. I am very sorry that they acted mean, how ever it was not my fault for I tried [to] persuad them to follow me as I was goin to Settra Kroo but it appears that after they went ashore and got some thing they would go no furtha then this place Monrovia. They have suffered a Great deal by Stoping here. W. W. McDonogh

105 / GEORGE R. ELLIS McDONOGH TO JOHN McDONOGH

[August 3, 1843]

We have now settled up the St. Paul rive. Our land was not given to us untill Feburary. We have not had oppertunit[y] of doing much but we are makeing all the improvements we can. There are good many moved up the river and a good many on the Cape and at other place on coast. I am sorry that we have brok promise we made you. I make no appoligy for myself. I was compell to Stop here both by Govener and the people. When we arrived here some of our young men came on Shore and being persuaided they went aboard persuaided others. On a friday I cam aShore to see the govener. He was willing for them to stope but he would not take the charge to himself. He left it with me to reason with them about goin to sinoe but they would not hear reason but theaten my life incase they should be prevented from stoping here. I Stated to the governer the theats that were made and said to him I would reather you [he] should send a note on board the next day and he did so for those that was not willing to go to Sinoe, & every man that was not willing, to Sind [sign] his hand to the note Stating that they were not willing to go to Sinoe. Every man siened [signed] no except, Mr. J. Gray & A. Lamberth and myself. Your answer will oblige you humble servant,

George R. Ellis McDonogh

106 / AUGUSTINE LAMBERTH McDONOGH
TO JOHN McDONOGH

St. Paul river, Africa. September - 1843

Dear friend & benefactor: I embrace the present oppertunity of writing a few lines to you hoping that thes will find you in as good a health as I am in at present. I have had the fever and am enjoying very good health. I have made a start of farming. I have cleard a part of my land

and have it planted down in coffee trees and cotton & potatoes and all kind of plants such as the country affords. I resceived your very kind letter dated may 1, 1843, and I was very happy to hear you were well and all with you. I heard it read with much pleasure. The things you sent me were all lost with the vesel. I would have been very glad indeed had I got the things you sent me for provisions are very scarce here at present. I still entend to go to Sinoe as soon as I can get some seed from what I have planted. You requested me to give your love to all but we live so fare a part that I have not seen any of them scince I resceived your letter. The Governor sent his brother up to take names of all that [were] willing to go down but he did not find one of them willing to go. They are scatered all about the country, some up here & some on the cape &c. Please to give my love to all, to fanny and here daughter Elen & all my friends and to Mr. Mc Lain. I intend to send some of all kiends of seeds the first chance. I have been very busy Since I got over the fever. That's the reason I have not sent you some be for this. Of all the seeds you give me not one of them came up. Julyann my daughter Sends here compliments to you and wishes you well. She has not had the fever yet. She is the only one out of all the emegrants that came out. Here boy is well. A. Lambeth sends his love to you also and desire you to give his love to his God mother & family. I have wrot here [wrote her] but have not reseived any answer from her. Tell her to send me some thing when ever she can make it convience or when ever she feinds an opportunity. My mother is well. She send her love to you and also to my God mother. My love to all. Nothing more at present. A. Lamberth[1]

[On same sheet]

I am very glad to hear that Mr. Dunford is coming out and wish you would be so kind as to send me some provision by him.[2] Provision is scarce. Phillis Watts[3]

107 / JAMES McGEORGE TO JOHN McDONOGH

Mr. John Mc Donough   Monrovia, Nov. 17th, 1843
                                       Liberia, W[est] A[frica]

Dear Beloved Benefactor: This is the first oppor[tunity] I have had to send a communication to you since my arrival here. Therefore I do embrace it hoping that these may meet you in good health. Mr. and Mrs. Fuller [James and Henrietta] are both well and are doing very well at present. And We are all Quite Sorry that We Have not done according to our promise We made when we was about to take our Departure from you in regard to the port that We were Destined to go to, Which was Sinoe. But We do Beg of You to overlook our wrongs in this matter. As it was owing to the Governor and many other persons here that We Did not Go thither for they informed us particularly that the condition of the place at that time was Such that we had better remain here for the population was So Scanty there and the Country people being much more Uncivilized than they Were here that during our Sickness in the fever We would be robbed of what few articles we had. But Since I had the pleasure of Receiving such an important an animating Correspondence from you Speaking of this matter, the Generality of Us are now resolved to Go there, Though I have commenced farming here and have a considerable tract of Land under cultivation.

Your Letters arrived here in the Latter part of September. But I am Sorry to inform You that the Articles you sent us we did not get none of them, for the Barque Renown never reached our port. But the vessel that brought the Letters here brings Us the intelligence that She was stove on a rock near an island, I suppose about 200 miles or more to the Nordward of Us, and it was with much difficulty that they succeded in Saving all the Emigrants but their cargo Was all lost.[1] Now Beloved father We do earnestly request of you that you will not forsake us for our Delinquency in not being as vigilant as you thought We might have been. But We do intend to mend our pace and act consistent to your Will. Since We have [come] to this country and got rid of the fever We like the Country very well and our only Grieveance now is for us to Get to Sinoe Which We have been prevented from Emigrating to Since We have got well on account of our Shortness for money to defray our Expenses. But We are trying to do all We can now towards Getting there. Please Remember my respects to George Kenney & Noell Ruffile and my best wishes and respects to fanny Grinos & my Dear old aunt Mary. And Remember my respects and Sincere wishes to all inquiring friends and tell them all to Remember me in their prayers for it is much needed in our land. But as paper is very Scarce With me now and the Barque now in our port is about to leave I must come to a close Giving you all the thanks for your Unspeakable Kindness and Goodness towards Us Which by me shall never be forgotten. Amelia Gray is dead & Sally Hives & Dabney & Peter Young, Maria Kelley & Lucy Kelley, Randal Brigs.

But I bid you all adieu and I do remain You most Sincere and affectionate and Beloved Son Untill Death. James McGeorge[2]

108 / JAMES GRAY TO JOHN McDONOGH

Monrovia, 28th Jany, 1844

Dear Sir: By the Bark Latrobe I write you a few lines hoping that they might find you well and in good health as they do leave me at present and family. Your favour of the 1st May, 1843, was duly received and I was quite glad to heare of you. I am at present residing at "Monrovia" and find it more profitable to remain here for the present than to do otherwise. In your letter you refered me to the Benefit that would result from my moving to "Sinoe," believing that the American Squadron would more generally visit that place.[1] But dear Sir permit me to in form you that the Commodore has made this place as the Centre of his opperation. The entire Ships of the Squadron has been here from time to time [to] receive their supplys of water vegatables &c &c which has been the means of circulating a great deal of mony among the inhabitants of this place. I confess that you must have been much disappointed in your people not going to "Sinoe." But I am of the oppinion that they will do as well here as if they had gone to that place. In relation to my property at "Gretnia" you will please make as profitable sale of it as possible and transmit the proceeds to me in Tobacco of the best quality. I rejoice in informing you that the Imports of Monrovia for the last 2 years has exceeded two hundred and twenty seven thousan dollars as per return of the Collector of Customs. My respects to all enquiring friends Dear Sir I Spok a Bove Bout the furst [shipment] of tobaco. But if the lef Is Long it will do here and I expet to Remaine here Un til the Ex Pen Disan [expedition] Com out. I have fore famleys that is Willin to Go Down to Sino if I go With them and I cud get more to go if they had mens [means] to go With, for they have Spent all thir mens to Clar ther Farmes.

Elizabeth Gray Sends her Love to all inquiring Frends and She thinks that she Will Be abel to Right to you herself soon. John Mc Donogh, opposite New Orleans, January the 28, 1844.   James Gray[2]

109 / GALLOWAY SMITH McDONOGH TO JOHN McDONOGH

Liberia, Febuary 3th, 1844, Sinoe

Dear Sir: I take the pleasure of writing to you to let you know how I am and I hope these few lines may find you and all the family well as I am myself at present, thanks be to god. I was very well situated in Monrovia and your letter which you sent me made me brake up and went down to Sinoe and I am know in sinoe and I am thire alone only me and my wife. I am married has a fine son and I could not persuad not one of my fellow man to go with me to sinoe. But I hope you will not forget me for I think sir I would be sining agains the all mighty god and agains him who may consider so kind and so good as to my state and my well bain hear after. All of your family are know well and they all are doing better than I am because I was doing very well and your letter compell me to brake up and go down to sinoe and thire fore sir do not forget me. I want no money. You people is all situated on the river saint paul and are all well. I ask them if they was going to write you by the bargue renown and they all said now they had no call to but I told them I would write as long as I heard one pice of John McDonogh name in Louisiana whether or not he send me anything for my part and I [am] hear. I think he has done a nuff to give us our liberty and freedom and so not one of them would write. My wife is harriet Smith. Eany kind of cloth is good, makes no order what kind, since this cloth cheep and calico and som of all kind of cheap stuff and som of them want shoe slipping. But such as want I shall let you know. I want som cloth and provision and some tobacco. The cheapest cloth will be as good as gold and tobacco as silver. My wife present love and kindness to [you] and wish you a long and happy life both in this world and eternal in the other. May the almighty and everlasting god keep you and perserve you in this life and in the world to com, which is my humble prayr th[r]ough Jesus christ, our lord, amen. Please to give my love to all my frends and tell them that liberia is a fine place and all who can com they had better com. Pleas to send me some shoes and some shirting and when you send them pleas to mark them Galloway Smith McDonnogh, sinoe. So fair the well and the all mighty take charge of you soul [is] my humble prayr, for christ sake, a man.

[Galloway Smith McDonogh]

110 / WASHINGTON W. McDONOGH TO JOHN McDONOGH

Settra Kroo Mission house, February 7, 1844

Dear Parent: It is with gratitude and respect that I transmit you these few lines in hopes that you are in as good health as I am at present. Give my best respects to all inquiring friends. The climate agrees with my health very well in many respects and again in som respects it dose not. In the rainy season I am troubled with the chils and fever, & in the drys also, but not quite so much. About one month ago no one here in the Mission thought that I would be living to day but, thanks be to the alwise creator of heaven and earth, I am yet spared to do his will. I was take with the bleeding at the nose. I have had sevrel attacks. During the last dry my nose commenced one Sabbath morning at 9 o'clock, bled from that time untill 1 in the after noon. I then thought it was done but alas & recommenced about 5 o'clock and bleed from that untill half past 11 at night. Mr. Sawyer done all he could do without effect after trying every thing in his power. He then offered up pray to him that orders all things to his own Glory. As soon as pray was over Mrs. Sawyer got some Alum and dissolved it in water, milk warm. She got a surenge & by squirting it up my norsels it stoped it. I resceived your very kind letter dated may 1 and was very hapy to hear that you were well and all my friends. My Mother and all are well. I left them on the 10 of january. [They] were all well and doing well, that is some of them. Mother I suppos by this time has gathered about ten or twenty pounds of cotton. You mentioned in your letter that I have either forgoten to writ you or that I have no affection for you. How can I forget the name I bear? How can I forget a Father? I assure you Sir that [I] will never forget to write you when ever an oppurtunity affords it self. The reason why you do not rescive letters oftener is because I am so situated that I donot see every vessel that comes on the coast. There is but two Americans Captains that stops here and when ever they stops I always have letters ready for you. I have now twenty eight boys in school & three girls. I exspect to leave this school in a week from this tim. I am going to commence a new school about 10 or 12 miles below this. Out of the 28 boy in school there is but 5 that cannot read the word of God. 2 of the girls can read the bible very well. The other can not read the bible at all. They are all native children. But alast for us death has been in our midts. The Rev Mr Sawyer has been called to his long and hapy home. He died after a short illnes of 12 or 13 hours. Still every thing is going the same as when he was a live. Your humble servant,   Washington McDonogh

111 / MARY JACKSON TO JOHN McDONOGH

Monrovia, February 20, 1844

My Dear Revered Father, Yes, my best benefactor on earth: Sir, I sit with emotions of much joy, to have these lines written unto you in answer to your kind letter of May first, 1843, which came safe to me notwithstanding the wreck of the barque Renown.

I assure you, sir, that on hearing your letter read it afforded me—yea, us all—an uncommon degree of joy. Particularly on reflecting upon what our good Lord has done for us, to provide us such a gentleman as you for our former master, one who, when we were sitting still, being contented with being the slave of a kind master, you considerd our cases, read, and thereby found a place on earth where we could be free indeed. You gave us our liberty, spent your treasures in giving or procuring us passages to this our now delightful country, and now condescend to write to us by the endearing appellation of dear children. It seems almost too much—it almost seems not to be reality. But we thank God that he ever put it into your heart to do us this great kindness. We are in our own free soil, where none can molest us or make us afraid. We are sorry that you do not seem pleased with our present location. We would have been glad at first to have landed at the place where we would have to settle ourselves; but when we got to Monrovia, the people there generally said, that as the Governor had made no arrangements for us at Sinoe or Blue Barra, that it would be a deathly undertaking to go down there. The Governor then thought we had as well settle on the St. Paul, which, on seeing, we thought a fine place. The land on the St. Paul is good—and now, after we have spent our little all, to break up and remove to Sinoe or Blue Barra, would certainly be ruinous to us. I believe nothing prevents many of us, seeing *you* desire it, from removing but this. Judge [Samuel] Benedict, our lieutenant-governor now, who has been more friendly to us than any other, in reading your letter, which we handed him for his perusal, seemed anxious for us to go down, saying that as you have done so much for us we ought to go. Which advice many of us would have followed, but we are moneyless.

We have our fields planted with potatoes, cassada, &c. Very few have planted any coffee plants as yet, although it grows finely. Judge [Samuel] Benedict's farm of coffee is truly splendid—a good sample for us all. Mr. Wilson and Willis has made some fine sugar and syrup. In the whole we are delighted with the country. Mr. Benedict has taken aunt Eliza and her son John to live with him on his farm, has built her a fine house, and she will and is doing well, if she only behaves herself properly. Aunt Philis is quite well; also Mr. Ellis, Lambreth, and lady. They have quite a farm, and every convenience on it. Sister Rebecca, Matilda, Jack, George and wife, and aunt Polly, all beg to be remembered to you. At least, all of our people are doing very well. I do not recollect of our losing anyone since you had the pleasure of hearing from us last. We rejoice to hear, also, from all of our old fellowservants. Do tell them all howdy for us. Hoping that they will all so behave themselves to you, and try and serve the Lord, that he may open the way for them to get to these lands of civil and religious privileges. The box you sent aunt Phillis, with something in it for us, got lost in the wreck, but the pamphlets came safe, which we have read to our satisfaction. We are hopeful that they may be of much service in the United States, particularly to the holders of our race. The wealthier folks in Liberia live well and seem to enjoy themselves very much. We have much religious enjoyment in the churches of different denominations, particularly the Methodists and Baptists. Other sects are fewer in number.

My husband unites me in love to you, and all friends. I have much more to say, but my sheet of paper is full, so I end by subscribing myself Your very grateful servant, Mary Jackson[1]

112 / JOHN ROBERTS TO JOHN McDONOGH

Monrovia, Liberia, March 8, 1844

Dear Sir: I with great joy send you these few lines, which will tell you where I am. I hope these may find you as well as they leave me. Mother is quite well. I am staying with Mr. S. Benedict, and am doing very well for myself. I like this place very well, and don't want to return to America; but my greatest desire is that I may see you once more in this world. I have nothing much to say, as I expect you have had a good description of this place; for many of our people have been writing to you. My mother [Elisa] sends her love to you and says she wants to see you very much, and that she would like to come over to America, but says she does not ever expect to see you again, in this life. She has been quite sick this three or four weeks back, but is better now. You will please remember my love to all your people, and take the same for yourself.

I expect you heard that we lost old uncle Peter; and, also, old uncle Richard has lost all his religion, and has turned out to be a great drunkard.[1] All join me in love to you and all. I have nothing much to say, but when I write again I shall try and send you some curiosities. I must close this by saying I ever remain your Most ob't and humble servant,

John Roberts[2]

113 / AUGUSTINE LAMBERTH McDONOGH TO JOHN McDONOGH

[Monrovia, Liberia, March 8, 1844]

Here, father, I write a few lines in love, and I am rejoiced to hear from you, and that you are in good health.

I am in good health myself, through the blessing of God, and I am from morning til sunset at work on my farm, clearing and planting. I have made a good clearing on my land, and have considerable corn planted, and will try, by the help of God, to stock it with coffee-tree plant. I have planted a large piece in rice. Father, I shall be much obliged to you if you will send me a stone or still mill; for I have tried to cut out a stone to make a mill, but could not.

I have written to my godmother and brother for some things, to be sent by some emigrant vessel bound for Monrovia. Father, you will please notify her to give it you, and you will direct it to me.

Julia Ann, my wife, and Jonathan, my son, send their love to you. They are in good health. Give my love to all my fellow servants.

I am very well satisfied in this beautiful land of our forefathers. In this place persons of color may enjoy their freedom. In Africa, if a man is industrious and experiences the regenerating influence of the Holy Spirit, he will be happy here, and hereafter.

I subscribe myself a servant of God, and the friend of my fellow men. This leaves all well except mother. I remain, with esteem, Yours most ob't and hon. serv't,   A. L. McDonogh

P.S. Father, I hope that after you have finished your course, and performed the work assigned to you by the Father, that you may take your flight to Heaven and sit at the right of God, with Isaac and Jacob, where you will be forever blessed. I hope we shall meet there to part no more.

114 / GEORGE R. ELLIS McDONOGH TO JOHN McDONOGH

Monrovia, Liberia, April 14th, 1844

My dear Father: We are all enjoying health. The African fever has touched us up several times but the Lord has preserved us and it is my earnest prayer that this may find you in possession of the same blessing although we are separated by wide waters and rugged mountains. You my dear Father are always present with me in mind and never while memory last can I forget the godly admonitions given me by My dear Father.

I am settled up on the St. Paul's river and have some fifteen or twenty acres of land cleared and planted in Potatoes, cassadoes, arrow root, corn and about two hundred cotton bushes and about six or seven hundred coffee plants. The cotton we have gathered a good deal from. Besides those things mentioned we have a variety of other vegetables. Mother has had pretty good luck with her fowls more so than the Turkeys. She enjoys tolerably good health. Washington is living at Settra Kroo as school teacher attending I believe to what you wished him. He has been up twice to see us and speaks well of the place but it is entirely out of my power to go now as our place was given us on the St. Paul's. I went straight to work to see what I could do to make an honest living and I have gone on too far to move again to commence afresh, as by moving again I should entirely exhaust my funds for moving is attended with a deal of expense and trouble in this part of the world.

I look up to you as a Son to a kind Father and shall ever expect assistance from you as long as we are enabled to hear from each other. I stand in need at present of help from you and I wish you to send me something by the first chance. Mother begs that you will send her something as she stands much in need. She is now past labour and says you are the only one that she has to look to for help. Please remember me to James Thornton, Pa Noel, and all friends who may enquire after us. Mother sends a thousand loves to her dear Brother John McDonogh and to all her friends. Please give my love to Mr. Andrew Dunford and family and beg him to excuse me for not writing him. My love to Mr. John Hutchison if he is yet living. I remain My Dear Father, your aff Son,

George R. Ellis

115 / BRIDGET McDONOGH TO JOHN McDONOGH

Monrovia, up St. Paul's River, May 10, 1844

Father: We have received your letter of May, containing your health, which caused us to rejoice. I have been partly blind ever since I have been here, and I have the breast complaint, the complaint I had before I left America. Will you be so kind as to send me some mustard seed and some flax seed for stomach complaint. Father, will you please to send me a pair of spectacles nearly my age. I am very much in want of clothing; will you be so kind as to send me some coarse clothing and some coarse shoes. I remain, with esteem, Your most ob't and hon. serv't.,   Bridget[1]

116 / GEORGE R. ELLIS McDONOGH TO JOHN McDONOGH

Monrovia, Liberia, May 14th, 1844

My dear Father: It seems to me that I ought to write to you as long as the vessel stays so as I have a little more time. I thought I would just tell you something about the animals in this place. I have been visited by a leopard since my settlement on my farm. He took of[f] two Goats and one hog. I watched for him for some time but could never see him. I have seen the handsomest snake since I have been here that I ever saw. He had three colours, Red, pink and black, and was between 15 & 18 feet in length. He was lying on the margin of the river. I was at the time on my way from my farm to Monrovia and unfortunately had no gun with me. The leopards make nothing of visiting Monrovia. They walk whenever they choose but mostly at night and generally commit great depredations; they often take of hogs in the day if they happen to go in the skirt of the woods. I killed a snake in Mother's house that measures 9 feet 10 inches in length and one foot around. He was black. This snake was shot by Washington when he was up here on a visit last October. We have quite a variety of birds. Some of them are very handsome. I am almost afraid that the Paw Paw seed will mould before they get to you as my time was so short that I could not cure them as I would wish to. However I intend to procure a variety and fix them as they should be and forward them by the next chance. The seed are dried in ashes. I Remain, My dear Father, Your Afft Son,   G. R. Ellis McDongh

My dear Father: Please receive threse new papers, one enclosed with the letters and two packages. I hope they may be interesting to you. Dear Father, by the first good chance will you please send me if you can possible get them two large dogs a male and female. They are much needed here. The one I bought died. Your afft Son,   G R Ellis McDonogh

117 / JAMES McGEORGE TO JOHN McDONOGH

May 20th, 1844, Monrovia

Dear Sir: I now embrace this oppurtunity of writing you these few lines hoping that they find you all well. Our people, my step father James Fuller, remembers his love to you and says that he is ever mindfull of the one thing needfull that is at all times looking forward for the prize and when he visit a throne of grace he then remembers you all. Likewise Mrs. Fuller remembers her best respects to you all and begs your sincere prayers for she is ever mindfull when at prayer. Alexander Jackson says that he has not had time to write since he left but says that the Lord has blessed him with a reason portion of health and is doing tolerable well and wishes to be remembered to you all praying that he may meet you all in glory. Mr. Fuller says please to send him a whip saw & cut saw a frow & drawing [knife] with the different files as he needs them very much and at this time presents he is not in such good health but by the next vessels he hopes to give you a more full detail of his situation and conditions in this life. I pray you as you are and affectionate brother that you will send me out of 2 white or more of Cotton and 2 ps Blue Cotton Knard. Mrs. Fuller requst you sir to send her out a spining wheel and Cards as the wheels and cards were not enough for us to use and keep us all employed. Alexander Jackson says that he has been employed at the trade which you Learn him and has made or help to make sugar at the Government's farm at C. Willis Millsburg and by not having means to carry it on cannot subsist by it at all without turning his attention to something else. We can rejoice and thank God that we have not lost one out of the family. We are all still living and have time and health returns him that thanks for so good favour bestowd on us by him that put us in existance. The famly sends their love to James thorton, Noel Battice, George Mc MKenny, George Calhoun, Fanny Grimes, Jerry Rent & Davy Crocket, Horace Leander, Sophia and to all our inquiring friends and tell them to pray for us and we will pray for them. Nothing more at Present But Remains Your friend, James McGeorge

118 / JAMES McGEORGE TO JOHN McDONOGH

Monrovia, May 20th, 1844

Dear Beloved Sir: I have a favourable oppertunity of addressing you a few lines by way of the Expedition vessels that brought out imigrants for Sinou River which vessels landed here about seventeen or eighteen and the rest has gone to sad place. We received your leter from the expedition vessel that was lost and was very glad to hear from you which was dated May 1st, 1843, which afforded us a great deal of pleasure in perusing it. But when we came to hear that the presents you sent was lost we were very sorry that is sent by our friend James Thornton. We all joins in this letter in sending our best love and rspects to you and all the surveing [surviving] friends and relatives. The vessel has not yet arrived from sinoe but we look for her every day. We will now give you a hint of our situation. We have settled ourselves up the river on the saint paul about 15 [or] 16 miles up the river and are very well situated and will in the course of time do perhaps as well as we might wish in a new country. But before my story [I am getting ahead of my story?] We are not in such a prosperous situation as might be exspected toward farming—that is so as we could exchange our produce for foreign produce. But we make enough to sustain us from starvation if so might be true. The land up that river is very good and all it would want would be means to carry farming into operation when Sugar, Coffee might be made and a great many other things for importation. Again we are very well satisfied but, if you in your wise arrangement thinks for us that we had better break up from where we are, we are willing, but we would have to have a little assistence. And our reason was for not going down to sinou when we first came out was that section of country was in an unsettled state. We all had to go through the fever and we thought it unsafe which causes us [to] remain in Monrovia until we was climated. But since the squadron came out there are no danger for they have gon ashore there and settled the dispute both betwen the croomen & country people which can and is a great advantage to our people going to sinoe river to settle. To tell you the truth the whole of the country amongst the different tribes are at war to this day. The place is named where [we?] live Louianna McDonough. Henrietta Fuller raised about five barrels of corn, some cotton, a quantity and cassada, besides beans, arroroot, tomattises, sugar cane, Butter Beans the first season that she planted and we think that she will raise this year nearly ten Barrels in addition to all above mentioned, sallads, greens, &c &c.

We have nothing more particular to write you at Presents, Yours &c, James McGeorge

119 / AUGUSTINE LAMBERTH McDONOGH
TO JOHN McDONOGH

Monrovia, Liberia, May 20, 1844

Dear Father: I avail myself of this favorable chance to let you know that I am well and sincerely hope this may find you the same. I was truly glad to hear by the letters you sent per the "Lime Rock" that you enjoyed good health and would have been still better pleased at receiving a letter myself from you as I have never had the pleasure of doing so since I have been here. When we first arrived here George Ellis, James Gray, and myself were all that would agree to go to Sinoe so we were compeled to come ashore and settle here, since that we drew our lands up the river, and expended all that we had on them in building and fixing. Notwithstanding that, I am still willing to go to sinoe but have not sufficient means. James Gray is not living up the river but George Ellis and myself lives joining each other and have a good quantity of land under cultivation for new beginners. Please remember me to Mr Andrew Dunford and family. Julia sends a thousand good wishes to you, also to Mr. A. Dunford. Aunt Philis sends her love to Mr. A. Dunford & his family. My Mother also sends her best wishes to you. And now my dear Father I must conclude by hoping you still enjoy health and happiness. your afft son, Augustine Lamberth

120 / NANCY SMITH McDONOGH TO JOHN McDONOGH

Monrovia, Liberia, May 31, 1844

Dear Sir: I avail myself of this opportunity of writing you a few lines to inform you of my health, and of all my family. I am now in good health, and I hope these lines may find you the same. Dear sir, please to give my best love to all my friends, and tell them to try to meet me in Heaven, that is, if I never more see them in this world. Please to give my love to Fanny, Ellen, Aggy, aunt Hannah, Sophia, aunt Sain, James Thornton, Park Nowel, Henry Mann, George Carpenter, Jerry and little Henry, and David Crockett and Charlotte Gainard and Randolph Temple, and to one and all of my friends and, above all, please to give my love to Mrs. and Mrs. Andrew Danford, and tell them I am well and hope they are the same. Please tell them I wish they would send me something, if it is only some molasses. I would have sent them some preserves, but I have not got the sugar. I would have sent you some, but the main means is wanting. I have received your seeds, and thank you very much for your kindness. I hope the Almighty may bless you for so doing, both in this world and in the world to come. Yes, I have reason to rejoice, for you have done more for me than my father. Yes, sir, for there are servants which have been serving their master for fifty years, who, instead of being set at liberty, are carried to the auction market, and there sold to the highest bidder. Yes, how many thousands have been served in that way. Sometimes, when I think of that, I often say, how good the Almighty was to me. Yes, he was more than good to bless me with the luck to have such a master as you. Please read this in the presence of all your servants, and tell them to look and see for themselves, that there is not another such man to be found under heaven as your master; no, there is none. I suppose you think that I am free, and that you are in bondage, that is my reason for so saying; no, God forbid it. If that is your thoughts, you must all remember that I have been under the servitude of the same master; and I am no stranger to his ways and fashions. Yes, I thought the Sabbath was one of the most burdensome days I ever wished to see; but I find it was for my good, and if the same is going on now, I say it is the most, best and important thing that can be carried on by you. Yes, I say never let your servants have too much pleasure on the Sabbath day, for it brings on sin and ruin. I have found, since I have been in Africa, that my custody on the Sabbath was for my good. Yes, and more than for my good, for it first taught me the way to God, and then enlightened my understandings. So all of you servants pay attention to your master, and go to school and learn. If such should not be obeyed, I think a little punishing would not be wrong. I, myself, was sometimes missing out of school, when sometimes you would put me in the barn; but instead of putting me in the barn, you should have taken me out and given me a severe flogging for not attending to what I have seen the use of, since I have been here. So if they refuse to go to school you must punish them, both old and young; for a man that is fifty is not too old to learn; but I suppose a man thinks himself too big to be among children. But if I myself needed understanding, I would go among dogs, if I thought they were capable of teaching me. So farewell. May God bless you and keep you, is my faithful prayer. Amen.   Nancy Smith[1]

P.S. My mother sends her love to you and all of your people. She is getting quite old, but firm in grace. George and Susan have joined the Baptist Church; also, Matilda and little Nancy. Old man Peter is dead, and Thomas Young has a bad sore foot, all the rest is well.

Settra Kroo, Dec 28, 1845

Dear Father: I have a great reason to thank God that I am yet spared to see the close of another Year. And I hope that by His blessings these will find you and all inquiring friends the same. I am at this time with the Mission at Settra Kroo, and we are all well at presint. I suppose you heard of Mrs. Connelly's visit to the States. She reached here on the fifteenth 15th of October last. She has been confined since that and has a fine daughter. On her return to this country She brought out a young Woman of color with her as my assistant and teacher. But, alast, she is not, for She has been called home to rest. She lived little over one month after her arrival here but we have every reason to believe that her end was peace. This is the third death that we have had in the Mission this year. In the first place We lost a boy with the consumption. The next one died very sudden. He was taken sick about ten o'clock in the evening with a pain in the stomach. We gave him medicens but all to no purpose, for he died in about two hours after he was taken. The first boy went home when he was taken very sick to his father and died in town. But the second died in the Mission yard which caused a great many of the Scholars to run off, so our school is quite small at this time. The people among whom we live are very ignorant and superstitious. If any one dies they will say that some one has bewitched [him] and very often will go of[f] to the gran devil man as he is sometimes called and get him to tell who it was that bewitched the person that died and if he choose to tell them a lie on any person they catch the person and give them what they call sassa wood.[1] This sassa wood is the bark off a tree that grows in the swamps. There are two kinds. One kind is very poisonous. If the person that is acused has a plenty of money they will give him the worst kind for the sake of getting his money. If he will pay them a good some them will give him the weak kind. But a poor person will be sure to come of badly. But they did not give it for either of the young men that died in the Mission. Now Dear Father I hope you will answer this by the first chance & I hope that by the Blessins of God you will be sapred [spared] not ony to answer this one but a great number more. Your humble servant,

W. W. McDonogh

P.S. I have not seen my Mother for one year and half. The last time I heard from them they were all well.   W. W. McDonogh

Monrovia, March 18, 1846

Honored Parent: I have embraced this opportunity of addressing you a few lines hoping they will find you in as good health as they leave me at present.[1] I came up here in Jany last on a visit to my mother's family. Mothers health is not very good at this time. She is troubled with the chills & fevers. Brother & Sister and their family are all in good health and join me in love to you & all enquiring friends. I wrote to you not long since by a letter that brought out the emigrants in February last.

We were greatly disappointed on the arrival of this last emigrant vessel by not receiving a single line from you.

But I hope Dear Father that you have not forgotten me for I never shall forget thee. I have read your letters time after time, and shall endeaver to follow after your counsel as much as possible. You need not be afraid that I shall forget or neglect them.

I am still striving to do all the good I can among the natives. I can speak a little of the Kroo dialect. I have been among them for nearly four years. Their language is very hard to learn. I can understand it better than I can speak it. But as the old saying is practice makes perfect. Now sir I close this letter by wishing you long life & a happy end. Your obt servt,   W. W. McDonough

P.S. I shall leave this place to day for Kroo country which is about one hundred miles from this.

123 / GEORGE R. ELLIS McDONOGH TO JOHN McDONOGH

Monrovia, March 20th - 1846

Hon. Sir: I have again taken up my pen to address you hoping they will find you in the enjoyment of Gods blessing for without them we are nothing.

Our family are in pretty good health except Mother. Her health is not very good at this time. They all joins me in love to you and all inquiring friends. I was very much disappointed on the arrival of a vessel direct from New Orleans and not a line from you or any of my friends. Dear Sir I hope that you have not forgotten me for I am looking out for a letter by every Vessel for it has been a long time since I had one from you. I did never expect to see a Vessel from N. Orleans with-out a letter from you for I Shall emprove every opportunity of writing to you. I am still striveing to carry on my farming such as Rice, Corn, Sweet Potatoes and Cassadoes, &c. &c. Sir I wish you would be so kind as to send me out some seed of all disscription, if you will please sir, and any thing which you may think proper to send me will be very exceptable for this, like all other new countries, is a very hard one.

Now my dear Father I hope that the Lord will continue to gaurd and protect you from all harm and danger in this low and sinfull world and at last receiving you into everlasting aboard [abode] is the prayers of your unworthy *Servt.* Yours truly, G. R. Ellis

124 / JOHN AIKEN TO JOHN McDONOGH

Monrovia, Liberia, August 7th, 1846

My Dear Master, and friend, Mr Mc Donogh: I take up my pen to write you a few lines, hoping they will find you in the same good health that I write them and that you may live a long number of Years, blessed by the Lord in every way, and to do more and more good on Earth. Oh Sir, your kind letter to me of January the 2d is received and I read it with tears of joy, to think that you write to one so low as me and call me your Dear Son. I read it to all your people here and it made us all to rejoice and tears to flow when we remembered you and all your kindness and we should never see you any more in this world, but we trust we are only separated for a short time to meet again to part no more.

You ask me to tell you all about this country—If it is a good country and what we raise. I will tell you Sir as well as I can. It is a fine country. The land is rich and produces everything but wheat. All kinds of Garden Stuff as in America, Cabbage, Peas, Beans, Cowcumbers, Melons, Onions, Tomatoes, Rice, Indian Corn, Cassada, fruits of all kinds. Oranges, &c., &c. The country is healthy for the Black people and our children is increasing in numbers. We are all happy and contented as we can be, Seeing that we are separated from you, our Dear friend, and father, and we would not change this country for any other part of the world. We have a plenty of everything but clothing, which is very dear. All our people send their love to you and all our friends with you, and tell you that their prayers are constantly put up to the throne of Grace night and day for blessings on your heads. I am in haste to write this as the vessel that carries it sails to day, but will write you Dear Father again soon. Oh, my prayer to GOD Is that he will bless and preserve you long in life, and at death receive you into heaven.

All from your faithful Servant and Son,   John Aiken[1]

125 / WASHINGTON W. McDONOGH TO JOHN McDONOGH

King Will's Town, October 7, 1846

Dear Father: I have again taken up my pen to address you a few lines, hoping that these will find you in as good health as they leave me at this time. I thank my God that he has still given me health and strength at this time to address you. We are all well at this time, that is, in the mission family Mr. and Mrs. Connelly, Mr. and Mrs. Priest.[1] Mrs. Connelly, you recollect, was in America last year. After her return to this country she was delivered of a fine daughter; but, alas, the Lord has seen proper to take it to himself. Mrs. Priest had a fine son, and he has been taken also. They could not have been taken in a better time, for they were both infants. Therefore, the Lord giveth and the Lord taketh, blessed be the name of the Lord. I paid a visit to my mother and family the first of this year, and found them in good health. I spent two months and a half with them, during which time I assisted my brother in clearing and planting a fine crop of rice, corn, and cassadas. He has at this time on his farm about 24 or 25 bound boys; some of them were taken from on board of a slaver by an American man-of-war. I think he has now about sixty acres of land under cultivation, or very near it. My visit was in January, February, and a part of March; I then returned to my labor among the heathen.

Dear father, I have just been reading again your very kind letter to me just before I left college. I do assure you, sir, that there is nothing on earth that gives me more pleasure than it does to think that I have such an adviser and friend as you are; for no one but a father can give to a son such advice, surely not; and the more I read it, the more I am encouraged to press forward in my calling as a teacher, and may the Lord give me grace to run and not be weary, for without Him we are nothing and can do nothing. I praise His holy name that my lot was not cast in a heathen country and among heathen parents, but in a Christian country and among Christian parents and friends, and that, too, in the hands of one who has been a father to me instead of a cruel oppressor. When I was young and foolish you took me from my father and mother into your own dwelling, and brought me up as a son instead of a servant. I often thought hard of it at the time, but now I find that it was for my own benefit and not yours that you took so much pains in bringing me up in the ways of truth and honesty, for I find now that truth and honesty is the best capital that a man can possess in this world. It is true that wealth makes many friends, but their friendship is deceit. An honest man is said to be the noblest work of his Creator. Had I been permitted to run about, as many of my age were, I should have been today as ignorant as they are; but, thanks be to my Creator, I was not.

And to you, dear father, words cannot express my gratitude to you for your care towards me during my younger days, for youth is truly the time to lay up for old age and I hope that I have commenced on a good foundation, for you have given me precept upon precept, and line upon line, and may the Lord give me grace to keep them all the days of my life. And now, dear father, permit me to give you an imperfect statement of the productions of the country, and then close for the night.

The first, and greatest, is rice; sweet potatoes, Lima beans, ochre, pease, raddish, cabbage, snaps, cucumbers, greens, cassadas or cassavas, yams, corn, sallads, cymblanes, arrow-root, carrots (few), the pawpaw, which grows on a tree, pumpkins, parsley, mustard. Fruit—watermelon, muskmelon, mango, plum, orange, rose apples, sour sop, guava, tamarind, plantain, banana, gramma dilla, limes, and lemons. *Domesticated*—cows, bullocks, swine, sheep, goats, duck, fowls, pigeons, turkeys (very few). I will not attempt to give you a list of the wild animals, and the different kinds of fish which we have here at this time. Should you wish to know, I shall give it to you at some future time, should my life be spared. I should like very much, dear father, to see you once more before we leave this world, for it would be a source of great delight to me, *but I will never consent to leave this country for all the pleasures of America combined together, to live, for this is the only place where a colored person can enjoy his liberty*, for there exists no prejudice of color in this country, but every man is free and equal. Please to remember me to all my friends and acquaintances, to Mr. Dumford and son, and uncle James Thornton, and Par Nowd, and all the rest. And now, my dear father, I close this letter, hoping that you will let me hear from you soon and may the Lord, who is able to do all things, protect and deliver you from all dangers, seen and unseen, and grant you strength for many days and years yet to come, is the prayer of your humble servant,

W. W. McDonogh

126 / GEORGE R. ELLIS McDONOGH TO JOHN McDONOGH

Messurado County, October 9, 1846.

Dear Father: I again avail myself of this chance to write you. I do assure you, though, that I feel at a loss to know what to say. I have written to you so often, and have never received but two letters from you since I left you. The first was by the Renown that was wrecked at Port Prays, and the second by the Lime Rock. And by Capt. Auld I wrote you two or three letters, besides those I sent to different persons, and I don't as much as know whether you ever received them or not; but one of the emigrants from Kentucky, who passed through New Orleans, told me that he saw you in New Orleans, and that you told him you had only received one letter since we had been here and that was from Galloway Smith, and I assure you I was more than surprised to hear it, for I have wrote you by every chance since I have been here by way of New York, Philadelphia, Baltimore, and direct from here to New Orleans. The same emigrant told me that you said you wished two of the young men from here would come to New Orleans. I should be extremely happy to come on myself, but I would rather hear from you first. My dear father, I really think some hard feelings against me on your part is the reason I have not received any letter from you for such a length of time. My brother Washington gets letters from you; he can tell me of your health, and I know I write to you as often as he does, as I generally forward his from here, and write myself at the same time, and he receives answers and I none. My dear sir, as I cannot see nor hear from you, I am almost disheartened about writing to you, but I assure you, sir, without any thing like flattery, that my affection remains the same towards you, and, in fact, I feel more love and esteem towards you, now we are separated by wide waters and rugged mountains, than ever I did. Now I know how to appreciate good advice received from you in my youthful days. I feel and know the truth of the Scripture that says, train up a child in the way he should go, and when he is old he will not depart from it. I hope that we shall see each other's faces again in the flesh; but if the Lord has ordained it otherwise, I trust we shall be among that number that John saw surrounding the Throne of the Lamb, where sorrow, pain and death are felt and feared no more. Julia and her husband and Lamberth have both joined the Church, and nearly all the rest of the people. Lamberth is one of the official members. We are all in good health, and sincerely hope you are enjoying the same. As this letter will reach you, I hope, by Christmas, I will conclude by wishing you a merry Christmas and a happy New Year, and that you may enjoy many more, with the blessing of God upon your head. Mother and Julia send their respects to you. I am, dear father, Your affectionate son,   G. R. Ellis

127 / A. JACKSON TO JOHN McDONOGH

Monrovia, Africa, November 11, 1846

Dear Father and Friend: It is with love I write you this, and all our friends join me in their love to you, our benefactor and kind master. The letter you wrote to Mr. Smith for us all, we read, and it made us happy to learn that you and all the friends we left with you at home are well. Sir, be pleased to give them our love, and remember that you share it with them. We pray always, giving thanks to the Giver of all good, for His blessings to you and to them. We hope that this letter will find you as it leaves us here, all in good health. You ask us how we are getting on with our farms. We are doing very well, sir. Have plenty of every thing, such as yams, sweet potatoes, corn, rice, cassada, garden vegetables and fruits of every description in the greatest abundance. Fowls in plenty, of all kinds. Hogs and goats. Our horned cattle are now beginning to increase. We have now fences made to secure them. When they ran out in the woods we lost them. As we have now got our plantations cleared and in good order, and our houses finished, we are beginning to plant coffee trees, and hope to be able to crop from them in two or three years, at least for our own use. This, sir, is a great and very fine country. The land is rich, and yields every thing in abundance, if the seed is planted and taken care of by keeping it clean of grass and weeds. Any man who will use common industry, and even work half of his time, can raise more of every thing then he can use, and have much to sell besides.

We should like to see you, sir, once more before we die, but we cannot hope for this. But we trust we shall meet again in a happier state, and be separated no more; for almost all your people have joined the church of our blessed Lord, and are made happy. We thank God day and night that he cast our lot under so kind a master as you, sir, who helped us with your riches to get here, to this free and blessed land of our fathers, where the colored man can be happy, if he will but love and walk with God. Our hearts overflow, sir, when we think of you and all you have done for us poor black people. But the great God whom you serve, whom you taught us to serve, has blessed you, wonderfully blessed you, and will continue to bless you through many days yet to come here on earth, and translate you when your days are ended, we trust, into His heavenly kingdom. All of which, we, your poor black friends here in Africa, pray for day and night.

I will now end this, and subscribe myself, your friend and servant, till death, A. Jackson[1]

128 / GEORGE R. ELLIS McDONOGH TO JOHN McDONOGH

Monrovia, Liberia, March 25th, 1847

My Dear Father: Your kind and cheering letter bearing date January 6th, 1847, came safe to hand on the 14 present Month. I cannot express to You the joy it afforded me, also my Mother and Sister. Mr. Ellis I have found out to be a fine man and I hope a good Christian. He preached Yesterday, it being the Sabbath. I also went to hear him and am much pleased with him. We are all well. Mr. Ellis is at my house and has been to see me several times. My Dear Father I have wrote You by every chance but have not received letters from you as I expected but as I wrote You in my last I hope You will do, that is to write and direct Your letters to me but to the care of Walter Lowrie of New York and he of cours will forward them to me as I am now acting Agent for the Mission at Settra Kroo. I have been very much disappointed in not receiving letters from You by the way of New York as You promised to communicate with me that way. I have received no letters but by vessels direct from New Orleans since I have been here. The letters of Andrew Dunford has been wrote better than two Years ago and if You had have sent it on to New York I should have received it long since. I have also wrote You to send me something and I wrote to You as a Son to a Father as I have no one on Earth that can render me the assistance that You can. I again repeat the request. You stated in Your letter that You did not know of the Vessel Sailing until about an hour before she sailed. I was suprized to hear it but I believe if you had have known it You would have sent me something if it was only a Yard of Cloth. So I hope as I am told this vessel will return You will send me something. Anything You may Choose to send will be acceptable wheither dry goods or Provision. I know that You cant send any thing but by vessels direct from New Orleans and I will certainly look for something by the first Vessel from there as the amount of three or five hundred Dollars would be of no consequence to a man of Your wealth and as I find myself so much in need in this hard Country and feeling assured that while I was with You I acted upright and just towards You and believing You know the same is my reason for making this request of You. I wrote You sometime since concernig Gray's Property in Gretna. The Children as I stated then are in My Hands and I find it difficult to support them and school them both so I beg of You to have the Property sold and send the amount out to me for the children in any thing You think suitable. I was in hopes that it would have been done before this time. My Dear Father I must inform you that I am married and living as comfortable as can be expected. Our people are doing tolerably well. They saw timber planks and Shingles and make farms. Cornelious is dead. The rest are all well. My Dear Father I remember the Good Counsel You gave me so often and pray that the Lord may bless protect and defend You through life by his unerring counsel and that when the voyage of life is over and he has no more for you to do on earth he will take You to live with him in glory. I did as You told me with Washington's letter and as an opportunity afford on the sixteenth of this Month I sent it to him. I got a letter from him about three weeks ago. He was then well. Mother and Julia sends a thousand loves to You and prays to be rememberd by You at a throne of grace. By this Vessel I would have come to New Orleans on a visit but I could not bring my buisness to a close sufficient to leave and I wish You Dear Father to write me wheither there will be any difficulty and how the law is touching persons returning to visit. I have between thirty and forty acers of my farm under cultivation. I have cassadoes, Potatoes, Arrowroot, Ginger, Groundnuts, Pepper Bushes without number, Orange trees, Mango, Paw Paw, Roseapples, Guava, Sugarcane, Lime trees and my dwelling on my farm is enclosed by a lime heage [hedge]. I have between three and four hundred coffe trees which I planted from the seed in a nursery and I drew them and set them out and they are now bearing from half pound to a pound each. I have also Cocoa Nut Trees. I have sent You a specimen of the coffe from my farm. Mother has done pretty well with her Turkeys. From those five she brought out, she can show twenty or thirty besides what she has made use of. She has some of the old ones also. This coffe I send just as a curiosity and to show that I took Your advice in farming. I have seen a man from New Orleans that I knew while there and he told me that our Old Judge Martin was dead, also Mr. Pollock the Notary, as well as many others that I asked him about. My Dear Father I wish to enquire of our old friend John Hudson. I hope he is well. Give my best respects to him if he is yet alive. I am very thankful to You for those newspapers You were kind enough to send me. I hope You will send them to me by every chance. I have sent You a few of ours. I hope Dear Father that You will send me also a few working Tools such as axes, hoes, spades and the like as they are very hard to get here and very useful. Dear Father I have sent some letters in your package for different persons which I hope you will give them for me. Madam Egrette lives just back of your house. And now dear Father I must bring my letter to a close. I hope to hear from you in short. I Remain dear Father, Your Affectionate Son,

G. R. Ellis McDonogh

129 / GEORGE R. ELLIS McDONOGH TO JOHN McDONOGH

Monrovia, Liberia, March 26th, 1847

My dear Father: When I wrote my other I expected the vessel would have sailed before this; but, as it has not, I again sit to write you, as it always affords me pleasure to do so and when I am writing I feel somehow as though I were near and conversing; consequently I derive pleasure from it. I neglected to tell you in my other letter that from the corn you sent in the "Little Rock," in 1844, I raised more corn than has ever been raised by our farmers since the settlement of the colony, namely, forty barrels of as fine corn as you ever saw raised any where in New Orleans. I neglected also to inform you that I have a fine parcel of cocoanut trees on my farm, also the granadilla, a very delicious fruit, and the sugar apple, a very delicious fruit, sour sop, also another excellent fruit.

I send you a small box of coffee raised on my farm. You may find it a little more mashed than the coffee generally, as we have to clean it by beating it in a mortar; but you will find it as good coffee as need be drank. Please give Lawyer Hennan a little of it, and tell him it was raised on my farm from seed sown by me in a nursery, and drawn and set out. Julia, my sister, has had a fine son since I wrote you last, his name was "James Watts."

Dear father, please be good enough to send me a grindstone and a corn mill, and the tools I mentioned in my other letter, as such things can't be got here. I have sent to New York once or twice for a mill, but can't get one out by order, and now I beg you to send me one. Mother joins me in love to Jim Thornton, Pa Noel, George Carpenter, Perry Fanny, and Ellen; she says tell Jerry, Fanny, and Ellen to recollect the advice she gave them before she left, respecting their duty to their master, and that they must seek the kingdom of Heaven and His righteousness and all things shall be added to them. I have sent enclosed in your package a letter to Mr. Tuton, your neighbor; likewise one to Mr. Banney. As I did not know their given name, I merely put their titles. Tell them you will receive anything they may wish to send me. Also, one to the Rev. D. Wells, of New York, a correspondent of mine. I received a letter from him by the Mary Wilkes, appointing me the agent for the Presbyterian Mission of Settra Kroo. I received things at the same time for the mission at Settra Kroo, and have them in my store until an opportunity offers to send them down. So, dear father, if you will write me even when you forward his letter, and direct it to his care, he will most likely find an early opportunity of sending it out to me. And now, my dear father, I close by wishing that He who conducted Israel through the Red Sea may protect, defend and bless you, and be unto you at all times as the shadow of a great rock in a weary land. Your affectionate son,

G. R. Ellis M'Donogh

130 / WASHINGTON W. McDONOGH TO JOHN McDONOGH

Nova Kroo, Nov. 13, 1847

Dear father: I embrace this precious opportunity of addressing you a few lines hoping at the same time that God in his mercy will spare you to read those and many more. I am still among the heathens trying to teach them the ways of God. But alast for us we see but little or no fruites of our labours as yet. I now have charge of a boarding School at this place which is about ten miles from Settra Kroo. My school is not as flourishing at this time as I could wish. However I am doing all that I can for the few that I have at this time. I have never seen the Revd. Mr. [H. W.] Ellis of whom you spak in you last letter as my Station is over one hundred miles from his. I have written to him but have never received a single line from him. The money that was sent to Mr Lowrie from you in the year 1845 I am sorry to say that I have never recieved one cent of it up to the present time. Why it is I cannot say but so it is. The last accounts I had from my Brother state that they were all in good health and that Elizabeth has been called to rest. When I say Elizabeth you will understand me to mean my older Sister's Child. She died with the swelling of her body the cause I do not know. Now dear father I hope these will meet you time enough to wish you a mearry Christmast & a happy New Year and as many as Shall be gathered together on that day. Give my best wishes to all my friends uncle James and ma[n]y others. With the best wishes of your humble Servt for yourself,   W. W. McDonogh

131 / WASHINGTON W. McDONOGH TO JOHN McDONOGH

Settra Kroo, March 7th, 1848

Hon Sir,   I have taken this opportunity of addressing you a few lines to inform you that I am still in the land of the liveing and enjoying the rightes of man for although I am in a land of darkness I have nothing to fear. My wants are few and of course easily supplyed, Not like you who are liveing in a land of milk & honey and yet never satisfied. I have lived in the same land myself and had the pleasure of enjoying all that the heart could wish for or that would make one happy and yet I was not willing to denie myself of the lease thing. But alas, what a change has since taken place. Things that seemed to have been of so much value to me in those times are no more to me now than idle dreams. When compared with my present views of them, all that I now wish for is just enough to make me comfortable and happy while I live in this world, for we are told in scripture that we can carry nothing out of it when we go hence. And now Dear Sir, I think that I have found one that is able and willing to help me on in my labours as a Missionary among the heathen. She is a young lady from the West. She was exspected out with the Revd Mr. Ellis by whom you wrote me a year ago. She came out last year, say in October, and has gon through her acclimating fevers very well and is now prepared for the business of a Mission, being brought up and educated in one of the best Christian familys in Cincinnati. You may know that she is worthy of your Dear Washington. She was brought up in the family of the Revd Mr. Biggs of the above named place. I exspect to marry her in a short time if life lasts, perhaps before this reaches you & I hope that you will be so kind as to send me out some thing to start on in the way of making a liveing or to live on for you know that my time is all spend in the Lord's service and not in worldly gains or speculations. Please inform me when you write me when you heard from David last and what is his occupation. Now Dear Parent I will close by wishing you long life & happyness with my best wishes to you and all my friends. Your obt servant,   Washington W. McDonogh

132 / JULIA SMITH McDONOGH TO JOHN McDONOGH

Monrovia, Liberia, W. Africa, July 1st, 1848

Dear Father,   I embrace this opportunity to write to you by this vessel the "Liberia Packet", hoping this may safely reach you being the first I have ever written to you since my arrival here. I hope in consequence of having neglected to do so will not by any means be astonishing to you when it reaches you though no doubt you will be somewhat surprised when you see from whom it is sent. I am at present in moderate health and all the rest of us except Sister Jane Henderson who has been very sick but is now recovering. John Jefferson Martin has married and has a fine daughter; I have by the goodness of the Lord embraced Religion and like-wise Orleans Martin and have joined the Baptist Church. Also John Jefferson Martin has embraced religion but has not as yet attached him-self to any denomination. I trust inasmuch as we have entered in the Warfare we may have faith & grace through our Lord Jesus Christ to hold out to the end, also patience to resist temptations of the evil one, and as our blessed Lord says, "take up our cross & follow him through Evil as well as good report." Gallaway Smith has gone to the U. States. He left here in the U.S Storeship "Southampton", shipped onboard and has never returned since. I have heard from him three times. The last time I heard that he was in Philadelphia acting as porter in some mer-chant's store or warehouse.

Dinah Young is dead. She died about two months since. The burden of repeating the ten Commandments, which we considered to be at the time when [we were] with you, [we] have found them to be of the utmost im-portance and are now more than thankful to you for the pains you took with us as a Father, and hope that the Lord will reward you for you kind-ness towards us. I have learned to knit since here I have been & I send you enclosed a sample of edging which is now much admired & fashion-able with the Ladies in Monrovia & even at the other Settlements. Give my respects to Mrs. Andrew Dunford and all enquiring friends. Sister Jane, Orleans and all of us send our respects to you. I am as yet single and am living with Genl. John N. Lewis. Would like to know whether or not the Sunday School & Sabbath Meetings are still kept up as they were when we were there. I remain yours affectionately,   Julia Smith[1]

P.S. Please to answer this by the first oppertunity. I send you also a sample of a Collar. Would be glad if you could give us any information about David Kenny who went to Philadelphia & was to have been here before us but has not as yet arrived. Mother is well and sends her love to you.   J.S.

133 / NANCY SMITH McDONOGH TO JOHN McDONOGH

Monrovia, July 3, 1848

Dear Father: I now set down to take my pen in hand to writ[e] you a few lines hoping that they may find you well. We are all well. I have written to you serveral times and have not had the pleasure of received one from you as yet and will you please to be so kind as to give my best respects to all the inquiring frends and will you please to tell them to send me some thing and you will pleas to send me something, as you have not send me nothing since I left but once and will you pleas send me something to insist [assist] me in building my house which I expects to begin in in the coarst of next year. If you send me any things will please to send them by Mr. Underwood and if the rest should give you any thing to give it to him allso. Give my love [to] Mr. Richard Southerfield [?] . Tell him will he pleas to send me some things which he promis when I left. Will you pleas to received them and give them to Mr. Underwood. I would be happy to come and see you but I am afraid I would be interrupted by the white people. But if they would not you will be kind enough to let me no so I can come. Pleas to in quire for Mr. Bolerson Washington. Tell him that his god Childe is well and is going to school and she which [wishes] you to send her some thing and she says she has not received a letter since she left. Give my love to Mr. and Mrs. Dunford and tell them to send me one Barrel of molases or sugar. Are [either] one will answer. All of my family is well. My mother is yet alive and my oldest Sister. My Brother I have not seen him for two years. He is gone to the states but I do not no where he is. He has a wife and a fine Daughter. Little Jane is dead and Precela also. I have nothing more at presant but remain your daughter,   Nancy Ann Smit[h]

Monrovia, July 3, 1848

Dear Sir: I embrace this opportunity of writing you these few lines hoping that they may find you well. It leaves us all that is living enjoying a reasonable portion of health and geting along tolerably well and would be glad to hear from you and all the acquaintances that lives near about you. We are all more or less is forever thinking about [you] and do feel sorry that we have not heard from you. We have been somewhat industrious for we are all living in tolerably comfortable frame dwellings and if you would consider upon us a little know doubt you would assist us for we live so far from you. This country is a butifull place. It is well watered and timbered and if a person could have a little capital or any assistance would do very well and I would my dear Sir plead with you on behalf of ourselves to aid us and it would be gladly received. Bro. Underwood will hand you this letter and if you should feel for us my Dear you will send it to us by him and we will be sure to receive it. Please do not forget to send us something and particular to write us. George Calhoun, your Grandson Benjamin Jackson, Davy Crocket & Poly, Matilda, Levia, Mary Jackson, Riny Carter, and all five of her children is well. George Jackson and family and his fine son Matildo Briggs & Rebecca Brigs, Jim thorton, Nowel and Aggy all sends their love to you and they are all glad that you sent them to the Land of liberty and the Lord has bless them to reach the Land and we all disires to be remembered to all the friends and th[em] that shall inquire after us. And if we should be so plessd to hear from you and that you should send something we shall be glad and if we [should] no more see you we hope to meet you in heaven. Nothing more at Present, But remains Your friend and Well wisher,

Simon Jackson[1]

135 / WASHINGTON W. McDONOGH TO JOHN McDONOGH

Settra Kroo, October 13, 1849

Hon Sir,   I have taken up my pen this morning in the intint, doubtfully made, to address a few lines to you. It has been nearly three years since I received a line or heard a word from you. If these lines should find you in the land of the living I will be more than glad to hear from you. I have writen so many letters to you at different times and receiving no answer I have almost come to the conclusion that you have repudiated me, Dear Sir. If these should find you in health please return me an answer by the shortest way. My Mother departed this life since I have heard

Monrovia Nov 24th 1849

My Dear Father

      I ~~again~~ avail myself of this
favourable chance to let you know I am well
and cherish the same feelings and hopes for your
health and prosperity as the day I left you.
      The people
of Liberia were much cheered by the presence of
the Revd Mr Gurley. I have had the pleasure of his
company several times at my house in this place
and yesterday I took him quite up to Louisiana
the residence of our people he saw them and took
down their names visited their houses and conversed
with them. on our way up we stopped at New Georgia
a village about four miles up the Stockton Creek and
also at Caldwell on the Saint Paul river the people
in every place regard him as a dear friend and benefactor
this letter I shall put into his hands to be forwarded
to you by him and shall forward with pleasing anticipa-
tations for an answer to the many that I have written you
at different times as well as this and shall expect that
you will also send something to me as you promised
when I left you to do, all of our people are well
are well, I must now close this if I dont I shall
be too late for Mr Gurley as he will start for the
vessel in a short time. I Remain Dear Father
      yours affty G. R. Ellis

George R. Ellis McDonogh's letter to John McDonogh, November 24, 1849.
McDonogh Papers, Tulane University

from you and a number of others. My mother died on the thirteenth of Sep. A. D. one thousand eighthundre[d] fort[y] nine. Thus you see the Lord has taken away both of my par[en]ts. Yet [I] Dare not murmur for it is the Lord's doings. The rest of the family are or were well the last time I heard from them. I am now married and I trust to one of the best in Africa for She is a Christian and hope a true one. We were mar[rie] d on Second of May, 1849, and are Still labouring among Natives. Mr. and Mrs. Connelly is about to leave here for the states and I hope you will have the pleasure of seeing them. In haste I close, Your humble servt,

Washington W. McDonogh

136 / HENRIETTA FULLER McDONOGH TO JOHN McDONOGH

Mr. John McDonough   St. Paul's River, New Orleans, Liberia
                                          October 24th, 1849

Dear Sir: Having an opportunity of forwarding letters to the United States by the Liberia Packet which will sail in a few days I embrace this good opportity of writing you by her. This Sir I am happy to say leaves [me] in the enjoyment of good health, also my family & wishing these lines may find you & yours enjoying the same blessing. Since we have heard from you we have had some deaths out of our Number. They are Mr. James Fuller, Alexander Jackson, Manuel Fuller, & Catharine Travis. The rest of our Number are all well & doing well. We are doing pretty well in the Agricultural line growing coffee, rice, Sugar, &c., &c. We have no right to complain of our situation. It is true when we first landed after the expiration of the Six Months Maintainance from the Society the[n] we found it a little difficult to do as well as we could wish. Yet we have partially surmounted the difficulties & no[w] are perfectly satisfied. We now are in the strictest sense of the word Free. We have A Church in our village where we worship God & a School house where our children are sent daily to recieve instructions. The individual whose deaths I have mentioned died in the triumps of faith & requested us to meet them in heaven. They left abright testimony behind them of being hiers to the Kingdom above.

You will please remember us to all our acquaintances & especially to our colored friends & say to them that Liberia is the home for our race & as good a country as they can find. Industry & perseverenace is only required to make a man happy & wealthy in this our Adopted country. Its soil yields abundant harvest to the husbanman. Its climate is healthy. Its laws are founded upon Justice & equity. Here we Sit under our own vine & Palm Tree. Here we enjoy the same rights & priviledges that our white brethren does in America. It is our only home.

It has been some time since I recieved a letter from you. I would be happy to hear from you at all times. With these few lines I close, wishing God in his alwise providence to continue to bless you & all the friends in America & also to continue to extend his hands of care over us & at last bring us to live with him where parting no more shall be. Respectfully Yours &c.,   Henrietta Fuller[1]

137 / GEORGE R. ELLIS McDONOGH TO JOHN McDONOGH

Monrovia, Nov. 24th, 1849

My Dear Father: I avail myself of this favourable chance to let you know I am well and cherish the same feelings and hopes for your health and prosperity as the day I left you.

The people of Liberia were much cheered by the presense of the Revd Mr. Gurley.[1] I have had the pleasure of his company several times at my house in this place and yesterday I took him quite up to Louisiana, the residence of our people. He saw them and took down their names, visited their houses and conversed with them. On our way up we stopped at New Georgia, a Village about four miles up the Stockton Creek and also at Caldwell on the Saint Paul river. The people in every place regard him as a dear friend and benefactor. This letter I shall put into his hands to be forwarded to you by him and shall look forward with pleasing aticipatations for an answer to the many that I have written you at different times as well as this and shall expect that you will also send something to me as you promised when I left you to do. All of our people are well. I must now close this. If I dont I shall be too late for Mr. Gurley as he will start for the vessel in a short time. I Remain, Dear Father, Yours Affty,

G. R. Ellis

5/LETTERS OF THE
ROSS NEGROES

Frustration and tragedy figure prominently in the experience of the Ross Negroes.[1] Their master, Captain Isaac Ross of Jefferson County, Mississippi, owned 160 slaves at the time of his death, January 19, 1837. His will provided that they should be assembled after his demise and given the choice of being sold along with the remainder of his estate, or being freed and sent to Liberia.[2] Money obtained from the sale of his residual estate was to be turned over to the American Colonization Society for transportation and maintenance of those Negroes who elected to go to Liberia and for the establishment and support of a school in Africa.

Ross's heirs, and those of his daughter, Mrs. Margaret A. Reed who died in 1838, contested the will on the ground that it was illegal and void in that it gave slaves the choice between bondage and freedom and made provision for their education. The American Colonization Society brought suit against the executors in an effort to force compliance with the will. Costly and prolonged litigation ensued. In the meantime the blacks continued in bondage under the control of Ross's grandson, Isaac R. Wade, the person to whom the executors had entrusted management of the estate. Finally in 1847 the American Colonization Society won its suit, but apparently returns from the sale of the remaining estate and from crops produced after Ross's death were no more than sufficient to meet expenses incurred during the long period of litigation. The migrants never received any money from the estate or from the cotton produced by their labor after their master's death.

The blacks belatedly freed by Ross's will sailed for Liberia in two groups. The first, numbering 35, left New Orleans on the *Nehemiah Rich* January 7, 1848, and arrived in Africa on March 19. A second group of 141 made the voyage one year later, on the *Laura*.[3] Both groups settled in Sinoe in and around the town of Greenville. One of the members of the first group described the voyage to Africa as "long but very pleasant," while another reported that it was "long and teadious" and beset by a gale so severe that "I thought we [should] never [make] land again." The second group had the misfortune of being exposed to cholera while in New Orleans awaiting departure. Several died before leaving port, and more succumbed to the disease while in transit to Africa.[4] Both groups suffered from "African fever" during the period of acclimatization but mortality was considerably greater among the second group than among the first.

Fifteen of the twenty-four letters written by the Ross Negroes were addressed to officials of the American Colonization Society: one to William McLain, three to John Ker who represented both the American and the Mississippi Colonization Societies, and eleven to Ralph R. Gurley. Of the other nine, four were written to Mrs. Catherine Wade, Captain Ross's daughter or granddaughter, and five to Isaac R. Wade, his grandson.

Most of the correspondents complained of lack of money, shortage of tools and farming equipment, precariousness of health, and the difficulty of sustaining themselves in the strange land. Some told of destructive encounters with native tribesmen. A few professed great enthusiasm for Liberia and that country's prospects as an independent republic. Some found their situation only tolerable. One man reported after ten years' residence in Liberia: "Sum time i fild [feel] happy hear and Sum time Cold and Dule and Sum time Cast Down in heart and mind." Most of his associates probably experienced similar ups and downs of morale. Certainly a majority were very much like him in looking to God for comfort and sustenance in their times of trouble.

The most grandiloquent of the correspondents in expressing religious and patriotic sentiments and in making other comments as well was Grandville Woodson.[5] On February 10, 1853, he wrote Isaac Wade: "Liberia is now spreading her rich perfume roun and about the big Valleys of the World and introducing and calling out to her suns and Daughters to rise and come up out of the Valley of ignorents and Hethenism." A few days later he wrote Catherine Wade: "Liberia . . . have awaken from the cradle and wean from the breast of the [United] States here mother and raising to the sumet of Civilisation and Dignification." In this and another letter he requested books, including a dictionary, grammar, atlas, geography, and biblical commentary.

A theme running through much of the correspondence is grievance at failure to receive funds from the Ross estate, in accordance with provisions of the master's will. Procurement of his share of the Ross money was the dominant concern of Peter Ross, the person who wrote more letters than any of his associates.[6] In seven letters to Gurley written 1856-1859 Ross importuned the agent to do whatever might be necessary to obtain the money due him and the other Ross Negroes. He laid major blame for the default on Isaac Wade whom he called a "meane man," but he also suspected American Colonization official William McLain of wrongdoing.[7] His bitterness increased with the passing of time and may have contributed to his death which apparently occurred late in 1859.[8] His amanuensis and son, George Jones (who in one letter gave his name as George Ross) after his father's death made apologies to McLain for

Peter Ross's accusations. It seems probable that the amanuensis assumed the role of principal in a letter to Catherine Wade bearing Peter Ross's name and dated January 14, 1860. This letter contained a request for clothing and George may have thought that the recipient, not knowing of Peter's death, would be more likely to respond favorably to a request made by the father, whom she had known a long time, than one coming from the son. A brief note of February 7, 1870, to Gurley (not reproduced here) filed in the American Colonization Society Papers and signed by "Reuben Ross, one of the Rosses Estate People" states that some of the Ross Negroes "Still Remains in Sinoe County" and that they request "Some books, clothing or whatever else you can conveniently Send."

138 / PETER ROSS AND ROBERT CARTER TO JOHN KER

David [John] Kerr, Esq.   Sinoe, Greenville Co., W. Africa
                                           [March] 23d, [18] 48

Very Dr. Sir: We have at length, after a voyage of about 70 days, arrived safe at our new home in this our adopted land, "Our father home." Our voyage, as you will perceive, was long, but very pleasant, for our good Captain done all in his power to make us comfortable & happy. We landed last night & have slept on shore one night, & so far as we can judge from what we have yet seen, we feel quite sure that we shall be satisfied & happy as far as the country is concerned. But this is a new country where we shall, as a matter of course, have to meet with many & [I] fear very trying difficulties. These, by the assistance of God's grace, we do not fear. What gives us the most unpleasant feelings is the manner we have been sent out to this country. We were told for the last three years that the avails of our hard labor was to be appropriated to our support in Africa, or to help us to establish ourselves in this country, but we find ourselves here without any means to help ourselves after we get through the fever. We hope you will be pleased to write us & explain this matter to us, so we may be satisfied as the disposition of the effects of our three years labor.

We shall be glad to receive by the earliest opportunity the guns & ammunition you promised us at N.O. We shall be glad to receive also a supply of nails to build our houses, as we have none & no means to get them; they are hard to obtain here & come high.

Mrs. P. Ross sends her best respects to Mrs. Wade. Also you will please accept from us our sincere & grateful respects. Yours, &c.,

                                           P. Ross, Robt. Carter

P.S. Remember us kindly to our colored friends, & tell them when they come out to this country to bring everything for housekeeping, farming & carpentering, &c., that they have or can get; they will need them, for they cannot be got here.

Mrs. Carter sends her best respects to Mrs. Wade.

Please hand this letter to Mr. Wade after you have read it.

139 / HANNIBAL ROSS TO JOHN KER

Dr. John Ker: Greenville, Sinoe, March 26th, 1848

Sir: I embrace this opportunity by Capt. Carlton by dropping you a few lines to inform you that I am at my journey's end safe, all seem to enjoy good health so far, except my son Winson, who was sick during the whole passage.

You will please inform Celia to bring her children up [in] the fear of the Lord, as he is greatly to be praised for having spared me to arrive on the shores of Africa safe, and give my respects to all the rest of our people; also give my respects to Mr. Isaac Wade & all his family. Mr. John Congo told me before I left that I could get my daughter Charlotte any time, and I hope you will obtain her from him and send her out in the next expedition, if you please, and should he demand payment for her please send me an answer by first oppty. And tell my children when they start to come to bring all & everything they can because everything is needed in Africa. I have not as yet had an opportunity of taking a view of the country, but, so far as I have seen, I like it very much.

Uncle Necter [Hector] Belton wishes you to give his respects to Mr. Isaac Wade & all his family [and to] Jane Ross. And tell Mr. Wade to send him something. And my son Charles is not dead, he is still alive.

Having nothing more of any consequence to say, I conclude, hoping you will use all the energy to send our people to Africa. I remain, Your obbt. Servt.,   Hannibal Ross[1]

P.S. I would like to hear from my son Thomas, because a few days before I left he was sick, also my son John and all my Granddaughters & their parents, &c., &c.,   Hannibal Ross

140 / SARAH J. WOODSON TO CATHERINE E. WADE

Greenville, Sinoe, May 11th, 1848

Respected Madam: I embrace this favorable opportunity of pening to you a few lines from the Benited Shores of Africa and to inform you of our Safe arival to our destine homes in Africa and to let you know that we had a long and teadious passage to Africa of Sixty Some odd days. And I Can assure you that we Experiance a Very Severe ga[le] & wind

On the passage out. The Gale [began on the] 30th of January. I thought we [should] never [make] Land again. But thank God [we reached] Africa Safe. We was very kindly [treated] by our Captain on the voige out

I Cannot Say much about The Country as I have been here Such a Short time. But i think that I will like the Country very well After I gets on My own place. We are now under the Doctor going through the African feaver at this Time. My husband and Son was up to our place on yesterday Cleaning up trying to get Ready to do Something in the way of Making a Farm to Make a Begining towar[d] farming. After I gets on My own place I thin[k] that I will like the Country very well. But at this time I will not Say Much but in My Next Communication to you I will write you More fully about the Country.

To your Children: Remember My Love to them and to all the prospect people and to all the oak hill people and tell them that I am in hopes that they will bring all of My Iron ware with them when they leaves. Uncle Hannia Halls[?] Daughter Lucy is dead; [also] Uncle March's son Riley is dead. To Mrs Ross: Uncle Charles that did belong to Mrs. Reed is a living. Granville & Pascal sens their Love to all the people. Tell the children I will Expects something from them when our people Comes and tell our people to Bring all their things when they Comes. And the children is all going to School Every day. Bring Some seed of all kind with you and Eny thing that you possible Can Bring out with you of your things. Bring them for you will stand in need of Them in this country. And Makiah Cely Says that you Must Bring out her feather Bed with her & Bring out Shoes and plenty of them. And do not Spend your Money on the ring[?] and do Not purchase without you really Stand in need of. . . . [Two or three lines faded out]. . . . [Tell Mr.] I. Wade that we came to this country very poor and he will please to send us Out Something. I am Very Sorry that I left My Bed and their is no way to get another in this Country.

Daphne send her love To her Mother and all of her children. Jefferson Belton's children Says that they are not able to Buy him but hopes that the Executors will open their hearts and Send him out. Nothing more at present and remain your obedient ser[van]t,   Sarah Woodson[1]

Bring out Some Castor oil

141 / HECTOR BELTON TO JOHN KER

Greenville, Sinoe, October 12, [18]49

Respected Sir: As an opportunity occurs by the Liberia "Packet" I embrace it by writing you these few lines to inform you that I'm still spared & alive, hope they may find you and your family enjoying good health.

Jeff is well and haughty, and is on his farm trying by the assistance of the Almighty to make a living, and his children are also well, and expresses their thankfulness to you for your kind & affectionate influence & contrivance of his being in Africa with them, where they have labored long under fearful apprehensions of ever meeting him in this life. Of the last of our people (i.e.) the Ross Set that came out here, twenty-five have died from the effects of the *Cholera* taken in New Orleans on their way out here.[1]

You will please write me by first opportunity how all the remaining Ross people are. Old man Hannibald is well & family and wishes to know from [you] if you have done anything for his daughter Cecelia.

Now, my dear sir, knowing you were always kindly & friendly disposed towards me, even when Capt. Ross were alive, and I now am old and helpless, cant work, let me intrude upon you, notwithstanding past events. Simply by begging you to send me a little Soap, Rappa Snuff & any old clothes that you may judge to be of service to the old man in Africa, and a razor. A number of the last emigrants that is our people died on their passage out here, among whom were as follows: James Cole, Grace, Julia (in N. Orleans).

This settlement (Greenville, Sinoe) is rapidly improving & increasing in population, &c., and have been upon the continued increase ever since I have been here, and I believe the Spirit & necessity of Education have been awaken considerable.

Now, dear Sir, I hope & trust by the very first opportunity to hear from you and let me hear from all of our people there. Having [nothing] more of interest to communicate I conclude, praying that the Lord may continue to add his blessings toward you. Yours very Respectfully,

Hector Belton

P.S. Old man Scipio & Sampson is dead.

142 / SARAH J. WOODSON TO CATHERINE E. WADE

Mrs. Catherine E. Wade   Greenville, Sinoe, April 1, 1850

Dear Maddam: As an oppertunity is presented I embrace it to write you, by which you may know that I am living and well. All my family is well, that is my husband and my son.

I have written to you once, but I believe you did [not] get the letter. I wrote year before last directly after we got out here. I did not find the country as good as I hoped for or expected but it is improving so fast that

I am becoming quite satisfied, and especially since I have got my health as well as I have. My health has improved very much lately, so much so that if I only had a little more meens to start with I should like Liberia very well.

It is a very good country considering it is new and so little improvements in it, so that poor people could get a start. There is a great many things which grow here that grow in America, and there is no winter at all so that the growths continue all the year through. Rice grows in great abundance. Corn grows well some places. Potatoes grow in great abundance. Some people live very well and some live very poor. We have all got our own land and the most of us are living in our own houses,

The last people of our estate who came out [on the *Laura* in 1849] are a great many of them dead. They came here so worn down with hard useage and disease that almost the one half of them were carried of[f] in the acclimating fever, Tell Rufus that Rachael send her love to him, and says you will please to tell him her father is dead, and all the family except three, that is Rachael, Sinthy, and York. Rachael says she is doing tolerable well, as well as she could expect, but is quite low spirited.

Please give my love to all who enquire after me and to all the children. Pasco sends his love to Master Isaac Ross Wades and begs that he will please send him a sane [seine] or something to help him a long. A sane would be as profitable as any thing he could get as fish are very plenty and very good here. Give my love also to old mistress and her daughter Jane, and say to Jude and Sissy that I thought they would have sent me Something as I have come to a new hard country.

I am much oblige to you for the dress you sent me, and as to the oranges I was to send you, I find none growing in the woods, and I am not able to buy them as they are not to be got without buying.

Say to Miss Catherine that Macciah send her love to her and her father also and tell sely that they are both yet living. I suppose I shall never see you all again in this life, but I hope [to] meet you all on the pleasent banks of deliverance. Do please answer my letter. Yours truly,

Sarah Jane Woodson

I wish you would write me en answer and promptly one w[h]ich I know you are able to do.

143 / GRANDVILLE B. WOODSON TO ISAAC R. WADE

Greenville, Sinoe County, Africa, April 4, 1851, from liberia

Mr. Isaac R. Wade: I take this opportunity of droping these few lines as a man of much respect. We land on the fare shores of Liberia safe and with a little difficulty. Sence the attact of the african fever I have enjoy good health, so have father. Mother had several severe attact of difren complaints but [is] now enjoying good health. Both of them send there love to you both hopeing that your latter days may be more prosperous than your former has been, glorous, honable, and independence. And Mother says she hope that the children are good and smart active children as they ware when she left them. Robert Carter have died last March, 1851. Sabinah Ross been dead about three mounth from the deat [heat?] and the husband is quite low at preasent. If you cant Make it conveint to send me some good chool Books I will thank you with most noble respect as I am poor and have advance in education to teach my self in common tudies.

Mother say she have wrote two letters to Mrs. C. N. Wade and have not receive no answer yet. You must excuse my hand writing. I was in a hurry as the liberia pacat had just return from cape palmas on her way back to Merican and had about two mile to go down the river to the lyseums to vindercate on the afirmative.   Grandville B. Woodson

144 / GRANDVILLE B. WOODSON TO ISAAC R. WADE

Mr. Isaac Wade   Greenville, Sinoe County, February 10, 1853

My Dear Sir: I take the pleasure to write to you this Evening hoping that this letter will find you and your Family Well as I am my Self and Enjoying aperportion of happiness and freedom which is alloted to all man kind. Dear Sir as the Liberia Packet is Expected to Sail in a few Days for your big state America I hasten to Droop you a few lines as I have intended for some time to give you My views of Liberia. In My Estimation this is a good Country, taking all things in consideration, asspecaly for the colored Man or the Suns of Ham Who have been So Long bound Down beneth the penatration of the Gospel light. As to health is very good. And it must bexpected and is reasonable to suppose that land will produce its own fruits well. This is the land of our fore fathers, the land from which the children went, back to the land they are Returning. Liberia is now spreading her rich perfume roun and about the big valleys of the World and introducing and calling out to her suns and Daughters to rise and come up out of the Valley of ignorence and Hethenism. Liberia is very productive in its own fruits. It fruits is Cassades, Pineapples, Sourersap, Gouvers, papoo, Rice, Plantens Bananas, Walnuts, and various kind[s] of groves in the forest, I know not what. They is Potatoes, Collard greens, Coffee and sougar is made here. The Palm oil is very pretty looking oil, especaly when new. It is Eatable, quite nice to the tase. I will have it this Evenig upon my table as you will your meet [meat]. We is Raising hogs and Sheep now. Cows, goats, sheep, hogs are here, turkey, Ducks, chicks, guinia fowls—all these things are here with the exception of horse. But they are close here up on the cape Vered Island. We have not made so greate a Start to Raising stocks as you would Eamagion—only two Sheep, two hogs. We are very likely now to Rais stock. [In] one [or] two mounth we will have more, for they on the way of increase. Liberia is now quite asstonishing to one who know the nature[?] of country only so add year and now she have declared her independence and Rankeing among the nations of the Earth. She have her Civil laws and Elections. It will take plase this year, May, 1853 [for] New officers to make new laws for the country and People. Liberia indeed is a good and free Republican government. The folks here is very gay and Dressy, salabrating the independence of the country with much Joy and gladness which takes place on Every twenty six of July. County Sinoe has a saw mill and have sawed agood dele of plank. But Dear [friend] please to send me some america News, good Book, historys, Religious and temporal. Father and mother both send their best Respects to you all now. Yours with Respects and this is my hand writing,

Grandville Woodson

Very bad pen.

Please to send me some of your American news, good books, history, Religious and temporal.

Please to answer this as quick as you possible could. Tell all of you folk howdy for me. Hector and oren, how are they?

Grandville Woodson of the Benevolent Society

145 / GRANDVILLE B. WOODSON TO CATHERINE E. WADE

Feb 16, 1853, Greenville, Sinoe County, Liberia

Dear Mrs C E Wade: I take my pen in my hand to write you hopeing you and your family is well as I am my self, And Enjoying aperportion of happiness which is alloted unto all Man Kind. We started for Liberia from New orlenes on the 7th of January, 1848, and we landed on the shores of Africa 19th of March 1848. The voyage was tedious yet something suggested that beyond the western valleys and rooling hills of the ocean We would meet some of the different arts and sciences which originated from the American sceene. We have a Republican government regulating as you know evey thing that comes under its Notice. Very good laws have we here, the same as you have. This year is Election which will take plase [in] May. I can't ascertin to you who will be the canidates as the time is some what Distant. We have smart men here in Liberia who understand how to transact business to the advantage of our young and flourishing Republic which is now sending the light of Morality back in the interior among the dolefull stations which has long since for goten there Creator, God.

Uncle Hanible died a professor of Godliness yesterday and during his affliction gave good signs of the Eternel happiness which his soul would soon reach. Uncle Hector died last March leving the same testimony and his hope beyarn this vail of tears which his sould shall soon reach in heaven.

The words of the past, How happy. Every child of grace who knows his sins for giveing, this Earth he crys is not my home, my home is in heaven where Savage pains and death are felt and fere no more. Religious and national piety is exclaimed and extended up and Down the cause of Liberia. Every Sabbath you can hear the charms of the church bells or horns echoing there sound throught the town and country as indicating to the Inhabitance of Africa the silver trump of Gabriel, the archangel of God, Who Shall call the nations great and small to the finel Judgement of rightiouness. Liberia is indeed shoing aprobabiltiy and a glorious Prospect of her future and civil enjoyments. She have awaken from the cradle and wean from the breast of the [United] states here mother and raising to the sumet of Civilisation and Dignification. Every considerate man or woman will admit that this is the fact.

I my salf is or have Joind the M.E. Church 2 years this coming sep. 21 and have Experience the hevenly powers which is to come and is a class leader or assistance and asteward of the church and trustee for the church. Then, seeing that the sponsibility of the church rest upon the official member of the church, I would ask you if please to send me some book, good ones, such as historys of temporel and spirituel, Dictionary, grammar, Smith atless and geography, Benson theology and comontary, for all this thing I stan kneed of and feel and believe and have expeires that the lord has great work for me to do in the feild of great labor. Amen.

Mother says & send her love to you all, Father like wise. She say tell your children howdy for her. Ask tude have he for got me, sisey like wise. I am sorry to say that I have writen to you two or three times and have not receive any letter from you yet. My health is much as it was when I left there but still remain a s[l]im traverlor. I would be happy to receive some thing from you as evry thing here is so Dear and my money is non because it is not here to make. I am raising coffee and hope in afew more years to be able to send you some of the african coffee.

Grandville Wood son, secretary of the Benevolence society.

To Mr. I. R. Wade
Greenville, Sinoe Conty, Liberia,
Feb 21, 1853

Dear Sir: I take this chance to write you hopeing this letter will find you and your family well. I plase the pen into the hand's of my sun to write you upon this most important and interesting subject which have not interude its self unto me giving me the cheering information that all things will work out for good in the future by your hands which is expert in all cases and hopeing this may be one as you is our friend I write you. It was understood and was Capt Rosses will for all of his folke to have so much money or Something in one way or the other and we have not Received any thing yet. When we came down to Nachus [Natchez] we look for the money which was willed to us by Capt. Ross and they say go Down to New orleans and you shall Receive what is Due to you. Well we came down to New orleans and required of it and requested of Mr Cowering to give us the money as he was our attendent and he said the cotton was not sold which was the last year, 1847, and he said when it was sold the Colonization Society Would send the money to us. Well we find that to be a rite Down untruth of Mr. Cowering.[1] I write because I think you is the proper one that you may know how the matter is and what is its color and its unfairness. Please to Remember that this is I P. Woodson write unto you with the greatest of effecunation.

You is there and I am here, so you will Please to Write me any how, how the matter Stans that I may receive some Information from you which I hope may be Cheering to me and to all the rest of the people. It is now aliving with the increase one Hundred and fifteen Folk. Please to tell me something of the residue of the People which was left behind. Writ me all the perticulors of the astate, Capt Ross's, how it stands. This country is quite poor especaly to those who have no mony and you know Such country with out money you can not expect to make any. I have been quite sick lately unto Death and my constitution is much Weeker from its effect. But [I am] up again upon my feet and brething the sweet atmosphere of life. A man have to under go a good deal of hard and laborous work to make any thing worth talking about. But it is a good country because it is aland of freedom and the land of our fore Father (the man Ham). The Good folk salabrates the country to the honor of independence which is every 26 of July, Beeting the Drums Playing the fife & onother instruments and Displaying the independent flag to the honor of the nation and glory of the Day. It is highly Pleasing to see the broodes which just came out from under the Hen's Wings giving a Indication of nathional power. All of the good People send out of that astate sends there besrespects to you.

Uncle Hanable is Dead, Died on the 15 of February, 1853, and uncle Hector Died Jan., 1852. So it is but a few of the old folks alive and aunt Herrit Hilsen, Caty or Citty McKiah, [leaving a] good deal of offorns [orphan] children.

My wife and sun joins me in love to you and your family.

I, grandvill Woodson, ask you to send me some books, historys, all such useful, for I am very deficient & scerse for books for this settlement.

Pascal Woodson Esq.[2]

147 / PETER ROSS TO RALPH R. GURLEY

Louisiana, Sinoe County, October the 10, 1856

The Rev. Mr. Girley, Dear Sir: I embrace this oppertunity in addressing you a few Lines and hope that this may fine you & all the family wel. Al So, My Dear Brother, you tell me to write you when you was in Sinoe and theifor i take this oppertunity to Say to you if Please to See that we Get Sum of that money where was Coming us. Doe, if you Please, for the Agent of the Society tell us that we wood be Shoe to Get the money that old Captain Ross Leaves for us at his Deathe, for we are [in] want of that money. If you Please to Send us Sum thing [or] Another for the Lord Sàk, for we are in want, if you Please to Be So kind. No more at present but Still Remain your Cincer freind,

Peter Ross, from Prospect, Clabon County of America.

148 / GEORGE JONES TO RALPH R. GURLEY

Louisiana, Sinoe County, October 11, 1856

To Mr. Girlley, Dear Sir: I take this oppertunity to Drope you a few lines to Say that i am interrested at this time a bout the money that old Captain Ross Leaves for us. I will be Glad if you will in ter seed for that money for us for the war have Done us Great harms. The Native hav Burn our housees and Destroy our farm and all the produce and we Got no help at all.[1] We have Labour and Labour Sence we have Bin out to Liberia and we hav not Recive one Sent. Now i beg you all if you Please to Send us Sum Relieff for we are in want. We are the Ross People that Came out to Liberia in the year 1848. Doe for the Lord Sake Send Sum thing out to us and by So Douing you will help us a Great Dele and the

Lord will bless you all. May you all Run [?] our Relief for the Lord Sake. No more at Present. Your humble and obedient Servent,

Georg[e] Ross[2] from Prosspect, Clabon County.

149 / PETER ROSS TO RALPH R. GURLEY

Louisiana, Sinoe County, May the 15, 1857

Bro. R. R. Gurley: We all have Received your kind Letter and was Glad to hear from you and to Read your kind and incor Rigeing words to Labour and trust in God. We ear quit thankful to you Sir, but My Dear Bro. ever Sence our feet have trod the Sea Shouer of Africa that have Bin our motto, to Labour and that is veary hard. But we thought that we had a Right to ask Sum Good hearted friend to See to our Right for us wich old Captain Ross Leaves for us and we can Satisfy that he did Leaves the money for us Becose Mr. McLain tell us that the money is their for us and [we] wood Get it. And Dr. Chanwich had us in his Porsision the Last Year we was in Slavery, wich was the year 1849. He tell us that their was money for us and we wood Get it and we Beg your Serious attintion to these few thing as thay Branch out Befor us. Mr. McLain Says that we in Coming out to Africa the Colonnization Society Spen more money in Setling the Ross People in Africa then ever he Recived from old Captan Ross estate. This May be So, but Consider one thing, My Dear Bro., and that is old Captan Ross Leaves one hundred thousand Dollers for his People Be Siad Land, stocks, &c. &c. and then we can not Get Twenty five Dollers of that money, after he placeing the Money in the Bank and Saying tow that the Money was for his People. My Dear Bro., the money is their in som of those Bank their for we ask you to Be so kind as to intersede for that money four us. We ear Glad to see your picture and we wood Be still Glader to see your face, but as their is a Great Gulf and Povety is So Low that we Can Not see you tho my head is Blossoming for the Gra[ve] and yeat i am in a Suffering Condision and if i Do not see your face a Gaine, ore your Picture, i hope we will meet in the Paradise of God where Parting will be no More. I was Duatful of writing to you, not knoing exzactly where ore what Part of the State you Live. We aer Glad for all the advize you Can Giv us but while we speak to you we feild that Africa, yea Liberia, is our home and we will not Give up, for Liberia is our home and the Rev. Set [Stephen] Benson is our President. I wish i had money to by Paper to write to [you] when i wanted to write. Now, my Dear Bro., i will ask you one thing—Please Do not Denigh me. Please send me one of those Dubble Boil [Barrel] Gun. Please Be so kind, in so douing you will a Blige me. No more at Present but still Rem[a] in yours truly,   Peter Ross

Louisiana, Sinoe County, May the 27th, 1857

My Dear Bro. [Gurley]:   I am happy to hear that you is trying to Do all you can in Sending addisunul emigration to help our weak Settlement. I have Seen your face in Africa once and i Beleav that you is Good hearted and a Religious and a hounourble guntleman, and Where hounour Be long, ther it Must be Store and i have not the money to Get Papper to explain our feling to ward you. Sum time i fild happy hear and Sum time Cold and Dule and Sum time Cast Down in heart and mind, but is writin in St. Paul writ and that we Must through Much tribula[tion] enter into the Kingdom of God. Tho i am Buffeted a bout, i have a hope big with immortality and Christ Said through his Servent John the Revelation 2, 10 v[erse], that i Must be thou faithful un to Death and i will Gi[ve] thee a Crown of Life. Hear i Must Stope for fear you will Get weary of me. B[ut] O Glorious hope of perfect Love, it Lifts me up to things above, it bears on eagles wings. Yours truly and Beloved Bro.,   Peter Ross

We ear Glad to Say, My Dear Brother, that we will Sing a[gain].

Louisiana, Sinoe Co., July the 11, 1858

My Dear Sir: I embrace this oppertunity to address you afew lines hopeing that this may fine you injoying Good health as they leaves me at present. My Dear Sir, i am Sorry that i have to trublile you so much about the one thing kneedful but i hope you will bar with me for a Little while. My Dear Sir, you hav writin one Letter to me and i receiv it as Good News from a far Country and i have wrote to you sevel times since and Receiv no answer as yet. But i hop for the future. Now, My Dear Sir, please answer this Letter with the Request that i ask of you befor. Please see to it that we Get our Right, tho we Labour much and very hard in this our Country and it is very Good Place for Living. If it is Posible answer this Letter for us. There was money Left for us and we would to God that he would enable you to be successful in interceding for us. Please answer this Letter for i want to here from you very Much. Can you, My Dear Sir, tell me Who Got the old captain Ross Place inpossion [in possession] and how about it. I would be very much gratfy to here from you and also the old man Place. Please do not disappint me and, my Dear Sir, i would be glad to Com and See you if you is willing and Can get money anogh to Com. In Concluion i will Say to you that i hope to meet you in heaven.   from Mr. Peter Ross to the Rev R R Gurley

Luisanna, Sinoe County, July the 13th, 1858

Mr. Girlay, Sir, Dear Friend: We know of no one else to write to but you as sometime it Seams almost no use to write to you. But being persuaded, Sir, in our mind that you are still our friend We all biages to you to please to intersied for us & do all you can for us. Suredly We would be glad for the smallest quatity of any things that may be Sat to us. We hav had our sufferings & our kneeds & meney of them know the wore [war] Which We had hear has left the Wedders [widows] the awphan [orphan] to Ress upon a wanting community. If you Could Send a little Cloth or a fish sane We will be very thenkfull. It is true that you hav told us in one of your litters the expens[ive] Lawsut has consumed all the monny. We beleves you [and] are willing to Cridet evry thing you say & we hope you will not think outher wise. But you said ther was some land to be sold. If it be possible try to do som thing for us. Ther is som old people a mong us yeat, surch as can not do any thing for themsilvs. When Mr. MacCowan wass heare the other day We told him somthing a bout these matters but We hav not herd any thing Since. We know of nothing more We can say at present. Yours Respectfully,   Horris Ross,[1] Peter Ross

153 / PETER ROSS TO RALPH R. GURLEY

Louisiana, Sinoe Co., July the 19, 1858

My Dear Sir: I am Glad of this oppertunity in addresing you a few lines. I have written to you very often Seance you hav wrote me the first Letter and i hav not Receive an answer from that time. Therefor i know not whether you hav get those letters ore not. Please write me the nex oppertunity. I will be Glad to here from you all. I am geting a long very well at this time. The Lord has bless me so fair. Africa is a Good Place to live in and also we are happy in the Serviceces of the Lord and we do thank him for his blessing toward use as a people. We are happy to say that we are injoying as Good health as we can exspect at this time. There are others who hav writtin to you at the same time. We Do not wish to trouble you too much by writting to you letters. But a Colonnizision Society, we think that you all are just. There for, we beg you all to See and know if there is enney possible meanes by wich we can obtain sum if not all of the money the old man Captain Ross leaves for his people. I do not know whether you get the last tow letters that i written you befor ore not, but i hope so. There was one houndred thousand Dollars wich the old man Captain Ross Leaves for his people, besides land, Cattle, &c.

&c. If we only Can get 50 ore 25 ore 12 dollars a Pace we would be much better sadisfy. But to here the awful sound, we Can Not Get enney, or there is non, It seame awful. I beg you all to See to it that we would Get sum of our money for we stan in kneed of it. Our object is to buil a ship to sail Cross the Atlantic osion. There for we beg you all to help us. Africa is a Good place, but we want to be much better. No more at this time. Yours humble Servent,

from Mr. Peter Ross to the Rev. Mr. R. R. Gurley   Washington City

154 / YORK WALKER TO ISAAC R. WADE

Mr. Isaac Wade   Monrovia, Libria
                                                        Africa, July 30, 1858

Dear Sir: I embrace this opportunity of writing you these few lines which I hope will find you well. I have not heard from you for a long time and dont Know you have not writen Me. I am still living and many of our people. Though a great Many have died Since we have been out here, We are getting along tolerable well, but have suffered great deal Since We have been out here, because we had a war with the natives in which we lost all of our clothes and every thing we had. I will be thankful to you if you would send me Something, as a barrel of our flour or meat and fish. You will also send me some clothes or cloth to make them. I have not forgotten You, nor do I hope You have forgotten me. If [you] send me any thing please send it in care of Dr. McLain and I will get it. Give my best love to all of our people and friends. I am now living in Monrovia instead of living at Sinoe where [we] were sent. I find that Monrovia is a better place than Sinoe and I can get along better here and besides its more handy to write to You. I will certainly look for a letter from you by the Caroline Steven. All of our old people are dead. Rachel, Emily, Lewis, Abram and some other are living. Ephraim is dead and Granville too. We all were doing pretty well before the war broke out but we are geting along poorly indeed. The Natives took all of our hoes, axes, spades and everything we had. Do send us some thing by the Stevens

All the people join in love to You, We wish Much to see You once more. Please let me know what [is] going to become of our people whether they are coming out or not.

I want to hear from My brother. Nothing more, yours truly,

York Walker.[1]

Louisiana, Sinoe, January the 29, 1859

My Dear Sir: I hav written to you sevel letters befor, but it Seams as if you hav not Received only one of them. Howbeit i am Sorry of all my labouring for nothing. I hope you will help me in sum way ore nother if it [be] only in and through your goodness in Sending me one Coat ore a pair of pants ore Shoes. We have a plenty to subsis on in Africar at this time, God will bless his people. I am quit thank ful to you my Dear Sir for your kind attention to ward me. My Dear Sir we hav wated upon all of those guntilemen that had to Do with the old man estate and it Seams after all that eavry one will Decive us. I know Sir that the Colonization Society hav Done sum thing for us but notwith standing they Could send us the money that Captain Ross leave in Banks for us. Eavry Set of peoples, more ore lest, hav Received sum things after leaving Americar but we, and our old master leaves So much money for his people. I am well awere of the mean ness that was in Isaac Wade but not with standing his meanness he could not hav power [to] Rule you all, Breatherine, and i Do not think enney one would surpose So. We hav not Receive our College and nothing like it. We hav done nothing to fofet our Right to the money that was leave for us. All the labour we did after the old man Death, Isaac Wade had know Right [to] it, not the lest, and the money that was in the Bank i Do [not] think he could hav power to take that out of the Bank. I Can not see where the Differcul[ty] lay in not Seling the Cotton that Mr. Mclain [mentioned] and McLain said that we would Get the money for that—i mean the last year labour. We hav not Received a cent for it as yeat. Do for God Sake Remember us, if you please, for we Stand in kneed of it at this time. Isaac Wade is and was a meane man, al tho i Do not know whether he are living now ore not. May God Save us all for his Dear Son Sake. I think i Shall Writ know more but leave it all in the hands of the almity for he is Merciful to his people. As i [am] bout to Close, please Do not for Get what i ask you for, for when the poor are crying, you let me beg you to here him for Christ Sake. Yours truly, humble Servent,   Peter Ross

156 / PETER ROSS TO RALPH R. GURLEY

Louisiana, Sinoe, August the 8, 1859

My Dear Sir: I Received your kind favour July the 29. Was very Glad to Receive a letter from you & al So hopeing that God had open the way that my Self ore all of us Would have Receive Sum thing. But when i opon the letter i found it to the Contrary. But not withstanding all of the

Disappiontment, i am Still in Courrige to write & whiles i write Preaying the lord that he would help me & that his Blesing would Rest uppon me. Now my Dear Sir i am happy to know that you are still living & i will ask you one favour. Do if you Please send me one gun. Not that i think you have aright to Do Soo but it is only afavour. I am enjoying good health at this time & the family the same. I have 5 in family. It may be that Mr. McLain knows more of the money that Captan Ross leaves for his people & i there say Mr. McLain hav agreat account to answer for at the Rain of Justus, Both here & hereafter, [about] the money that the old man leaves for his people. We will furst enter a law suit with Mr. McLain for having in his possesion our money & would not gav it to us & againe he had the Power ore it was leaves with him & others, there for it would be Justust for Mr. Mclain to Send me Sum thing if it [were] only one suit of cloth. The lord has Been very murciful & kind towards me sence her i have Been, but his murciful chair will still be to ward me, eaven her & her af- ter, this is my preay. It is true i Do not charge you My Dear Sir with in Justust about the money that was left for us, but Mr. Mclain know all about it. Sevel other of my Company have written to you but i know not what for. I will look for sum thing from you by the Steven the nex time, not that you hav aright to Do so but i Simply ask of you that much if it [be] only one cage of butter, ore apair of shoes, ore a Barrel flour. Do plese Send me Sum little things by the Steven. I am under tenthosand ob- bligation to you for Your kindness in writing to me. My Dear Sir, Dont think hard of me in this letter. Had i knowen where Mr. McLain live i would have writtin him porsonel all that i have said in this letter as Regaurd to the money that was left for us. I think you will do this much. It was will him to Sold five hundred Cotton bail When the first people Com out [to] Liberia & the Sam thing when the last People Com out, which made one thousand. My Reason for writing to you i thought it may be that you could hav Seen Mr. Mclain, get him to Send ore gave Sum Sadisfaction about the money ore cotton. & another thing again he was told to let us have enney things we wanted in Olean [New Orleans] & he would not Do that much and it is sum thing strange to me & that is this: It have Been thoughted [by] me & others that Mr. Mclain was a Just man, but i am Sorry to Say that he are not & far, far, far from it. There- for i will Say no more of Mr. Mclain to you, but leaves it in the hands of the Great Judge of quick & Dead. My Dear Sir you said to me in your let- ter that you would be Glad to Know how meney people of the Reed & Ross are living when they went to Sinoe ore befor they went to Sinoe. There was 2 hundred & 50 heads of them, i meane of the Ross people. & be side we work 13 Years after the old man Death which he Did not cal- culate for his people to do enny thing attal after his Death. I thank you all for the kindness that you all have Done. Yours humble Servent,

Peter Ross to the Rev R R Gurly

157 / GEORGE JONES TO RALPH R. GURLEY

Louisiana, January the 7, 1860

My Dear Sir: I am glad to have Received your kind letter on the 23 of December & to know as yet that you still hav an intress in our Case & i think my Dear Sir that i hav Said a enoff in Relation to our old Master Property. Therefor i will [not] Say enney thing more about the matter. I will leave it with the lord. He is our judge. You hav acted a Juntilman. After all i hope you may get to Heaven. Mark the perfect man and behold the Up Right for the end of that man is Peace. I have said to you befor in my last letter that i Did not know Presily [Precisely] the number of the Reed People that are living now in Liberia at the Present but the Rosses people there are 11 family living in Louisiana and about 100 persons living now. Sum of them is not living at home Just now. I am sorry that you hav not Been able to do anney thing toward what i ask you. The old man [Peter Ross] hav Died Sence he Received you kind letter befor this last one. [After] you wrote to him he was Sun Struck and did not live long after that desease taken him. I hav heartofore wrote all the letters that he wish me to wrot you, therefore i thought it know harme to answer the last letter the Best way i know how and my Dear Sir as i have always write letters to you for old man in time Past and he Seames to have Been very famillair with you, therefor i thought not Robry to answer the letter as i hav all Ready Stated to You. If there are enney thing you wish such as Coffee or limes of Pornanah, Very probly they Can be fix So as to reach you befor they spoil. Then it is witt you to say, then of cose i will Send them to you. I would hav say or said Sum thing to you befor now, but the old man he thought it was best not. The old man or my father Claim the name of Mr. Ross So that you may know that he was one of his people. Old Captain Ross was my father master and were not his father. My father's father name was Mr. Jones. We all are Ross people but hav our father title. Yours truly,   Georg[e] Jones

Or Please your Honour you will oblige me much if you will gave me sum imployment. If you or enney other guntlleman want enney ceder plants or Cantling [?], Gave me the order, if you please.   Georg[e] Jones

158 / HORACE ROSS TO RALPH R. GURLEY

Luisanina, Sinoe County, June 3, 1860

Mr. Girlly, dear Sire: I Set down to write you a few lines a gain. I who is one of the farthers of the Rosses people Spent all my Strenth thare working for those who ware lord of that land acording to promisses maid by Mr. McConn & Mr. Chare did Ralay [really] expeted to Receve Sum thing from you all long Sence, but we hav wrote & worte till it all most seem to be usless. I am a ware of the fact that old Capt Ross did left a Som of money for his people. It dos all most seem impossible to us that all the money should be gone and we hav not recived as munch as one sent. Somtime we thinks that Why we are treeted So be couse we ware poore, mancipated & ignorent people. If so, God will Judg beteen us & you who are members of that Society. I am not willing to multiply words but as you wishes to know how meney of us are a live I will try to give you a correct statement. Ther is a bout 65 of us a live that was imigrated to this Country of the Ross people. If you all would send us any thing we will be Glad. Of course we are Glad to think that you all went to much truble to get us here &, if we never Receve any thing Else, I most Say that I am thenkfull to you all. But we hav So meney old women and widows amoung us that it would be a grate help to us if you all wold Send us any little thing. Yours respectfully,   Horric Ross

We prewy for You all.

159 / GEORGE JONES TO WILLIAM McLAIN

Louisiana, January the 8, 1861

My Dear Sir: I am happy of this opportunity in addressing you a few lines hopeing tow that they may find you well as they leave me at the Present. I am at this time a fartherless and motherless Son. Also my father has said wrong Respectting matters of the old Captain Ross Estate. I am Sorry that he have acted thus & i hope you will forgive him what he have said. I am very thankful to the Colonnization Society for what they has Done for us in sending us to Africa. May the blessing of God or the lord Rest uppon the Society for good. I will be very glad to hear from you. I do not know any thing about the old man Estate, being very young when i left America and therefor i can not say any thing. Will you be so kind as to Send me a theologicle Book if you Please. Yours truly friend,   Georg[e] Jones

160 / PETER ROSS [GEORGE JONES] TO CATHERINE E. WADE

January the 14, 1861, Louisiana,
Greenville, Sinoe County

My Dear Madam: I am glad after so long a time [to] have an oppor-tunity in writting you a few lines hopeing two that they may find you and the family well as they leaves me and my family at Present. It has Been So long Since i have heard from you, So much so untell i know not whither you are living or Dead. I Can not hear from you all by no Means. I have wrote again and again and i no not what is the matter. I Can not Say much at this time because i Doubt it whether you will get the letter. My son Georg[e] is married and got one child. If i thought you would Receive the letter i would State to you the Condition of all the People, but i Doubt it very much. How is all the children and Mr. Wade? Due write me if Please. This is my Son Georg[e] writing. How is all your Servent? I would like to hear from all and if you Plea[se] to be so kind as to send me Sum things [on the] Stevens when She Set Sail fo[r] Africa again i will be very glad in[deed]. Sabinah send howdy to You and Mr. Wade and his Son and Say Please be so kind as to Send hear a Dress or apair of Shoes. I shall close by Saying My love to all. Say to My Couson, Tansy, She have not write to me. Tell her howdy Do for me. Ny name is Georg[e] Ross. Yours truly friend,   Peter Ross[1]

To Mrs Catherine Wade
Mississippia, Jefferson County

161 / YORK WALKER TO ISAAC R. WADE

Greenville, Sinoe, Liberia, April 21st, [18]62

Mr. Isaac Wade, Dear Sir: I Embrace this opportunity of writing you these few lines informing you of my health which is very good at this time, and at the time hoping they may find you the same. This is indeed a fine Country for the Coloured man but we have to live by the sweat of the brow for every thing is scarce and high, such as provisions clothing, &c., and I stand in need of many things. Notwithstanding I tries to be industrious. Their is not Enough douing to enable me to procure them. You would theirfore, Sir, Confer a great favor on your humble Servant by Sending me a few articles.

If you can make it Convenient, pleas to send me a whip Saw and some Close and a pair or two of Shoes and any other thing that you may think proper to send will be thankfully Received by Your Humble Servant,
                                                                    York Walker

To Mr Isaac Wade

6/LETTERS OF THE
RICE NEGROES

On February 11, 1851, William W. Rice of St. Mary's Parish, Louisiana, turned over to the Louisiana Colonization Society thirty-three Negroes for transportation to Liberia. These blacks ranged in age from one to forty-nine years. They were slaves at the time Rice placed them in the custody of the society, but the document by which they were transferred provided that they were to be deemed free on their arrival in Liberia. Rice gave the society $1,600 to help pay the cost of transporting the blacks and maintaining them during their first six months in Africa.[1] Shortly after completing these arrangements, if not before, Rice moved to Ohio. His brother, John M. Rice, a sugar planter who was opposed to emancipation and colonization, remained in Louisiana.

Most if not all of the thirteen letters reproduced in this chapter were transmitted through agents of the American Colonization Society. Possibly these agents requested return of the letters so that they could be preserved in the society's files. The poor handwriting, composition, and spelling afford convincing evidence that these are original manuscripts and not copies.

The Rice Negroes sailed from New Orleans February 12, 1851, on the *Alida*.[2] After a voyage of fifty-five days, marred by an outbreak of smallpox which took the life of one of their number, the group arrived at Sinoe. Several more died from fever during the first months in Africa.

Reactions of the migrants to Liberia varied, but most of them complained of hard times and shortages of food, clothing, and tools. Their letters to William W. Rice, for whom they seemed to have continuing affection, were replete with requests for a wide variety of articles, including shoes, cloth, hams, pork, fish, molasses, tools, weapons, cooking utensils, and books. In some cases requests were accompanied by offers of compensation. When Rice responded negatively to one appeal for assistance, on the ground of his poor health, he received the reply: "We would like to hear from you whether you have anything [to send] or not, that is our motto."

The greatest hardship experienced by these blacks resulted from destructive attacks by hostile natives in 1855 and 1856. Some settlers lost their homes and virtually all of their possessions from these incursions.

The colonists took great pride in their schools and churches. For them, as for other groups seeking to establish themselves in Liberia, religion was a source of continuing strength and hope.

The letters of Titus Glover, extending over a period of seventeen years, are the most informative. Glover and his wife, Katy, were each forty-nine years of age when they went to Liberia—older by six years than any other member of their group. They were accompanied by five children, ages eight to sixteen. Titus accepted responsibility for two other juveniles in the party, Jack Haines, age sixteen, and Washington Morton, age ten, both of whom were bound to him as apprentices. His wife died of fever shortly after her arrival in Liberia, but not until after giving birth to a son who was named George Washington Glover; this child died in 1856.

During his first five years in Liberia, Titus cultivated a plot of land near Greenville, but in 1855 he became the manager of a farm in the vicinity of Monrovia. Shortly after he moved, natives attacked the community where he had first settled and burned the home that he had left in the care of two of his daughters; they escaped, but the invaders destroyed all the property left in and around the dwelling. For a while Titus entrusted all of his children except one son to the care of acquaintances, presumably with the understanding that they would work for their keep. Sometime later he returned to the Greenville area, and there he was living in 1869 when he wrote the last of his three extant letters. At that time he told his former master: "I must tell you something in reference to our adopted country. It is a very good country, indeed, for a man to live at any rate but not without any money. . . . So I must appeal to [you] for alittle assistance." He did not specify the kind of assistance desired other than "what you think is necessary for me in Liberia."

Titus Glover was a humble man, deeply religious and ambitious for his children. The fact that he survived with little complaint the troubles experienced in Liberia indicate that he was a person of exceptional strength and stability.

162 / JAMES RICE TO JOHN RICE

Mr. John Rice   June the 3th, 1851
                                                Greenville, Sinoe Co., libaria

My Dear Friend: I embrase this chance to let you now that we are all in a bad state of hethe [health] at present but i hope that we will be bether in a fu Days. We havent got threw with the African fever as yet but I hop that these fu lins may find you in the good helth [in which] I now wright you. We hav lande[d] after a long voiage [of] 55 days. We had a very plesan voiage with the exsept[ion] of the small pox. There want but seven that had it but there [were] 53 cases [of illness] and only 2 Died and 1 with the brain fever. I hop that you have got a good crop on ha[n]d. I want you to send me a barrel of pork and a bolt of bleach Domestic and I will send you 2 barrel of pam oil. Pam oil is plentyer than fish oil is in america and I have now [no] Dout that [it] is bether or as good [as] the fishoil.

Nothing More at presant, but gave my best respects to your brother thomas and to my brother thomas Miller, and to James page and Samil Moton. I want you to gave Mr. John rice [William Rice] some money to send to me and when I get Able to triville [travel] I will return the value of it. gave my Compliments all inquiring friends.   James Rice[1]

163 / TITUS GLOVER TO WILLIAM W. RICE

Greenville, Sinoe, September 20th, 1851

Respected Sir: Yours bearing date of the 19 of April is now before me. I address you with afew lines hoping that they may find you in a State of perfect [health as] good as there is. [We are] in a tolerable State of health at this time. We have had the acclamating feaver of the Country to contend with since our arrival to our New and destined home in Liberia.

We all join in this letter to you though we are at agreat distance from you. But yet Sir we know and feel that we owe to you a debt of Gratitude in which we are afraid that we will never be able to repay you back again for the kindness that you has bestowed upon us in giving of us our freedom and sending of us to Liberia.

We rejoice to see and to know that you feel such a deep interest in our future welfare and that we are willing to receive at any and all times any instruction that you may see fit or proper to write us at any time that may offer. We certainly had a pleasant passage across the Atlantic Ocean and I must further say that Cap. Sales acted and treated us all very kind indeed.

We had a misfortune happened [to] us. That is the Small Pox broke out in the Ship. We had one death of the Small Pox on Board and I myself had it ve[r]y bad. If you was to See me at this moment you would not know me from this fact [that] it left my face marked up in Such a manner. I have lost my wife in going through the acclamating feaver. Henry Smith lost his two children, the oldest Daugh[ter] Isaac and Martha. His family has been the worst off of any [of] us with the feaver, that is all of us that [have not] Died.

According to your wishes we have all gone to farming and we work

Every Day upon our Farms as we see that is the only thing to build up Liberia. Two thirds of the people in this Country are farmers. We are in hopes to let you see some of the produce of our Farms by the next season if God wills. We are trying as much to please you as we did when we was with you. Our children goes to School regular Evey day and Some of them has made considerable improvement and they also attend Regular the Sabbath School.

Our farms seems to be in a prosperous state with the produce of the Country and the Land and Soil of Africa seems to be as good as the Land in any Country. James Paterson has drawn a poor pice of Land and he has been quite dissatisfied but has become quite reconciled since his family has recovered. I wrote to you by the Barque Baltimore but I was that sick at the time I could [not] finish the letter but sent it off so. But I am in hopes this will reach you in safety. I will be able to write you twice a year by this Packet as she will [be] here that often.

You will please [send] us out a cross cut saw and a whip and if [possible] to send me out a Barrel Flour an Barrel of Pork [by] the next Veaesels that Sail from New Orleans, and write also to Mr. James Rice and ask to him give me a little assistance if he his able.

Washington and Jack are bound to me and are smart boys. Write to Washington father and tell him he is well and doing well and he is a very smart boy. Ruben sends his love to Mr. John M. Rice and wishes for him to send him out a Barrel of Molasses and that he will pay him for it with the produce of his farm next Season if life Last, and to send me out one steel corn mill. Maria Ann lost her Daughter Ann.

Henry Brashears Say You will please to write my Sister that lives at the Huttons and tell her that I am well and hope this may find her the same. My family is all well and Expects to move on my farm in a few days from this and am in hope of hearing [from] you as soon as possible. Give my love to all the white family. Little Ruben sends his Love to William and he talks about him evey Day. Titus Glover sys please to send us out some seed corn if you please Sir and some Cloth to make Clothes, any kind.
Yrs. Humble Servant,   Titus Glover

164 / JAMES PATTERSON TO WILLIAM W. RICE

To Mr. W W Rice,   Sept. 29, 1851
State of Ohio Hurricane Coun[ty]

Dear Sir: I State to you that we are in tolerable helth except my Leg & I have suffered very much with my foot & leg. I think it is worse than it was when I was in the United States. It pears to me that my famly wil come to suffer if I dont get some asistance from you. The doctors says that they cant cure it in this country for the climate of this country does not suit old sores. I think that if you wil assist me to get to New York it may be that I can get it coured. If I cant get it coured I will oblige to suffer. I give my respects to you and your wife hopeing that these lines may fine you & family enjoying the blesings of helth. I state to you that we did not find the country as we exspected. Pervisions is very high and very scarse. In fact new comers cant get it for lov nor money. My pervisions is scarse and my money is scarse & my clothing is geting scarse. My wife givs her respects to Mr. Rice and Mrs. Rice, so Nothing more until death.   James Patterson[1]

165 / REUBEN [WHITTEMORE] AND [HENRY] BRASHEAR TO WILLIAM W. RICE

Greenville, Sinoe, Sept. 30, 1851

Dear Sir: We write you this because we see at once if we do not ask you for some little hep that we shall suffer for the first year. So you will please Sir to send us 2 barrels of Flour and two Pork. We are vey well satisfied with the Country, indeed. Yrs. Respectfully &c,

Ruben & Brashear[1]

166 / HENRY SMITH TO WILLIAM W. RICE

Greenville, Sinoe County, Liberia, July 21, 1852

To Mr. Wiliam rice, Dear Sir: A few lines to you that we are in tolerable helth hoping these lines may find you in good helth. Dear sir, my crop is faild very much. And al so Thos. rice, our respects to you. I am doeing tolerable wel according to the handing of the country. Times is hard [and] have bin. My wife wishes for Thos. Rice to send her one barrel of Pork, one barrel of fish. My res[p]ects to John Rice and family and to all my friends in the Plantation. Dear Sir, I have bin your servant. I want [you] to send me one barrel of molases, one barrel of sugar, 2 pear of shoes no. 9, one pear no. 8 for my wife. Frances Smith wants 2 pear of shoes No. 6 & one barrel of corn meal, 6 baken hams, one bolt of common handkerchiefs and one bolt of checks. To Mr. W. Rice—I want you to send me all kinds of sead. Dear Sir, I recevd your letter concerning that yellow corn and it wil doe very wel her. I feel wiling to try it. I want you to send me one steel mill that we use to use in the plantations, & send me some books and Sign The names on the Books that is the one thats to received them, one bolt of Coal rain [coloring?]. James Patterson took the whipsaw from the company and sold it. The Brode axe and the Kooking utentials I never seen. Yours &c.,   Henry Smith[1]

167 / TITUS GLOVER TO WILLIAM W. RICE

Belleview near Monrovia, Jan. 19th, 1856

Mr. W. Rice, Dear Sir: We are well and I hope this may find you and your kind family in good and perfect health as it leaves us. I should have written to you some time ago before I left Greenville, Sinoe, but for the want of chance and time. So I hope by this you will be glad to hear from me and my little ones, Frances and Peter, Mary, Samy, all [of whom] is here with me in this part of the Republic, as I move up here to attend to a farm be long to Mr. Jno. B. Jordan, where I expect to stay sometime to come as yet.[1] I will now mention about our present situation. Since I left Sinoe County there are now war with the natives and the Colonists. They have killed several of the Americans and burnt down different villages of ours and all my property. Now I [am] left without anything, so I hope you will take deep interest in my case at this present time as this country is very hard one except means to carry out person object, I means money; I like this part of the country better than I do my former resident as it is more near to our Capitol which is Monrovia City. I have just lost one of my children which is the youngest on the 14th of this month who I name Geo. Washington Glover, the Lord gave and the Lord taketh, blessed is his kind name. I must degress alittle from my first subject. The time the war taken place two of the children were at my former resident, which was Frances and Mary, where I left them to take care [of] my place but they had to leave in haste by the war which I mention in the above.[2] Now I have put all out to other persons but Peter who is still with me at the farm, to assist me to overseer the place and also to attend to my domestic affairs whenever it is practicable. Since I left the place Mr. Jas. Patterson have also left, without his family but he is looking for them by every chance which I hope they will be up before long, by the assistance of the great Jehovah who knows all things. R. Whitmore is married and have fine son and I am not able to inform you how they are in health as I have not hear but once since the war. All the friends that come out with me are all well when I heard from them. Do dont listen to every tales others persons will say about our Republic because it is fine place although it is new country like many other new country, so as you know there must be some persons who have objection of Liberia being settled. I should like to know how all my old felow servents who [were] left behind when I come away, and especially from Thomas and John, who I should like to hear from individually, and all the news about that part of the country where I lived. I hope you will present my best compliments to all the enquiring friends. I should say more but time will not permit me to do so. The children send their love to the people. The war is not settle as yet. The President and his troops just left here on the 26th of this month for Sinoe, to put down those natives who rise against the Americans to fight. Your dear friend,   Titus Glover

168 / REUBEN RICE TO WILLIAM W. RICE

Mr. William J. Rice   City of Greenville, County of Sinoe,
                                                                    Jany 20, 1859

Dear Sir: I take up my pen in hand to inform you concerning of my health in which is Good and my Family at present and hoping that these few lines may find you the same. Dear Sir, The War at Greenville, Sinoe, has been very distressing insomuch that I has lost every thing that I had even to my house in which I had erected in a Small Village called Lexington were Burnt up to ashes by the Natives and I wish if you will be so kind as to aid me in some little thing so that I will able to put up my house again for it is a Very Distressing time in this City at present and if you have any thing at present to Send you can Direct to The Rev'd William McClaine, Washington City, for me and i will be sure and Certain to get it. Old man Smith are well and his Family. Tilmore is Well and his Family. James Patterson is Dead and Nelson Brooks, Jack Haynes also. Since the war all of the Old Folks is move away with the exception of me and my Brother. I have a wife and two Children. No more at present. I remain your friend and will wisher,   Reuben Rice[1]

One of my Child is name William and the other is John. If you send any thing to me you will [be] so kind as to send [it] in my name, not in the [name] of Titus Glover or Henry Smith.

169 / STEPHEN RICE AND HENRY SMITH
TO WILLIAM W. RICE

Mr. William Rice   Greenville, Sinoe, Liberia
                                                                 Jany 25th, 1859

Dear Sir: We are happy of another opportunity to write you these few Lines hoping they may find you all well as they Leave us. Many have been my wishes to See you Since here I been But this wish Seem to be in vain. I am as Yet in Sinoe doing all I can for a Lively hood. I was Getting along very well until the war, which flung me Back very much But I donot dispare [for] the Same God that moved your heart to Set us free and Send us to our own Country I hope will keep me from want and Sufferings, and allso raise up friends for me Even in the distant Land of America.Our health is very Good at this time But times are very hard with us Just Now. Yet in the midst of all our discouragements we are trying to work and not disgrace the Goodness of him who Set us free. I am Stephen Rice. You will Be kind enough to Send me By the Mary C. Stephens a few pare of shoes, a Bag of so of shot and a few yards of cloth and in short any thing that you think fit to Send us. We can assure you any Little thing from you will be Joyfully Received. I, Henry Smith, the old plantation servant joins in writing this Letter. Write me where you are and I will try to Send you some African Coffee. You will please show this Letter to Mr. Thomas Rice and all of the Brothers. Franky Smith, who nursed Mr. Thomas Smith, Beg leave to remind him of his Promice which was if she ever stood in want he would help her. She is now In want and Begs him to send her Something. Shoes, Cloth, and indeed any Little thing. You will Please Send me with my wifes, franky, things a Little powder and shot. Levi is alive and is trying to do what he can to Live. [Please send] a double Barrel Gun, even if it is an old one I beg for. You may think what is our condition after the war with a savage tribe. James Paterson, Henry Bushear, Jack Haynes are dead. All the rest of your people are well and on their farms trying to live. Let us hear from you if you please By the M.C.Stephens. Should you Send us any, thing please direct it in care of Mr. B. A. Payne, Greenville, Sinoe, Liberia. We remain Yours Most obediently,   Stephen Rice & Henry Smith[1]

170 / REUBEN RICE, HENRY SMITH
AND STEPHEN RICE TO WILLIAM W. RICE

Greenville, Sinoe County, Jany 26th, 1861

My Dear Friend: I take up my pen in hand to inform you concerning of my health in which is Good at Present and my wife also is in Very Good health and I do hope whenever this letter reaches you that it may find you and all of the Family Enjoying Very Good health. I myself and Family do like this Country well. It yields its products in abundance Such as coffee, yams, corn, Potatoes, Rice Bonanes, Plantain, Corsarders [cassadas]. There are Several other articles to Numerous and to Tedious to be mentioned—Stock in abundance, Viz., Cows, Calves, Sheep, Goats, hogs and if a man will half do he is bound to Get along with a very small Capital, that is provided that he intends to work. We wants working men here besides the Capital for God Said in his holy Law that by the sweat of his brow he Shall Eat Bread. My Dear Friend, I am really Sorry to hear that your health is so bad at present. Thos. and John we would like to hear from, [those] that are on the Old place. Henry Smith & Franky Smith Sends their kind love to you and Family and beg of you to [write] us often and as soon we receive your letter we will be certain to answer you by the first opportunity. My Brother Rubin wife has 3 children. Ann Rice has one. My Dear friend, you Stated in your Letter that you will not [be] able to Send us any thing at present, that your health has been Some what impair, but on the other hand We would like to hear from you whether you have any thing [to send] or not, that is our Motto. No More to Say at present. Remember me to all Enquiring Friends. I Still remain your friend and well wisher,

Reuben Rice, Henry Smith, Stephen Rice

171 / HENRY AND FRANCES SMITH, STEPHEN RICE AND LEVI SEAY TO WILLIAM W. RICE

Mr. [W. W.] Rice   Republic of Liberia, Sinoe County
                                                         Nov. the 10th, 1863

Dear Sir: I avail my self [of] this opportunity to address you these few lines & do by these presents acknowlage the recpt of yours dated April 22, 1863, & we thanck devine proverddance that he has afford us another oppertunity to heare from you and the rest of the family. We have from time to time bean thincking about you and it has imployed much of our conversation. In perrusol of your letter we finde much information in relation to the present war now in your Country and we do thanck you for them & also render thancks to almity God that he has taken us out [of] The reach of it and plaste us on our four father's Soil away from all of its calamitys. I will now proseed to give you a short description of our country.

We are now resideing in Sinoe County, the same place that we landed on our arrival to the Country. Sinoe, thou[gh] not so thickly settled as some other parts of Liberia, is a fine place and is cappble of much improvement althou the present war in America has provnted [prevented] any Emergration to this part of the republic. But its inhaitance [inhabitants] is generally industrious people and is straning every nerve to set if affloat. But im sorry that I have the occation to mention the Deths of so many of our poeple. James Patterson is dead and we are hapy to say that [he] reseigned his work a Christain. Jack hanes, Emily Baldage, Peter Glover, and Jinny Smith are those that have falen assleep since you hear from us last. In your next leter you will be please to let us know about al[l] of our acquantances and if Tom Miller is allive. Stephen tilmore health is verry bad at present. Washing[ton] Rice is marrid and has a fine daughter name Tames. Leavi See is marrid but is verry much under the wether and has bean so for the last two years. He has two chrildin, a Boy and Girl by the name of Allice. Rhueben Rice is one of the ablist amoung us, the oanly one that has bean able to render any milatary duty to our Country. He has bean a volentear in two wars. He is now marrid and has fore chrilden, William the oaldist boy, John, Mary Elizabeth (Eliza) & Francis are his childen.

The rest of our poeple is all well or allive and tender thair best reguards to your and the fiamily and call your attention to our condition as settlers in a New Country and that by the next oppertunity you will remember us. Rhuben Rice writes that he is sorry to hear of the death of John Rice but is glad that he has made his Home in Heaven with the angles of God. May God be with you all. We Remain yours Respect-
fuly,   Henry Smith, Franky Smith
                                         Sephen Rice, Levi See [Seay][1]

Rhueben W. Rice Wife sends her respects to you and the family. Delia Whittemore, We also take this oppertunity to inform you of our connection to the Bapist Church. Ruben Rice was the first that join. Levi See is now a Preacher of the Gosple in the same Church. Stephen tilmore has made membership also.

172 / EDWARD JAMES PATTERSON TO WILLIAM W. RICE

Mr. William W. Rice   Monrovia, April the 2, 1868 [1869?]

Dear Friends: I recived your kind leter by Rev. John Seays. He has delived ous your kind leter and we was happy to here from you all. Since A long time has pass and Gone and you want [to] no How we [are] getting along. Well I can say that we is getting [along] here by very hard labor indeed an then kin hardly live affter that. And it takes aman to live here that has aplenty of mony. Withe out that, you may as well not to coeme here. To live in liberria withe out a little money, sometimes you can get alittle start here. But as to undertake to make the money here you neve will Getit because when you here [work] Right hard, then you pay tuice befoer you can getit, then you bege for you can [not] Getit aftr you don work for it. Sir, Mother is liveing yeat an She sends her best Respects [to] you all, all so. Dont laff at my pouer marks. I had not the time to go to school as Regular as I want to go. I hope you can make these fue lines out. Wish you would send me some Good bookes to read. I have to improve my learning and I have no Books to leren in. I have been up to Cape Munt [Mount] to war this year withe president, [James S.] payne, and we had a small fuss withe hethen, kill some one or two persons, and by the treatment of the president payne was so g[oo]d and kind to us I had nothing to Gromble at.[1] He is the finest man I ever seene.

I was in camppaign one monthe with president James payne and he is Brave man, an good, God ferring man. And [I] Beg you please to send me some painters tooles. one Blander [blender?] and set combes and some ombrig and some outher mixtures of pouders that you can get, an some paint Bressers [brushes] larg and small, and please get me one Panter's Booke, some of late workes. And please send me the Bill. Put all in old man Seays hands and I weel Get thim if you send them for me. Levie Seay is dead. I have writen off the list of all that is dead [and] Give [it] to Mr. Seays; wther [whether] he send to you or not I dont no. Particular Aske uncle titus to [write] by the first mal Boat. Wether he don it, I dont no. I will be soure that I will see that you get this one. Nothing moore. Remain Yours Friend,   Edward Jamese Patterson

173 / TITUS GLOVER TO WILLIAM W. RICE

Louisiana, January 16th, 1869

My dear Sir: I received your letter some time ago, and I wrote you in 1867, but I have not received any answer from it, so I thought it was best to write again, since the Rev. John Seys, the American Consul General, have inform me where you now lived. I have been wondering what had become of you, as I had not hear anything definitely, and when person write he must know the place where to directs his letter or letters so it might reached you exactly as sometime it may be miscarried. I would be glad to hear often from you, if it would be convenient, as I always would be glad to know how you and your family are [at] any rate, and also about matters in that part of the world. We here in Africa loved to hear news especially from an old friend of mine, who I know are so well adapted into it. I know Ohio is [a] great place for intelligence of any kind in the world, as I have heard from every sources.

The Republic of Liberia is not like the new world as I may call it, if I am allow to do so. We are here, it is true, but it is like new beginners for news. as we have no other medium to know or to hear anything of important nature except through our friends on the other side of the great deep, no newspaper to circulate to us the things we ought to hear to encourage us in this dark and benighted land of ours. Most everything we have to do here, are more like it is too hard to end it at all, which seem like is impossible to keep up our news, as we are not in the proper form for those important things we ought to know for our future benefit in this our world.

I must tell you something in reference to our adopted country. It is a very good country, indeed, for man to live at any rate but not without any money [manuscript torn] . . . person who wants to make [manuscript torn] . . . in the world, but when there is scarcity for money, and you know no nation can do anything without its use, as it is given to us by our Maker to make certain used of it but not to put our whole mind on it which I know would not be proper in any way whatever, as frail creatures as we are in this world of ours. You requested the Rev. Jno. Seys to ask for the number that have died. I have gave him the number of persons in writing, which he told me he would send to you by the next chance. Mrs. Patterson and two of her children is living at Monrovia, and the rest is at Greenville, Sinoe County, where we were first landed after our arrival in this country. I would sent this letter from the time it was written but I had no ready cash to post it by the way via England. I must tell you how I am situated here in this country. I have been trying every since I came to the country to make a living for me and family but time is so hard poor man can scarcely make any thing to carry out his end. If they live at all it is under great restraint. So I must appeal to [you] for alittle assistance. If you please to send me out what you would think is necessary for me in Liberia, such would be beneficial to any one that situated as I am now is. I would write more news but I think it is not worth while to do so. I will try to avail the chance next time. Next May is our election for President, Vice President, Senators and Representatives. Mr. Payne and Mr. Roye again is before the people, as they think justice was not done to Mr. Roye last election.[1] I am yours Respectfully,

Titus Glover

174 / EDWARD JAMES PATTERSON TO WILLIAM W. RICE

Monrovia, March 30th, 1869.

Mr. William, Dear Friends: I recived you last leter here came by Mr. Seays, came [to] Titus Glover.

But I red the contents of it and all so like it verry well. But I reather see you if I could. I have a very lite Eeducation But you may make this out. But at same time I hope you family [are] all well. You was telling me something a bout your childdren. I [was] Glad toher from them. Tell them tha must her from me now, being this is [not] the first leter that I ever [wrote] to you and all. I have writen you sevil lteres [letters], But I never could get ansur from you all. So that disencourged me so that I would write nomore. But Mr. Seys says that he will see that you would get these leter whe[ne]ver I would write them to you. Nothing more, But Remain Yours,   Edward James Patterson

7/LETTERS OF THE ROBERT E. LEE NEGROES

   Almost all who are familiar with the career of Robert E. Lee know that he was opposed to the institution of slavery and that before the Civil War he emancipated most of his Negroes. Relatively few know that he offered to send the liberated blacks to Liberia and that one family accepted the opportunity to emigrate.[1] On November 9, 1853, William C. Burke, age thirty-six, his wife Rosabella, age thirty-four, and their four small children embarked from Baltimore on the ship *Banshee*, chartered by the American Colonization Society.[2] Late in November they landed in Monrovia. They tarried for two months in the town and then moved a few miles up the Saint Paul's River to the settlement of Clay-Ashland, named for Henry Clay, a champion of colonization, and for Clay's home located on the outskirts of Lexington, Kentucky. There Burke built a small house on an elevated site that he named Mount Rest, set up shop as a shoemaker, and planted a garden. In thus striking out on his own soon after his arrival in Africa, instead of subsisting for six months at the expense of the colonization society as most emigrants did, Burke gave evidence of his unusual initiative and drive.

   Both Burke and his wife were deeply religious and their reliance on Divine Providence helped them to cope with the discomforts and dangers of establishing themselves in a new country and provided solace for them in the loss of one or more of their children.

   Burke, who obviously was a person of superior intelligence, sought diligently for self-improvement. Late in 1856 he enrolled in a newly established theological seminary in Monrovia, commuting a distance of fifteen miles at considerable inconvenience to himself and his family, in order to study Latin and to learn to read the New Testament in the original Greek. He began to preach early in his Liberian sojourn and in 1857 he was inducted into the Presbyterian ministry by the ceremonial laying on of hands. He helped educate his own children and assumed responsibility for instructing members of his community in both religious and secular subjects. Unlike many American settlers, he did not disparage native Africans. In January 1858 he took several native children into his home "to civilize and Christianize them, so if possible to do something for the heathen around us." In September 1861, in reporting to Ralph R. Gurley the arrival of a large number of recaptured Congoes in his community, he stated: "I have twelve in my family . . . men, women & boys & I have the most lively hopes and prospects in the most of them." His concern for the unfortunate, both emigrant and native, was evidenced by his proposal to set up a public almshouse for the care of the aged, the ailing, and the needy.

Burke had a streak of poetry in his makeup. "My opinion in regard to the Country is an exalted one," he wrote in 1857. "It is a Land of Cooling Brooks and Sunny plains where the melody of Birds are sweet and where the Leaves are always green, a Land that will aboundantly satisfy the Husbandman for his toils."

While adjusting to life in Liberia, Burke continued to manifest a great interest in his Lee connections in America, both white and black. When he learned in 1858 that Custis Lee, father of Mrs. Robert E. Lee, had died, he offered to help the Negroes emancipated by the will of the deceased to become happily established in Liberia. Indeed, he proposed to have them settle near him in a new community that he wanted to call Custisburg. Earlier he had written Gurley: "We have had a fine daughter added to our family. . . . Her name is Martha Custis Lee Burke."

Burke's letters to the Lees and to officials of the American Colonization Society indicate a genuine and enduring affection on the part of him and his family for their former owners. This affection reflects credit upon both master and bondsman. In character, ideals, aspirations, and demeanor the Burkes were very much like the Lees. The success achieved by the Burkes in Africa was due in part to skills, attitudes, and other attributes they acquired as slaves, and in part to the adaptability, resourcefulness, and faith that were a part of their innate strength. But, however pleasant their recollections of past associations in Virginia, not once did they indicate disillusionment with their freedom or a desire to return to the land of their birth.

175 / WILLIAM C. BURKE TO WILLIAM McLAIN

Rev'd Mr. McLaine, Washington, D.C.

Monrovia, Africa
January 16, 1854

Dear Sir: This is to inform you of my safe arrival on the shores of Africa. We had quite a rough time during the voyage; but for my part I feel thankful to Almighty God, and also Greatful to the Society, for the safe arrival of myself & family on the shores of Liberia, and the comfortable support that we have received so far & Expect to get during the space of six months.[1] If the Lord should bless me with Lief & health, I see no reason why I should not be able to live Comfortable, after a while. This certainly is a fine place for any one that has money or goods to sell, to get along very fast. At the same time, I am happy to say that the poor man may also Live if he has health and will be industrious. The Emigrants up to this time are all in pretty good health. Myself and family at present are all in pretty good health. Hoping these few Lines may find youself & family in good health, I Remain with high consideration your humble friend & servant,   William C. Burke

[P.S.] You told me in Baltimore that any thing I wanted from the U.S. that you would send to me that I was to see Mr. Dennis who would Give me the necessary Instruction. He told me that whatever I wanted to write to you for & you would send them to him & I could pay him for them on Delivery. The first thing is you will please send me a Good Counter platform, patent balance scales that has a tin on top to weigh sugar &c & an[d] the beame & platform will weigh as high as 200 [pounds?]. They cost from 6 to 8 dollars. You will please also send me one barrel of Good Pork, one of mackrel, one of hard bread, 2 tins of flour, the amount of which I will pay over to Mr. Dennis on delivery. Your attentions to the above favours will greatly oblige your humble friend & servant,

Wm. C. Burke

Be Good Enough also to send me about 100 lbs of Brown sugar as you furnishes the Emmigrants with.   WCB

176 / WILLIAM C. BURKE TO ROBERT E. AND MARY C. LEE

Liberia, Africa, August 20th, 1854

Dear Madam and Sir: It is with much pleasure, that I take my pen in hand to acknowledge the receipt of your two letters, which gave both Rosabella and myself great comfort to hear from you all.

We receive very few letters from our colored friends and relations. We have been here eight months and we have all been very sick, with the fever, but, I am happy to be able to say that we are still alive and enjoying as good health, as we might expect. For four or five months after we arrived in Africa, my children looked better than I think I ever saw them; they were so fond of palm oil and rice, and eat so much of it, that they fattened very fast. Myself and Rosabella also, enjoyed very good health for four or five months of our residence in Liberia. I must now try to tell you something in regard to how we are getting on, up to this time; as I have no doubt, you will like to hear. You inquire in your letter, what I brought out; and if they were the right sort of articles. When I arrived in Baltimore, preparatory to sailing, I had, with what you gave me, a little over one hundred dollars, but after paying board for two weeks, and buying some things necessary for house keeping, and paying off all my accounts for moving, and getting a few things to the amount of $10, I found, that when I got on board of Ship, I had only $33 left. When I arrived, I spent two months at Monrovia, which is a very expensive place to live in, having to pay for your wood and water. I found *this* would never do for me, so I got the favor of the agent to allow me a room, up the St. Paul's river, where I was to settle for the balance of the six months. When I was moved, I had only $3 in cash. The health of myself and family being quite good, at that time, I went to work to cut down my lot and clear a spot for a house, not knowing at that time how I should go about it, having no means. Many persons however advised me to go to *shoemaking*, as it would not do for me to be out from eight till four o'clock. I took their advice, and when the six months were out, I had a house of my own to live in. It is 22 by 13 feet and though very rough, yet it is very comfortable. I have found my trade to be very valuable to me indeed. I do not know what I should have done without it. The greatest drawback is the want of *leather*.

If the Lord continues to bless me with health, I have no doubt that my hands can administer to all my temporal wants. Everything in this country, as I suppose is the case in all new countries, is very high and very hard and inconvenient to get. A little money here, can do but little with regard to farming, and that is certainly the surest and best avenue to wealth, ease and comfort. The only farmers here who are making anything for sale, are those who come to this country with money. Farming is more difficult now than it has been, as all the land on the St. Paul's river has been bought and the emigrants now, have to go back in the forest some two, three and four miles, and whatever they may plant, is destroyed by the wild hog, the wild cow and many other wild animals. We hope, however, that the time will soon come, when persons will venture to settle a little back from the river, and beasts of burden will be brought into use. At present, there is not one of any kind. In telling you about my house, you might think I was in debt for the whole. It cost from 80 to $100, and I owe about $12 on the whole. I hope soon to be able to live much cheaper than I do at this time, having now everything to buy. I have commenced gardening, raising fowls, &c., and hope soon to be independent, in the way of chickens, vegetables, and bread stuffs. Great has been the sufferings and mortality among the emigrants, who came out with us. There are many causes for it, which may not be interesting to you to know, nor my business to write. I could write a pamphlet of considerable size of what perhaps might interest you, but as writing is not good for me, passing through the fever, I must conclude for the present. I am very much obliged to you for your corrections in my writing—please correct me always, as I am a self-taught writer. Please present our kindest remembrances to the young ladies and gentlemen and the children. Please write to us by every opportunity and let our friends and relations at Arlington hear from us, when you write to them.

William C. Burke

177 / ROSABELLA BURKE TO MARY C. LEE

Liberia, Africa, August 21st, 1854

Dear Madam: According to my promise, I take this opportunity to write you a few lines, to let you know how I am getting on and how I like the country, &c. During my stay of two months at Monrovia I was very much pleased, except that the people were too gay and fashionable for me, I being not able to rank with them. I was honored with an invitation from the President to a tea party, which we accepted and were highly gratified.[1] I was, however, much better satisfied when we got up the river, as we were anxious to be making some preparations for the future, knowing that the sooner the better. I am very much pleased with the little town that we are now making. It is known at present by the name of Clay-Ashland. We have quite a good sort of people about us at present, and we have a lot and house upon a beautiful hill in the township, which we have named Mount Rest. It is about 200 yards from the river, looking down in the river, and overlooking the town. Around the house, where we are making our garden, the ground is so full of white flinty rocks that it is with difficulty that we can make a garden. I have no doubt it will be a healthy spot. We have a plenty of churches—one very fine Episcopal Church, one Baptist, one Methodist and one Presbyterian—and on the way to them four schools, though I am sorry to say that they are very badly taught. I have not sent my children to school as yet, as they are acclimating, and I thought it best to wait till they got quite well. We have all been blest, so far as regards our health. We have all had the fever, but not very badly or long at a time. The baby got along finely, and was almost walking, until he took the fever—since that he has lost nearly all his strength. The rest of the children are tolerably well. The things I brought out were not exactly the right sort, though they have been useful to me. I wish I had brought more calico, bleached and unbleached cotton. It would have been much more profitable. I was much disappointed in not hearing from sister; when you write please let us know her whereabouts. From your humble servant,   Rosabella Burke

178 / WILLIAM C. BURKE TO RALPH R. GURLEY

Rev. R. R. Gurley   Clay-Ashland, Liberia, Africa
                                                    June 8th, 1855

My Dear Friend: Your welcomed letter of the 15th May is now before me: I am always delighted to hear from you or any of my friends in America. I was somewhat surprised to learn from your letter that Mr. and Mrs. Lee had left West Point.[1] I am glad however, to hear that Mrs. Lee is at Arlington. I hope she has received my letters that were directed to West Point. I did not get a single line from her, or any one from Arlington. I suppose the Rev. J. B. Pinney has given you accounts of every thing in Liberia; he was at my house twice. Our Presidential election is just over, which was a very exciting one. Mr. Stephen A. Benson is the President and Beverly Yates Vice President.[2] Our old long tried friend, J. J. Roberts, will retire to private life. We are still progressing slowly in our little town. Myself and family continue to enjoy good health, and we feel quite satisfied with our new home; we have never suffered for any thing since we have been to this country. I think the people in a few years will learn how to make themselves much more comfortable than they are at the present.

It may be gratifying to you to hear that I have been duly licensed to preach the glad news of salvation to this benighted people; may the Lord help me to be faithful. I have charge of the Baptist church in this place, (with about forty-five members) which is increasing. And now my dear Friend, I must in addition to all of your kindness ask you to try and get me some books on theology, such as you know I need at present. I have none but the Bible.   Wm. C. Burke

179 / WILLIAM C. BURKE TO RALPH R. GURLEY

Rev'd R. R. Gurley   Clay-Ashland, Liberia, West Coast Africa,
                                                    June 27, 1856

My Esteemed Friend: It is with much pleasure that I am now seated for the purpose of dropping you a few lines to Acknowledge the recept of your Kind Letter rec'd by the General Pierce on the 10th of May Last. Your Letter gave me much comfort in hearing from yourself & family besides the Information you gave me about Mrs. Lee & my friends and relations at Arlington. If it were not for yourself & Mrs. Lee I should hardly ever hear a word from Arlington the home of our youth as our Coloured friends do not write. This leaves myself, Rose & the children all in pretty good health. Since I Last wrote to you we have had a fine daughter added to our family, which is quite promising. Her name is Martha Custis Lee Burke. You see now that we have the same number that we brought to this country.[1] My three children goes to school and the oldest which is the girl Learns very fast and the boys are doing very well for their ages. We are all getting along pretty well at present. Times are unusual hard at this time in almost every place in the Republic for various reasons. I have no doubt but what you have heard of the war of Sinoe which Called of[f] almost every man that could stand Traveling and they were gone from home for several months at the time they ought to have been planting there farms.[2] Shortly after they returned the rains came on when they were unable to clear of[f] & burn there farms. In consequence of which Bread stuff is very scarce & hard to get. Besides the natives have failed in there Crops for the Last two years in Consequence of the seasons Changing so much. The seasons are by no means uniform now as they used to be. It rains during the dry season. The war is now over with but Little Lost on our side. The People in Sinoe County have suffered much in Consequence of the war for some time. Our Little Town is still improving. It is thought that it will soon go ahead of Monrovia. We want population and those of the right kind with money and enterprize & we shall soon have a flourishing Town. They are raising sugar cane pretty extensively on the St. Paul's. They have Introduced a steam sugar mill which I Expect will do a good business. Besides they are getting Cows & oxens. With some little help I think we will go ahead.

My dear Friend, I hope you will not think me strange and ungeatfull in not settling up the accounts between my self & Mr. Haben for those goods he sent me. You know that I had very recently arrived in the Country and was not fixed in my own house in Consequence of which I had to keep them Longer on hand than I ought to have done. Besides, as I was a stranger in the Country I did not know who to trust. I shall however Expect to make a full settlement with Mr. Haben in September after which I Expect he will send me more goods. Rose desires to be remembered particular to your family & believe me Yr Greatful & Obt servant,   Wm. C. Burke

180 / WILLIAM C. BURKE TO RALPH R. GURLEY

Rev'd R. R. Gurley   Clay Ashland, Dec. 10th 1856

My Dear friend: I rec'd your Kind favour of the 1st which as usual afforded me great pleasure to here from you and others in the Land of my nativity of whom you mentioned. I cannot help feeling glad whenever I receive a letter from one whom I know feels the deepest interest in myself and family and have made it manifest by so many acts of kindness. There is nothing that I can do to Compensate you. But feel asured that you will in no wise loose your reward. I am happy to be able to say that my family Continues to enjoy very good health with the exception of the youngest. You may be somewhat surprised to Learn by this Letter that I have become a school boy in my middle time of Lief. There is a seminary built at Monrovia by the suthern Baptist board through the agency of the Rev. John Day for general education for which there is a Theological department, Rev'd John Day principal.[1] I have entered the Theological studies with the determination, God being my helper, to read and understand the Greek Testament if no more. There are three of us in anthons Lattin first Lessons. We have an excellent Teacher, G. W. Blyden, a young man who have received his Education in the Presbyterian high school. Rev. A. D. Wilson [is] principal. It is quite inconvenient for me Liveing as you know 15 miles up the river and my family must of necesity suffer inconvenience from my being away the most of the time. But I feel the necessity of being able to understand properly the word I preach and as we cannot do any thing productive of good without inconvenience and self denial, I feel willing to suffer inconvenience and hardships in order that I may accomplish some good in the end. And besides we are in a progressive age and I feel the want of that wisdom which is needful & profatable for the Lief which now is and that which is to come. I attend the Church at Clay-Ashland as usual on Sundays. Our little town is progressing slowly. They have commenced to clear of[f] the spot for the creation of a colledge for Clay-Ashland which will be quite an improvement. It is a short distance from my house on the same hill. I suppose ere this you have heard of the death of the Hon. G. R. Ellis, the hotell Keeper.[2] He died after a short illness. He was much beloved in the Community and his Lost is deeply felt. I received the Book sent by Mrs. Lee safely and shall Endeavour to write to her by this opportunity. Rose joins me in the kindest regards for yourself and believe me your Humble greatfully and obedient servant.   Wm. C. Burke

Write by every opportunity

181 / WILLIAM C. BURKE TO RALPH R. GURLEY

To the Rev. R. R. Gurley   Clay Ashland, Dec. 27th, 1856

Most Excellent Friend: There is a vessel now about to sail for the U.S. and having just received your kind favour of the 7th of Nov. I hasten to drop you a few Lines to acknowledge the recept of it and to thank you for your promptness in writing to me by the various opportunities that offer. I feel blessed to have someone that will take the trouble to write and Inform me of matters and things generally. I am very sorry to Learn from your Letter that Mrs. Lee was suffering from Rheumatism.[1] I hope however that she has recovered before this, Knowing as I do that she is so formed & enjoys an active Lief so much. I had flattered myself that Mr. Lee had returned from Texas before this and was quietly siting down at Arlington. I hope that it will not be Long before he will. Myself & family Continues to enjoy good health with one slight exception. I wrote to you by the Shirley which sailed about 2 weeks ago. We are Looking for the Emigrant ship every day. I have just returned from the Baptist Association which met at Edina, Bassa City. I had the pleasure of meeting with Jacob Vanbonn and Lewis Cary Crocker, two natives who have been Educated by the Northern Baptist Board at the school up at Bexely. It seems to me to be a pitty that that school should have gone down. These two Reverend Gentlemen seem to be Entirely Civilized and Christianized and there Influence must be very great as they are considered Kings or Chiefs of the country around them. Lewis Gary Crocker [is] Chief of Little Bassa and Jacob Vanbonn of Grand Bassa. I was much pleased with what I saw of them and feel sadisfied that the native African can be made anything and everything that is necessary that man should be. Rose desires to be remembered Kindly to Mrs. Gurley, to Miss Mary Gurley and all the family. Any paper, book, pens &c, &c, will always be very acceptable. Please write by every opportunity. And believe me as ever your Grateful & obt sv't,   Wm C. Burke

Everything is going on quietly in this Republic at this time. I have just sent Mr. Haben fifty Dollars and have written to him fully on this whole matter which I have no doubt will be satisfactory.

182 / WILLIAM C. BURKE TO RALPH R. GURLEY

Rev. R. R. Gurley   Clay Ashland, March 6, 1857

Very dear sir: I again take up my pen to write to you upon a Subject that have presented itself to my mind very forceable. In one of your Letters I received a short time since you Speake as Though you were willing to engage in Something that would be beneficial to Liberia generally. Notwithstanding the many benefits her Inhabitants have already enjoyed through your Instrumentality, I Looking around yeare after yeare and observing the Condition of Orphans and Widows in this Country I am Led [to] the Conclusion that nothing is more needed and nothing wold be more beneficial than an *Alms House* or any Kind of house that you might chose to call it that could have for its object the general good of orphan children & widows. You are aware, my most excellent friend, that in many of the expeditions from the U.S. to this Country there are old mothers & fathers at the head of Large famileys of Children and those aged persons' Constitution generly broken down. After arriveing they Like a butterfly flap about for a few days and then pass away leaveing there Children to the mercy and Cold Chariety of the Country and particular that Kind of Chariety which might be expected in a new Cuntry where things are hard and inconvenient to come at and where every one feels that he has as much as he can do to Look out for himself & family. It is true that the Law of the Land does make some provision for orphans as far as to bind them out for a term of years to persons as mechanicks, farmers, &c and whilst it should be there business & duty to Look after them and indeed it might be the duty of any one to Look after there welfare, Yet I Regret to say that it often appears to be no ones business to care for them and Thence they often drag out a most miserable existence to the Grave. Cannot Something be done in these ends of the earth? Is there not another John Steavens in the Land whom God has caused the Tide of fortune to flow upon?[1] And who is willing, nay anxious, to bestow a part of it in some way that will redound to the honour and glory of God, the Giver? I sincerely hope that one may be found. It is not uncommon to see Boys and Girls in our streets running at Large haveing no particular home and no one to Look after them, and thence they Learn to pilfer and often become Candidates for the Jail. Alms Houses are most usefull and most beneficial institutions in all Countrys where money is plenty and Chariety abounds. And would it not be more usefull in a new Country where money is scarce and few persons that are able to bestow half the Chariety that is really needed & desirous? I do not wish by this to be understood that the Country is unfavourable to prosperity and happiness. My opinion in regard to the Country is an exalted one. Both in regard to the healthiness of it and general benefits it affoards to man kind. It is a Land of Cooling Brooks and Sunny plains where the melody of Birds are sweet and where the Leaves are always green, a Land that will aboundantly satisfy the Husbandman for his toils. But there are many that are coming to our shores year after year that after the C. Society have taken care of them for six months and they then being bereft of there only guide it is then they need to have a place where they may still be cared for and guided in the way that they should go that when they gets older they might not depart from it. The good people of America have done much for us in Endeavouring to build us up as a Christian nation in Africa and I feel asured that the hearts of many of the Philanthropy of your highly favoured Land still yearns for our present and future good. I beg that you will give this matter a more carefull consideration. Should there be anything worthy of your notice; if not, Let it fall to the ground. As the M. C. S[tevens] is to sail on tomorrow I have not time to say any more at this time.

Your two Last Letters came safely to hand which affoarded me great pleasure to here from yourself & family and of our friends at Arlington though very sorry to here that Mrs. Lee is still suffering from Rheumatism. Please write often, in haste, W. C. B.

My family is in pretty good health, hopeing that yourself and family are in the full enjoyment of health & happiness, I have the honor to remain as ever your humble & ob't sv't. Wm. C. Burke

Just after finishing this Letter my Lamp turned over, which will account for its appearance.

183 / WILLIAM C. BURKE TO RALPH R. GURLEY

Rev'd R. R. Gurley Clay Ashland, Aug 22nd, 1857

Very dear sir: The M. C. Stevens is now ready to sail for the united states, much sooner than I expected and I have only time to drop you a few Lines to thank you for your Kind remembrance of me in sending me that useful Book by Mr. A. D. Wilson and for your favour by the M. C. Stevens. I had quite a long talk with Mr. Wilson, he telling me of meeting with you and talking over matters and things in regard to Liberia. He Looks remarkable well. There seem to be a good many persons going back in the fine fast sailing ship. I should have no objection to takeing a trip in her myself if I could effect anything by so doing. I have not been very well during this rainy season, being Troubled with chills & fevers. My youngest child continues quite feable. The rest of my family are pretty well. It has been very cool here during this rainey season. Times have been extremely hard for some time pass; indeed quite a famine. But things are now much better. The rice crop is now being harvested and the natives are bringing it in in small quantities. Remember us Kindly to your family and except the Kindest regards of myself and wife for yourself. From yrs. Wm. C. Burke

184 / WILLIAM C. BURKE TO RALPH R. GURLEY

Rev'd R. R. Gurley Clay Ashland, January 29th, 1858

Reverend & Dear Sir: It is with much pleasure that I am now seated for the purpose of acknowledging the recept of your kind letter by the M. C. S[tevens] telling me of many things of interest. The death of Mr. Custis though might have been expected from old age. Yet it must have been quite a shock.[1] He lived 7 years beyond his allotted time and I have no doubt enjoyed as much of this Lief as any man ever did, so fare as health, food & raiment is intended to make one comfortable & happy. But my Idea is that it requires more than all these to make a man truly happy in this Lief and if we would be happy in the world to come we must have a foretast of it in this Lief. In regard to his making a will Concerning his servants, He certainly has done so to my Knowledge. The summer he went to the north before going he went to Wash[ington] and had it written, brought it home in a small box and gave it to Daniel charging him to be very carefull to put it in the Bank for every thing as regard him or us depended on that.[2] In his Lief time he has talk a great deal with me in regard to his servants particular those at the White House and I have always been impressed from what he said that he intended at his death for all of his servants to be free and to go to Liberia.[3] However, I have no doubt but that it will be attended to in a proper time. Should they be coming over to this Country at any future time I could wish to come over previous to their Leaving for this Country as I well know that I could be of great service in prepareing them for the voyage as well as for there settlement in this Country. (But this is only a thought.)

The half barrel of Pork which you spoke of in your letter I have never been able to get in Consequence of not geting an order from Mr. McLane or Mr. Dennis. It would have been and still will be a most acceptable present as I have had to give 28 cts per lb. for pork. Times is still very hard in Liberia as regards money and other Provisions. I have at this time and have had for some months pass a plenty of Tania an excellent bread stuff raised by myself. I expect another year to have more than my family Consisting of eleven Can destroy. I have some native children in my family which I am trying to Civilize and Christianize so if possible to do something for the heathen around us and it seems that this is the best method to take as this way has been the most successfull way. You will no doubt be happy to Learn by this that during our association in December I was set apart for the ministry by the Laying on of the hands of the Presbytery. Our Little Church is still increasing in number and I hope in true piety. But now our house of worship is become two small for our Congregation and what shall we do? This we will do (the Lord being our helper), we will pull down our small house and build a greater one. But how shall this be done without money? We intend doing all we can our selves and then trust that the Lord will enable us to go on to Completion. A wood house being so perishable in this Country we have thought it best to try and build a brick house and we are now makeing bricks and geting wood to burn them whilst others are geting Timber and other materials necessary for the building. But after doing to the utmost of our ability we do not expect to be able to go on to Completion without the aid of our friends in the Land of our nativity. Therefore, my most excellent friend, any thing that you can directly or indirectly do for this object will be thankfully received and aplied. I have written to Richmond and Baltimore upon this matter and however Little may be raised it will help to some extent. In regard to the Little box which you spoke of in your Letter, nothing will give me more pleasure than to have you one made and sent as soon as possible. I might have sent it by this trip of the M. C. Stevens But I could not bear the idea of sending it empty and knowing how fond you are of Coffee I spoke to Mr. Thomas More of Grand Bassa to let me have enough to fill it as the best Coffee is raised in Bassa City. We have a very fine son 4 months old and our Little Girl who have been sick so Long is now quite well & walking. Rose with myself and all the family with some slight exception are enjoying pretty good health. Rose desires to be Remembered kindly to Mrs. Gurley & family. You will please except of my highest regard for yourself & family and believe me always your greatful serv't.   Wm. C. Burke

185 / WILLIAM C. BURKE TO RALPH R. GURLEY

Rev'd R. R. Gurley   Clay Ashland, Liberia, West Coast of Africa,
                                                    July 26, 1858

Reverend & Dear Sir: The good old Ship M. C. Stevens arrived in our port on the 13th of June some two weeks sooner than she expected bringing me your Kind Letter which as usual affords me much pleasure in hearing from you and many others in the land of my nativity. I also received with much Comfort the 1/2 bbl of nice Bacon you was so kind as to send me. It came at a most exceptable time as Bacon were selling in Clay Ashland just before the arrival of the Stevens as high as 37 1/2 cts per lb. You will please except of my wife's sincere thanks together with my own for such an exceptable present. I also received some Nos. of the African Repository all of which I feel greatfull to you for. You did not publish the Letter of mine on the subject of Alms House. Though I have no doubt but that you had good reasons for not doing so, I thought perhaps you would have published an extract from it. You can publish too any times any Letter or extract of any Letter that I may at any time write to you that you may in your good Judgement deem proper. I was mortified & disapointed at not getting a single Line from any one at Arlington and but for the Little information you gave me in regard to the health of Mrs. Lee I should not have known any thing. I am happy to Learn by the papers &c that all of Mr. Custis's servants are to get there freedom within the next five years. I sincerely hope that many of them may be able to better there Conditions. In regard to there coming to Africa and in regard to Looking out for a healthy region of Country for them and in useing my influence to induce them to find there homes in Africa must be a matter for future Consideration. I would Like first to know if it was the will of the Testator that they should come to Africa and what is to be there outfit &c. A people coming to Africa Totally unprepared in body & in mind Cannot be expected to do very well. Should Mr. Custis's will be published will you be so kind as to send me a copy? Mr. Wm. Fitzhugh's people of whom you spoke of were Liberated on very favorable terms to come to Africa haveing 2 years to prepare there minds & there Bodys for freedom and if true, as I always heard, that they were to have if they came to Africa 50 Dollars in hands young & old at the time of there embarka[t]ion which some would have given to the heads of those having Large familys an amount sufficient to have established them quite Comfortable in Africa and it is my firm belief that many of them might have come to Africa under those favourable Circumstances and have done well.[1] In regard to the Arlington people of whom as you know I have many near relatives and those of the White House of whom I Lived with for ten years, I hold myself ready & willing to do anything and everything for there advantage that I can do Consistantly. Mr. [A. D.] Cowan brought out two Little Cottage Receptacles and have had them placed about 2 miles just behind Clay-Ashland.[2] The Country still farther back is quite mountainous and I have no doubt but that it is also quite healthy. I could wish that we could get several Thousand of the right sort of emigrants to settle back of us. Observation and experience have taught me since I have been Liveing in Liberia that it is fare better to settle the people together as much as possible so as to have strength amongst themselves sufficient to make such improvements as is really necessary for the Comfort of the people such as opening roads and keeping them in a passable Condition and makeing Bridges across the Little Creeks, &c. The best Bridge perhaps in Liberia is in this settlement and one of the reasons is that we are the strongest in number. I believe that all the emigrants by the Last trip of the M. C. Stevens have gone out to Carysburg. The weather was most favourable for there going out. The rains are very much behind the usual time this year. Up to this date we have had very Little rain and the St. Paul's have not risen hardly any to be perceived. The seasons in Africa as well as in America are Continually changeing. I am truly happy to Learn by your Letter and papers sent me that there is such a wonderful display of God's power & Grace felt and seen throughout the united states and since it is so universely I sincerely trust that the power of sin and satan may be so destroyed that the kingdom of our Lord and his Christ may be built up in every part of the Land. The churches every where in Liberia are in a rather cold state. I sincerely hope and trust that a Cloud may rise for good in this our barren Land and a gracious shower of God's Grace may be poured out on all of our churches and many may be brought into the fold of Christ such as eternally shall be saved. Many matters Continues very hard throughout Liberia and I am at a Lost to know what we shall have to resort to at Last as money is the grand pendulum that puts in motion and keeps in motion the machinery in which we are all engaged in and for the want of it almost every thing is at a stand still. Our Government have been Lately thrown into a state of excitement and trouble by a French ship purporting to be an emigrant ship seeking emigrants for the Island of Burbon which ship is a Slaver to all intents and purposes.[3] She has been runing up and down the Coast for some time and I have no doubt that that she has done a good business in the Slave trade. Nevertheless the Great King who rules upon earth among the children of men seems to be overruling the Cunning Craftiness of man that there sins may find them out. I have no doubt but that you have heard all about it before this time yet I thought it would not be amiss to give you a full out Lines as they have come to my knowledge. The matter have been examined Carefully in our Court and the natives say that they were sold by the Chieffs and Carried on board the ship in sticks, ropes and in Irons against there will and all the men say 25 to 30 were put below and kept in sticks & Irons. Those answering by the names of boys, say from 18 to 20 [years of] age, were permited to go Loose on decks. The ship was Lying of[f] Cape Mount when the mutiny arose, the Captain being on shore with some of his officers Looking out for more Slaves. The natives say that one of them went to the Cook house to Light his pipe when the Cook Cut him with a knife after which one of the crew stabed a native man from which he died instandly. The natives said one to the other what does this mean? Did they not tell us that they bought us to work And now they are about to kill us. Let us fight with sticks of wood, blain [belaying] pens and anything we can get hold of. The Crew seem to be aware that they intend to fight in there defense. They immediately shot down seventeen of the poor natives at which time the fight became general. Those that were below in the sticks & Irons came up and soon killed all of the Crew, threw them over board and took possession of the ship. The number of the Crew that were killed were 9. The ship was brought down to Monrovia and place in the hands of the Government. The French man of war have taken her away without Leave knowing that they were stronger than we. I sincerely hope that this may be the breaking up of this abominable slave traffic in human flesh, particularly in this disguised form. I have been quite afflicted Lately by the death of my youngest Child a very fine Little boy about nine months old. He was a most remarkable fine, Large, healthy Child. He was taken sick and died very sudently. I am not prepared to say really what his sickness was. Bishop [John] Payne of Cape Palmas was at my house a short time before his death and said that my family was the most healthiest family that he had seen in Liberia. We are all quite Complaining at this time with bad colds, the weather being very Cool and my oldest daughter Cornelia has quite a bad wound on her ankle.[4] I hope your self & family are in good health. Please remember myself & Rose Kindly to Mrs. Gurley and all of whom may enquire after us & believe me always with the highest Consideration yours Humbly & greatfully,   Wm. C. Burke

This is not good paper. I hope you may be able to understand all of it.

186 / WILLIAM C. BURKE TO WILLIAM McLAIN

Rev'd Mr. McLain   Clay Ashland, July 31st, 1858

Rev'd & Dear Sir: You will please Allow me to introduce to you a very worthy citizen of this place. Mrs. Caroline DeCounsey being unacquainted with you have requested the favour of me to give her these few Lines of introduction. Will you be so kind as to accept of her order and send the articles which she will name for which she send you a draft of Twenty five Dollars ($25) on the Episcopal Mission payable at New York. By so doing [you] will very greatly oblige her and your Humble servant,   Wm. C. Burke

187 / WILLIAM C. BURKE TO MARY C. LEE

Mrs. Mary C. Lee   Mount Rest, Clay-Ashland,
                                                               February 20th, 1859

Dear Madam: Your letters, and those of our friends at Arlington, that ought to have come by the *M. C. Stevens*, came by the *Stephen A. Benson*, that sailed from Baltimore some time after the *M. C. Stevens*. The letters did not reach me until after the *M. C. Stevens* had left for the United States. Therefore I suppose you received my letters, telling you of my disappointment in not getting a letter from you. Your letters gave us much pleasure to hear from you all once more; also to hear that you were so much better of your rheumatism. I am truly sorry to hear that you have so much unnecessary trouble in regard to the expected freedom of the servants.[1] They will all find that at the end of their time that many of them will not then be prepared for freedom. There are many out here who are getting on poorly because they have no one to act for them, and they are totally unable to act for themselves. I sincerely hope that those of our friends and relatives who expect to be free, will embrace every opportunity of improving their minds and preparing themselves in every way to act for themselves. Should any of them ever come out here, I shall be most happy to do whatever may be in my power to help them along.

In regard to the country, of which you spoke in your letter, wishing to know my opinion in regard to its prospects, &c.; my opinion is that it is a glorious country, one that God has blessed to its inhabitants. Though, like Canaan of old, it is not free from famine, war, sickness and death, and other troubles incidental to mankind. In regard to the healthfulness of the country, I think it will compare favorably with any other part of the habitable world.

I have now been living in Africa for a little more than five years; you will doubtless allow that to be time sufficient for one to form an opinion. My experience and observations is the ground upon which I form my opinion. Upon the whole, we have enjoyed most excellent health for the last five years. The aboriginees of the country are the most healthy people to be found anywhere in the world. I do not pretend to say, nor would I imply, that one can get every comfort in Africa that they can get in America; far from it. Persons coming to Africa should remember that it is a new country, and everything has to be created, and they should naturally expect to find things inconvenient and uphill. The country has the elements within it to give to man everything that he could possibly wish, but as yet its resources have not been developed, and persons coming to Africa should expect to go through many hardships, such as are common to the first settlement in any new country. I expected it, and was not disappointed nor discouraged at anything that I met with; and so far from being dissatisfied with the country, I bless the Lord that ever my lot was cast in this part of the earth. The Lord has blessed me abundantly since my residence in Africa for which I feel that I can never be sufficiently thankful.

In regard to Careysburg, of which you mentioned in your letter, I have no doubt but that you have a better opinion of it than I have, from all that you have seen published concerning its healthfulness, &c. I have traveled for many miles about Careysburg, and do not see why it should be more healthy than anywhere else. The hill or mountain on which they first settled, is quite high; but that is very small, and the country all around it is very low, and wet during the rainy season; and besides it is not far enough in the interior to make any difference. By a late survey it is only found to be eleven miles from the St. Paul's River, and about as far from the sea as Millsburg. The first emigrants sent there got through with but a slight mortality; but the trial was by no means a fair one, compared with emigrants sent to other places. The Rev. Mr. Seys, from Baltimore, went out there with them, and continued with them during their acclimation, and did not suffer them to want for anything necessary for them.[2] The last emigrants sent there have not done so well. My opinion is that emigrants would do pretty well anywhere in Liberia with the same attention they had at Careysburg.

Our climate, as a general thing is quite pleasant, the weather never so warm as the warmest weather in the United States, and of course never so cold. Our mornings and evenings at this season of the year are quite cool, and remind us very much of September and October in America. Our water is very cool and pleasant, much better than the water in America, without the use of ice in summer. Fowls of almost every kind thrive well in Liberia, particularly chickens; also cows, sheep and goats; hogs do not thrive so well; they grow fast and get very fat with what they pick up about the yard, but when about half grown they die off from causes unknown. We might have a plenty of sheep, goats and cows, if we had fences which we might have. I have a very fine cow and calf, which Rose is quite proud of; she furnishes us with milk and butter, besides we sell a little milk every day. Cows in Africa, as a general thing, give very little milk, but a great deal is owing to the management of them. I have quite a number of hens and chickens, vegetables, fruits, &c., and upon the whole I feel quite comfortable upon "Mount Rest." I am very much engaged, having to rise early in the morning, shoemaking or at work about my garden until nine o'clock, open school and teach until two o'clock, then shoemake or do something about the place, then try and study at night by a dim palm oil light. On Sundays I teach Sabbath school once, and try to preach twice. Thus you see that my time is pretty well employed.

I shall write to my friends and relations at Arlington, not to advise them to come to Africa when they may have it in their power to do so, but to tell them that it is a fine country, a goodly land, and if they like what I like, and can be satisfied with what satisfies me, they will never have cause to regret having come to Africa. Many have come to this country through the advice and persuasion of their friends living out here, when they have become so dissatisfied that they were no comfort to their friends nor themselves, until finally they would manage to get back to the United States. Seeing so much of this, forbids me ever from advising any one to come to Africa. Every one that comes to Africa should be a volunteer, determined to take everything just as they find it, and be satisfied.

This is now the dry season, and may be considered our summer, so far as being the warmest part of the year, but it also corresponds to our winter, the grass being dried up by the hot sun and the absence of rain, the trees also shedding their leaves. This is the great farming time with all that farm in this country. The natives are very busy cutting down the bush and burning off their lands, preparing for sowing rice in March. They leave their towns early in the morning—men, women and children, leaving a few old women to take care of the town, and straightway they go to their farm lands, carrying their pots, &c., to cook in; at night they return to their towns, often bringing with them jugs of palm wine, which after supper they drink, get a little drunk, sing, dance, beat drums, &c., until midnight, then retire to rest. I have slept in their towns frequently, and have often drank of their wine, and thought it very good.

I have tried in vain to crowd in this sheet of paper all that I want to say; and finding it impossible, I shall be obliged to add another half sheet, hoping you may be able to understand it all. I have heard you say that you did not like to get short letters from a distant place.

In regard to vegetables, those that we have in the United States do not thrive so well in Africa, with the exception of sweet potatoes; they grow in abundance, and are quite as good as they are in America. Lima beans thrive very well, the first time they are planted from fresh seed brought from America. We have a vegetable known by the name of eddoe, or tania, very much like our Irish potato, a very excellent breadstuff. I raise a quantity of them, which my family live upon, they being very wholesome. Bread stuff can certainly be raised much easier in this country than in America, as there is nothing to be done, as a general thing, after planting until gathering time, with the exception of rice, which has to be watched by boys to prevent the little rice birds from destroying it.

Please remember us kindly to your young gentlemen and young ladies—which I suppose they must nearly all be by this time. Please, also, write often, and tell us all the news; and be kind enough to inform us what has become of Mr. Williams' people. Our friends write us but little news. Your humble servant, Wm. C. Burke

188 / ROSABELLA BURKE TO MARY C. LEE

[February 20, 1859]

My dear Madam: William has written you quite a long letter, yet I thought I could not let this opportunity pass without writing you a few lines to inform you something in regard to myself and family.

I am at the time, and nearly at all times, in the enjoyment of most excellent health. My children are as fat as pigs. Granderson is nearly as broad as he is long; Cornelia is not tall for her age but is quite stout. Alexander has begun to grow a little, though he is quite small for his age. They are all going to school and seem to be learning quite fast. Little Martha does not go to day school but is very fond of going to Sunday school; she can say some of her A, B, C's; she has got entirely over all her sickness.

You could hardly believe how cool it is in Africa; it is equal to the coolest October nights and mornings in America; we can hardly keep warm in bed at night.

In the morning I get up early to milk my cow, feed my chickens, &c. The last time I churned I had to put warm water in the churn to make the butter come.

I have thought and dreamt much about you lately. I hope you have got over your rheumatism and the many troubles which you spoke of in your last letter.

Please remember me particularly to all of your children, and to Mr. Lee. I often think of them all. Please give my love to Mary Ann and tell her for me that she must try and behave herself, that it will be for her good in the end. When you write please let me know something about Catherine and Agnes.[1] Remember me kindly to Aunt Eleanor; tell her that I love Africa, and would not exchange it for America. What has become of Julian? when you write, please tell me all you know about father; he never will write to me. I would write more, but have no room. Yours humbly,

Rosebell Burke

189 / WILLIAM C. BURKE TO RALPH R. GURLEY

Clay-Ashland, Liberia, February 20, 1859

I rejoice that an opportunity offers that I may address you a few lines, in answer to your kind favor received by the M. C. Stevens. I am always delighted to hear from you, and whenever there is an arrival I am expecting a letter from you.

This leaves myself and family in pretty good health. My health and that of my family, are generally good, quite as good as it was in America.

The season has been very cool and dry up to this date; the showers will however soon commence. Every body seems to be busy cutting off and preparing their farms for planting in March. The natives in this county may by no means be called a lazy people, for they work very hard at some seasons of the year. We have a company of emigrants from Cambridge, Mass., who have taken quarters back of us in the little cottage receptacle brought out by Mr. Cowan; they expect to settle back of us, somewhere in the vicinity of the Receptacles. They are a promising set of emigrants, and will become useful citizens. I sincerely hope they may do well, as much depends upon their reports in regard to many of their friends coming from the North: such emigrants as those we need to build up the country. There has been but little mortality among them up to the present time—only two old women have died.   [Wm. C. Burke]

Rev'd R. R. Gurley   Clay Ashland, August 24, 1859

My Dear Friend & Brother: The Stevens is here on her way to the U.S. much sooner than I had expected. I cannot fail however to drop you a few lines in answer to your kind favour of the 9th of May. Myself & wife feel sorry to hear that Mrs. Gurley's health have been so feeble for so long a time. I sincerely hope that ere this time she have entirely recovered her usual health. You never mention Wm. or your Daughter. What have become of them? This leaves myself & family in pretty good health at present though we have suffered a little from chills & fever during this rainy season. My wife have a fine daughter two months old, the 3rd one born in Africa. I have now five children Liveing and five dead. I have now been liveing in Africa for almost six years and I am happy to be able to say that I have never for one moment regreted of having come to Africa. We are certainly improveing in our little Town. We have quite a herd of fine Cattle in our little Town, some of them fine milch cows, besides a number of fine sheep. The women have Commenced spining and weaveing; several Looms are in operation and during the Last year some very excellent Cotton Cloth were manufactured by them. One of our Citizens that came out when I did have grown Tobacco and have made segars for which he received a premium at our last National fare. Hogs do not thrive as well as we could wish, that is to say they die when about half grown from Causes not exactly known. Yet we often kill fine fat shotes weighing from 75 to 100 lbs. In regard to agricultural operations I am happy to be able to say that it seems to be improveing daily. There are two steam sugar mills in operation besides four other to go by hands or oxen. I have not said anything on this subject before because I fear I am afraid always of haveing two much Colour in the brush. But for the last few years there seems to be such a spirit of farming manifested by nearly all of our citizens on the St. Paul's River that I think I can safely conclude that in a few more years sugar and Coffee will be raised in such quantities as will greatly increase the prosperity of our Citizens. Besides these articles of expotation there are others such as ground nuts, ginger, arrowroot, &c, &c. [that] will also be raised as soon as a place is established to purchase it and pay cash for it, and will buy from 1 pound to 100 pounds.

You will I have no doubt be pleased to learn by the united effort of my little church and with the assistance of $200 kindly given to us by the suthern Baptist Board and $129 by our tried and indefatigable friend Mr. Wm. Crane of Baltimore we have been able to erect a brick edifice 38 by 28 (walls 15 ft. high) with plank floor and a full set of benches & pulpit and are now useing it for worship. During the approaching dry season we want to plaster the walls and Ceil the roof. We are now fixing up a small steeple to place a nice little Bell just sent out [as] a present from Mr. Wm. Crane of Baltimore. I believe I wrote you in my other letter of the death of Rev. John Day. Since then our esteemed John H. Cheeseman of Bassa with several others found a watery grave while crossing the river at Bassa.[1] Mr. Cheeseman is truly a lost to Both church and state. I received with pleasure the Book you sent and will read it with interest. You will please except of my thanks for your kind expressions in regard to the matter I wrote to you about. My wife joins me in the kindest remembrance to yourself & family and believe me as ever your Humble & greatful friend & Brother,   Wm. C. Burke

191 / WILLIAM C. BURKE TO RALPH R. GURLEY

Revd R. R. Gurley   Clay Ashland, Jan., 1860

My Dear friend & Brother: I received your kind letter by the M. C. Stevens and the nice half barrel of Pork you kindly sent me. You will please except of my thanks together with my wife's for such an exceptable present. I gave, according to your request, 8 lbs to Mrs. Ricks for which she was much delighted at your kind remembrance of her.[1] I am sorry to hear that Mrs. Gurley's health Continues so feeble. Myself and family Continues to enjoy good health. Our Government seems to be getting on quietly. The College of which there have been so much Controversey about is now I believe entirely at rest and the building is now to be erected at Monrovia. Should the White House & Arlington people ever come out here in a large number I should like to be an especial agent for them and establish them some five or ten miles back of this place where the Country is most beautifull, Calling the place Custisburg. In traveling back in this beautifull Country for some miles these things come to my mind and I speak of them to you only. I sincerely hope that the large debt to be paid by the estate may be satisfied and the servants may get there freedom at the expected time. The people seem to be quite busy up and down the St. Paul's grinding their cane, making there sugar, picking there Coffee and many of them are makeing bricks to build with, finding that wood houses will not last.

What have become of your son William and your oldest daughter? You never mention them. The saw mill at Junk owned by Messrs Payne & Yates is doing quite a profatable business furnishing lumber to almost every body that wants it and very excellent lumber. The saw mill at Buchanan, Grand Bassa, is gone to reck. I spoke to the President about it and he told me that so many persons owned a part in the mill that it being everybody's business to look after it that it turned out to be no body's business and thus the whole things has gone to destruction. I think it is a pity as there is so much timber on those rivers to get for many years. Please remember me kindly to all of whom may enquire after me, and believe me as ever your Humble & greatful friend & Brother,

Wm. C. Burke

192 / WILLIAM C. BURKE TO WILLIAM McLAIN

Rev'd Wm. McLain   Clay Ashland, Jan 24, 1860

Dear Sir: I received your letter by the M. C. Stevens with the half barrel of pork you sent me by the request of Mrs. Gurley. All came safely to hand and in good order for which you will please except my thanks. This leaves myself & family in pretty good health and doing as well as we could expect, though not as well as we could wish. Hopeing that yourself and family are enjoying the blessing of good health, I remain your humble servant,   Wm. C. Burke

193 / WILLIAM C. BURKE TO RALPH R. GURLEY

Rev'd R. R. Gurley   Clay Ashland, Aug. 31st, 1860

Rev. & Dear Sir: The Stephen Benson expects to sail for the United States tomorrow. And as I failed to answer your kind favour by the M. C. Stevens on her return to the United States I thought I would now avail myself of the opportunity of doing so. I have just returned home from Monrovia where I have been sitting on a Committee for the distribution of over fifteen hundred Africans of the Congo tribe taken from the ship Mountain King and Era. I have never witnessed such a sight in all my lief. The horrors of the slave trade is more than I can find language to express. We have endevord to put them out with such persons as we have Confidence in that they will do them good. I have taken some of them myself which I trust my lief may be spared to Civilize and christianize.

The ship Lake shore has just arrived from the United States with recaptives. She had not anchord before I left, therefor I could not learn any thing particular in regard to her. As the Marion leaves this port for the United States tomorrow you will doubtless hear all about it.

I received the Book you kindly sent me by the M. C. Stevens published by Mrs. Lee, which I shall read with much interest. Please remember me kindly to Mrs. Lee when you see her and tell her that I have not received a line from her for more than a year nor any of my friends at Arlington.

Rose desires to be remembered kindly to Mrs. Gurley and hopes her health has improved. There is nothing else of interest that I could communicate at this time. We are getting along quietly and prosperously in our little republic. This leaves myself & family in the enjoyment of prity good health. In haste your humble servant,   Wm. C. Burke.

194 / WILLIAM C. BURKE TO RALPH R. GURLEY

Rev. R. R. Gurley   Clay Ashland, Sep. 23rd, 1861

Esteemed friend: The Steavens not comeing out as usual makes it appear a very long time since I heard from you. I hope however that yourself & family are in the enjoyment of good health and I wish that I could say happiness but I know that it would be vain to suppose that you were in a state of happiness in the present unsettled and distracted condition of your country and although we are fare of[f] in the eastern world yet it being the home of our youth and the land of our nativity, we feel deeply interested and our prayer to God is that he would interpose in this great strife and cause peace once more to be proclaimed. This must be the severest affliction that have ever visited the people of the U.S. and must be a sorce of great inconvenience & suffering and although we are seperated from the sean by the Atlantic yet we feel sadly the effects of it in this country. The Steavens not coming out as usual was a great disappointment and loss to many in this country. But while these troubles & afflictions are abroad in your land we are by no means free from them on this side of the great waters. Just last year we had to go to war with the natives and although our loss was small everything considered, yet we being few in numbers feel the loss very much. We loss some very useful men out of this little town. A short time since our Government Captured a Spanish Slaver a short distance above Capt Mt. but could not get her out of the river. The English hearing of it, came down and destroyed the vessel. The Spanish knew that the English were sufficiently strong for them and supposeing that we were few & feeble came in our Harbour to visit there revenge upon us. They fired upon our Government vessel (the Quail) and as The Lord we trust would have it, we gave them such a warm reception from the Quail and from Fort Norris that they soon steamed of[f] to parts as yet to us unknown. So you see that you are not alone in the unpleasant apprehention of war. The Number of Recaptures that have been lately brought into this Republic by the American Cruisers are now scattered almost in every family.[1] I have twelve in my family of which there [are] men, women & boys and I have the most lively hope & prospects in the most of them. They seem to be very fond of Civilization. I cannot but regard the whole matter in regard to these natives being brought among us as a wise and gracious act of Providence designing them to be a blessing to us and we a blessing to them. Our churches and sabbath schools are every sabbath crowded with them and in a few years many of them doubtless will become to know and worship the true and liveing God. Many of those that were brought here a few years ago by the ship Pons are now respectable citizens and members of the church. I could write much on this subject but I must forbare for the present. I see by the papers that a potion of the U.S. Army is stationed at Arlington. What a state of things must now exist! Please write me fully in regard to all these matters. We are all well. Rose joins me in Kind remembrance to your family and except for yourself my highest esteem & believe me aways your humble ser'vt,   Wm. C. Burke

195 / WILLIAM C. BURKE TO RALPH R. GURLEY

Clay-Ashland, Liberia, February 21, 1863.

Esteemed Friend: I received your kind favor of the 10th of November, 1862, which gave me comfort to be able to hear from you once more, and the health of your family. My own health and that of my family are very good. R[osabella] is getting quite large. I feel quite distressed at the long and continued war of the United States; we feel it very much, though far off as we are. The Southern Board has stopped all of their operations in Liberia for the last two years. We are getting along as well as might be expected, everything considered. Mr. E. Morris, from Philadelphia, has given several valuable lectures on farming operations. He has gotten a good quantity of coffee from the St. Paul's river. The attention of almost every farmer has been lately turned towards raising coffee, and I regret that they have not done so before. I am operating on a hundred acres of land, about three miles back from the river. My wish and intention is (should God permit) to plant at least twenty-five acres in coffee. Should my life be spared to see it come to perfection, I shall doubtless realize a handsome profit, and should I die before receiving the profit, it will be a good legacy for my children. I am truly glad to learn that the attention of many of our friends and relations are being turned towards Liberia. We need thousands, multiplied by thousands, to fill up and build, and cultivate this vast *waste* . In regard to the healthiness of the country, I think it will compare favorably with any other part of the known world. This may appear strange to those who have always believed that Africa's air is always filled with poisonous and deadly miasma; but my reason for so thinking are these: in the first place, we have comparatively no doctors nor medicines in this country; yet we, as a general thing, enjoy good health. For my own part and that of my family, we enjoy excellent health, as good as we could expect anywhere in the world. In regard to interior settlements, I think that persons coming from the mountains and high lands of America, would do well to go to the mountains or high lands of this country. I have just returned from my third visit to the settlement of Caryesburg, and I find that the air is very strong and bracing on the top of that mountain, much more so than on the low lands. I believe, however, that emigrants may do well in this or any settlement in Liberia, provided that they are prudent in all things, and have good attention. My opinion in regard to the healthiness of this country, I have not arrived at hastily, but it is from observations and experience of almost ten years. The country just back of Clay-Ashland is high and rolling, and the water cool, pure, and excellent; the natives strong and healthy.

The Government is just furnishing a very large and well arranged receptacle on the road to Caryesburg, about five miles from the St. Paul's river. The bridges to Caryesburg, numbering nine, are all in good order, and I could wish that they were constantly being traveled over by carts and wagons. Our election for President and Vice President will soon come on; the candidates are D. B. Warner for President; J. M. Priest of Sinoe county, for Vice President; opposition, B. J. Drayton, of Cape Palmas, for President; A. F. Johns of Monrovia, for Vice President.[1] I trust in God that the best man for the general good of the nation may be elected.

Will you, my most excellent friend, be so kind as to see or inquire about my mother, whether she is still living at Arlington, or elsewhere. I have written again and again, and have not been able to hear a single word. I must now conclude, as my paper is so bad I fear you will not be able to understand this bad writing.

Please remember us kindly to your family, and believe me, as ever, your humble and obedient servant,   Wm. C. Burke

P.S.—Rose begs that you will also be so kind as to inquire for her father.   W. C. B.

196 / WILLIAM C. BURKE TO RALPH R. GURLEY

Mount Rest, Clay-Ashland, September 29, 1863

My Most Excellent Friend: Yours of the 7th of May was duly received by the M. C. Stevens, which as usual gave me the greatest pleasure to hear from you and your family, and that you were all enjoying the blessing of good health.

You will please accept our thanks for your kind agency in looking up our relations at Arlington and elsewhere, and causing them to write to us. I was much gratified in receiving a letter from Selina [Burke's sister].

She writes me that the place abounds with contrabands.[1] I wonder if they could be persuaded to seek a home in this the land of their fathers; it seems that they must ere long find a home somewhere. We cannot but look forward to a great number of our colored friends seeking a home in this country; but we were rather discouraged in seeing such a small number come out in the last vessel. As regards the contrabands, I suppose they are waiting to hear what the Government thinks they should do. I pray that it may be their own voluntary choice to come to Africa. Many of our old settlements are going down for the want of emigrants; besides it is so necessary to build up new settlements.

The rains, which are now going off, have been very favorable. The growing crops are very promising; the rice crops are just coming in in small quantities; the coffee crop this season promises to be very good. The planting of coffee is now receiving attention from almost every farmer in Liberia. I regret, and it seems to be the regret of almost every farmer that they had not attended to planting coffee many years ago. Mr. Blackledge seems to be the only man on the St. Paul's river who has a coffee farm sufficiently large to yield him a comfortable support. I have planted a goodly number of trees this season.

The Southern board of missions have entirely abandoned their operations in Liberia. The schools and churches have all suffered in consequence of it; yet we are still going on, trusting in God for the future. There have been some intimations that the Northern board (now in a prosperous condition) will at some future day do something for Africa.

I feel quite anxious to hear of the settlement of the great difficulties now existing in the United States. My prayer is that the day for the termination of all those troubles is near at hand, even at the door. My wife joins me in the kindest remembrances of yourself and family, and believe me, Your obedient servant,   Wm. C. Burke

8/LETTERS TO OFFICIALS OF THE MARYLAND STATE AND AMERICAN COLONIZATION SOCIETIES

The first six letters of this chapter were written to officials of the Maryland State Colonization Society by blacks who were transported to Liberia under the auspices of that organization. The others, with two exceptions, were addressed to the Reverend William McLain, who in 1843 became treasurer of the American Colonization Society.

These letters provide some interesting detail on conditions in Liberia and the varied reactions of the settlers to the country of their adoption. Some correspondents asked for provisions and tools, others sought assistance in contacting former masters, and still others asked for help in obtaining emancipation of wives and children still in bondage in the United States, so that families could be united in Liberia. One man, Alex Hance, was able with the help of the Maryland State Colonization Society to return to Maryland, arrange for the emancipation of his children, and escort them to Liberia. Some correspondents complained about the failure of the sponsoring society to make adequate provision for their sustenance in Africa, but none expressed a desire to return permanently to the United States. Several expressed appreciation of the freedom that they enjoyed in Liberia. One settler wrote: "I am anxious to see my friends and relations but never wish to be unde[r] the presure and the ty[r]anny of the white man." Another directed: "If any of my friends enquire about me tell them I am under my own vine and fig tree [where] none dare molest me nor make me afraid." A third, who wrote a long letter and requested its publication, defended an agent of the American Colonization Society against charges of mistreating and defrauding the settlers. This correspondent, after citing the abundance and variety of provisions available in Liberia, added: "I can not see what a man of Coller want to go Back to the united States to Live for un Lest he has no Sol in him for Whare thire is a sine of a sole With in a man it Panc [pants] for freedom." The most interesting letters are those of Sion Harris, an articulate carpenter, remarkable for his resourcefulness and valor.[1] Almost single-handed, he repulsed a large group of hostile natives who attacked a mission station at Heddington in March 1840, and killed their chief.

The most unusual letters in the chapter are those of H. W. Ellis, who was born a slave in Virginia, grew to manhood in Tennessee, and moved to Alabama when he was about twenty-five years old. He learned to read on his own and somehow acquired a knowledge of Latin, Hebrew, and Greek. Because of his erudition he was known as the "Learned Blacksmith of the South." He became a Presbyterian preacher and his renown as a minister caused the Synod of Alabama and Mississippi to purchase him and send him to Liberia as a missionary. Accompanied by his wife and daughter, he arrived in Monrovia in March 1847. Five months later he became minister of the First Presbyterian Church of that city. He died at Cape Mount on March 8, 1870.[2]

197 / JACOB GIBSON TO JOHN H. LATROBE AND WILLIAM McKENNEY

Messers Latrobe & McKeeny[1]   Harper, Cape Palmas,
                                                   August 31st, 1833

Dear Sirs: We arriv here 23 of the present month after a pleasant voyage of 56 days. We touched at Mesurado and remained there four days. The Captain was kind to us through out the voyage & it would be well if you would employ him in future. I can say that I have realized all I expected. The soil has the appearance of being good—the climate is pleasant & altogether our prospects are flattering. We have just drawn our five acre lots & are pleased with their situation & soil. The long house which we now occupy & which has just been built, is comfortable & pleasant. My children will go to school to Mrs Wilson, it being nearer to us than the school at the Cape. We have a good church and Mr Wilson preaches for us. I will be ten thousand times obliged to you if you will make an effort to get my children freed & sent out to me. Neither of you, perhaps, know the pain which a father feels at being seperated from his own offspring. I was disappointed in [not] getting a whip saw here—they were all sold. If you will send me one by the next expedition it will be esteemed quite a favour—& a few wrought nails of a large size would be very acceptable. The whole of our company are satisfied & pleased. I hope you will go on in the work of colonitation. I look upon it as the cause of God & the hope of benighted Africa. Yours very affection-aty,   Jacob Gibson

198 / ALEXANDER HANCE TO WILLIAM McKENNEY

                     Cape Palmas, Maryland in Liberia, 19 March 1835

Mr Mc kiney, Sir: I take opertunity to write a few Lines to you hoping thay may find you well as I am unwell my self at present. Sir I want to inform you that I have found most all you made mention of Except team and that article is much wanting heare as we have no way to till the ground without them. And if you will b[u]y my children and send them to me, and if I can get team to asist me, I will pay the Board whatever expenss they go to for me for I Cannot bear the idea of Staying heare without them. For if it is ten or twelve years to com I will go Back Again to them.

But if I can get them out heare I dont think I Ever Shall return again thar to Live. I met with a Lost [loss] coming out hear. I had my Looking glass broke and also my teaketle, and have Lost my keys Since [I have] Been heare. I have sent my 2 Locks to you for to get keys to fit them and also I want you Send me one trunk Lock if you pleas and pleas to Send me a bed tick, as I have non and nothing to make one With, and aney other nesarys that you think proper, such as a Litle molases and flour and So on, as I Shall be of[f] the colony and nothing to Subsist of. And pleas to send me some Shirting Coton and 2 Handkercheefs if you pleas. Those articles that you send to me, put my name on them. I want you [to] write word whether or not you can get my children and be [sure] to not disapoint me in that. My Love to all my freinds and acquaintances. I feel destinated to meet them on the banks of deliverence Where parting Will be no more. And all those that weants to come out must come as I did, especily those that have children and want them to be any thing, they better Come out hear. I want you [to] take it in consideration amongst you Selvs that 6 months rations is not Long enough for Emagrants Coming to this Country. We will have to go in debt and no way to get out. I Want you to Send me out Some Leather and Salt and tools if you pleas. I Remain your,   Alexander Hance

199 / ALEXANDER HANCE TO WILLIAM McKENNEY

Harper, August 30, 1835

Dear sir: I Recived your letter on the 24 nst [instant] and was glad to Recevie your restructions Concerning obediance knowing that it was my responsible duty to be obedient to God and man. I did state to Mr gould that things was not hear as you tole us. I also think that six months is not long anough to find [furnish] any person here thats not got means to start with. My greatest grevence was that I had to go in debt and no way to pay it hear. [There] ar some that are not able to live hear without asistance, for inst there's Mary Watkins. I Recived the clothing that you sent and I believe that thay all were thankful for them as thay needed them very much. I want you to send me the shoe tools & leather what you promste me that you would send me. We are most all out on our farms with the exceptions of a few & I think with a little asistance thay will get along.

My love to you & all & family and all my frends both white and colerd and tell the colerd people this is thare home. I want you to try and do all you can towards geting my children. No more But Remane yors forever,

Alexander Hance

200 / ALEXANDER HANCE TO J. H. B. LATROBE

J. H. B. Latrobe Esq.   Cape Palmas, April 7, 1838

Dear Sir: I embrace the opportunity thus afforded to rehearse a few lines in your hearing by which you will be informed of the present situation of the colony which at this time is far different to what it was when I left here for america. On my return it had altered so much that it really astonished me to see it in that time how the colony had fallen from its former prospects. And it now is in quite abad sutuation both in regard to provisions & Government.

The new Emigrants that came out with me are now on quite a small allowance. They only get one pint Rice per Day & the other part of Bread stuff they get in tobacco which is by no means sufficient to support people in as sickly a condition as they are. Some of them the reason they are now put on that small allowans is because there was not a sufficient quantity sent out for them & the natives themselves are rather Put to it for provisions. The Tobacco they can get nothing for as the natives charge whatever price they chose for their articles and they have by that obtained a sufficient quantity of Tobacco to last them untill the next season. Rice is now one dollar per croo & when I left There it was only fifty cents. If this continues we will suffer considerably from the consequences. One fact is this: the natives do not like to be governed by a colored Man and they do just as they please almost. When I saw you personally I endeavored to explain to you as much as [was] in my power & Just as I stated to you so it is. We want aid. If there is any thing to be done without, we are nerely done [in] some r[e]spects.

The agent & selectmen examined the public school kept by Capt. O. A. Chambers & think it in quite a flourishing State. If we had aid it would not be long before we would regain our for[mer] standing & I do sincerely hope that help will be given us, as I know you feel a deep intrest in [the] welfare of the colony & will lend all the assistance in your power. The colonist generally are very much disatisfied especially the new emigrants. They are all extremely so. I regret my trop [trip] to America, for the new emigrants connected with some of the old colonist would deprive me of my existance were it in their power. They have raised a great many false reports about me & have attempted to excommunicated me from the church. I hope that you will make it know that I am not as they reported me to be. I am with the Utmost Respect, Your Obt Sevt.

Alx Hance

P.S. Everything is double the price Just 100 per cent higher than it was when I left. My family are in tolerable good health except one daughter who is not quite over the fever. I return my sincere thanks to you for your trouble and the rest of your colleagues. I would be very well satisfied was not every thing so dear.

201 / PAUL F. LANSAY TO JOHN H. B. LATROBE

Cape Palmas, Jany 16th, 1839

Dear Sir: I have taken this opportunity according to promise of writing you a few lines hoping it may find you as it leaves me at present in expressing myself to you. I can But Say I do feel myself verry happy that my lot has fell were [where] it is. But in one thing only I can Say that I am not Satisfied in that is my wife and children that I have left behind me being Slave as I was but hav not the chance that I had of geting their freedom. There is one thing I should like you to write me about, that is if I Could not make it convenient for me to come over next fall to See if I could not do something for them. Perhaps with a few friend I may be the means of getting them out of bondage by next fall expedition. I Shall try to return to america by your permission to See if I can do So. I have got my farm partly cleared down and my house twenty by twenty six almost finished and I hope that next time you hear from me I shall be able to tell you more about africa. I should be glad if you could make it convenient to send me a quire of this kind of paper that I write to you on and if any of my friends enquire about me tell them I am under my own vine and fig tree [and] none dare molest nor make me afraid and doing well as I can expect. Father and mother and sister give their love to you and all of your family. Remember me to Mr Kennard and Mr Mason also. Dont fail to answer this Letter if it is convenient for you to do so and you will oblige yours While I Reman, Yours truly,   Paul F. Lansay

202 / STEPHEN HALL TO WILLIAM McKENNEY

Mount Tubman, Cape Palmas, West Africa, May 21th, 1839

Dear Sir: I avail myself of this opportunity to let you know how I am at present. I am enjoying tolerable good health and can say that I am not subject to as many diseases as I was when I lived in America. My strenght has failed me in a great measure. As for the likeness of this place I cant say much about it at present, yet I am far better sattified to what I have been. I dont see anything to render me unhappy at present and still hopes for beter times. I wish to hear from my Master family my brothe and sisters by the next expedition for this is the fifth letter that I have writen and received no answer except two. I am anxious to see my friends and relations but never wish to be unde[r] the presure and ty[r]anny of the white man. You will pleas to let me know how many have have died out of my neighborhood and list their names if convenient. Let me know wethe Thomas Norton and Aron giles and Russle Hill, George kin and family are all well, in particular. You requested me to keep upercorespondence with you. I Should be very glad to see your face once more that I might commune with you respecting some particulars. You will pleas to send as much you can of what I wrote for before and above all thing send me a sow pig and a box of hard soap. I suppose that you will think that my request is very unreasonable. I only take you at your [word] when I was with you you told me to write for what I ever I want. I exsect to be there in years time if god spares my life.

Sepen [Stephen] Hall

203 / SION HARRIS TO SAMUEL WILKESON

Mr. S. Wilkeson,[1]   Caldwell, April 16, 1840
Washington, D.C., America

My Dear Sir: I am at present enjoying good health. My family also is well. Yours of January 31st came safe to hand stating the reception of the skins, &c., and that you ordered the things I wished, which I have not received. Since that time we have passed through various scenes and dangers helped by the providence of God. After Our removal to Heddington my wife as school teacher and I as Carpenter I built the mission houses, &c. After various t[h]reatenings from Goterah & Gatoomba the town of Heddington was attacked by about 3 or 4 hundred warriors Composed of Botswains, Mambo, Veys & Deys, headed by Goterah and 4 other warriors. They made their attack March 7, about day break. On the sixth my wife was very sick. I was up quite late until about 4 in the morning. Sleep departed from my eyes, my wife having asked me several times to lay down which finaly I did across the foot of the bed. I had hardly got down before I heard a gun fire at a half town a mile off.[2] I arose quickly & went to the window but it was too dark to shoot and at that moment I heard a voice crying War! War! is come, which proved to [be] a woman and man from the half town. I quickly called to Mr. Brown to [get] up and Load guns. He asked what was the matter. Load guns was the command. At this time two boys were dispatched to see [what they could discover] who hardly got out of the yard before they returned and said it was at town already. I snatched my gun and shot bag and hastened Down and ran in town. By the time the boys got back crying war, several picked up muskets and ran, the Headman with them. At this I cried if they did not bring back the guns, I would shoot them. At this 4 only returned. By the time I returned out of the town or from the back door I Jumped over a picket fence in the front of the Enemy on whom I poured a double load of one ounce balls and about 25 buckshot. By the time I loaded and fired the second time Brother Benny Demery, whom I had employed to assist in building at Heddington, an Elegant marksman who took his station by me in front after which a general battle commenced. After firing the third gun, I and my Colleague retreated in the front door of the mission house, before which a little storehouse was built about 10 y[ar]ds off, no kind of shelter for us whatever. Day began to break. After firing catriges at natives not 2 rods from me, taking good aim, which they returned house on the house, having called for more cartriges, now being out, I got 7 which took me about a minute and a half at which I flew from my post to a large chest in which I had six lbs of buck shot and the same quantity of powder of which I filled my large pockets and filled my bosom with too, and flew back to my post and called for catriges no more. In this time my frind had fired 12 of his own loads and 3 cartriges which he had received from Brown. The native army, or a part of it, now [tried] to get behind the church about 40 feet from the dwelling house at which I left my station and flew for the church but found it locked and the shot of the Enemy whistled by to such a degree I had to get behind a large stump from which I gave them 3 loads of 50 or 60 buck shot each, they not being more than two rods off. I then flew to my old post in the door at which time they broke through the fence and two came in, one of them a head man. Demery droped one and I the other in about a rod and a half of the door. At this time Goterah appeared B[e]llowing and roarng. Demery was out of Ammunition and both our guns empty. At this time one of the four natives that stoped in town came in shot, by name Baker, and said "Dady look." His bowels was out and he left his gun by me as I bade him go up stairs. It was loaded with 3 slugs about an inch and a half long (I had seen them the day before) made Just to fit the musket. Goterah came without fear, at which I reach for my axe at which I laid hold of Baker's loaded musket, not knowing that it was loaded, which I pointed at him and he jumped behind the kitchen, shaking, growling, bellowing, calling his men to come up, [claiming] the town was his. When he steped behind the kitchen I opened the pan and it was primed good. Fear left me. Demery cried there was the head man. Goterah returned back to the kitchen which he seized and shook with one hand and brandished a dreadful knife with the other, about six inches broad. And about a hundred and 50 men came up to the fence to whom he said, let us go in. I took deliberate aim at him (he was half bent, shaking) and brought him to the ground, cut off his knee, shot him in the lungs and cut of[f] his privets[?].[3] To this time about 6 guns had been fired from above or up stairs and ceased, Zoda [and] Nicky, the natives who fired them being shot. I thought all up stairs was dead Until I cried Brown! He answered and I asked him for God's sake to fire, at which he fired four guns and stoped. During this I had supplied Demery with buckshot and was playing with two muskets as often as I could. One was English, with a large mouth, which I used most and kept the other loaded. At this time we had to fire in order for fear they would rush up, first I and then he (and we must have been killed had it not been for the house before me and that the warriors fired at the upper window thinking our smoke came from thence). You can Judge how we were now. They came to take their warier, Goterah, 20 at the time on which we would pour loads of 50 or 60 buck shot, and they would fly, as many more come catching at him as if he were hot Iron, on whom we would pour the same compliment and open order amongst them. They would carry him a little by little which only gave our shot room to scatter. We gave them 9 or 10 shots each befor they got him & I cried Battle is done now. The head man is dead. But not so. They retreated to the Church which they wanted to shelter them from our shot. The men that took Goterah left teeth, hair, fingers and brains in abundance [?] at which I flew to my stump with two loaded muskets and they poured shot in the stump right oposite to me, one passing through my hair and I gave the fellow that done it the contents of one load in his back. When I returned back, Demery was gone and I thought he was dead. (I gave up to God and commenced firing expecting to be dead, my comrade B[rown] above not doing anything). I was soon comforted again at the return of Demery who thought they would come in town and had run to fetch his trunk. At this time a third warrior came in at the gate about twenty yds of the house, at which one of the two remaining contry men fired and shot too high which only made him growl and run, at which I took a good aim and put 32 buck shot in his cloth and 5 in his head (which cloth you will receive as I gave it to the Gov.) and sat him dow[n] against [a stump] as if he was keeping guard at which all flew. I went and asked the dead guard if he wa[s]nt gone and why he stoped, seized him by the foot and turned him over. 10 or twelve shot passed through and through the house, one close to my wife and one in 5 inches of my head. I then took my bugle, a large french horn, and blew it, which made them fly. The natives came from all quarters and said Harris is not dead, we hear his horn. The natives came and licked my feet, said i had greegree [charms] and asked me for some. I told them I had none but what God gave me. They carried off 22 dead beside their lost head man, left four dead on the ground and the wood stank in places where the wounded had died. And about 12 o'clock 15 of King Governors men followed them and found Goterah whom they had hid about 15 or 20 miles from Heddington with the other dead. They returned about sundown and wanted a headman to go cut of[f] his head, they being common men would not. About 15 American came by this from Caldwell and we started with Zodaquee, a headman, a recaptive. On the path we went about 15 miles and returned. Zodaquee went on after Goterah's head and returned saying "here is Goterah's head. You have killed him, for true. You have done this country good," and shouted. Many wished the head but I reserved it for the Governor with Greegrees, a great quantity, which I delivered to the Governor and I expect you wish them, Sir. I would have published this but Mr. Brown, who was shut up in his room somehow published, and throughout the whole action he knew nothing save the four guns he fired. I have given these facts as they were, being in front. I cannot say I was not frightened when the Alarm first came, I examined myself and saw all was right. No thought entered of leaving my wife. We all, I thought, wold die together. I did not pray while in action, only that I asked God to let the sun rise and then that the dense fog not of smoke, mite pass off.[4] The reason I write or take the privilege to do as my Father in law was acquainted with Mr. Gerly and you are the same as he and have condesended to write us. Yours, Dear Sir, in Love,   Sion Harris

P.S. I desire to go to America to see my frinds who are in East Tenasee, Knox County, and I would like your advice about it whether it would be safe or right. I have no Family but Myself and wife and [no] means to come. If you think it difficult to go to tenesee I would like to visit America anyhow, somewhere or other. I have not received what I wrote for which you Ordered which [I] need now very much, being out. I would have sent you some Curiosities worth looking at but this war and being engrossed at H[eddington] for nearly 2 months, I have not had time. I however delivered a good many fine ones to the Governor. On the return of the Saluda I will send them. I would be very glad to have a frind to exchange Curiosities with or give Curiosities for other little things because I have in my power to collect many. One reason for my asking to go see my frinds is I write and I write without answers and I have often [been] told of Mr. Gurly by My Father-in-law who was well known (George Erskine). Yours in Love,   Sion Harris

Rev Mr McClain   Cald[well], Jan. 5, 1848

Dear Sir: I write to inform you that I received your letter by the
Packet. I was glad to hear that yourself & family were well & that you
were still Stryving to help us. I might have come in the Packet But It was
the rany Season of the year. I thought It was not good to go in the winter. My health is very indifferent So I think It would help me to spend a
year in the United Stats. You know It is not easy to leave home at any
time, most perticular a farmer. As you told me what you would do I will
come provideing I can get there when the Packet returns. You know I can
do much with my Collard friends in convinceing them that Africa is there
home, the Land of our fore Fathers. I am able to do much more than I did
when I was there before. I am more experienced about Africa, more convinced that this is the Collard man's home. Therefore I could tell them
much Stronger. I know the opposition that I will meet with. I am prepared to meet them all for they have no foundation to theirs, talking
about things that cannot belong to them nor do not enjoy It. [Of] those
emegrants that the Packet brought there have been 2 deaths. Jack Myrl
from Lynchburg, he was very old. The rest of his family are well. Another freeman, Mr. Drew, that is all [who have died] as yet. There is such
a few comes I have not seen nari a load since I left, for a great many of
these that comes are my old converts. Some I converted & some I convinced befor I left. They are Still comeing yet. But I think the time is
comeing that you will not have to beg them to come. But as you stated in
your letter, the conditions that will do I will come providing I can get a
pasage in the packet when she returns to Spend one year or eighteen
months & if so, I will bid America farewell & Shall try to do all the good
I can in telling my Brethering the truth & increase our number in citizens.
You will please write to me. Inform me how times are & sending me some
papers and notice. I am yet Stryving to Serve God & in weakness to
preach the Gospel. Let me tell you how the Lord has been working in our
little number. The increase in Methodist Church this last year [is] about a
hundred & Sixty. Those last recaptured Congoes, a great number of
them that is a little good the United Stats done us. The Baptist Church
[gained] something like a hundred. I must Say the Lord is blessing us in
Liberia. Though she increases Slow in number, yet we will be a people.
Pray for us that The Lord may still bless us. Sinat & the Representatives
met yesterday. We have 2 houses now & the oath was ministered to the
President & a Salute of 24 Guns. If But Slow, we are climeing. For is It
posible that a Collard man can Say he is free in America when these
things that I see & enjoy and pertake he cannot talk about? That is the
reason they are So easy whiped in conversation. Let me ask you is Mr.

Pinny dead?¹ I cannot hear from him. If he is not dead he must be Asham to write. When the Kentucken came out he sent out a recommended woman to me by the name of Mrs. Simpson from New Orleans, Stating to me that her husband would be out in the fall, wishing that I would Keep her at my hous and that her husband would be fully able to pay when he came. I cannot hear from none. I have written until I am tired. I still have the woman. She is well and Harty, viz. Ailry Simpson. Her husband name is Samuel Simson, lives in New Orleans. If Mr. Pinny is living will you pleas to drop him a few lines for me. Inform him of the circumstances. Perhaps he has forgotten It, informing him if Mr. Simpson is not coming please Send me one hundred dol[lars] for bord and I will have no more to Say; if he dont I shall talk a plenty. I Shall Send a bill. You will do me a kindness if you will attend to this for me and write to me at any time. I have no more to say. I will come to a close. May the Lord bless you in your labour & undertaking. Give my love to your family. Is Mr. Walker dead, the young man that travild with me? I remain yours,   Sion Harris

205 / SAMUEL D. HARRIS AND POLLY D. HARRIS TO WILLIAM McLAIN

Bexley, May 3rd, 1849

Mr. McLain: I got your letter and the garden seed that you sent me by the request of Mr. G. E. Dabney. I am a thousand time Oblige to you for sending them. You say something to me in your letter about some of the persons in Lexington want to hear from me how I like this Country. I must say when I first Come out here I was well plase with this Country. It is a butifull Country, well timber with Oak and Poplar and Mangale and hickory, and timber of many kinds that i have not Spoke of. Mr. McLain, I hav not bin out here more than 2 years and a half. I have got a butifull farm Contain 10 acres of good land on St. John's River, 5 miles from the sea; I have planted a fine Crop of arrow root and ginger, 150 coffee trees, karsaders and pertaters, and a fine garden of growing vegetables, and Miss P. D. Harris have bin Blessed through the mercy of God to have bin so good to her that She have been able to rais a fine Chance of poltry, of Ducks and Chickens. Her stock have bin at first about six and have increase to 50 to 70 and 100. Still we have a fride Chicken and a Roast Duck when we feel like killin them. Enny person Can live here with their industry or his industry, but if persons Come out here they must make up their minds first that they will meet with Dificultys and trobles, for this is belong to human nature while on earth we stay. Look at the trobles the Bless Savour Borde for us while he was on earth, and all his apostles, for trobles and difficulty belong to all persons, To the Christian is trobles according to his faith, for if he or she is a Christian they must expect to meet with trial. When i come out i meet with trobles and Dificulty that i wish myself back again. When i come to reflect on the case, troble belonging to everry boddy, so i have made myself Sattisfide. Now you Coud not get me and my family to Come Back to the United States to live againe; all though we live as well as enny Coullard person in the States. Mr. G. E. Dabney and lady, Miss C. M. Dabney, treated there Servant as they live themselves, but i thank God that they was so good as to give me my family to come out here. It was one of the Bes things he ever did for me, all though he and his lady all ways was very good and kind to me, But the Best kindness he ever did for me [was] when he give me my Dear wif and five Dear little Children. Now i must bring my letter to Close. The Lord may Bless him and his Dear lady, that their live may be long upon this earth, servin God and doin all the good they Can for the Soul of man, and at last when they have don all that God have Commanded for them to do, then he will take them up to heaven with him to rest, is my pray for Christ sake. Nothing more to say, But Remain you Bro and Sister in Christ,

S D Harris, Miss P D Harris[1]

Mr. McLain, i expect to Come in the nex packet and Bring Some arrowroot and ginger of my own make since i bin out here. I want to get som gentleman in the States to take my arrowroot and ginger and Coffee that we make here and i want to make some Contracts with him so when i Send the produce he Can Send me what i want. No more to Say but Remain you[r]s truly,   S. D. Harris

I will make 400 lb ginger and 600 lb of arrowroot, one Barrel of Pepper. But when I Come in to the States i Can tell the people in Lexing[ton] all about it. Please to have part of this letter publish w[h]ich you think Best. My rice and Karsarders and pertaters will be for family use at home.

206 / SION HARRIS TO WILLIAM McLAIN

Rev'd Mr. Mclane   Cald[well], May 20, 1849

Sir: I write to inform you that I have got home Safe after 28 days and nine hours after we left Hamelton roads [Hampton Roads]. I can say that I thank God that I am at home in Africa. I found my family well. I never expect to contend with the collard man in America no more. If they come, well; if not [it is] well with me. I expect to die in Africa where the free air blows, for here are liberty. The Presadent had got home before I did. He has just come from ware from New Sess. [He] have broak up the great slave factory and liberated a great manny slaves. There was none of our men lost [and] none crippled. They burnt up a great many towns. [A] great many told me when I was in America that we could not take the Spanyards. We have got them in our town wating for tryal. It proved as in all of the wars that God is on our side & if he be for us who can be against us. We have been oppressed long enough. We mean to stand our ground & contend for our rights until we die. O if my cullarred friends would only believe and feel the love of liberty they would not stay in the United States. We are so Ignorant that they won't even believe when they see. You know well how it is. It is not worth while for me to say anything more on this. You wished me to write you how things were in your department. There is mighty great grumbling with the emigrants that went out with me. They say they can't get nothing to eat. They are all sick But have got up. They gives them no coffee, no sugar, no tea. They can't get more. They all like the contry but not the far[e]. [Of] Mrs. [Jane C.] Washington's people, Charles Starks is a smart man.[1] I believe he will work to mentain his family. I have let him have coffee an sugar occasionly. I beg him not to write to his Mistis yet. [I told him] that they would do better when Mr. Lewis comes home.[2] He is gone to the leward. Mr. [Marshall] Hoopper from North Carlina went down Saterday to see the captain to return Back. He could not get anything to eat here, a pint of meal a day. They told him they thought when Mr. Lewis came they wold give him more. He says he paid for It and wants It; if not, he will return to the United Stats. There is But one died, hellems wife from Lynchburg, Virginia.[3] I don't think any more will die with the feaver. It is a great pity that you hadent some one that feel for the emigrants & see that they were tended too. But men becomes carless. Mr. Lewis is engage in the menopolist [trade monopoly] & he is gone down the co[a]st. I am appose to It & It makes hard for the poor man. He can't get a pound of tobacco without getting a haxet [hatchet] and get a musket with his getting a box. It is only good for the merchant. I have been Elected by the people for Representative since I come home. If I live I will do all I can to brake It up. Give my love to Mrs. McLane & all the children. I have not had time to get any lemon juce yet. I will send some by the next opportunity. I got my dogs all home safe except one I lost in pasage. William Butler that left Washington, he is liveing with his cousin, the Vice President. He has had the feaver and has got up. He is well satisfied. Good by. I have no more business in America. But I will talk with you here. I will be glad to hear from you any time and thank you for a bundle of news papers. My wife [sends] respect to you, hoping you are well. She says you must send her Chrismas gift. Yours truly,   Sion Harris

Monrovia, Liberia, West Africa, November 20, 1849.

Rev. and Very Dear Sir: As I cautiously take the liberty of writing, I humbly solicit the condescension of your honor and reverence to accept a communication from a transmarine stranger; and I hope, sir, that you will take the subject, together with its circumstances, for my apology.

The subject, sir, is the College. I think, sir, that the idea of giving to Liberia a college, is one of the grandest and most wise, more fraught with the economy of universal benevolence than any idea that perhaps ever entered into the hearts of any men, in any nation. The scheme is too grand, yea, entirely too large, to have been developed in the hearts of Liberians; too high for England, and too deep for France; but just let a few of Columbia's expanding-hearted sons environ it, and it is borne aloft at once; thus a comparatively few men in America will effect more for Liberia than England, France and Russia combined! The B.F.M.P.C. [Board of Foreign Missions, Presbyterian Church] has given us a school, called the Alexander High School; this has been going on one year; they have now given an iron school-house! ("Benedic anima mea Domino! et noli oblivisei omnes ejus beneficientia.")[1] I have 16 promising students, whom I have been teaching ever since 1st January, 1849. The greater part of them have read through the Historia Sacrae, and are making rapid progress in Greek, besides other sciences; we go in school at 9, and often a half hour sooner, and we come out of school at 2 P.M., teaching generally 4 1/2 hours a day. The minds of youth in Africa are, if possible, more susceptible of literary and scientific improvement, than any other part of the world; they cannot study intensely, I think more than 7 or 8 hours in 24. They may, with a short time of intermission and recess, study 8 hours a day very profitably.

Rev. R. R. Gurley is here; he is a wonderful man; his coming to Liberia brought a general influx of joy through all the Republic. That portion of our people who are intelligent and good, who love themselves as they should, love Liberia their country. They are worthy and useful citizens, and these are they who love America! Now there is this remarkable fact about it, that those of the above named quality love America from proper motives, and for proper reasons, but would not go back there upon any terms whatsoever; but you know that we, of course, have some trifling, indolent persons here, as well as every other place, who never were, nor ever will be any important use to themselves or country; these always are murmuring and grumbling, even in America; they grumble here—yes, every place!

But, my dear sir, do not suppose that I am murmuring at, or underrating my population; very far from it, sir. I was observing how the different classes of men received Mr. Gurley; all so joyfully, but their fruitive excitement, arising from different sources, exhibited from different motives, of course produced various effects on the good man.

If you have any correspondence with Rev. John H. Gray, of Memphis, Tenn., please mention me to him, and tell me about him in, or through, whatever medium you may choose.

Our B.F.M.P.C. has a very excellent station at "Kentucky," in Africa. We have a good and useful young missionary there (H. W. Erskine). We have recently organized a Presbyterian church there; it is certainly the best place for those good people who have a disposition to make a good living by farming; even those whose means are very small, it being a beautiful and elevated site on the St. Paul's river about 12 miles from Monrovia; rich land, well-timbered, and well watered, near, and on the same side of the river with Virginia, on the opposite side from Upper Caldwell. I think this is decidedly the best place that I have yet visited, (and I have visited from Cape Mount to Cape Palmas.) Dr. J. W. Lugenbeel can tell you all about Millsburg and White Plains—a select site for extensive operations of the M.E. Mission. Now Kentucky is situate 9 miles below Millsburg, on the same great river. I wish you would inform some good people who may desire to know of the best place in Africa, here they have the most salubrious air in the day, and then, at night, we have such a cool breeze that we cannot, like many other places, sleep without cover. Here we have excellent neighbours, both Americans and natives. Here we have Virginians, Kentuckians, Tennesseeans, &c. We have (natives), Golahs; Pezzeys, Bassas, Veys and Boatswains (often called Bosons), choice people. The Methodists have a church here.

Tell them (the people who may come) that I love them as my dear countrymen, and am working and paying to provide for them. Here is a good Presbyterian church and school, plenty of rich land, good timber, and cool water! Come and be happy!

And now, that high blessings from heaven may pour down upon you, and all yours, temporally and spiritually, soul and body, in time and in eternity, is the prayer of your missionary.   H. W. Ellis

208 / SION HARRIS TO WILLIAM McLAIN

Rev'd Mclane   Cald[well], Nov. 29, 1849

Sir: I write to inform you that I and family are well. I was very glad to learn that you was well. I do not know what to tell you. But Liberia is increasing in number. Virginia an Kentucky has almost met. I means the houses. The Emegrants dies very few more. Ther [is] a great fuss about that same complaint: "I don't git my rashions." [Of Mrs.] Washington

Servant[s] that went out with me, there are 3 dead, Lewis and 2 of the children. Lewis went to sea aboard of the man a war before he had the feaver. He was there but a few days & died. Charles Stalks lost 2 children. In the family that came from Lynchburg, Helems, 2 of that number died. That is all that died out of the number that stoped with us, 30 some odd. I believe things are gitting along tolerable well. You said you was going to send me out a lemon Squeazer & I was to send you some lemon juce. I have not seen it. I am just now gitting at leasure after returning home. I am just gitting time to lay back on my Sofa and Hamack. Congress meets next week. Mr. Butler is gitting through the feaver. He is clerk on the man a war. He think of paying a visit in a few year. He is a great deal better satisfied. You will know through the Rev'd Mr. Gurly the condition of the colony. Pleas give my love to Mrs. Mclan & the children. I would have sent her a dozen bottles of Lemon juce But had not the bottles. No more at present, But remain yours,   Sion Harris

[*In same envelope*]

Mrs. S. McLan

Dear Sister: I hope you are well & children. I had some feaver after I got home, But are well. I dream of seeing you often & would like to see you. But I could not concent to come to America. My love to you & all the children. How large is John? I love him. I wish I could see him. When he grows up he must send me a present. My respects to Rev'd Mr. Mclane. Yours,   Martha A. Harris

209 / ISAAC ROBERTS TO WILLIAM McLAIN

Greenville, the County of Sinou, Apr 2, 1850

Dear Sir: I now take up my pen to address you with a few line hoping that they may find you and family enjoying good health. My self and family are now getting smart. I am now living in my own house and am well pleased with my situation. I am located not very far from the sea beach. I can stand in my house and see the british and american mana-wars passing by at sea. Our harbours are often visited with trading vessel. The palmoil trade is good business here. Our schools are tolerable. The lord's day is strictly observed by this community. Our congregation are very good although wee have no special manifestation of the spirit of grace poured down upon us yet i believe it my duty and priveliege to advance the redeemers kingdom [among the] benighted sons and daughters of africa. I have held divine services among them several times. My dwelling being very near theirs they appear glad to attend preaching at any time and as far as i can judge pays strict adherence to the word of god. Early this morning King Davis visited me. I was Just about to hold family prayer. I invited him in and he bowd with the family while at prayer. Wee are now about to erect a market w[h]ich will be a great improvement to this place. The expedition of the [barque] huma proved themselves to be vigilant men. They have cut down trees, cleared their lands, erect their houses and [are] living in them with the exception of a very few families. They have formed themselves into a military Co. They applyed to the legislature for a chart[er]. Kernel Yates was sent to examine them and gave them much credit for their improvement [in] so short a time and told them that the president was expected down in a few weeks and made no dout would grant them a chart[er]. At the expiration of a few weeks the president arrived and examined them himself and reddily granted them a chart[er]. Liberia is the home for the colered man. A few days ago the lark went down to the leeward [and] came in contack with a vessel that had violated our revenue laws by not coming to the port of entrance w[h]ich forfeited the vessel and cargo but the Capt. pleading ignorance of our laws and upon a promise that the like should [not] take place again he was let of[f] with the fine one thousand dollars. Agriculture is on the increase. I have been informed that you have received a letter to this effect that you sends too much provisions out, but take my word for it, Sir, always send as much beef and pork with all your expeditions for what is not consumed by the emigrants will always find reddy sale. Twice i have written you and received no answer. You would oblige me by sending in lue of the funds w[h]ich you have receivd for my lumber the things w[h]ich I hav prescribed in my first letter. Please send me the respository and all other papers that you can spare. I hope soon I will be able to write you more fully concerning this place. The palaver is now set with the president and the men of blue barre concerning the settleing of that place. Our climate is a most delightful one. I have never found the heat as oppressing here as in the States. In the morning wee have the land breese and in the afternoon the sea breese. No more. I remain yours with respect,   Isaac Roberts[1]

210 / H. W. ELLIS TO WILLIAM McLAIN

Monrovia, Liberia, West Africa, April 15, 1850.

Honorable and very dear Sir: Your very interesting letter of inquiry, dated July 24th, 1849, I received per Liberia Packet. Everything contained in this friendly communication was gratifying in the highest degree; and I now write in answer—which letter leaves myself and family well, and I trust that a good Providence may conduct it safe to you, and may find you and yours in the enjoyment of health and happiness. I shall try to answer your inquiries in order. And first, as regards the intellectual condition of the people, and whether they manifest much desire for intellectual improvement? And here, sir, when we bear in mind that we seldom see much exhibition of intellectual strength, in the entire absence of literature, and mental culture, I can safely affirm that Liberia, in this respect, is a grand exception; for after we shall have made an investigation of the people's general intellectual effort to honorably sustain the national position which they have been providentially called to occupy, we shall be brought perhaps to the Jews' inquiry: "How knoweth these men letters, having never learned?" Having a great love of liberty and republicanism, their national intelligence is called into exercise, and thus many show surprising mental faculties, even without any education whatever; but several of them can read and write, and but very little more; and some again, and of these a majority, that understand arithmetic, have labored to improve themselves by readng history, law, &c. Our men of the best business are chiefly of these. There are, however, a few who may, in this country, be called educated man. Some of our chief officers of government are of the latter, together with a few Gospel ministers and school teachers.

Secondly. You wish to know whether the younger portion of our community desire intellectual improvement? I answer: our youth far surpass our elder men in this trait. Our elder men are compelled to use what intellectual knowledge they have at command, without much effort for improving, only so far as this can be effected by use. Our youth think, and very correctly too, that the amount of education that the seniors generally possess is inadequate to the task before them; so that they (the youth), many of them (but not all), are using every means in their power for intellectual improvement.

Thirdly. You mentioned those who have grown up in slavery. Now, of these, strange as it may appear, many are our most useful citizens, fill high offices and places of trust faithfully, with honor to themselves, and benefit to their country. A majority of the people have been slaves.

Fourthly. What is the probable number of books in Monrovia and what their general character? A[nswer]: We have in this place four schools in all: one kept by a citizen lady (Mrs. Frances Moore); a second by or under the auspices of the M.E. Mission; a third, and by far the best preparatory school in this place, is kept by Mr. B. V. R. James under the auspices of the "Ladies Benevolent Society of New York City"; and a fourth, kept by myself, a classical or high school, supported by the "Presbyterian Board of Foreign Missions," at New York. In the first two schools they have perhaps 150 common school books; the third ("N.Y. Ladies' "), have perhaps 300 books of the best kind. There are, in all, 450 books; but our high school has a library of two thousand volumes, consisting of all kinds of books, maps, globes, a philosophical apparatus,

&c., &c. You wish to know if the citizens generally possess libraries. A: Nearly all those of Monrovia have tolerable libraries, and several have extensive libraries.

Again. What is the general capacity of children? A: The children of Liberia are exactly like those white children in America; and as this part of our community have the best opportunity to equal the corresponding part in America, their equality can be better seen, and as remarkable as this branch of society is, old persons had not the opportunity of seeing much of it where we came from, so that many think our children have more penetrating minds than those of America. This supposition arose out of the above mentioned circumstances, but it is not well founded. The fact is, if there be any difference, it is in this: perhaps the children in Liberia learn as fast, if not faster, for the first few years; but it may be that the young Americans continue their mental improvement the longest. I think, though, that there are circumstances by which we can, after awhile, better account for the facts just alluded to. I think it most probable that the "Lambs stop eating because the shepherds get out of corn!" The children stop learning, when their teacher cannot teach them any further—but this sad state of things does not exist at present.

You wished to know what would be the principal articles of commerce? A: The products of the soil, of course. But which? you may ask. I must name what have been and are now, which are these: Palm oil, camwood, ivory, &c.; but our chief dependants are sugar, arrow-root, ginger, and coffee, all of which are certain.

You inquire whether the labor of the natives of Africa could not be turned to some profitable channel? I suppose for our benefit and that of colonization. This induces me to mention a scheme, which we (not to say the Republic), an individual society, have in contemplation, and for which we implore assistance from our white friends in the south—a scheme that will facilitate the colonization enterprize, and benefit Liberia perhaps more than any thing that has been attempted in Africa. Which project is to open a road into the interior, say 150 or 200 miles at first, and extend when we can. This will ensure and secure to us the benefit of native labor. Give us access to native territory; push forward civilization; give to us their "corn and wine," their rice, their cassadas, goats, sheep, and oxen, fowls, &c., and their gold in the bargain. The advantages accruing to the natives from intercourse and trade with us would cause the slave trade to vanish like chaff before the wind.

Perhaps I have written more than you are willing to read, but I have a word of advice, and, I think, of consolation too, to my colored friends in Alabama. I am a pure and undefiled African, in every honorable sense of the word; I hope to live, labor and die in Africa; I love my color indeed and in truth; and my unadulterated friendship and gratitude to the white man of the South will endure, if possible, longer than this mortal life. I strove, when with them and under them, to make myself agreeable and happy; and now I am a thrice happy freeman. And by making yourselves agreeable and happy, causing all around you to be happy also, the Lord will provide for you, and your superiors likewise, and you will learn, as your friend has, this comfortable truth: That the path of duty is always the path of safety; and that all those who wish to be lovely must learn to be good. As long as it appears to be the will of the Lord, make yourselves and all around you as contented and happy as possible, where you are. I do not think it to be the will of our Heavenly Father that you should leave home and go to any place except Africa. If your superiors say, Go to Liberia, come right along. But, excepting Liberia, go to no place, from Alabama, under Heaven.

I close with feelings of continual gratitude. Your most humble servant.   H. W. Ellis

211 / SION HARRIS TO WILLIAM McLAIN

Rev'd Mr. Mclane   Cald[well], April 16, 1850

Sir: I write to inform you that we are all well, hoping you & family are the same. I am glad to say to you what I could never say before that we have found out another power beyond man's power. That is, for the first man in Liberia, I am working of horses plowing. I have got a nice horse & mar[e] & the mar[e] has got a fine colt. I also have 2 yoaks of Oxens. I am halling timber out of swamp which has killed up hundreds of men toten it. They draw as well as any of your oxen in America I have Scars come to see. I have planted about 12 achers of rice. I have corn & ginger now planted. You have at the publick Stoar in Liberia numbers & Scors of plows. They are rotning. Thear has never been any use found for them before. Will you make me a present of one or two along as I will use them? You also have a number of waggon & waggon wheels laying about the publick store. There is never been any use found for them. Will the Society make me a present of some of them or of a waggon to use? When done with it I will deliver it back. I am glad that I can tell you that I am the first man that have found use for them & I hope from this move that you will see use for hundreds if you consent for me to get them. Write to me & to Gen. Lewis. He is wiling for me to have them But he wants me to pay. But I don't think it is right for me to pay for they are lying there roting & no one has no use for them. I only have to get the thing agoing, get it started. Some one has got to start first. I am bound to keep on with it & Mr. Mclane, the fact is you might send me out a pear of Birth [Girth?] bands, 4 geers. They are hard to get here & present my case before the Board of Manager & tell them they might make me a present of an old gig with 2 wheels & some friend send me an old Saddle. Now this will do more good than sending some of my old Brethering, one that are dead when the[e]y come. You ought to be here to see the native Africans. Looking at them as me working. He claps his hands & say ten men no fit tote that stick that Bullock tote he cry out thanky daddy how some Bullock can make work. I think they do eat them that be all what mat[t]er all Amarica man no do so he no eat them. The Lord is on our side. You can pick this & give notice in the Herald and [Re]pository that the way is open to the Mandingo Contry & cattle & horses are coming down. The cattle is cheap. I have some 8—9 now. They cost from six to seven dollars apiece. Some of them will weigh 3 hundred. The horse cost from forty to fifty & sixty [dollars]. I Hope to hear from you. Pleas write to me if you know what have become of Mary Moore. I shall send you lemon juice. I have just got bottles. I am so busy now that I have no time to atend to it. No more But remain yours,   Sion Harris

My respects to you & family,   M[artha] A. H[arris]

212 / ISAAC ROBERTS TO WILLIAM McLAIN

Greenville, Sinou, 17 Apr 1850

Dear Friend: I received your letter on 6 of Apr. The pac[k]et left here on the 2 of Apr. I have received all the goods with the exception of the alpacca. Leaving out the alpacca i am in debt to you 18.36 w[h]ich I would have forwarded on had the packet been here. At the arrival of the bark chieftian i had an interview with the capt. of the chieftian expecting I could send it on by him but he told me that he was going to west indies. Mr. mishael request me to say to you that he have received one piece of alpacca 28.3 yards. The chieftian has discharge her cargo. All is well. I must inform you about the health of this place. We have lost but two by death in the space of nearly three month. The prayer of people has been answered by the lord. I am extremely obliged to you for your kindness toward me, and in any way that i could make myself servecible to you i would be happy to do so. The chieftian increased her number. There was one birth at sea. I remain yours,   Isaac Roberts

213 / SION HARRIS TO WILLIAM McLAIN

Caldwell, Sept. 20, 1850

Sir: I received your letter and was glad to hear from you. I am much oblige to you for the cart and plow. I made a better crop this year than ever I made in Liberia. I made about a hundred and fifty bushel of rice; will make about four or five thousand pounds of ginger, a plenty of cassada and potatoes. I raised some corn and a quantity of peas. Horses still keeps coming down, now and then, from the interior. I have not got time to give you all the particulars. A heap prophecied and cried out that Liberia could not stand. But I tell you that she is in better health now than ever she has been since I have been here. I mean the Treasury, and also the people. As little as is said about it, Liberia will be a country and a great and mighty nation. For the Lord, with his mighty arm, is on our side. I have a large Boa Constrictor. I caught him. He is larger than that one that is in Dr. Hall's office—19 feet long. I have had it going on six months. It eats hearty. What is it worth in your country? Don't you want a pet for your children to play with? She blows as same as a steamboat letting off her steam. She had about forty-four young ones in her den, and great many eggs that was not hatched; some larger than goose eggs. Mrs. Harris' love to Mrs. McLain and children, yourself likewise. No more at present but I remain yours truly,   Sion Harris.

214 / SION HARRIS TO DR. JAMES HALL

Dr. [James] Hall   Caldwell, Sept the 26, 1850

Sir: I write to inform you that I am well and family hoping you are the same.[1] Dr. I have not heard from you for somtime. You are my Good friend though [I] have never told you so before. I would be glad to hear from you at any time. I hope you will write to me. I have been hard at work since I got home. I have got as much money as I had before I left home. I had But little But I am making more to It. I have large farm. I made 2 or 3 hundred kroos of rice this year. I have about forty akes [acres] in ginger, Rice, & casadoes & sugar cane. Have 2 fine horses. I have a yok of oxens. Some 10 or 15 horses has come down out of the interia this year. I plow my horses. I find It much easer than the hoe & make as much again. I must stop here now Dr. Let me tell you Buckky Buckker I have got you a great big snak, A Bour constrictor. I have not got time to tell you altogether how I cought him But I will tell you a little. I was out a hunting. The hounds was running a deer & I run & jump on a Bugabug hill to Shoot the deer & the top of the hill broke in & the dirt fell in & she Blowd as same as a Steamboat Blowing off Steam. I peeped in at the hole & I saw the M[on]ster. I thought about you. You told me to try to ketch one. I snatched off my coat & stoped up the hole & looked a round for some more & found 2 others. I stoped the[m] up good & secure. I broak [for] home studing what plan how to ketch him. I cauled my boys & all my hands. I made a large Box twelve feet long & broak [brought it?] Back. I dre[w] up some forks & made one of the holes la[rge] enough to poke the end of the Box in. I [had] a trap door in one end & then I built up a big fire at the other hole. After roa[s]ting the old fellow well She run out in the box. I shet down the doare & give 3 Chee[rs]. "I have got you!" She is nineteen feet long. Sh[e] was a setting. She had forty four young on[es] that I saw. A great many run in the box with her. She is large[r] than the one in your office that I gave you. She eats well. I have her now going on six month. I caught her a few days after the packet left. Before I sold one small one for fifty dollars to Captain Foussigh of Philadelphia. He was about twelve feet long. You can have this for a hundred & fifty. I will Keep It untill the packet returns. By that time she will be prety well tamed. You told me if I would git you one as large as that you would give me five hundred dollar & pay the frait. Now give me a hundred fifty. I will send her. You know what we [word undecipherable]. Write to me. I will be glad to hear from you at any time. No more, your truly, Sion Harris

[The following postscript is crossed out]

Dr Hall,   Sir, pleas to send me one Barel of Rhy Whiskey & I will send you the money. My wife best respects to you. I will pay you for your trouble. You must count the percents & tell me. S. H.

215 / MARTHA A. HARRIS TO MRS. WILLIAM McLAIN

Mrs. McLain Cald[well], May 12, 1851

Dear Madam: I & family are well, hoping you and yours are the Same. I received the Lemon Squeazer. I have prepared the juice to send you. I hope it will Suit you and I want you to give Dr. Lynsy one bottle full. You know he came to see me when I had the measeals. Though he stand far off frome me, yet I wish him to have a bottle of It. My respects to all the Children. How is John? I expect there is another John or Mary on the way. My respects to Aunt Corah, your Sisters also. If you like it, let me know. I want you to send me one dress by Gen. Lewis, a white dotted or notted muslin. I do not know what you call It, & edgeing to suit It. Do not forget It & I will send you more if life last. You can have as much as you want. Mr. Mclane Send me a Keg as full of Cheap wine or something. I have nothing to put It in and I will send it back full of Juice. I had to buy the Jugs. Mr. Harris Returns his thanks to Mr. McLane for his cart of wheels. He would send you a piece for his Journal But he is preparing & fixing a peice for Dr. Hall. If he has time he will drop him a few lines. No more a[t] present, But Remain Yours,

Martha A. Harris

Possibly Martha A. Harris, wife of Sion Harris.
American Colonization Society Papers, Library of Congress

Mr. Harris says he beg Mr. Mclane to send him a buggy with 2 wheels and he would have kept his Journel full of interesting peices but he want [time].

216 / EDWARD Z. WHITE TO WILLIAM McLAIN

Rev. Wm. McLain

Monrovia, Liberia,
Wed. April 3, 1852

Dear Sir: I humbly trust that you will excuse the apparent liberty taken with you, but tho perhaps the care of a poor bondman may apologize for me. Sir, I have a brother in the City of New Orleans who is a Slave and Said to be a Good Man, and Member of the Presbyterian Church in that City. His name is William Z. White, and I think [he is] under the Pastoral Care of Rev. Mr. Stanton of N.O. Now, what I wish to say to you & ask of you is this. My brother has nearly enough money to purchase his liberty but not quite enough. He has been anxious to Go to Liberia, but his mistress charges a very high price for him, which has prevented his freedom hitherto. But if you will write to Rev. Mr. Stanton, or C. C. Lathrope, of N.O. that they may influence the auxiliary Colonization and Missionary Societies [and] assist him in oblaining his freedom. What ever that amount may be, in reason, I will refund the some to the proper person, or persons, in Palm Oil, paid over to who ever you direct. Yours &c.,

Edward Z. White[1]

217 / ISAAC ROBERTS TO WILLIAM McLAIN

Feb. the 21, 1853

Dear sir: I embace this favourable opportunity of addressing you these few lines hoping they may find you and family enjoying good health and the smiles of a kind benefactor. I have been troubled occasionaly with chills and fever but not so as to prevent me from preaching. The association convend here for the first time. The brethern all laboured faithfully in preaching all through the settlement and I hope that their labours will be blest. I have ben unable to forward the amount for value receive. I hope you will indulge me a while longer. Provission is very high, 25 dollar a barrel for pork. I have lost all my first stock in town and now I have made another start on my farm. I have ditch in a small pasture wich I hope in time will prove beneficial to me. It is the first ditching that have been done here among the farmers. I have ditch the whole front of my farm. A quarter of that I have ditch east, west, north, south and placed my stock there. You will oblige me by sending me one barrel of pork, one barrel of flour, and half barrel of brown sugar. I hope the time will come when I will be able to pay you all that is due you. Yours affectionately,   Isaac Roberts

218 / SION HARRIS TO WILLIAM McLAIN AND J. W. LUGENBEEL

Rev. W. Mclane & Dr. Lewgenbeal   Cald[well],
                                                                    March 3, 1853

Dear Sirs: I am not very well but my family are well hoping this will find you well. I am yet trying to work. I have bough[t] one hundred & ten achours of land on St. Paul's River. I have just Raised me a Brick hous upon it. I made a fine crop of corn last year an I made abbout 80 Bushel off of About four Achours of grown [ground]. On the same peace of grown I made Ab[o]ut one hundred Bushel of rice. I Judge I have About A thousan Bushel of Casada. I expect to move on my farm in Clay Ashmun right Against Oreleans. I have just commenced to plant corn Again. I want to make a crop this year. That is the great fear that my collar [colored] people have of Comeing to this contry. They say we have nothing to eat. But when they can know truely that hogs & corn will grow here & freedom Abounding then they will be willing to come. I grown [ground] on my little hand mill last year & sould in market About forty Bushel of meal in 2 months, Beside what I sould at the mill. If I should live to make this crop I shal give you something to hand to them. I am trying to get A little heav[i]er mill & I am going to fix It to run by water. I can do It myself. No more in this head if they don't Believe It, Mr. Ball, a [w]hite Babtist Missionary called & saw It growing. He went home in the last trip of the Liberia Packet. Dear Sir, let me request of one of you or both to do me A favour. Now you can do It with A very little trouble. Dr. Lewgenbeal, I am informed that you & Mr. McLaine are Acquainted with an Agent in North Carlina, Rolly, by the Name of Rev. Mr. Haze that Sent out Some of my kin foaks in the last vessel that come out [in the] Bark Malinda Steward. There was a man that came out in her by the name of Anderson Harris, had a wife and 6 children & Another young man by the name of Nathan Harris. He was from Fayettevill, North Carlina. They are my Cosins. They all have had the feaver. They are living in my house. He tell me that my Brother is living in 3 or 4 miles of Rolly, who are well acquainted with Mr. Haze, the Agent, and Mr. Haze with him. His name is Leasure Harris whose Mother was name Bailie Harris who had a sister by the name of Sirene Harris. She never had But the 3 Children. My sister is dead. I thought they were all dead. My Grand Father & Grand Mother moved Away to tennessee when I was About five years old. I can remember It well, though, of seeing My

Mother. My Grand Father name was Gipson Harris who run off with a white woman for A wife. Her name [was] Libithy Calvin. He had another Bro. by name of Soloman Harris that went with him to Tenessee. Anderson Harris Grand Father & my Grand Father are Brothers, also Nathan Harris Grand Father & mine were Bro. The reason that I request of you they tell me that he got ready to come, had some dispute with a white man & struck him. He had thirty dollars to pay & they stop him & A white gentleman stood his security & kept him out of Jail. They tell me that he says he is coming next fall if any vessel sails. I would be Mighty Glad to See him. I have a home for him. Please to write to Mr. Haze & tell him all About It. Tell him to tell Leasure that he need not be Afraid. I have been here something like 23 year and is not dead yet & if they leave It to me I am going to sit here under my fig trees & orange trees About five hundred years longer & then bid Africa good by & try to go to Heaven to live forever. I would be glad if you would forward this letter to Mr. Haze After you are done with It, stating my request. You Both can tell him who I am. If you throw It down on the table & loose It I will come as Strait to you hous I will be there befor 18 months if [I] live & if you do not wish to be Bothered with me you better Attend to It. I have got so much work to do I have not got time to come But if you don't I will do like the old woman. I will risk my lif once more. How was that she got marrid & the first child was Born. The old woman had a very searis time, so the Dr. told her if It was ever the case again she would surely die. So her husband went & prepared Another Room. He went & staid in one & she in the other. He had gave up all hops. After 8 or nine months the old woman gits up in the night & wraps the doore. He thought some one had come to rob him, crying out, "Who is that?" "Who is that?" She says "Me, my Dear. I have come to risk my life once more." I Just give you this lower peace [of paper on which the joke was witten]. You need not send It to Mr. Haze. No more at present, But Remain Yours Truly, Sion Harris[1]

219 / SIMON HARRISON TO WILLIAM McLAIN

Revrd McLain,   Buchanan, Grand Bassa Co., Liberia
Agt. of the A.C. Society   September 10th, 1853

Dear Sir: As I have safely arived on the shore of Western Africa in the above named place, I thought it my duty to say a word to inform you how I like this Quarter of the world. I suppose I need not trouble you with a History of my passage over the Briny Deep.[1] But one thing I suppose would not be amiss on that subject. You are aware, sir, that if a

Colered man don't know any thing else, he knows when he is pretty well used. Consequently, I would Just say I liked the Banshee trip, and think Capt. Wilson, the Commander, is a gentleman, or was toward myself & family. I hope he did not come to Africa for the last time. When I arived at Monrovia I anticipated that I was at the end of my Journey. But there I found that from your consignment I had not gone far enough, that I could not yet be released from another water passage. I had while there an interview with Revd. Wilson on the subject of my mission, & in conclusion [it] was decided that I should proceed on my Journey untill I would arive at the Place of my destination. As I had long since learned the lesson of obedience I was willing to submit, feeling that Him that had never left me when I would try to do his will, was the same in Africa that he was when I went to the Choctaw Nation. I submited the Case & said with *one* of old, I can but perish if I go, and am resolved to try. After a few days we weighed anchor & soon lost sight of the Capital of the Republic. But it was not long untill anchor was dropped in sight of the place where I am now located. To me at first sight the place looked lonesome & when I was called upon to go ashore & did so, I thought I was ashore sure enough, & as they say in the south sometimes, this is running the thing too far in the ground. The inhabitants was very clever. But the Houses was principally thatched, and not too many of them, & plenty of Bushes within sight, & you know a Colered man likes to see a good many fine houses, even if he dont have any himself. But I am here in the land of Naked people and all I could then say was, well God is everywhere. I have been here nearly three Months & now thus far I will say a litle about this Country & people. As for the Country, I firmly & religiously think that this is the home of the Colored Man & I also think that he is blessed indeed by his Creator when he sets his foot on the soil, notwithstanding all the disadvantages. If he came here Healthy & gets the fever, if he is prudent, I think it is possible for him to master it; & if he dies, he might have met the same fate in the States. If he is industrious, the advantages he meets with will outweigh the Sacrifice he has made, & then he stands here erect as a *Free Man* to boot. I think the location is decidedly better than that of Monrovia; & now I hope to bless God that he so conducted your mind to send me to Bassa County. I speak for myself, although when [there] I doubted my liking it. But the Cloud has already began to break. The prospect looks better than it did a few weeks ago; & I am not the only one that has made like expression. There has been some Deaths among us but, leaving out one family, we have got along thus far beyond our expectations. They tryed to make us believe at Monrovia that death would be certain if we came here, but I find it is no more so than many places I could mention in the States. I must not forget to state that you have an agent here that does Honor to his Office. Under his administration I think I can pass through my six months without a murmer. I tell you Mr. McLain, Stephen A. Benson is a man of good sense, & the least I can say He is a Gentleman & a Christian in my Opinion. I found here when I cam a Lot secured for the Presbyterian Church but there is no church on it. I hope there will be one got on it of some kind soon. There is a few members here but, having no Pastor and no house of there own, they feel desirous that something should be done for them if posible. I ask you the Question, what can be done for the Church at Fishtown in Western Africa? I have no doubt but that you have ofttimes made use of this Expression, He that giveth to the Poor lendeth to the Lord. Now, sir, I am in the pleasant and healthy vilage of Central Buchanan (for I understand that this place will be devided of in three districts, to wit, Uper, Lower & Central) & no resources to depend upon of my own. The Society's hand will in a very litle while be closed & in Consideration thereof I wish to go to work & get something ready but I cant get what I want here. I must now call upon you, Sir. I wish you to purchase for me One good sise Cooking stove for private family, One Barrel flour, One Jack plain & Two other planes, 1 drawing Knife, 1 Broad Axe, 1 square, 1 Compas, 1 Keg 6d nails, 1 Keg 8d nails & send me a Bill of them to price. You are aware that you can corespond with Mr. Kingsberry on the above purchase & I would ask the favor of you to inform Mr. K. at the same-time that I now need some Money & if convenient to transmit some to me. & now sir, in conclusion, I beg leave to be remembered to all the Church of Christ & those that are laboring in the vinyard of the Lord. Pray that the God of Jacob will sustain his Servants in benighted Africa. My utmost regard to the Mission of the U.S.A. and the American C. L. [Colonization] Society. My sincere Prayer is that they will not slack their energies & that Elijah's God will bless their every effort. I bless my Heavenly Protectors that I ever fell in their Hands; & for the encouragement of Brethren of a Sable Hue, I say to them Africa is not what many term the Grave yard for the Colored man, or that he must Die as soon as he comes here, & as to the place where I am located, a handsomer spot cannot be found on the Cost. I believe it to be Healthy & a finer prospect for agri-culture cant be scared up, & what is quite as encourageing, the inhab-itants is more on a equality. In a word the people is a working people. They dont apear to be one part of the Community going around to see if his neighbour has a Jackson Mint Drop, so that he can shave him out of it or steal it from him. But he goes to work and tries to earn one too. I am speaking in a general way, so I think you are doing Emigrants a special favor when you send them to Grand Bassa County. I say this because I would like to be a friend to my own Color. There has been a few frame Houses put up since I have been here & they are working on the Streets. In fact things begin to look like living. Please let me hear from you in ref-erence to the favor asked at your hands. Yours with the greatest Respect, Simon Harison

Revd. Wim. MCLain   Louisiana, August 17th, 1857,
                              Republic of Liberia, Montserado County

Hon'd & Dear Sir: Suffer me to drop you a few lines by way of introducing myself to you by saying that myself & father were liberated by
the agency of the Rev'd Nathaniel Dodge of "Bates County Missura." My
father is ded and as I am the only surviver, I would be happy to oppen a
communication to the said Rev'd Dodge through you. I am well an hop
to her from all of my friends. Tell Mr Dodge and all of his family i am in
Joying Good health. Sinc the Death of Father i hav taken a wife. I have
alsow had 5 Children. To of them is Ded, &c. I hav not much to say at
preasent ontill i hear from you. Pleas to answer my Leter By the first
opertunity, &c. If you hav any thing to Spar I would thank you kindly
for any thing in this wourld you wish to send to me as I am in need of
something about Bilding a Hous. Nothing more at present, Yours,

                                              Phillip F. Flournoy[1]

221 / JAMES W. WILSON TO WILLIAM McLAIN

Revd. Wm. Mc Lane,   Robutsporte [Robertsport],
Baltimor City   August 5, 1858

Dear Sir: I Write you a few Lines Hoping thay may find you and
your Dear famley enjoing the bleseng of good helth. My Self and famley
is in good Helth at Present. I have never under took to Write a Letter for
Publickthion [Publication] and Would Not at Present if it War not For
the Report of the Watson men, James & William, Which left here in Forty
dayes after thir arivel.[1] I Larn thire is a Report floting in the unided States
that the agent of the Colonizathion Society had Pursaded them to
Pucherd som Chep Calico & Brest Julls [jewels] and on thir arivel thay
Ware disopinted and thair by defroded out of thir money. I have ex-
zamoned and Enqured in to it from Limos Watson, Dr. Watson, Rile
Watson, gary Watson, Olin Watson, Adim Watson & Cornelyous Watson w[ho] is his Brother. All Sayes that thay had no Such advice from
anney one and thay gart thir money from the Exeters [Executors], Josep
D. Peas [and] R. D. Smith and it War given to them on bord of the
Stemborte [steamboat] and thir fore thay could not Spind thir money &

they have not Ben Seen With no Such thing but Have uised a Part of thir money to Build thim good fram huses. In Regards that is all so denied by the Hold of them, in Regard the Lands, thay Pur ferd [preferred] Town Lots in Stid of farm Landes. The Report Sayes thay Was ill Treted bad. Thay Say it is a fals hord [falsehood]. So far as it Con san [concern] thir Eting and Tret ment in the Recepticle, I saw them Sind [sign] a document Dning [denying] than had Ben ill & Badly treted or did not have a noff to Eate Whilest thay Was in the Reseptlee. With no disrespec [to] the Writer of the Report he Will at mit thoes [w]ho have ben hear 7 monts to know as much a bought thing hear as William & James Watson [w]ho only Was on Shore 40 days [w]ho had not Cureg to Walk over the Small Settlment. You know, Sir, the Children of iserel Wanted and Wish for the flesh ports [pots] of Egyp, not With Standing god had Promes them a Land that floes With milk and huney & he that Will not Try to make him self Satis fide With the kind Providenc of God Would not be Satis fide if he Was Placed in heaven. I am all so despose to think [that] he that Would not Work for his on [own] benefite will not Work for others unlest he is forst With the Whipe. But if it is thir path to have som one to make thim work for a Liven, Let it be so far as thar path is. So shal it be un to you sayes tha Criptures. As for my Part I do not know What William & James Watson return for unlest it Was for the Whipe. It cannot be for som thing to Eate, for We have the Sweet Potato, Casad, Rice, Corn meal. We can Rase Hoges, Sheps, gotes, & Cow, Fouls a Plenty, Turkey, ducks, gees. Be sids We get from the States flour, meal, Bacon, Pork, mackrel, Herinng, Che [Cheese], Buter, Lard, and a variety of thing. We Rase in this Cuntry and all So impoted [food-stuff] that is too tedus to menthion. I can not see What a man of Coller Want to go Back to the united States to Live for un Lest he has no Sol in him, for Whare thire is a sine of a sole With in a man it Panc [pants] for fredom in this Life & the Life to come. As for my Self, I Ware Rased in Augusta, gorgia [by] the Wider marks & War Emancapeated By hur & thar Son Dr. D. W. Marks. I Ware Rased as tho I Ware hur son, So far as Li With in hur Pour [power]. I Ever Shall Love & Rember them Whilts [whilst] memery Holds it onn [own]. No man nead fear he Will Starve if he Will Work and a Lazey man is a nusen in Any Cuntray. As Regards Cap mount it is as Helthey as Anny Part of Liberia & mor so than a good maney Pleases. We have the Best of Water & Pure. [This] are a Butfull Locathion. I would ask What is Beter in the known World than good Helth. You will Pleas Publish as much of this Leter as you think Proper. I say so Becas I am now [no] Scoller What Ever. Thar fore you will Excuse the Bad Spelling & Writing. I must Com to a Close by Saying give my Love to old Springfeell Church, Augusta, georgia, Richmond County. I Remand yours most truley, &c.,   Rev. J[ames] W. Wilson[2]

Rev. Wm. McLane   Robutesport [Robertsport],
                                                              Feb. 28, 1859

Dear Sir: As Chanc affords me anopportunety of Writing you a few
lines to inform you That my Self and famley is quit well And I hop thes
few lines may find you and your dear famley enjoying the Blesing of
good health. Sir I am happy To in form you that Cap mount has Improve
considebal. The pepols Show A Spiret of in dustry. Hear and thair you
can See good small fram houses going up, not With Standing the dark
Clouds that has ben throwed over Cap mount by her enimenys. I fell
That god Will cause the Sun to bust Forth yet in hur meriding Splender
And drive back the dark Cloudes that Had ben throwed over hur. I am
happy To in form you that pusones [w]ho may Emmagrant to this Place
can get farm Landes amediately on thir arivel In this Place, as it Ware.
The greates objection that could be helt up a ganst Cap mount [is the
quality of the land?] I know of no other. We hav a buttifull locathion,
fine Warter and a helty plac. Sir, I realy bleve That emmergrants can and
do pass throw The fever With more safety and eseyer Than any Place in
the Republick of libria. Hear is a woman that cam out on the Elasier
Ames With the Wartes Pepols that never had the fever. Guen Waters say
She has not ben sick with The fever one day Senc She cam to this Country. Cap mount has the atvanteg of the first news at the arivel of the
Stevens and the last oppertunety of Writing when She is going back.
That of it Self is great. As for my Self, I do not bleve that any Settel ment
has improve more than this in the sam time and under the sam dis-
atvantegs, that She has had no farm Landes [one word undecipherable]
of and falst Reportes Cerclated a ganst hur Which neserely In flounc the
Emmergrants to other Places. But I have h[e]ard Som When they arive
To this Place with thay had not con sined them selfs to other Places in
Stid of this. In fact the pepols in this county are turning thir attenchion
more and more to agarcltur. In Dec. Last I visete Monrovia and went up
the Sant Pual River. The farmes War good. I Saw that the farmes had a
plenty Around them to make them comfutbel. I saw fine cropes of Suger
cane. I have no doupt Suger can be bought At 9 cts. pur lb by the barel
and Suyurp at 50 cts. pur gallon. I all so Saw fine Tobacco and cotten
groing on thir farms. I visete the Soap factury and I saw Fine qulety of
soap as ned for wishing. By this few lines you may say that the pepoles
are tring to do somthing for them Selvs and country. Dear Sir, I have the
panful task of informing you of the death of Rev. John Day, agent of the
Southen Baptis Mishinery bord. He is a great lost to This Cuntry as a
minester of the gospel. I fell that he fought under the baner of King Jesus
untell he was call to Stak up his armes and com home to resev his reward. I would Write more but I have not the time Just now. I must Com

to a close by Saing give my love and Respects to all. I reman yours &c.,
&c.,   James W. Wilson

223 / GEORGE WASHINGTON TILLS TO WILLIAM McLAIN

Rev. Wm McLain,   Greenville, Sinoe,
Washington City, D.C.   Jany. 10th, 1860, Liberia

Dear Sir: I take this chance of writing a few lines, which I trust you
will Plese Parden me for my neglect of not writing as often as I said I
would write. Trusting these few lines will find they way to you & find
you and your family all well. Sir, permit me to lay before you my
deploable circumstances I have expearinced in this day & time from 1834
[1843], the year I came to Liberia. You was presant at the time when I
took shiping at New Orleans in the Bark Renown, which after so long a
Journey of 5 months we was shipwreck at Porto Prier (one of the Cape de
Varde island). I lost all at that time but what I had on my back. However, the Blessed Master spared my life, so I got to my long home & thare
I dig & strove from time to time in an honest & honorable occupation. I
did tolerable well until the year 1855. The war broke out & corned [cor-
nered?] us, broke me up. Our executor in Mississippia, the Rev. Zebulon
Butler of Port Gibson, promes me he would send us our money when he
sent the balance of the people to Liberia, but I have not received one cop-
per cent or nothing eles as [y]et.[1] I have rote Mr. Butler from time to time
but have [not] received an anssur from him. I cant tell why. I will write &
write again. I trust that the good Master will fix all things Right in this
Matter. I would not wory your Patience with this bad spelling & writing
but I trust you will make every allowance for that fault you will find in
this letter. I trust you will understand what is the purpose of it. True it
has been a long time sence you saw me. I was born & raised in George
Town, D.C. My owner was Mr. Henry Addison, a wholesail & Retail
Dry Goods merchant in Geo. Town & then in the City of Washington. I
have rote this Gentleman several times but have not heard from him. I
cannot say whether he is alive or dead, but I will rite him again & again.
Mr. McLain, I think you are acquainted with this Gentleman because I
knew you when I was there & in his service. Plese Give me some information of him. He is my friend indeed. He raise me & all my family. I
have a Brother I left with this Gentlemen in Washington by name Wil-
laim Tills. I should like to learn of him if Possible. I am well acquainted
with Dr. J. W. Lugenbeell & also, if you Plese, do me the kindness in this
perticular. Sir, I feel no way at all ashamed to ask for help now. I need it.
I am confident that misfortune will be fall us at times & I am aware that
you know these things. Therefore I beleve you to be a frend to me in this

from what I know of you. Plese do what you can for me in the way of geting a sta[rt] again in this life & if you [please] send me some leaf tobacco, Bleach & unbleach Cotton, Provisions or eny thing that will help me on. I will send you some Palmoil. Allow me a little time (Try me). I remain yours with due Respect,　　　　　　　G[eorge] W[ashington] Tills

224 / GEORGE WASHINGTON TILLS TO WILLIAM McLAIN

Mr. W. W. McLain,　　　　　　　　　Greenville, Sinoe, Jan. 28, 1860
Washington City, D.C.

Sir:　　Yours of the 5th April is received stateing your wish. God grant that you may Get your wish! Soon! Indeed, Sir, it would be folly in me to requeire impossiblitys of you when I know it to be inconsistence to Common sence. When you & I was in Norfolk [in] 1843 you ware in the act of fiting out the Barke Renown for Liberia! You tole me you had some knowledge of the matter! Perfect or imperfect, I am not able to say. You talk with me very free on the subject & spoke of Mr. Butler [saying he] had not done what he should have done & [when] I saw you in New Orleans the same year you also stated the same thing! Mr. McDonough of Orleans said about the same (that is, we had not [received] what belong to us) & the old gentleman told me at the same time he would see Mr. Butler about the matter, that we ought to have what is right for God sake! Mrs. M. A. Reed *decese* made us acquainted with the thing & what was her desire long before her death. You Represented Mr. Butler as an honest & an honorable man! I have never yet said that Mr. Butler ware not a honest & an honorable man, but I say Mr. Butler has not gaven me my money. What he should have done, & he knows it, is a stated fact! Nor no person eles has paid me for him in this case.

　　Sir; You spake so possitive in relation to Mr. Butler honesty [that it] coused me to say so much & the want of my money! Mr. McLain, Sir, I have know you for a number years [since] when I was a boy & I have never once tampered with your name or couse [course]. But this is one involve a deep intrest in me and I hope to find my rights at your instant! I am extremely oblige to you for the information you gave of Mr. Henry Addison. [I] did not expect for you to go about to look him up. I rote Mr. Butler last Jany. on the subject. I have not receid a ansor yet but I hope to get one soon from him & others in Miss. as he was the Cheaf Executor of the Estate [of] Mrs. M. A. Reed *decese* of Mississippi. I feel Greatful to you for your kindness. Your obneant Sert.,　　George Washington Tills

P.S. Will you Plese ansor.

225 / MARY KING TO WILLIAM McLAIN

Mr. McLane   March 10, 1864

Dear Sir: You Probably Recollect a woman and four children that used to belong to Mrs. Madavill that resided in August, Ga., that came out in the M. C. Stevens in May, 1860. If so, you will please forward the enclosed letter, if possible. This is my husband's name, A. B. King; he is the man that they wanted 3,000 doll[ar]s for at the time I came out, and in consequence of the war I have not heard from him since Nov. 1860. I direct this to you with a hope that you may be able to forward it by some means that I know nothing about. By so doing you will oblige yours most respectfully,   Mary King and four children

226 / LANDON WILLIAMS TO WILLIAM McLAIN

Rev. Wm. McLain,   Monrovia, Feb. 7, 1867
Agent, A. C. Society

Sir: Your being a man of note and having the power of authority by virtue of your connexion to the American Colonization Society, therefore I see or know no man who would better suit to lay this subject before than yourself.

I have three children in the State of Georgiz, viz: Nancy McClow, Falla McClow and David McClow, formerly owned by Francis McClow, a Georgian—owned a place on Ageeche road, fourteen miles from Savannah, turn out at the eleven mile stone and the first plantation you come to known as Wildhorn, a cotton plantation—He owned the next plantation on Ageche river known as "frog camp," a rice plantation is the place where I left my two daughters.

The boy I left in Savannah, Georgia, but I learnt since he was in Athey, Georgia, near Macon.

I and my wife are the persons sent out here by you on the M. C. Stevens, first trip. My mistress died and left me to come out to Liberia. Landon Williams, A Blacksmith, by trade. I only add this to refresh your memory of my person.

If you go in the city of Savannah and inquire about my children, Jacob Godfrey or his wife, or any body, can point out my children to you. Do, if you please intercede and send them out to me. You will find me in Monrovia, a resident therein. Consign them to the city of Monrovia, Liberia. Yours,   Landon Williams[1]

9/MISCELLANEOUS LETTERS

The twenty-four letters in this chapter reveal a variety of experiences and reactions. Nearly all of them tell of hardships of one kind or another. Accounts of reversals and deprivations are usually accompanied by requests for assistance.

Some of the correspondents were unhappy in their current situation and pessimistic about the future; others expressed satisfaction with present circumstances and great hope for the future. Several stressed the importance of hard work in achieving success and criticized associates for lack of diligence in trying to improve their plight. Religion and education were frequently mentioned. Some of the writers manifested continuing affection for former masters and most of them revealed deep and abiding interest in relatives residing in America.

Twelve of the correspondents are represented by only one letter each and in a few instances the writing was done by an amanuensis. For each of six correspondents—George Crawford, Jacob Harris, Charles Jefferson, Wesley Horland, Seaborn Evans, and Lucy (Lucinda) Clay—there are two letters.[1] Crawford, who before his emancipation belonged to John McCalla of Lexington, Kentucky, wrote his former master in May 1834 that Liberia was "not the place for a general imagration of the coloured people." Two years later, after having built a comfortable dwelling and while enjoying vegetables grown in his own garden, he seemed more content; still, he reported that "the colony . . . is not as flourishing as i could wish . . . chiefly owing to want of horses to plough," destruction of sheep and goats by leopards, and scarcity of provisions. Jacob Harris, also from Kentucky, observed July 4, 1848, that "all of us are highly pleased with the country. . . . Our country I believe to be the Colored man's home." Seaborn Evans, a Georgia black, wrote his former master, Josiah Sibley, September 19, 1853: "I See very plain this young and infant republic bids fair to become a grate people. . . . Liberia is the Star in East for the free black man." Evans, in his second letter, written three years later, stated that conditions in Liberia were improving and that "I am much pleased with my new home." He added: "It is true Some people come to this country that complain against the country and Say they cannot live here, but it is nobody but lazy people who had the overseer to drive them in America, and the misfortune is they have no overseer to drive them here."

An unusual letter is that of Virgil P. McParrhan [Bannehan?], former-ly the slave of Paul C. Cameron of North Carolina. Virgil had acquired some medical experience treating sick slaves on his master's plantation. When he went to Liberia in 1848 it was his intention to pursue a medical career, but his initial experiences as a practicing physician in Africa were discouraging. After considerable travel in Liberia he wrote: "I fine prac-tice anuf in this place but no pay. Mony in Africa is out of The question. Every Boddy wants Drs. But non Can pay them. I have at this Time 5 pathints and The five is not worth $5. . . . This is a very fin Country for sum peple but I am a frad it will not sut me."

The longest and most informative of the letters is that of Richard, a teacher-preacher from North Carolina who after his arrival in Liberia changed his surname from Blount to McMorine and added "Esq." This communication, dated June 1858 and addressed to James Johnston Petti-grew (who later became a Confederate general and was mortally wounded during Robert E. Lee's withdrawal from Gettysburg) stated that Liberia was a good country and that it was making commendable progress. "All it wants now," McMorine wrote, "is a little money and the people to Go on their Farms & Go to work." He added: "There is many people here is very poor. Many of them have had masters Barn and Smoke house to Go to and now when they have to Look to themselves for Every thing they do not no what to do. . . . We must do Some sort off work if we want to live." He advised against people over fifty years old migrating to Liberia and stated that planters who contributed money to migrants should give it in small installments, as a safeguard against reckless expenditure and costly theft. "I never saw people steel so Bad as the people do here," he observed. He attributed the widespread thieving to tardiness of colonization officials in providing sufficient land to yield a livelihood and aversion to labor resulting from prolonged idleness pend-ing land allocation. McMorine closed his long letter with a request for money to help build a good house for himself and his wife.

227 / GEORGE CRAWFORD TO JOHN M. McCALLA

Monrovia, Liberia, May the 3 [1834]

Dear Master John: As Mr. Jones is a bout Return to a ameriCa, I feel greatly desirus that you should know the situation of our affars. I feel it my duty to write a few Lines to you on the sub Ject, hoping that i my find you and the family well. I am happy to inform you that god has favered us in Land of sorrow. out of a hundre[d] and fifty emegrants that came out with us their are but thirty remain. The fever has takening them way and the dear missionarys [manuscript torn]. . . . Mr. Right and his wife,

Mr. John Cloud, Mr. Land and his wife. Dear sir, we are in monrvia and still have attacks of the fever. I am working very hard. This is not the place for a general imagration of the coloured people. Please to give Love to all my friends.   George Crawford[1]

228 / GEORGE CRAWFORD TO JOHN M. McCALLA

Mr. John McAly, Lexington, Ky.   Monrovia, Sep. 25, 1836

Dear Master John: I have by the arrival of Mr Heron in the Brig Lunar and a young man of colour both from Lex[ingto]n [received news of you]. They inform us that you [manuscript torn] . . .well and in good health [manuscript torn]. . . . [We are] all well and glad to hear from [you] and all my freinds. Give my Love to old Mistress and Miss Maria and Mrs. Clark Andrew and thomas and miss Elizabeth and aunt Jane. You please to write by the Brig when she return. We intended to have sent you and miss maria two boxs of Lemons and some shells and sea weed but the gentleman could not carry them. I will send them by the way of Bev-[manuscript torn]. . . . The Captain of the brig was in [manuscript torn] . . .not time [manuscript torn] . . .you the particular but [manuscript torn]. . . . [We have] by hard labour and econemy and my wife frugality bin able to build a comfortable Little house and good garden. We have some butter beans and we have a quantity of sweet po-tatoes and arrowroot, pine apples, and soursops. As it respects the col-ony it is not as flourishing as i could wish. I am not prepared to say from what cause tho i think chiefly owing to want of horses to plough. The forests is as yet very dense and full of leopard wich destroys sheep, goats [manuscript torn] . . . wich makes provison very hi[gh] [manuscript torn] . . . colony is imported [manuscript torn] . . . as possible to draw my farm a [manuscript torn] . . . but have been prevented as I am not able [to] get tobacco and Course cotton cloths to pay the natives to help me clean it. I hope to see you all a gain if nothing happens. If not, Let us all through grace try to meet in heaven. I am yours,

                                                          George Crawford

229 / MALINDA REX TO DUNCAN CAMERON

                                   Caldwell, Liberia, November 3, 1839

Dear Sir: I have met with the oppitunity of writing to you to inform you that I have arrived safe in Africa.[1] We all had a safe passage here but we all have not enjoyed our health since we been here. Benjamin has been very sick but he is geting on the mend. I am not satisfied. I have not found nothing as they said and never will like [?] it. My Dear Sir if you had of known that this place was as poor as it is you would not [have] consented for us to come here. If I had of known myself when you was telling me I would not of been so willing to come. But I thought I could git along like I could there but I fond it to the contrary. Dear Sir, we understood from you that all our provision were paid for but I find it to the contrary. Our Governor Buchanan says that we must pay for all our provision, likewise all the expenses. I would wish to learn from you if thos are facts. If it is so, such [h]as never been known in the colony before. I did think you was not aware of them. If you were I thought that you would not suffer it to be so. You [are] aware if we have to pay for all our expenses it will consume all. If we do [not get] all what is coming to us we shall never be enable to pay all expenses. My respects to you, Your Obedient Servant, and if I have to pay for all of the expenses and all the provision, you will please to inform me by writing by the Ship Saluda. We [are] informed she will return as soon as she gits there and gits in her load. It was understood here at the decease of my Master there was some quantity of money left to be divied. I never was able to understand how many thousand dollars it were. After the Governor understood this they then say they expenses shall come out of that money as I was aware my self that there was some money left. I was sorry to hear this. I met with a friend and he told me that I had better inform you of this and if it were not left in the will, though you are a great way off from us, I hope you will not suffer this to be. You are all my dependance at this time to receive information, [therefore I write] this letter. William Thompson said that all our provision were paid for. Now they say it is not so. They have multiplied how many pounds it takes to serve one one week. They [al]low one three pounds as they may know what quantity of our money to take to pay for it, flour twelve and half cent per pound, pork 25. You know if we have to pay for all of this it will mount to a great sum of money. Sweet potatoes [are] one dollar per Bushel. Truly I am in Africa where I cum to be free. I am well satisfied on that head but I beg you to write me as quick as possible by the [next] vessel. Our vice Agent, namely Anthony Williams, he is willing that we should be dealt by just[ly], but Sir they low him no privaleges. He is treated so ill he says he intend to leave in december wich [means] my friend is gone. We have been bless with friends by the orders of Mr. Williams. Ellick [sends] respects to his wife, namely Jane. Please to inform him if she is coming out. My respects to your wife. I have not been sick since I arrived here. Nothing More remains at present, But remains your obedient servant,

Malinda Rex

Bassa Cove, Jan. 18, 1846

This leves me well, and I hope you ar the same.[1] I was very glad to hear from you indeed, and more asspeshel, becaus that wase the first letter that I reseved from you sace my arival in this countray. Semes to me that the pepel have forgot me altogether. I hope we will be abel to cepe up a regular correspondence with each other hereafter.

The firs thing that I will consider is the condition of the collonay. From the information that I have reseved since my arival, I am hapay to say this is a very good countray; and any man may make a living in this countray, if he will.

Let us notice the land. The land is good. The land in one mille of the ocion is good enufe to rase any thing most on it; and the father you go back the better the land is. The land is not very large timber, but verry good. I have some timber in this countray four feet in diameter. But I do not think that is as large as timber in the U. States, therefor I say it is not verry large. The land is verry well timbered, that is, thar is a plenty of it.

Hillay Land. The land is not very hillay. It is as level as any countray, or as any part of the U. States as I have scene. Thar is a chane of mountains that runs from the norther extremety of Africa to the Cape of Good Hope. Thes ar verry large mountains. This I have from moderron travelers.

Produce of Africa. There is palm oil, rice, casander, yams, potaters, coffay, cabbish, water mellons and many other things that I might name, sugar cane, &c., &c. Cattle, sheep hogs, goats, and fouls of various kinds, &c.

Crimes. Thar is indeed some crimes in this countray of a very bad natcher, but not a grate menay of them.

Religion. This pepel is a religis pepel; thare is no queston about that. They ar a Church going pepel. They go to meeting evry Sabbath. I had the plesur of being at the last Anul Conference at Monrovia, on the 9th instand, and I remaned thare for some days, and was verry mutch graitefide, hevving some verry abel ministers.

The number of the settlements. Thar ar ten or fifteen settlements, but Monrovia is the larges; that also is the seat of government. We have legislatter every yere, commensing on the 5th of this month. The business is maniged very well, indeed; this I am a witness to. I have been in the legislater and seen them myself. My self and my mother's family: my mother is well, and my sister and two brothers; Asberry[2] and mother. [Of] the pepel that came to this countray with us, the Majers, there is three men and two wimmen alive; Hopkins, two alive; Alexander Horland, mother and two of his sisters—he is dead. The most of his pepel did not die with the fever; some of theme was shot in the last ware with the natives. As for the pepel, they ar all emplyed in doing something. Thar is not any of the[m] very lazzy. By this do not understand me to say there is no lazzy ones among us, for thar is. I expect to come to the U. States before long, if you think it advisable. I am doing a littel of most everrything. I am yours,   Wesley Horland

This letter is not all I will send, I will send another letter soon.   H.

Mr. James Moore, Kentucky, Christian County.

231 / WESLEY J. HORLAND TO JAMES MOORE

Bassa Cove, Jan. 19th, 1846.

I told you that I would say something more in my next that would afford you more satisfaction, as it regards this countray. The next that I will notice is the situation of the settlements. Monrovia is the Cappetel of the Colony of Liberia. The pepolation of Monrovia is about one thousand men, wimmen and childring. This settlement is on a Cape extending in the Atlantick ocion and it is a verry elevated place. It is bound on the north by the ocion, on the este by the Sent Pal's river and on the west by the ocion. The buildings is made of wood, stone and bricks. The pepel that live here is those that follers merchandizing. The revenue is somewhere between eight and ten thousand dollars a yare. Thare is mechanickes also in the place of almost everry kind, so thare is not much need of me moveing the different employments. There is also three or four settlements up the Sent Pal's river. There pepel are farmers, so they live without having any thinge to do with trading. These settlements is about 18 miles, the fathis settlement; thar is some mishingnerry stations the other side of the settlements. Marshall or Junk: This settlement is somewhare about 50 miles south of Monrovia, situated on the Junk river, bound on the south by the mane branch of the river, on the west by the Atlantick ocion and on the este by the north branch of the said river. Ediner: This is a fine littel settlement 40 miles south of Marshall, situated on the north side of the Sent John's river. The pepel of this settlement is improving verry fast, both wase. They ar the most of them farmers. This settlement is one that have been blest; they have never had a inserecshen sense the settlement of that place. It is situated on the north side Sent John's river, bound on the este by the Meehlen [Mechlin] river, on the west by the ocion. Bexley: This settlement is six miles from Ediner, on the north side of the St. John's river. Bassa Cove: This little place is had more to contend with than the most of the settelments. It has bin consumed by fier by natives; but we have nothing to dred at this time. This settelment is the cappetal of the country of Grand Bassaw. This is a verry fine settelment and the best that I have seen since I have been in this countray. This settelment is one mile south of Ediner, situated on the south side of the St. John's river, bound on the este by the Benson river, on the weste by the ocion. Senoe: This settelment is somewhare about 100 miles south of Bassa Cove. Cape Palmas: This settelment is somewhere between 200 or 150 miles south of Senoe.

Monrovia [was] settled twenty yares ago; the popelation [is] 1,000, without the upper settelments; the upper settelments have between 5 and 600, Marshall 80. Ediner have been settled ten or fifteen yares; popelation between 75 and 120. Beeley [Bexley] have been settled six yares; it has somewhare about 150. Bassa Cove [has] somewhare about the same. Cape Palmas have somewhare about 150 or 100.

This I think will answer for the settelments. As for myself, I am by endevering by the assistance of God, to do the best I cane. I am indevering to Preach the Gospel of Crist, and this I think nothing less than my duty. I am a member of the Methodist Church. I have not been sick two weeks since I have been in this countray, and if the Lord is willing, I intend to see yore face once more. I do hope you will advise me what to do in this respect. I would like to come thare verry well; but I do not know the law that you have among you as yet. I would be glad if you would wright me all the newse. Wright to my pepel for me. This leves me well. I remane yours truely with respect,   W. J. Horland.

Mr. James Moore, Kentucky, Christian County

232 / MOSES JACKSON TO ELIOTT WEST

Mr Eliott West   March 22, 1846, Kentucky, Liberia,
                                                        Western Africa

Dear sir: Having arrived safely in Liberia I seize the present spare moment to write a few lines to send to you in which I shall give you some account of our voyage and of the state of affares here.[1] We had quite a favourable voyage and met with no misfortune worth mentioning. We were just 48 days on our passage. We all had the Sea Sickness and it lasted some of us more than half the way out but none of them lost thier lives. And When [we] got through with our passage the most of our people were in better health then when we started.

Our Capt., Mr. Lawry, is without doubt one of the finest Captains that the society has Ever employed. No man Could be more attentive [to] the entire welfare of a people then he was to ours and should they ever send out an other emigration I do not hesitate to say that they cannot send it [in] Charge of a better or more worthy Captain.

The present state of affairs here is not very flatering. The people here from all that I have seen and heard take but little interest in the improvement of the country. They Generaly engage in trading with the Natives for Camwood and Pam oil which they barter agane for such things as they need with merchant vessels and neglect almost entirely the Cultivation of the ground. The generality of the farms do not exceed 5 acres and the largest that I have heard of does not exceed 15 acres. 15 acres is considered a large farm and so it is for one man [to] tend the way that they tend it with the hoe. They use neither horses, mules nor Oxen and they say that these animals cannot stand it [to] perform labour in this Climate. This is the majority. Yet their [are] some think that if they were properly managed they might be profitably employed here. Which of these opinions is Correct I Cannot say, but one thing I Can say, and that is that there is none of those animals in use here & but two horses in [the] Colony that I Can here of.

Now sir you may judge how a man feels who has been raised to the use of these animals in Cultivating the ground and you may also judge how things are progressing her[e].

Please tell Absilom Woodfork that I cannot as a friend recommend him yet to come out here untill I have seen farther and that I would advise him not [to] make preparations to come untill I write to him agane.

I look upon you as a friend and now I am about to ask you to act the part of a friend, which I hope you will do, for all those [who] are doing any good here are those who have and who are befriend by people in the U.S.A.

I wa[n]t you to send me out some grindstones and Choping Axes by the Expidition and I [shall] place the mony in Governor Roberts' hands to be sent to you by the vessel when she returns. and if you do not send them yourself please make some arraingment with the society to send some out and I will pay the mony for them for they are verry scere [scarce] here and not a grindstone in reach of us to Sharpen our tools on.

We are sttled about 12 miles from Sea Shore on the north bank of the St. Pall river in a perfect wilderness living in bamboo houses.

Tell Colins Day that I am [in] exelent health and all my family except my wife and is now in better health then we started. Tell all my enquiring friends the sam.

I am no[t] [e]ntierly out of [heart though] I feel doubtful whether we shall be able to do much good here or not. 6 of those who came with us are so much discouraged that they are going return on the Same Vessel, Some of Fishback people and some Mr. Martins.

Tell Uncle Plesant that we have snakes here from 15 to 20 feet and can swalow a man, Dear, or hog with ease. Deer are as comon as hogs or sheep in pasture in Kentuckey and there are a good many lepards also and monkey without number.

My respects to yourself and all enquiring friends, Yours,

Moses Jackson

233 / NELSON SANDERS TO SUSAN FISHBACK

Mrs. Susan Fishback   Monrovia, Liberia, Western Africa,
                                                          January 5th, 1848

My Dear Friend and Benefactor: As the Liberia Packet is about to sail from Africa to America, With the greatest pleasure I embrace the opportunity to write to you agreeably to your request. As far as myself as an individual am Concerned, I am now in the enjoyment of Comfortable health, for which I give praise to the Supreme Ruler of the Universe. You have perhaps been informed previous to this inteligence concerning the large number of Kentuckians besides those of your family of blacks who embarked with me, some of whom have fallen victims to the African fever, but we who survive are doing very well. I am aware that some persons have [written] falsely concerning us, and have given woful accounts of Liberia. If such inteligence have been given it is entirely wrong. Liberia is unquestionably the happyest teritory for the black man that could be selected on the globe. We enjoy liberty here in a degree which it is impossible in the order of things for the Negro to enjoy [in] any other Country. Here is the place the Whence the man of Color, especially a black colour, originated. Here he should teminate if possible. The Beneficent displays of Almighty providence are so visible in Africa for the perpetual benefit of the black man that [no] inteligent Negro, I am persuaded, could take a view of them without feeling in the language of the Bible, that "His tender mercies are over all his works." Africa is like all other countries in one restet [respect]. It has for its inhabitants those who are wise and those who are foolish, they that be indolent and dishonest, Consequently poor, hungry and naked. On the contrary, it has those who are industrious, economical and enterprising and as a natural & necessary consequence they [are] wealthy, useful, & happy. But, as to myself as an individual, [I am] laboring on a fine stone building belonging to the Revd H. W. Ellis, who writes my letter, [t]he Pastor of the First Presbyterian Church in Monrovia, and the best friend that I have found in Africa.[1] My Ship mates and Country men, viz, Ware, Jackson, Scott & others are geting on finely & wishes to be remembered to their friends in Kentucky. They are living in Kentucky in Africa.

Myself, am living in the Town of Monrovia with my good friend above mentioned and expects to continue with him untill such times as I can venture out on "my own hook." I usually perform the duties of Sexton of the Presbyterian Chruch, for which I recieve a Stipend. The political affairs of this Country have undergone a considerable change since my first arival. The Citizens of Liberia have declared their independence, but with dire and [un]becoming exceptions on the part of Benevolent America.[2] The 24 August was the beautiful, happy, Grand, and Memorable day, on which this declaration was Celebrated. The Meeting of Congress took place 1st day of January 1848. We have a Senate & house of representatives. Both houses have convened and organized and proceeded to legislative negotiation. And now I take leave of you for the present, but I hope not forever, for I trust you will condescend to write to me in Africa at least once more, if only to answer this letter. No more at present. I remain, your ever grateful servant,   Nelson Sanders[3]

234 / ELISA THILMAN TO EDWARD BRETT RANDOLPH

Greenville, Liberia, May 11th, 1848

Sir: I take this opportunity of Writing to you hoping this may find you Well. I have Written you before but have not yet received an answer. I wish you to write to me how all your Family is and give my love to Virginia. Tell her I wan to [se]e her. I am yet on the lord's Side and hope to continue so if it be his Wishes. I am alone by mySelf but still I have some friends here. I desires very much to hear from my Mother and all my people. Please to tell them they must Write to me. I have been very sick & never thought I Would recover, but through god assistance I have been raised. I was sorry to hear that your health was bad but you must trust in God and he Will preserve you . . . in Sickness or health. Tell my Mother to Write me and tell me Wether any of my Sisters is religious or not. Tell my Mother I Write to her to let her know that I am still alive. Tell her that my Sister is dead. I am sorry to Say that I had not much hopes of her death; and all her children is dead. And give my love to my Fathe[r] and tell him I trust he is found Christ precious to his Soul. Be of one heart and one mind [and] the god of heaven Will bless him. Tell my Mother to tell me all [about] my sister's ch[ildren]. Tell her that my head is much bowed down but looking up to Christ. He [is] able to raise it up again. I have no more to Say at present. I remain Your Friend,
Elisa Thilman[1]

Mr. P. C. Cameron Eqr   Grand Bassa,
                                                                    May 29th, 1848

My Dear young Master & friend: I Take up my pen To drop you a
few Lins from This place To inform you That we all reach hear quit saf
and all well. I wrote you by The Brig Bound for New York on my arrival
at Monrovia. The Brig was histing sails To go To seea and I had To write
in grate hast, Tho I hop you was able To make it out, Tho it was badly
writen and worst Spelt. The nex day after we dropt ancorag at Monrovia, I went on shore To visit The Town in company with Capt. Good-
manson and Walker. We Spent The day in visiting The native School
and The publick Buildings, The churches, &c. The nex day we wer invitead To dine with Rev. Mr. [Hilary] Teage who gav ous dinner in Th
American Stile. [We had] Tea in The Eavning with Col. [Beverly Page]
Yats. The nex Morning [we were] invitead To Brexfast at The president
hous by Dr. [Henry J.] Roberts, The Presidents Brother.[1] The President is
gon To The U.Stats. This day we dind with gen. [J. N.] Lewis, Sacatary
of State.

The nex day [we] visits The Setlers on The St. Paul, 20 Miles from
Monrovia. Up This River is all The farmers and planter. The St. Paul is
as Larg as The ronok. On This Stream all The farming of The Country is
Carad on. The Land is very Rich in deed producing Rice, Corn, Cas-
sadars, ginger, and arrow rout. Orang and other fruit Treeas Loocks
very well and is loaad with fruts. This is the rainee season in Africa So I
Cannot go far in The Country To look at it. But The river lands is good. I
reach grand Bassa Cove on the 23 in The mor[n]ing. Found The Bar very
Bad indeed. Had To land The Emagrants on The Beach and let them walk
up To Bassa and Then Lan The Cargo over the Bar as Then can get The
chancs. I had my bead [bed?] and all my Clothing mad as wet as watter
Cold [could] make Them and Like To Lost Them at That. The Bote
Turned over in the Sea with Them. As Soon as I Can I intende To go up
to Bexly and Settle up Ther. It is 8 mills from The Cove in the Sam County. I went up the river The other day as far as Bexly. The St. John is a
butiful stream 1 mile wid. Well, The Land on Both Sids is verry rich indeed. I Think Bexly much The Best place for me That I has seen in The
Country. Judg [John] Day has offerd me a room in his hous until I can
Build one of my owne. I am not sertian wher I shall Buill yet as I dont
Know weather I shall reman hear or not. I may go To Siroleone [Sierra
Leone] or return To america. I am not Surtian. I have visitead all The
farms on the St. Johns and Benson River and intend going up The Mack-
ling River as soon as I can do so. I find practice anuf in This place but no

pay. Mony in Africa is out of The question. Every Boddy wants Drs But non Can pay Them. I have at this Time 5 pathints and The five is not worth $5. I Think farming is The Best Buisness for This Country But I cannot go into That Buisness yet. The Land and Labor is verry cheap in this country. I hop I will be able To write you in my nex sumthing new in regard To my remaning in africa. It is a verry fin Country but I dont Think it will sutt me at Present. I may be com satisfide with it but it is doutful at Present.

Remember me To all, old Master and Miss Margrat and Miss Mildred and Miss Ann and the children, all so [to] all my colard friends, my Brothers and ant and ther children, Sip and Phily, old Ben Parks, Ben umstard, Daniel watsan and his family, hernry Dixson, David Bell and uncl Luk and all The Black famly. Allso remember me to Charity, Moly, old Patty York, and grace and her family and write me who you hav sent To The South. Rememer me to E. Tilly, John Ray, and all my old nabors, all so my frend William, Harris, Mark Tate, S. Pipir, and William Pipir and ther familys. Remember me to Mr. Green and Richard Ashe & Mr. McDall [?]. I cold call 100 moor names but tell them all how day for me. I hop in my nex I will have sumthing To write you. This is a very fin Country for sum peple but I am a frad it will not sut me. I am at Present Bording with The Rev. A. P. Davis, The Baptis Mishioner at Grand Bassa, Tho I will Leav hear in fiv or six days for Bexly. I remain, yours,   Virgil P. McParrhan [Bannehan?][2]

Remember me to ovid and his family all so Pats and Demtredy

236 / JACOB HARRIS TO N. M. GORDON

Rev'd N. M. Gordon   Monrovia, Liberia, July 4th, 1848

Dear Sir: I take this oppitunity of writing you a few lines the object of which is to inform you of my helth and Condition up to this date. George, Frances, and my Self are all having the acclimating fever and have all bin down but I Give thanks to all might God that we have bin sparred and raised to our feet againe. I all So state that all of us are highly pleased with the Country and flatter our Selves that we will be able by useing industry and Good Economy to Secure to our Selves a Comphortable and honorable living. This Country I believe to be the Colored man's home. Why should we not be Contented? Please to make application to Messrs. Casady and Rainey Store in Louisville by which application you will assertain that things were left off—and a cupple of working tools and a cupple of watter buckets, one pare of shares [shears] belonging to frances and the silk handerchiefs and all So a box containing several dozen of blacking. Give my best respects to inquiring friends particularly my Colored friends. Tell them that we are all well Satisfied and we have grown to the full stature of men—an experience [they are?] unacquainted [?] with and will continue to be so long as they [remain] in America. I have the honour to remain your humble servant.

Jacob Harris[1]

237 / VIOLET GRAHAM TO JAMES HAYNES, JOHN RAMSEY, AND THOMAS HALL

Caldwell, Liberia, November 9th, 1848

Mr. James Hanes and John Ramsy and Thomas Hall: We are All Well that are a Live and we hope to hear from youall. Mily Orston, Melenday and Her 3 Children and Eliza and martha ann any [and] Daughter them are all ded. My Famely are all well. Jacob and James Keley, Ralph Maderson Sends there best Respects to James Michel and his family. James and Justus have got converted and Join the Methodis[t] Church. Violate Huston, Mary Mariah Huston and Charles Jeferson, Samuel Henderson and Lucinday Jane, Ann Roxana—all are members of the M.E. Church. If we never see youall no more in this world we hope to meet you all in the kingdom of heaven. Sister Clary and Sister Rebeca and brother Steven, If youall are not found the Lord, never Rest until you find him. This is my letter that I write to you. Brother Lambus Sends his best respects to his wife and Children. John Huston is well but he remains a Siner as yet. We all Sends our best Respects to all the Inquiring friends &c. We all dezirs for you to Send us Some thing. We have never had no Leters nor nothing sense we left home. We are all pleas with Africa and Satisfied &c. Violet Huston is maried [to] Jery Mire [Jeremiah?] Graham and now my name is Violate Graham.

To Miss Dicy Hanes: Lucinday Jane, the girl that [is] your age, are maried to A yong man by the name of Thomas A Morris. My love to Steven McClenon and his wife and all his Children. John Wesley Can now begin to Reade a little. Little Adline Has Begun to Spell and the other children have not had the chance of goin to School as yet being a widow and having to work hard. Me and my Children have improved my land and got a deed for it. Please to ansur this Leter as Soon as you can. No more, remain yours in love and respect. Mrs. Violate Grayham[1]

Mr. Josiah Sibley   Greenville, Sinoe, Liberia,
                                                          September 19th, 1853

Dr Sir: I find an opportunity of sending you a few lines and I think it
my duty to do so. My self and wife Mary and all the children are all well
at present and dowing as well as can be expected in a new country, and
we are better satisfied than we ever was in our lives. I hope this few lines
will find you and your family well. I will not omit to informe you of the
massacree which toke place on this cost [coast] some time in July last, but
it was out of the bounds of liberia about 50 or 60 miles north of Cape
Palmos, at a place called tabboo, whear the English trade with the africans; that is, it is one of their trading places and they had a larg lot of
goods in store at that place for the purpose of bying palmoil and Ivery
and calm wood. & one Capt. Jackson, an englishman with a four topsel
Schooner, droped anchor at that point and went on Shoar to look after
his buissiness and the Savages conspired agains him and Severed his head
from his body and then Some 75 or 100 armed themselves with weapons
and got in the cannoes and went on board of the Schooner and murdered
all the crew, but one, that kept himself in some close place and they toke
charge of the Schooner and all the cargo. In a short time their came a
long a nother english trader and when he found what the Savages had
don, not being able to recover the property no other way, he flattered
them and told them that they had don right. So he bought the Schooner
and the cargo from them up on the best terms he could and has gone to
england with the sad news. It is though [thought] that the english government will Seek revenge soon. I must say and tell the truth liberia is improving very fast. The people lern Some thing more about cultivating the
land. The peoples mines [minds] are much upon coffee. Cotton do not do
very well on the cost and we are not full handed a nough to go back in
the up country yet, but hope we Soon will; but by being industrious we
make bread, plenty, such as the country affords. [We have] the Sweet
potatoe and Cassada, which is Some thing like corn bread, and they are
fine for hogs and cows. I See very plain this young and infant republic
bids fair to become a grate peopl. Our laws are modled after the laws of
georgia, with but little exception, and the people oby [obey] them. It is
all idle talk and not true when it is Said that the black people can not
govern them selves and you would Say So if you could inspect liberia or
visit this republic for a short time. I must Say to you I have Seen a white
man from georgia traversing the Streets of Greenville and he came out in
to the country places a mong the farmers and Spoke hily of our new beginning. I am not acquainted with the gentleman and I omited to lern
what office he fills on the man a war Constitution commanded by Com-

modore Mayo. They Stoped on the 20 of August and left in a few days. The young man I think you know and it looks as if I ought to have known him, but it is So, I do not. His name is William R. Gardner. The officers all came on Shoar and they looked well. I hope I shall hear from you the first opportunity, and if it is not saying too much, do send Some old School books to the children, for in this new country such thing are thankfully received, for Some times they can not be had for money nor love.

I must close by Saying that Liberia is the Star in East for the free black man. Do rely upon what your Servant Says about liberia.

Seaborn Evans[1]

239 / A. B. HOOPER TO SAMUEL TILLINGHAST

S. W. Tillinghast   Monrovia, Sept. 27, 1853

Dear sir: With Much pleasure I Drop you a few lines to in form you that I am very well and I hop you are the Same and your family likwise. This letter I Dorp [drop] with pleasure bause [because] you were a great friend of my Master Thomas C. Hooper whoes name I love to Beir in Mind. Years have Roled out Scince he has pased a way and I am in the land of my Farthers. His name shall never die in my mind. He was a friend and a Farther to poor me. When thir was none to watch over me he keep an eye on me for good. He advised me tho I was his little slave. His treatment was that of a Farther. The name of Hooper stands hight in this Republice. I am very Happy to in form you that the Republic is advancing and our trade commerce are Reapidely increasing. Liberia must be come a powerful Republice. The Europen powers have gott thire eye on us for our commerce. We have Jusst recd one 1000 Stand of Armes from France one 1000 suits of uniform and one 10 gun Brig of war. These are Signs that the united stats government ought to look at [us]. France and England are watching Each other in Relation to the trade of Africa. I am Duing well. I am planting coffee and suger cane, ginger and AroRoot, ground nuts. I have one of the Most Beautifull coffee Farmes in Liberia, 4000 trees given coffee and 100000 young trees, 50000 of them to be planted out nex season on a farm of 200 acres that I have Just purchesed to plant coffee on. I perposed planting 20 or 25 Acres suger cane also nex season if nothing hapens. I Must close. Monrovia is Becoming to be a Fine city. Brick house after Brick house are goin up and the Same up the Beautiful St Paules. The St. Pauls are one of the fines Rivers I Ever saw. Fancy you see the Hudson River and then you see the Beautiful St. Pauls.

Do sir if you please Remember [me] to Mrs. Tillinghast and your kind sister Mrs. Hank and all the young gentlemen of the family and Ladies, and to all of my Masters friend, doe if you pleas Remember me to them. Dont for gitt to call my name to old friends E. Winslow Esq., Jon and Warran Esqrs., Mr. Sanuel Hanley, Mrs. James H. Hooper, Mr. Joseph Hooper and James Husk, E. J. Hale, Esq. and Ladie, and to all that I have for gotten. Dou if you please lett me hear from you very Soon and if you can I wood be very much a blige to you if you wood send me a small Box of seed of all kinds and in the Same Box some corn [and] grap cuttings of all kinds that grow in Fayettville. Please to say to Mrs. James Hooper [that I] will write to hear next month via England. Marchell and wife and Daughter are in good health and he and wif begs to be rememberd to you and family. I am very happy to in form you the people that came from Fayeettvulle are all well and well satisfide with thier new home. They are all settled on thir Farmes near Millsburgh. Old man Robbin and wife are Booth Ded. He died with bowlel complaint. T[el]l all my colord Brother to come home and take posesion of the land of our Farthers. Tell them to come and lett us Build up a great Replublice to our Selfes. Sir I remain your obd Servant,   A. B. Hooper[1]

Send your letter to the Cear of J. N. Lewis, Esq.

240 / MARY ANN CLAY TO "MR. CLAY"

Monrova, Sept the 27/53

Mr. Clay, Dear Sir: I again attempt to address you Again with a few lines as I have wrote you three or four times and have not receive not one line from you Since I left you. I hope that this will be receive by you. It would give me a greate deal of pleasure to receive a letter from you if it is but one or two lines. I can asshure you that I am very much please with Liberia Since I have had the feaver, and I can asshure you that I am more thankful to you for Sending us to the Land of our four Fathers and where we can enjoy our fredom. It is true that I have been a great deal of afflicted Since I left America But I hope that I will Soon be well again. I am now residing In the family of Gen'l John N. Lewis, and I am very happy to Say that they are very fine people. I could not wish to be in a better family. They are very good to me. There is nothing Strange worth relating. I write you to let you know that I think a grate deal of [you]. I lost my two Children in the feaver. Lucy lost hers Comeing out with the Small pox. Please to give my respects to Mr. Joseph Pen and hope that he is well, also to Mrs. Ann Clay and your Daughter Martha Clay and I hope that they are well, also to William and all of my people, to young Sidney Clay, Darison Clay, Green Clay mother and please to let me Know weather She is liveing, also to all the friends. and please to let me Know wether Cousin Anna have made up her mind to Come to Liberia with her children.

Mr. Clay, Mr. Canerday tole us that you gave Mr. Cowen money which was given to the agent. We never have got [it] and he tolde us if we did not get it we must write you.

If you ever write me, please to direct it to Gen'l Lewis.

I would be happy to receive any thing from you. You had better take a trip to Liberia and I can asshure you that you will be very happy with the country.

No more but remains your Moste humble Servant,   Mary Ann Clay[1]

241 / LUCY CLAY TO BRUTUS J. CLAY

Brutus Clay Esqr   Monrovia, Liberia, 29th Sept. 1853

Dear Friend,   Feeling assured that you would be pleased to hear from me, I concluded to address you a short letter by the barque "Shirley" which sails from this port in a few Days for Baltimore. This makes the fourth letter I have written to you since I have been to this country, and I have not received an answer to either of the former letters, but being anxious to hear from my old home and friends, I am encouraged to make another trial and In all probability I may be successful in this attempt. Myself and Aunt has been much afflicted since we have been here, but notwithstanding I feel quite satisfied with the place, and like it very well. I have not as yet regretted that I left my native home, though I have often been unwelcomly circunstanced. One of the children died with the small pox on the voyage out, and two with the fever after their arrival here. The articles of domestic use you gave for our use here, I must thank you kindly for, though I am sorry that I have to say that we were compelled to barter them away during our sickness for such necessaries as we required, being not able to obtain them otherwise. I should be more than thankful if you would send me some domestic goods for my own purpose if you can do so. I am sorry that I am under the necessity of asking aid from so distant a quarter, but my circumstances obliges me to do so, believing that by asking in a becoming manner I will get some assistance. Please remember me affectionately to Mrs. Ann Clay, Mr. Sidney Clay, Mr. Robert Kenaday, Miss Isabella Clay, and all the friends I have not mentioned, also my Aunt Louisa.

Hoping you and family are well, I subscribe myself Your obedient Servant,

Lucinda [Lucy] Clay

242 / CHARLES JEFFERSON TO THOMAS KENNEDY AND JAMES HAYNES

Dr Thos. Kenedy &
James Haynes

Clay-Ashland, Liberia,
Near Monrovia, March 31st, [18]55

D[ea]r Sirs: Since our arrival in Liberia we have been in tolerable health; viz, after we passed through the fever. Athoulth [Although] Uncle Austin and his mother, Mellet, they are both dead. So far we all seeme to be well pleased with the country but so far as getting along we find it quite hard, i.e., a man has to labour very hard here in this country. And now the money which we were to get here after we arrived here the next fall we have never seen or ever even heard of it and the reason of it we can not tell. The money also which Doctor Kenedy gave to Maria and her children, into the hands of James Haynes, Esq., we have never seen it as yet, the amount being $500. If you have not sent it, will you please to do so, and if you send it not in cash, please send it in goods or things suitable to your convenience. Maria has been very low, say about the 13th of Feb'y, but since then she is much better. Please state to my father that I am well, and doing well at the present. And if he can make it convenient to come out so do, as I will be glad to see him here. My love and kindest regards to all my enquiring friends, and tell them I am well and am trying to make a liveing as well as I can. The money that was to have gone to Vilet and her family, they have not received any thing as yet.

Please if convenient when you send their money, seperate Mariah's from Vilet's. Vilet and all her family are well and she sends her best respects to you. Please tell father that I have now arrived [at] the manhood and tell him that the things that he promised me he will try and send by the first opportunity as I am in need of them. Lucinda Jane is well and doing well and she sends her respects to you. Rena Paralea she is also well and at present doing well. She also sends her regards to you. Lucinda Jane sends her respects to Miss Mary Jane Haynes and tell her many a day has she longed to see her. I state to you that Alinda and her two children are dead. Master James Haynes, your favourite Chas. Jefferson has now become a man and wishes all the help you can let me have. I wish to hear by you from all our people there, how and if they are well. Please write me by the 1st Opportunity, &c., either send or write. Yours Respectfully,

Charles Jefferson

Please direct them to S. F. McGill & Bros., Monrovia, with this direction, Chas. Jefferson, Care of S.F. McGill & Bros, Monrovia

243 / RANDALL KILBY TO JOHN R. KILBY

Mr. John R. Kilby Lower Buchanan, Grand Bassa County,
Rep[ublic] Lib., W.A., June 26 1856

Dear Sir: I Embrace this the present opportunity In writing to you to inform you that I am well hoping by these few lines to find you and yours Enjoying the best of health. In ansuer to your Request what are the Bunch's people doing and where do they live, &c.: Lucy lives hear near me in town. She is doing as well as can be Expected though she has not a very good House to live in. Fanny is also living near me. She has a good House to live in and is doing tolerable well for an old person. Rufus is not doing so well. He lives three miles from us. He married a widow named Brown. Ben Bunch is not very well himself & his wife is in a low state of health. They live so near that I can stand in my door and call them. Davy is dead. Martha Ann is living. Joshua is dead. Hanibal is dead. Josiah, born here, is living. Lawrence Bunch is Living at Junk Marshall some thirty miles from here. I [hear] from him that he is doing well. He is married. Myself and my wife are well at this time. My wife is sitting with her two little ones on her Knees Lap; the other I do not know where she would put it if it was living. John Early Wesley Gray Kilby was born Nov. 25th, 1855 and Amelia Ann Kilby was born Nov. 25, 1855, Both at one an the same time, and also Commodore Perry Kilby was also born at the same time, so you see that I had Three at one birth. Abram Joseph is dead. He died on Board of the vessel. Solomon McGuire Kilby, George Washington, Moses Abner, my Children are living. I Recd the Barrel of flour and the Box safe. In Regard to coffe, it is in the Rainy Season and we can not Clean &c; nor gather Coffee. But as soon as the season Returns I will send you Some. Tell Mr. Joseph Kilby that I am glad that he is well and am happy to hear that he is married. Tell Mr. Madison Bailey I hope that he and his family are all well, Archibald Reddick and his family, Captain Cutler and his family. Tell Dr. James Brown that I and my family are well at the present time, hoping to find him and his family Enjoying the Best of Health. Please inform him that we are greatly troubled with the chills & agues and please ask him if he will be so kind and obliging as to send a few of his pills. My best Respects to Mrs. Corbell, to my sister Jenny and her children, to her husband Fabous Lewis Norflett and his family, Tom Copeland & family, Esau Smith, Jacob Smith and to all

Enquiring friends. Please tell Tom Copeland to write me what he is doing at the present time and howe he is getting along at this time. I am Lying with my head on my arms and my arms on the Holy Bible. I hope that all are well, Excepting Elijah Hampton for the Five Lick he gave me and tell him to send me my half dollar that he owes me for my Hound. I hope that Julius Gordon & family are well. So no more at present, but God be with you all. I am dear Sir your Humble Svt,   Randall Kilby[1]

244 / SEABORN EVANS TO JOSIAH SIBLEY

Mr.Josiah Sibley   Greenville, Sinoe County, Liberia,
                                                          November 5th, 1856

Sir: I embrace this opportunity to Send you a few lines once more as I wish to informe you how we are geting a long Since the war. My self and my family are all well and much better then one could Expect taking under consideration the great war. We have [had war] in our community for Six months. It is true numbers of our neighbors Suffered very much for Some thing to Eat and clothes to wear as the Africans Run them from their houses, comeing upon them unawares, and after taking out Such things as they wanted they burned the houses to ashes. But I must Say with a heart full of gratitude to him who rules all nations, I was able to maintain my position at home, but by hard fighting and runing great risk. But they did not hurt me nor none of my people. But after the President came to our ade with all the forces of Liberia we took up the line of march and went through the country all round us and burned 92 Towns and destroyed almost Evry thing they had to Subsist upon and they Soon came in and Signed a Treaty of peace.[1] And now we have then under our control as we have been wanting to get theme Every Since I have been here. Now they stand in fear of us. I have a better crop growing now than I Ever had Since I have been in the Country and my coffee is doing well. I have lerned by Experience that, if a man will work, he can make a living, and a good living, after he has been here a few years. And I am happy to Say the time is not far distant when men may Even make fortunes by growing Coffee, and a variety of other vegetables, which grow in a bundance here. Hard work is a good medicine for the black man in this country, for I have better health here than I Ever had in my life. Since I have been in Liberia, I have been able to improve my Self so that the Methodist Missionary Society have Employed me to teach School in my Settlement, and I have been appointed Justice of the peace in Sinoe County for the last 4 years. So I must say, upon the hole, that I am much pleased with my new home. This is the place for the free black man to bring up his children. We are badly Situated at present in this country on the account of books, as we have no book nor paper manufacture, and the people are all poor and have but few books and Some have none, and Especially the poor African, who Seem of late to be anxious to Send their children. Notwithstanding the Missionary Society Send books to the different Schools, their is a great many children that wish to come to School that do not for want of books. Seeing all this my Self it drives me to do all I can for the rising generation in this young Republic. So all I can do at present is to beg. So I appeal once more to your Sympathy, and I pray you will condesend, if I am not asking you for too much, to Send me Some books and writing paper. Such things will be greatly [gratefully] receved by my Self and others in this poor country. It is Strang but it is the truth, the africans children lern the book faster than the American children, and the better it will be for us the Sooner we get the Africans civilized, and to lern them the book is the fastest way to do it.

I must say again I am well pleased with this country and with the climate also. The black man have better health Journaly [generally] in this country than he had in America, notwithstanding he may be born in America. It is true Some people come to this country that complain against the country and Say they cannot live here, but it is nobody but lazy people who had the overseer to drive them in America, and the misfortune is they have no overseer to drive them here. I Remain you humble Servant, With Respect,   Seaborn Evans

245 / SUSAN CAPART TO JOHN KIMBERLY

Mr. J[ohn] K[imberly], Chapel Hill   Mar the 1st, 1857

Dear Sir: I am happy to say to you that I am well at present and hope that these few lines may fiend you in the same state of health. Here I have bin 7 years and I have not heard from none of you yet but I heard that Truston Kimb[er]ly was dead. I often think of the children. I have 3 Children a living and they are well at the present. Andrew is able to help me right smart. Harrett my daughter is a going to the school on the mishion on saint Pauls river in a little place called Millsburgh to a white woman by the name M. Wilkins and she is highly esteame by her teacher. As for me I am a geting a long very well, living with a man by the name of Filoph Coper on saint pauls river. But my land is in Virginia [in Liberia] farming on the smalls, but I am a doing Very mutch the same work that I did when I was in the america and the longer that I live in Africa the better I like it. I see a great meny white people from the north but I cannot see eny one that can tell me eny thing about you.

Mother and father is yet a live and a doing very well and family and sends their compliments and is able to raise his own swetening and & other thing to teadious to menchion untill I can hear from you. George died last year. I would like to send the Children sumpthing but it is ilconvenient to get eny one to carry it, and if you are eny ways near to Mr. Cullin Caphart and family, boith white and color, an Mrs. amstud and family an also all that may enquire for me, I or we send our love and compliment. I have writen to you all often but cannot her from none of you. Mrs. Magill and Mr. Burns & meny others exspects to come to the America soon. I see so meny come out here and other people sending their people sompthing that has bin out here so much longer than we has it makes me think that you all has for got us all. We still bare the name of Caphart.

William Kimble is well and has one Child. Myself and Harrett is a member of the methodis Church and Isaac, but he has joinde the babtis Church. And this you fiend [find] within is the hand writing of Harrett [which] she desired you to see. But I must say to you all that I am not Maried yet. And tell Mr Bauldin Caphart that I would like to here from him.

I heard that you had about a year ago you sent my father sompthing, but he never got it. If you did and if you send eny thing else, I hope that you will remember me. Yours most obediunt friend,   Susan Capart[1]

246 / JACOB HARRIS TO N. M. GORDON

Kentucky in Liberia, Monstasado County, May 15, 1857

Rev and Dear Sir: I embrace this opportunity of writing you a few lines. I am settle in Virginia Settlement. I have my house up and living in it with my family. I like this county very well. The only thing a man wants is to have a little means to enable him to farm extensively. I would be glad to know of Georges' whereabouts. I havent heard from him Since he went back again.

You promised with Mr. Hill promised to send us Something after we got settle here. We are now ready to receive thankfully whatever you may be pleasd to send us. We need it now very much.

Tell all of our friends that may emigrate here that they should prepare themselves well. This is a new county. Let them provide themselves with hoes, axes, clothes, provisions, and Leaf tobacco and some money. All are necessarily useful here.

My wife and myself Give our Joint love to you and yours and wish you much health and happiness in this life and eternal felicity in the life to come. Yours obt Sevt,   Jacob Harris

Dr. Ellis Malone   August 2d, 1857, Cape Mount, Liberia

Sir: Its with the greatest pleasure that I write you from this Land of Freedom. After A Short and pleasent passage of 34 days I arrived at Grand Cape Mount, A new Settlement having been formed here not quite one year ago. But it has far outstript many of the Older Settlements, as it now numbers upwards of 400 inhabitants, A happy, industriious and free people, who seem determined to show that even in Africa there is and can be a nation of Free and happy Children of a hitherto downcast and oppresed Race. I feel glad and happy That I ever heard of and came to this goodly land. The half has not been told of this country. I forebear to say much but where I now am, the prospect is flattering and with the amount of goods, &c., That I wish to get and hope that you will Interest yourself in, I shall in a short time reap a handsome fortune. I enjoy as yet the best of health. Have had no Sickness whatever since I left North Carolina and did my Coloured Friends only know or could they have seen what I already have seen they would not hesitate a moment to come to this Glorious Country. I would wish you read or let Mr. Daniel Hill read this letter and give my respects to all of that family. Tell them I now begin to enjoy life as a man should do. I look upon you as my friend while I am in this goodly land. Now is my time of want and these things will not cost more than 70 or 80 $ and will bring back in return to 4 fold. It will bring back what is much needed in North Carlina. We have here mahogany, Rose wood, Ebony, Brimstone And Gum Arabac, Catauche or India Rubber, the white kind, all of which I will either send or bring myself. I have seen cotton Trees here measuring 30 feet around And I intend to collect a box of Curiosity for you. Mr. Campion the writer of this who has been here some time kindly volunteers to assist me. He has travelled with Revd. John Seys and understands the country well. It is as cool here as any place need be within the tropics and I beleive that I shall not only benefit myself but also my freinds at home as well as here in Africa. I never knew before what I was indebted to you for what knowledge I now porses. I can never thank you as I ought, but whenever I think of you and the little mule and Old Buck It will stimulate me to do great and good things. I have some Idea that the practice of medicine will be my future study, having an Eye also to the Judicial Bench. Yours Truly,

Henry Chaver[1]

I wish that you would be so kind as to furnish me with the following Articles, by the return of the M. C. Stevens in November and I will forward you by her return double what they may cost you, in Ivory and Cam wood, Palm Oil, Gold dust, &c. I wish to commence trade and the following Articles will just Set me up: 500 lb Tobacco in the Leaf, 4 Or 5

Blls of Flour, 1 Bll Black Eyed Peas and Chowders, 10 peices Calico prints, 10 Peices Narrow Stripe Homespun, 1 Box Pipes, 1 Bll white Beans, 1 Keg musket Powder, 1 US Musket, 1 Small Box women's shoes, No. 5, 6, 7, 8, 1 Peice Madras Handkercheifs, 10 lb. Mixed Glass Beads. Now, Dr. These things will be of the utmost help [to] me to make you ample returns by the next vessell. Now, Sir, I am at a stand. I wish to say a great deal more but fearing that my freinds may think i exaggerate. My respects to all Miss Nancy Thomas family, White & Coloured, All my relations at Dunsans up Tar River. And try and persuade them to come to Grand Cape Mount right on the Beach and live, for they are only a staying where they are. Particlarily tell Hilray Dunsans to come and bring all his tools and all such things as i write to you, for I only regret that I did not come to this country 10 years ago, and bring all the children you can.

248 / LUCY CLAY TO BRUTUS J. CLAY

Monrovia, August 19th, 1857

Mr. Brutus Clay: I now avail my self of a favourable opportunity to address you with a few lines this being fifth one hoping that these few lines my find you and all the family in good helth as they leave me at present. I would be happy to be informd wither or not Mr. Sidny Clay is dead or not also all inquireing friends. Pleas give my respects to M. S. Clay and all his people on the plantation. I have bin informed that you have herd that Mary and myself ware booth dead but thanks be to God we are booth yet alive. Mary and my self follow washing for a livelyhood at twenty five sent a day, sowing nine pence a day. We canot make much at our wok for the provishion is high, pork the lowest price twenty cen, fl[o]ur from a nine pens to ten cents a pound to 1 dollar and half per pound, sugar twenty five cents a pound, butter seventy five cents per pound, lard twenty five cents per pound, coffee twenty five cents per pound. We have had a famine in our land and if it had not of bin for the fruit many would have died with hunger but thanks be to God the times is better than they have bin 6 months past. As to my self i cannot say that I have bin a day without something to eat if it was fruit only. If any of the family have any regard for us we would like to see it exibited your assistance to us. It is true we both drawd land but was not ab[l]e to improve it and in consequence it went back to the publick again. As to the little affects that we brought out we had to dispose of them in our affliction for nurishment which left us destitute. I have bin afflicted five years some part of the time not able to walk. I had to crall as a child but thanks be to God i am getting better but I am quite feble as yet for want of strong food. I am not maried. I rema[in] in the Clay's family yet and Mary also is not married. I would be happy to receive any donations from any of the family that they may feel dispose to send such as flour, bacon, shugar, mackerel, tea, butter, corn meal, dried beans or peas, some calicoes, some white shirting and yellow domestic & pair of shoes [size] seven, 6 pair of cotton stockings. Mis Ann Clay pleas to send me a white counterpin or a blanket. Pleas send me a bonnet to suit your fancy, also a white mul muslin dress. My respects to Miss Marthy Clay and tell her to send me some pockit handkercheifs, mits, ribbion lace and spool cotton, pins, neadels, edging, 1 cordid skirt and hook and eyes. Pleas tell my father Harrison to send me a pair geanings [jeans?] or a hansom dress either. Tell aunt Luwesea to send me somthing. We herd that she had something to send me but herd that we were dead. Tell her that I am ready to receive them with thanks. We herd that Cassy and rillea was coming and we herd that they were sent to Massippi to be acclimated. I shoul be happy to be inform whare my Mother was and what county she is in as I would like to rite to her. Pleas inform me. Tell Cousin Amy her husband is well in health but not in condision. He livs 40 miles from me. I see him but seldom. Give my love to Uncle William, Uncle Richard, Uncle Abraham Matson and all inquiring friends and if i never more see them i live in hops to meet them in a better world to come.

Pleas send me some dried fruit, dried appels, peaches, pars, quin[c]eys, damsions, cherrys and some walnuts, chesnuts and hickrynuts. I would like to send you somthings but my surcumstances will not admit of it at present but when it is in my power so to do i will. I ad no more but remain Your Humble Servant,   Lucy Clay

249 / RICHARD McMORINE TO JOHNSTON PETTIGREW

Buchanan City, Palm Grove,
Liberia, Grand Bassa County, June, 1858

Mr. Johnston [Pettigrew], Dear Sir: As it seems that the Letter that I wrote Have not Been Recievd I write you again As you said that you would Like to hear from me after I had Been out Some time. I wrote Yo[u] some two years AGo But have not heard from you. But I wrote to Mr. E. M. Forbs at the Same time and he Says that he did not Reciev my Letters. So I think that you did not Reciev yours & so I write again. I hope that you will Receive this & that this may find you in Good health & all of your people. I my self injoy as Good health as I could Expect in this Country. The Country is a Good Country. I have no Fault to find with the Country. It is a Good Country, But it is a new Country. It is hard to live in all new Countrys at first. But it is much Better to live here now then it was when I first Came here. All it wants now is a little money and the people to Go on their Farms & Go to work. I said that the Country was a Good Country. It is. We Can Raise all most any thing that we can in the US Stats. I have seen all most Everything But wheat. It will Grow But it will not head. But Every thing Else will Grow and will Grow well. It is true that on the san Beach whare we live things will not Grow so well. But Go up the River whare the Land is good and all these things will do well. There is Some of our people Removed up on their Farms and Some of them is a doing well. People here that Go on their Farms Can do well and I hope that more will Go on their Farms. The time have Been when the people Could not Go on their Farms for the natives ware so war Like. But I think that there [is] no danger now. When I Came to this Country we Could not Go on A Farm. But now I tink there is no danger. There is many people here is very poor. Many of them have had masters Barn and Smoke house to Go to and now when they have to Look to themselves for Every thing they do not no what to do. But the people here have Been all a trying to trade for a Living. But they Be Gin to find that all Cannot live By trade and so some have Gone to their Farms. Now we here from palmas that the people are a doing well at their Farms, and from Sinoe they are adoing well, and From St. Palus [Paul's] River we no that they are adoing well for we Get our Syrup and Sugar from them as much as we send for. And why not Bassa do the same thing? I do not see why we should send to St. pauls when we have the same land and the same people. All it want is the people to Go to work. I myself have the Palm Grove Station in Charge during the absence of the Revnd j. Rambo. I am Living at the mission house and have charge of the Church during his absence. I meet with the people in Town on Sunday and in the week with the nativs in the Bush. I have been doing missionary work now for two or three yars. I do not no whare my station will Be when he Return. Bishop [John] Payne was with us a few days aGo and took a trip up the River to See the Country. He and my self Both thought it a Beautiful Country up a bout the mountains. The Land is high and we thought fertile and we thought it a helthy place. We Saw a butiful crop off Rice on hy Ground and we saw tanger, [tania?] Casada, all Growing well, Some fine sheep, some fine Cattle and Goats, the Best Cows & Bulls that I have seen since I have Been in the Country.[1] The Bishop thinks that he will make a mission station up there and I do not no But I may Be sent up there to preach to the nativs or to keep a School for them.

If so then my labours will Be to the nativs in tirley. Here my Labours is one part in town and the other in the Country. But I Shall not no About this until january next. I have not had as Good an opportunity To Look at the Country as I would have Like to have had, For when I Came out here the Ship that Brought my things was Lost and all that I had was Lost. So I Could not go about to Look at the Country as I would have done. But I have not faild to in quire off all that I Could to be well in formed about the Country. I know that the place that I Live is a Good Country. All it wants as I Said is a little money and the people to Go on their Farms and Go to work. The Land is Good. The Country is not so hot as it is in our Country. I have never seen it But 88 in this Country. But I have seen it 100 in our Country. I have seen it in E. City up to 100 hunred which I have never seen in this Country. And so I think that this after all a Good Country. But it is like all new countrys, has two sids. All new Country is spoken Bad of at First Becaus there is so many that go to a new Country that want to Live without work. But I find that we Cannot live without work in no Country. We must do Some sort off work if we want to live, for God have said in thy seet [sweat] of thy Face shalt thou Eat Bread untill thou Return unto the Ground from whence thou was taken. So then we find if we do not work we Brak Gods law. But it might be said do you work well? I Can say when I came out here I Built me a small house the first thing that I did, then went to work and help to Build the mission house, then took c[h]arge off a school at Fish town and keept Sunday School Every sunday and after mrs. Rambo died then took Charge of the mission house as agent of the place whare I now live and now I have Charge of the Church at this time Sunday in town & in the week in the Bush [I preach] To the native man. This is my work. Some Days [I] walk 20 miles, preach 4 or 5 times. I think that you can tell By this if I work or not. This will show what I do for the Country, whether I work or play.

As to people being sent out here, I think that no one ought to Be sent out here after they pass fifty. They are to old to Get a Start to Live. When we Come to this Country we have to Begin Life again and if we are old we cannot Get A Start. Before we suffer. So old people ought not to Be sent to this Country. There was some old people Came out from U.S. when I came out. Some of them have died for want off such things as they ought to have and there [are] Some of them alive as yet and they suffer for want of food to Eat. The Lord have Blest me so that I have it to help them, Quite often to keep them alive, people that I never saw before. There is people sent out here with money, But many of them have not had money Before and they do not no what to do with it. So it is Best for those that send their people here and is agoing to Give them money to keep it and give them But little at first and after they have Been here about one year then Give them their money and it will do them som Good.

Now when I Came out there was some people Came out that had some 2 & 3 & 4 & up to 8 hundred [dollars] and not one of them Can to day

Save one dollar of it. It is Gone and they do not no whare. But some of them had some Left and that they will Get now in afew days and if they Get that it will do them Som Good. They now have Learn the Country and so they will no how to tak cear of it. But I never saw people steel so Bad as the people do here in my Life. There is hardly a day that we do not hear off Some one having Lost some thing. But there is two things that I think have Brought this state of things. First that the people Could not Get their Land So they had to set down on 1 1/4 of an acor of Land So they Could not live on that. Sect [Second] they had so Little to do when the time Came For them to Go to work they did not want to work. So they had Rather Steel ten [than] to work. I think that there is some if they had Been able to have went on their Farms they would not have Bee[n] steeling Like they have. But I hope yet for the Better.

Now it is true there is no anamil Labour with us as yet. But a man can, if he will, Go in the Country whare the Land is Good [and] he Can with his hoe make as much as he and his Family Can Eat. But the people Say that we have no meat. If we will we Can have meat, but the Country is warm and we do not need as much meat as we did in a Cold Country. But if we will Go into the Country and will try we Can have as much meat as we may want. We have here in town some Fine hogs some that will way from 100 to 200 pounds & we have Sheep & Goats, Cows, Beef, all most Every week plenty off wile [wild] meat. We Can make our own Sugr, Syrup, & Coffee and our Bread and why cannot we Live? We Can. If we will make our own Cotten and our own Cloth thy [why] then Can we not live? I hope that people will not Say any more that we cannot Live in Africa. God did not make a Country for the man of Collor whare he Could not live.

Mr. Johnston, Dear Sir, I Take a little more off the Time of my Station to ConClude the Letter that I had Be Gan to write you. I hope that it will not Be so long that you cannot Read it. But I thought that I would say something about the Country. Now I come to A close hoping that this may be what you would Like to no of the Country. I do not think that the people here are what they might be, but I hope they will Be Better.

Sir, now I Have told you all that I do. You know that the people that Live By the preaching of the word, they Get But Little. Now the mission Gives me what I Can Eat and Cloths But I Cannot Save anything. So I Cannot Build me a good house. Now I Said that the First thing i did was to Build me A house. So it was. But it was not such a one as I would Like to have when we Come to this Country. We have to Build Such as we Can. But After that we want abetter one So I am not able to Build me one. It will Cost double in this Country to Build what it will in the united Stats. So to Build such a one As I would want would Cost about 700 hundred and so I Cannot Get one. But you no who I am and that my people are with you. So If it would not Be asking two much I would ask you if please to Be so Good as to Give me some thing To Help me to Build me A house. I do not no how Long that I may live and if die my wife will Be Put out off the mission and will have no whare to Go. So if you Can Find it in your heart, please to help me. I now think that I must Stop. So Give My Love to All off your people and now I Remain your umble Servant

Richard Blount. But now Richard Mc Morine, Esqr.[2]

If there is Any thing that you would Like to Give me you Can Send it to Bishop Payne at Cape Palmas or to Mr. G. W. Hall of Baltimore and I will Get it.

250 / CHARLES JEFFERSON TO JAMES HAYNES

Mr. James Haynes   Clay-Ashland August 2nd, 1858

Dear Sir: I again sit down to address you with a few lines in answer to a letter which I received from you dated January 5th, 1855, which letter was truly [the] source of much rejoicing among us all. My mother is yet alive & all the children. Vilet is also a live & all of her family and doing tolerably well. There seems to be a misunderstanding about the amount of money due us. We did not understand that you spent any of our money in the paying of our passage, that you did not inform us of before we received your letter. When we parted at New Orleans you told us that our money would be on the next fall after we left. We have been looking with strong anticipation for it ever since we have been to the country which has been about twelve years & has [not] gotten any thing yet. We were sent away poor & necked and today we remain poor. We yet ask you if you can send us any thing please send it; it will be very acceptable. We are poor & need all the help we can get. We do ask you to send us money but any thing like merchandise or provision, such things are money in this country. I truly hope this letter may find you & family in the enjoyment of perfect health. Please give my respects to Dr. Kennedy & family, Esq John Ramsey & family and all the inquiring friends in the neighbourhood.

Dear Sir this is the second time I have written this year. I wrote [by the] last packet but don't know whether you received it or not. I must close but before doing so I must tell you something about the country in which I live. This country is a great place for hunting. If you can make it convenient to send me six hounds they will be of great service to me in this my new country. My occupation is hunting, getting shingles & farming. &c. I shall wait your answer with the greatest patience. There is a maile vessel that runs from Liberia to Baltimore three times a year. I am now a married man withe one child. We subsist on a root for bread called cassadas & potatoes, plaintain & Bananas. Thous you may understand that I am in a hard Country. The aborigines of the Country since I have been [here] have stolen every piece of Clothes from me. Please to send word to my father, Bob Wilkes that I am well & all his daughters. I now close, Yours Respectfully,

Charles Jefferson

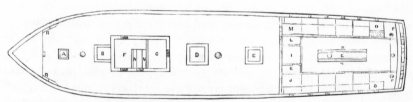

A. Forcastle Hatch. B. Forward Companion-Way to Steerage. F. Cook's Galley. N. Cook's Berths. C. Store Room. D. Main Hatch. E. After Companion-Way to Steerage. M. Captain's State Room. L. and K. Passages leading to Saloon Cabin. I. Pantry. J. Mate's Room. G. Table. H. Sofas. O. Steward's Room and Stairs to Poop Deck. P. and R. Water Closets. Q. Bath Tub.

The *Mary Caroline Stevens*, packet constructed by the American Colonization Society to carry immigrants and supplies to Liberia. American Colonization Society Papers, Library of Congress

10/LETTERS OF A
GEORGIA PREACHER

Ministers, many of them ex-slaves, played a very important role in establishing and sustaining the American settlement in Liberia. Representative of this influential group was Henry B. Stewart, of Savannah, Georgia. His letters for the period 1849-1868, of which twenty-two have been found and are reproduced in this chapter, afford interesting insights into the activities and aspirations of an articulate emigrant preacher who resided in Sinoe County. Stewart began his ministerial work in Liberia as a Presbyterian, but in the fall of 1850 he took the lead in organizing a Congregational church in Greenville—the first to be established in Liberia—and became its pastor.

Stewart and his family embarked from Savannah on the *Huma* on May 14, 1849, and arrived in Greenville on June 27. The ship's roster of passengers lists him as a manumitted carpenter, age forty-two. His wife, a thirty-two-year-old seamstress, was listed as freeborn, as were her eight children who ranged in age from less than a year to fourteen.[1]

In his first letter, written four months after his arrival in Liberia and addressed to William McLain, Stewart expressed gratitude to a kind Providence for enabling him and his large family to settle in this "land of liberty where I can inJoy Equal Rights and worship my god without fear." His devotion to God and his pride in the freedom found in Liberia increased with the passing of time and became the two most notable attributes manifested in his correspondence. In September 1851 he wrote: "Liberia is the home for the Colared man . . . there is no other place for him." On July 4, 1854, he quoted from the Scripture: "The Lord hath done great things for us whereof we are glad." His religious faith helped sustain him in his troubles, among them the loss of his infant son soon after reaching Liberia, and engendered optimism about the country's future. His outlook for Sinoe County was especially hopeful and one of his persistent complaints was the failure of the colonization society to send more emigrants to his home region.

Another of Stewart's salient characteristics was a belief in hard work. "The mandate is unalterable," he wrote on one occasion, "by the Sweat of thy Brow shall they Eat Bread." He chided fellow colonists who did not follow his shining example of unremitting industry. "There are some few fault finders," he wrote on May 10, 1857, "Speaking great things and doing nothing," and on January 20, 1858, he informed Gurley: "The gratis Difficulty in getting the people to work [is] finding that they Can Eat with so Little Labour." On December 19, 1856, he wrote: "We have no use here for *Carriage Drivers*, Boot *Cleaners* & Bottel *washer*, &c."

Stewart was a strong believer in education and self-improvement, for himself, for his children and for all other Liberians. Early in his African sojourn he wrote proudly: "My children are all going to school and are doing well." In 1860 he sent his fifteen-year-old son, Thomas, to the United States to be schooled at Oberlin College. He repeatedly wrote William McLain to send magazines and books for the entertainment and enlightenment of himself and his family. He attended public lectures to increase his knowledge. The breadth and depth of his intellectual interests are indicated by references to the writings of Jonathan Edwards and to Hugh McCall's *History of Georgia*. On two occasions he ventured quotations from Latin sources.

In 1851 Steward lamented the fact that "thear is not a School in the hole Country for the Native Children." He represented the natives as friendly, orderly, and respectable and encouraged them to attend his church. He took great interest in the recaptured Congoes and praised them for their attentiveness and good behavior while attending religious services.

His ability and civic-mindedness were recognized and rewarded by his appointment to serve two years as "General Superintendent" for Sinoe County.

He was truly a remarkable man—a dedicated and accomplished minister, an admirable husband and father, a tolerant, adaptable, and talented civic leader, and a high-minded patriot. His enduring devotion to his adopted country is apparent in his letter of January 24, 1868: "I have a free and good will for all Liberia. . . . Under her Lone Star Let me Live and Die, and I ask no more."

251 / HENRY B. STEWART TO WILLIAM McLAIN

Liberia, Greenville, Sinoe County, October 20th, 1849

Dear Sir: It is with great delight that I take up my pen to Right you a few lines hoping that it may find you and family in good health as it leave me and mine. It is the first oportunity that I hav hade to Right to you since my aRivel. We hade a very pleasant pasage. We aRived at Sinoe on the 27th of June making a pasage in 46 days. We was well treated by the Capt. He did all that was in his power to make all hands on Board Satisfide. Sir, tow much cant Be Sade of Capt. Henry in takeing ous to the Shores of Liberia. I can confidently say that you cold not get a Beter command. The only thing that we had to Regret was the water owing to the caske not being properly Burnt ought [out]. Sir, on my aRival I was Received into the Republick with many feeling of greatatud. On the 26th of July I Set don to a publect Diner got oupt by the City of wich the capt. and super cargo whear invited. It was the day of thear independenc. Toaces [toasts] and speeches[?] were givin in thanks to the colinization Society for seteling this coliny. As for my part I am truly thankful to god in inabeling me with my large family in coming to this land of Liberty Whear I can inJoy Equal Rights and Woship my god without fear. The Laws Ear good and Ear farly administerd without parshality. I has not seen Eny riotus person since I have Ben in the place. In fact I have seen Beter order hear since I have Ben hear than at home. The peope Sems to Be more [a]frade of the Laws hear than at hom. Sir, I am glad to Say to you that I had the pleasure of Seeing the Reverend R. R. Gurly on the present month. He addressed the citizen of Sinoe in publect meeting and States the he was Sent By the President and Secertary of States to inqure in to the arfairs of the Goverment of Liberia with a veiw I think in som das [days] not distent [of recognizing her]. I hope she may find faver in her to Reck ornise her independence. In leving [the] Sout[h] in Such a hury I forget to setel with you for the Repository. I wants it very much. You will dou me a great favor in sinding it. I had the may number, I wants all the Back number and I Shall Sete[l] with the Rev. R.E. murray who is your agent hear.

I am hapy to say to you, Sir, that on my aRival I found a young presbytearon Church Latly Erected hear By the Reveran James Preast abought 18 mounth ago.[1] It Bid fair to Be a prosperous Branch of the Lord Jesus Christ. It numbers sum 29 or 30 members. I am truly Sory to say to you that thear is a very great dissatisfaction hear in Regard to the Six mounth Rasion. The Rashion falls Short in three mounth after our aRival. In Lest than three mounth thear was no flowrer nor meal and it has Bin the generl complant in most all the Emigrant privus [previous] to ous. It tends to do a very great injury for thear Ear many [w]ho comes [out] to this place have now [no] outhere dependence for a living to cary them throu the Acclamating fever than the promis made to them By the Society at home. Sir it has cause a greadill of dissatisfaction among the people. Mr. Murray Says that yor provi[sions] dos not hold ought, that you Sinds so much to giv ought and so much to Sell.[2] Every thing is Scarce. Porke is nearly ought. Grone person have Ben geting 6 pounds a weak, children half that quanity and from the Looks of things it will have to Be a greadill Less. You will do wel to Correct this state of things. It is not my designe to [be] finding fault. You hast the Charge of things nor [two words undecipherable]. But theay is a very great mistake som whear.

No more at present, But I shall Right you from tim to tim,

Henry B. Stewart

R P [Republic], Greenville, Sinoe County, Ap 8, 1850

Dear Sir: I Recd your Leter dated Savannah 13th febuary By the Cap. of the Emagrant vesel Gest apeard in this port from Georgia all well & safe. It aforred me much pleasure in Receving your Kind Leter & allso the papers that you sent me. I receved a package of papers by the Baltimore packet marked to me & now [no] Leter accompaned it. I was at a Lost to know who sent them Gaging [surmising] that you must of sent it. I have put it down to you for wich I Return you many thanks for they are very Excepable heare. You allso say to me in your Latest that you have or would send me ought the Reposatary free of Charges. I have Recd the febuary number threw the politness of Rev. [R.] E. Murray & was much gratifide to see the deep interest manifested in the late anull meeting of the Colonization Society in the Behalf of the Republick of Liberia & asspesaly the name of the Rev. W. Bethune, D. D. faverabley non to me many years ago in the city of Savannah, Geo. & allso the Rev. R. R. gurly who had Recently visited this country a few months ago. It is Really Chearing to ous to see such a spirit manifested toward the poor degraded sons of ham. Sir, it is my wish & prayer to god that you may never want for frinds. As Regard things in this place all is Quite. The few that seem to Be somewhat dissatisfide at first now are perfectly satisfide. As for myself I wold not go Back to Am[erica] to live if I could. My children are all going to school and are doing well. 4 of them are making Rapid progress in gramer and Geograph & Atlas, Aritmatick & other parts of Lerning. Most all of the Emigrant that came ought with me have got ought thear houses & are doing well. I have put up my house & are living in it on a Butiful hill. We have not as yet Experenc a revival of Religion since I have Ben heare. But Devin worship ar regulary perform. I have Righten this Leter not nowin wether you will get it as the packet Leves a few days Before the Emagrant vesel got heare for monroe[via]. If this Leter Reches theare Before she leaves you will com in persesion of it. That vessel anchord heare on the 6 of Ap.

No more But Remain your friend,   H. B. Stewart

to Rev W. Mclain

Greenville, Sinoe, Rep[ublic] Liberia, Sept. 20, [18]50

Rev. Dear Sir: I Rec'd your leter dated the 27th June on the 5 Sep. and was very glad to hear from the U.S. We ar all well & are doing as well as can Be Expected. Thear is nouthing new Since I last Righten to you. You intimated in your leter that my leters to Savannah had a favorable effect upon the mind of my Acquaintences in Regard to this Delightfull home of my choce. I have Endevered to flater now [no] one that in coming to this country that he would have litel or nouthing to do. Far from it. In Some instance he would be doubly call uppon to labour. In the first Instant on his a Rival it will Becom nesesery for him to Bill himself a house & Clare his Lot or farm & though a house can Be Put upt Considerebel Cheaper here than in the States, yet in a new Country wheare things are Scarce he must Exsert himself. I no of no wone that have Come to Sinoe and made upt his mine to make him Self Comfortable that would be willing to leave this for Eny outher place in Liberia & we would Safely Say to Emigrant Coming ought that we would Reckormen them to Greenville, Sinoe C[ount]y as the healthies place on the Cost of Liberia. On this point we will not Say much as Dr. Lugenbeal in a late number of the African Repository has Seteld that.[1] He declars it to Be the most healthis of Eny of the Reast. But we leave all to Judge for themselves. But a word to our Charlston & Savannah frinds for me that they will never get ust to Climing that Ste[e]p Rock if they Stop Shorter than Ga., S.C. [?] I wants you whilst the frinds of Education all are for the Capatol City to think of Sinoe. We have Som very good teachers so far as they can go. But we Ear geting Proud. We like to go farther in our Studies. I am glad to see So miny interests that are manifested toward this Republict By the People of the U.S. I hope that the day is not distant when the Congress of the United State will not only Reckoniz ous But will Send ous that ade for which we Stand So much in need of. But I must Com to a Close By makeing one Remark to that Branch of the Church to which I Belong. It might not be non [known] to many that thear is a Small Presbyterian Church in Sinoe under the Care of the Rev. James M. Preist, Missionary of the Assembly Board. When i first Came to this Country this Church was not more than 18 month ould, a litel mor than one year ago. Sense then meny more have Ben aded to it an outhers are inquiring an asking what they must do to Be Saved. This Church have a very Enterresting Station a Bought 3 miles from the town, So much So that we would like to Bild a house of woshipt thear. But we are not abel at the Present. Mr. Preast is in Evrey way competent for the task and is much Esteamed By all that Knows him. He has commence teching a Day School. He cannot continue it long onlest the Board ades him. We are not yet able to give him Eny thing. Outher Denomanations have a Schooll in this plac & why not a Presbyterian?

I Shall all ways [something omitted] of yours by Rightng me At Eny time. You have my Best wishes at all times.   H[enry] B. Stewart

Rev. W. Mclain, Washing[ton] City

Rev. C. C. Jones   Sino, Greenville, April 7, 1851

Dear Sir: I Deem it my duty and also my plesure in Righting you a few lines and more Especially so when I call to mind the former days of my life.[1] Believing that you take a great interrest in the cause of foreign missions I avail myself [of] the opportunity of giving you some Account of the progrest of the gospell in this part of the Globe were my lot have Bin Cast. I Leaved Sav[anna]h in the Spring of 1849 & arive hear on the Last of June the same year safe and well by the Kind Protection of an overseeing Providence. I leave the States with 8 Children, 4 girls & 4 boys. They are all living But with the Exception of my Younges Boy 10 mounth ould [who died] with the Acclimation fevers. We all had the fever But not very Bad. I do not think the fever are Eny worse then in the Lower part [of] Georgia with proper Care & prudence. There is Never Eny danger of Emigrant Coming from Georgia & South Carilonia. In the Experdision that I com ought with of the Savannah not more than tow death of adult upt to this Date. As Regard the Climet, it is fine. Nature Seams to hav adapted it for the Colored man. The Eavning & morning [are] very p[l]esent in the Days very hevy with fogs, But soon vanishes at the Rising of the Sun. Very hot from 10 of the Clock to P. meridin & then we have a Swet gentle Brese with gradull [gradual] in Crease all night so that thick Covering is nesessery. I hav Scarcely never slep witought Covering in the hotes Seasons of the year. As Regard the State of Re-l[i]gion, I am hapy in Saying that we have a Bundent Reasion to thank God for the Succes that have attend the gospell in this Darke and Benited Land. The Word of Life is Statedly & Regualery p[r]eached on the Sab-bath & at stated tim in Weake Knight. I was all So much Blest in finding a young Presbyterian Church in this place under the Care of the Revd James M. Priest [w]ho having Ben Recently Remove from a mission Sta-tion a few miles Below this to fill the vacation Accasion By the death of Revd Wilson som 18 mounth Before I came. I met him greatly in Nead of [a] brake. I was inform By him that he had a Bought 18 members. I Ren-dered him all the Ascistanc that Lade in my Power. Since then God hast Bless ous much in ading from time [to time] souls to this litel garding [garden]. We number now Between 40 & 50. Our Congregation is well attend on the Sabbath, if Eny thing on the in Creace. In adition to this fiel[d] of Laber we have tow places up the River, very interresting feald, So that his Laber is much Devid[ed], he Being the only ordained Preacher hear of our order. He is indead a very interresting young man fully con-petant for the task. The Board could not [have] sent a Beter. [He is] much Belove By all the peopl . . . [four words undecipherable]. I must say that the Board have over Look ous in Som mesure in Regard of Schools hear.

We have not a singel one we can call as Presbty for 160 mils or more. It is true thear is School and [a] good one Suported By the Baptist Board & M.E.P.C. [Methodist Episcopal Protestant Church?] and they make now [no] Disti[n]ction for which we are thankfull. We are not yet abell to support a teacher nor a paster. But i must bring my leter to Close. Thear is not a School in this hole Country for the Native Children. The Native is perfecly frindly and are much under the influance of the Colonist. My tow oldest Daughters have join a fue month ago. You will Do me a very great favor By inquiring of my Mother & Sisters & Brother fore me & Send me word how thear are & tell them ho[w]dy for I Bought [wrote] them a leter soon After my a Rivail & have not Recd an answer. My Wife Joins me in Comp[li]ment to you and Mrs. Jones [one line, marked through, is undecipherable]. Should this leter Reaches you safe I will be very hapy of an a[n]cer. Send me som papers & Book. My love to Mr. S. J. Casel and all the Bertheren in Christ. No more, But yours in Christ,

Henry B. Stewart

C C Jones, Riceborrough, Liberty Conty [Ga.]

255 / HENRY B. STEWART TO WILLIAM McLAIN

Greenville, Sinoe, Sept. 26, 1851

Reverend And Dear Sir: It Afford me much pleasure in Righting to you from time to time. And more so when I see that you have not forgotten me. I therfore Return you my sincear thanks for the thirty fourth Annual Report of the Am. Colonization Society meetting. Believe me, Sir, Such favours Are greatly Appreciated on this side [of] the Atlantic. Sir, it would Be a Lost of time for to state the various Expression of grattitude by the Citizen of this Republic in Behalf of Colonization (Society) and the Am. People At Large for the welfair of this infant Republic And allso the frindly Tone of Expression of the State Legislator and the Diferent Ecclesiastical and Judicatury of the diferent Churches not only in America But in outher Forerun Countrys so it is no longer a doutfull Question w[h]ether Liberia is the home for the Colored man or not. There is no outher place for him But Africa. He may of injoyed a letel more priviledge to the North, in Som things than what are alowed the free Collord man to the South. But what is that to Be compared with a free Liberian Citizen very Litel Beter than a water man. But, Sir, it ware Abought Sinoe, on the 22d May last, I had the pleasure of wellcoming several of my frinds from Savannah, Georg[ia], among them my old frind G. & Lady an family & allso Mr. Edward Hall & Lady.[1] Mr. Hall Brought with him a steam saw mill, landed safe. Prepperation are afloat to have it Erected as soon as posable. Mr. Gorg soon After his arival, say one month, Lost three of his Children, his oldist Boy & tow younger. But [they] Are perfectly Resigned to the will of God. I only Regrets that no more of my frinds did not Avail them selves of that opertunity. I understand it that there are many more that ar Redy to Leave Sav[annah]. I hope that you may have the means to send them A vessel the Nex Spring so that they may have An opertunity in Coming to this Land of fredom for I know that the free people of Sav[annah] Georgia Do appreciate fredom & will Bee satisfide to Remain a month without the Residencal Chair unless pr[a]epedio, prae, pes, ire, ivi, itum.[2] Sir, this county, tho the last that has any attention pa[i]d to it save that of the Emigrants, Bid faire in No distiant day to Bee the metropolist of Liberia. Her advantages are Beter. Her internal trade once open must Bee Beter. One great Advantage her Baar [shore] Are Accesable At all times in the year with a very Litel Exception. As to the health of Sinoe, we think we hazzard nouthing in saying that It have Been proven to Bee Beter By all that is not prejudicial to her growing Entress. It would Astonish the Eye of an old Return[ing] Absent visittor to see the wonderful improvement mad in the Last 3 & 4 years past. A few Days ago, ought of Curiosity, I Counted no Lest than 6 or 8 new well Constructed Board houses put upt By the last Emi[grants] By the Barke Baltimore. It is true the war[?] Did pinch us a Litel this Seasion But not as Bad as one may think thou it all serve for a good perpos; it made us put a greater Value upon our own farming & Least on the Natives. So I can safely say that in no preceding year has there Been such a Qundity [quantity] of Crops planted as this year. The people are All alive, Bene, melius.[3] The times take Courage and are Looking with Anxious Desire to the Day when the Long Despurse sons of ham will Return to the Land of there four fathers. The people of Greenville are By no means Rec[k]less to the Advantages & Disadvantages of the perpetuity of A Republican government for the Cultivation of Litterature. They Adopt this method to improve their Deficince in Early Life. Corse of Lectures on Weake Nights on Diferent Subjects of General interrest, on Domestic acconamy, on agriculture, Civil Goverment and the importance of Education, &c. &c. I was much pleas in Lisening a few Eavning ago to a very anamating discussion in the Corse of a Lecture Between the Rev. James M. Priest & Dr. James Brown on the word Emulation, introduced By the former, that the word Emulation may be Applied in a Bad Sence or a Bad [good?] Sence.[4] The Later Gentlemen (Dr. Brown) Disagreed that a good Emulation & a Bad Emulation that they Are not stricly Belonging to the same family, A contridiction in tearms &c. Sir, it was amusing To see how Each tride to sustained their point Jhonson & Webster & som tim a Little Latin, and so you will see we are not asleep all ways. In all this I am happy to say the gospell is Regulary & I hope faithfully preached. Pray for us. I am sory to here of your Bad health. I hope Are [ere] this Leter Reaches you your health will Be Restored. Evry things gos on smothly. The Presidencal Election went off smoothly. Myself & family Are all well & what makes it Beter we are not Devided. We Loves Liberia, Because heare we are free. No more at present, But Joins our love to you & family.   Henry B. Stewart

To Rev. W. McLain, Washington City, U.S.

256 / HENRY B. STEWART TO WILLIAM McLAIN

Greenville, feb[ru]ary 23, 1853

My Dear frind: For sum time past I have Been thinking how Long it was since I had Received a letter from you. Reflecting on the Subject I Begin to Apprehend that I written or Done som thing that has made my frindship Appear to you in A Questionable shape or At Least Deserving of some Correction which seams to Resolve to inflict By maintaining this Long silence which I Assure you was sensibly felt By me. Since then many things have Accoured, Both as Respecting the Government And the Church, But nothing of Discouraging nature. Among them Are treaty with foreign Nation, the Rappid increase of Commercial intercourse with other Nation, the increased interest in planting and Raising Stock of various kinds, the improvement in our towns in the Erecting of Commodious Dwelling houses And new Churches. I think I can safely say from the present state of things, from what have Been Done the Last few years past, that it will not Be Long Before Sino, the Last of the other two Counties setled will not Be Behind Either if not Ahead. Our City is As healthy As Any in the Colony, if not more so. In proof of it we have only to consult aur Book of mortality for the Year Ending Last [December?]. In A population of the Rise of 1,000 inhabitants not more than 30 Adult and 16 Children from 1 to 13 years old [died], making in all 46. This, I think should speakes well for a new Country. But I must Ask you what have Become of the Georgia free people of Color? I Did once thought they Could Appreciate freedom But i must forbear. But I must now tell you some thing About this newly organized puritans Church. For the first time in the history [of the] Young Republic, through the kind providence of And over Ruling hand, we have Affected the organization of the first Independent Congregational Church in this place. We have therefour sent you a Copy [of the announcement] for publication in your valuable Journal that the frinds of the Redemer may know that we are not forgetful of that form of Doctrine and Government of the Church that we imbibe whilst in the Land that Gave us Birth.[1] We are as yet Deficent of means to put upt A house of worship And would Be very thank[ful] for Any Ascistance through you to us which will Enable us to prosecute our much Desirable object. We no not who to Appeal to Better than those that Believe as we Do. Without Any Comment I have submited the subject to you. Yours truly in Behalf of the Church,

Henry B. Stewart

W. Mclain, Washington City

257 / HENRY B. STEWART TO RALPH R. GURLEY

Greenville, Sinoe County, Liberia, May 20th, 1856

My Dear Frind: Your very valuable Packet by Capt. Sears of the Schooner King Fisher was received on the 18th inst. together with a Letter by the same conveyance. In what temper of mind these truly acceptable favours found us, and how they affected us, Solomon has described when he says hope deferred maketh the heart sick, but when the desire Cometh it is a tree of Life. Nearly six months had passed since the Date of my Last Letter. During a great proportion of that time we had been Looking with some measure of anxiety and impatience for some incoriging information from you and not without painful apprehension from the Great interval that my Letter might of been miss carried or that you had Disregarded our pressing wants, but it was not so. What thanks do we owe to our good God who has so Kindly Disappointed our fears and Exceeded our hopes in permitting us to here good tidings from you. I say good because it is the first we have had from any Reliable sorce since the organization of our Church. In this we cannot think hard of our frinds for not aiding us when they have not been informed of our wants. We have written, but our Letters have not fallen in the wright Chanel, not being acquainted with any of our ministers of the Congregational Churches named in your Letter, for which I am more than Extreamly oblige to you. I shall avail myself of Every opportunity of making Known our wants to them, and also through the press, that most valuable organ of the Church. I am very Sorrow, my Dear Bro., that the urgency of the Capt. to Leave will not permit me to write at this time particulars but I shall do it the first opertunity I have. Suffer me to say to you that we are doing the very best we can. Our house of worship is upt, shingled and matted Flow [Floors]. Windows & Doors are yet wanting. The matting, you no, are not comfortable in the Rainy Season. We would of done more but the Recent Wars has throwed us greatly back.[1] From this hasty sketch you see our wants and Dear Bro, who shall we go to for help but to our own people. If we appeal to A, B, C & D they say, & say correctly, Go to the Congregational Societies. I know that our people have the means to sustain a Congregational Church in Liberia. And I feal confident that they will do it and I am further Glad to see that you have not Relaxed your Efforts to collect means for our aid. I hope are [ere] this Letter Reaches you that you have been Successfull to some Extent but I must close and only Beg of you that any Remittances Draff [Drafts], Clothing, Books, Papers, Dry goods, provisions sent must Be Directed to the undersign, Pastor of the Cong. Church as in the margin. But I must ask one more favour of you & that is that on the Recept of this Letter, that should there not be an Early opportunity to write me, you would oblid[g]e me much by forward[ing] me a line or two by the mail via way of England & a few papers, the Independent, New York and the New England Puritan, Boston. I know that that Rout is very Expencive but it will Serve To Enliven & Cheer the minds of my Congregation, that the Church has frinds in America. No more But I Remain yours in the Bonds of the Gospell,   H. B. Stewart

Rev R. R. Gurly Coln Office, Washington

258 / HENRY B. STEWART TO RALPH R. GURLEY

Greenville, Sinoe Co., Liberia, July 4th, 1856

Reverend & Dear Sir: Knowing that you Take a Deep intrest in the Prosperity of Liberia and its Citizens, I avail myself of the oppertunity To inform you that Since my Last, things has Takeing quite another aspect. The war That has Been waging Between us and the Belligerent Tribes have been Settled and that throught the Judicious management of his Excellency, President Benson. June 9 a treaty of amity and peace was Entered into with Little and Grand Bootoa [Butaw] & us and on the 21 & 23, the President being here himself, the two Remaining tribes that we were in Difficulties with, viz, Blue Barre and the Sinoe tribes, was also settled with a pledge never more to Rase arms Against us. They were severally find as Aggressors. I would assure you, my Dear Sir, we were all more than Glad that Pease is in all of our Borders, for we were very Peculiarry Situated with Preservation of our Lives. Soly to him who holds the Destiny of all things in his hands and in the Language of one of old, not unto us O Lord, not unto us, But unto thy son we give Glory for thy mercy and truth Sake. Prior to the above statement the Superintendent, Hon. R. E. Murray, appointed a day of humiliation, fasting and Prayer To almighty God that he would avert from us the heave jud[g]ment that were hanging over us. It met a hearty Response from all, when all of Every name and denomination assembled in the M.E. Church and Implored the God of heaven To Look with Propitiousness upon us. And thus we are anable To Say Blessed be the Lord, the Lord who hath not given us as a Prey to their teeth. Thus was our mouth filled with Laughter and our tongue with Singing, for the Lord hath done Great things for us whereof we are Glad. It has already given an impetus to Every Branch of Bisness, trade is coming from Every quarter, merchant are Cleaning there old Cash, School are going on with its usual Regularity, the Churches are all open, Sinners are invited to come to Christ and we say to all your Colored frinds, come to Liberia. But before I close you will be Please to accept of the *One Dollar herein Inclose as a Subscriber to the Repository*. Once more if you have Received my Letter of May Last by the King Fisher you are in the Poss[ess]ion of my wishes and Desires. I Remain the Same and Shall Expect an answer from you as Soon as possable. May the Good Lord Bless and prosper the American Colonization cause that you may be anable To Send us Scores of usfull Emigrants. We want an increased number in this County, To occupy the Acquired Country of Blue Barra, Recently Acceded To us in the Last treaty. We have Been Looking with considerable anxiety for Emigrants from Savannah, Georgia. I hope that the war has not frightened them. If so, that is all pass. This makes me my Seventh years in Liberia and I only wish I were Seven years sooner. I Remain, Sir, Yours in the Lord,

H. B. Stewart

Rev. R. R. Gurley, Washington, D.C., Colo Office

259 / HENRY B. STEWART TO WILLIAM McLAIN

Rev. W. Mclain   Greenville, Sinoe Co., Dec 19, 1856

Dear Sir: As the King Fisher is now up for the States, I have Been Requested To write you a few Lines by way of Inquiry. Information of a Reliable Source have Reached us that Henry M. Mitchell, or Clarke as he Sometimes calls himself, who Left the Republic of Liberia Some 18 months Ago or more, has Abandoned the Idea of Returning Leaving his Lawful wife & Poor mother upwards of 80 years of Eage upon the Charities of the Public. If so it's horrible in the Extreme. I hope it is not so.

Knowing that you are Acquainted with him, Being an Emigrant from Savannah, Georgia, I think in 1851, he Left here with the idea of Soliciting Aid To Perchasing some of his Children in Georgia and at the same time other Important trust was Commited To him.

You are therefore Requested by his much Distressful wife & mother in making Every Possible Inquiry as to the truth of these Reports & you will be Please To Let us Know by the first Opportunity.

The Last Letter he wrote To his wife was by the General Pierce June Last.

As Regard things in general, we are geting along quite Prosperously. Their is quite an Augmentation To the husbandry from the Affects of the Late War. We now Realize the benefits of farming. In fact things never Appeared more flattering in this Country than at the Present. We have the interior trad of not Lest than 100 miles when a few years ago we were Circumscribe To the narrow Limits of 20 or 30. You Knows my views as Regard Africa. It is the home for me. Eight years Experience is Sufficient To test its feasibility. It is true we have felt the Pinch of the Shoe but never, never so as To be willing to take it off. We have no use here for *Carriage Drivers*, Boot *Cleaners* & Bottel *washer*, &c. We are here To Build up a free, *Civil Christian Country*. You will thus see what kind of Emigrants *we want*. Such is greatly needed in this Count[y]. I hope you has not forgotten us in this Particular.

But befour I close it Becomes my Painful Duty To inform you of the Death of the Hon. Judge [R. E.] Murray. His sickness was short, on the seventh, Last [he became ill] & on the fourteenth he was a Corpse. His Lost was & is Sensibly felt. Yours truly &c.,   H. B. Stewart

260 / HENRY B. STEWART TO RALPH R. GURLEY

Revd R. R. Gurley   Greenville, Sinoe Co., Liberia,
                                                      December 19, 1856

Dear Sir: The King Fisher is now up for The States. I avail my self the opportunity of writing you a few liens. In doing so I hope you will not think that I am too obtrusive in the frequency of my Communications. It is an old saying and I think a Just one that necessity knows no Bounds. And Like the widow mention in the Scripture, mine's an urgent Case.

Not Charging you with any neglect nor those that we are soliciting aid from—in my Last communication, July 4, I Sent you one Dollar To make me a Subscriber to the Repository—and at the same time a Renewal of our Request Praying the Congregation[al] Churches To Aid us in the Completion of our Infant Zion.

I also Sent a Letter To the Independent & one to the Puritan for Publication, Together with Several Letter[s] to Different Clergyman of our Denomination.

And for fear that any Doubts Should of arisen I have Reffered them To you. I have also Sent my Subscription To the Independent for which I Receive one Number, which Assured me that my Letters have Been Received. W[h]eather our Appeal has Solicited any attention it is yet a mystery To us for I am not in Possession of Pro or Con in the matter.

I would not Be understood that I am by any means impatient or Discouraged for the Cause is God and if we Pray aright he will Raise up frinds in our behaf, but we must use the means. I have thought Several times of trying so to araing my Buisness so as to come To the States, and this for several Reasion. One is that I might do more than [by] writing. The nex grand Reason is To Affect ordination. It is true we have Been Blessed by the Kindness of the Rev. B. R. Wilson in administering the ordanance for us & gave us free invitation to his Church.[1] Yet in this Perticular we are wanting.

In the year 1854 (Dec.), the Rev. Henry M. Adams on his way to the Gaboon mission stop A short time here & took the whole matter under Deep Consideration. And After an Examination I Received a License from him, according to the Calvinist Congregational faith, with the hope that ere this Some of our minister would of visited this Place, or some arrangement would be made.

I have mention these things, my Brother, for Advice And instruction. The Church is small in number but Sound in the faith, not made up of Proselyte from other Christian Societies. Will you be Please To write me on these Important Subjects for what we Do it must be done quickly. It is my Prayer To get the Church on its firm foundation. Two or three hundred Dollars would set us agoing. I have no Disposition in visiting the United States unless for the good of the Church.

We are all geting along finly. The People Seames To be awake To the importance [of] farming. Traid is Brisk. I supose by this you have herd of the Death of Hon. R. E. Murray. His Sickness was short, only 7 days, Died on the 14th November Last, Much Regreted, He was a warm hearted Liberian. His Place is not Easily fill.

Before I Close Suffer me To Say a Report is among us that Causes much uneasiness. It is this; information Reached us by the Arrival of the King fisher that Henry Mitchell who Left here nearly two years Ago, has Abandoned the idea of Returning, leaving his wife & Poor old mother whose Solle Dependence was on him for a Livelyhood. Should it be Proven to be the fact, it will Cause much Distress & Greaf in his family. He left here with the idea of Purchasing some of his Children in Georgia.

You will do us much favour To make some Inquirys and Let us Know. Other important trust of the Church was Committed To his Care. Yours with much Respect, H. B. Stewart

261 / HENRY B. STEWART TO RALPH R. GURLEY

Greenville, Sinoe Co, Feb. 27, 1857

My Dear Sir: The Receipt of your kind favours were Duly Received. I would assure you, Sir, that such Reciprocation is heart Cheering To one in a foreign Land Like this. Thoughts arises in my mind at times that my frequent communications would be Burdensome To my friends, but on a more Carefull Refflection, I am Encouraged because it is the Cause of God & that Life is only valuable when it is Spent in a good Cause. In Every thing there is a beginning. This is Emphatically So of this Branch of the Church of Christ in Liberia. Not that their are not those that favours this Polity of Church Government but quite to the Contrary, many thinking men when the Government of the Church is Clearly Stated gives it a Decided Prefferance. In fact it is my opinion, not To say nothing of Apostelical Churches, it is the best form of government in a new Republican Constitutional Government as ours. Because its Authority is Better Suted To the Limited Capacity of Each individual Church. That is, that Every Separate Church is the Soul Judge Relatin[g] To the interest of that Church *alone*, the bible Being their Soul Rule of faith and Practice (to the Law and To the testimony). It is better Because it Places the government in its Primitive State. This Long Ecclesiastical Court, that would Require one To Go to Rome, England, or America, etc. could be solved within her own Doors (Matt. 18:15, Luke 17:3)![1] It is the Best because it holds no Compromise with transcendelism. Such, in few words, are some of the views maintain in this Cong[regational] Church. The Doctrine, faith & Government of the Church I have in a former Report Sent To the Rev. Dr. Burgess, Mass. organization with a Request that he make Such disposition of it as best suits him. This Church Entered in To a Covanent of organization with Seven members, three males & four feamales, Average age of from Sixty to Sixteen. Total number has been Sixteen [in the] Congregation on Stated worship, very Encouraging. So as to the future Proserity of the Church, their Can be no Doubt. The only throw back is the want of means to Carry out our Designs & we firmly believe that had all thing worked as we then wished our number would of more than treble. We are more than glad to See the interest you manifest in behalf of this Branch of the Church of Christ in the Land [at] hom[e] by Giving Publicity of it. It assures us that you have not Relaxed your Efforts in our behalf. But we must Exercise Patience for Patience giveth Experience in the End. As Regards the work of grace among us there has been no special intimation of the out Pouring of the Spirit among us save an increase attendance on the Preaching of [the] word. Pray for us that the word of the Lord may have free Course & be glorified with us Even as it is with you. Things here Goes on finly. The health of the People [is] much improved. We are truly glad of the benevolent aid of the Society (New York) To the needy in this County. It does not seem from this & other acts of Kindness [that] frinds has Entirely forsaken this County though we had well nigh given up the Idea of Seeing & [an] Expedition of Emigrants any more. It seams that Sinoe is the Last of thoughts.

P.S. Since writing the above your Excellent Ship, Mary Caroline Stevens, from the Leeward (Cape Palmas) moored in our harbour on the

26 inst. Just as the Sun was Seting and will Leave this afternoon for her Destine Port. With Every wishes for her Safe & Speedy Return to the Propritors & the Beneficence Donor, though Dead, Lives in the Affection of the Liberians. With Every Regard for your health & Prosperity, I Remains your, &c.,   H. B. Stewart

Rev. R. R. Gurley

262 / HENRY B. STEWART TO WILLIAM McLAIN

Greenville, Sinoe, May 10, 1857

Dear Sir: Your Letter of Feby 16th Came Safe to hand Per Schooner Antelope Informing me of the facts Relative to the foul act of Mitchell. He ought to of been in Some Public Gazette that his villinay might be made known.

The things alluded to in your Letter was Brought to his wife Safe.

Since writing to you Last, his mother Died. I had her Buried decently. His wife Speakes of Returning to the States.

We are all geting along Quite fair. Reasonable men are Satisfied. There are some few fault finders as in most any Place Speaking great things and doing nothing. I am glad to See that your attention is now turned to Sinoe and at no distant day I may Cherish the Pleasing hopes of Seeing more of the Sable Sons of ham Returning to their fathers Land. We are not Perticular in what Section of the Country they come from So they are the Decendent of ham. As it is Said by Some of the wise, we Belong their if any where atall.

We are geting along quite Smothly. His Excellency is now on a visit to the Annexed County (Maraland) and on his Return will give us a visit. I Remain yours, &c.,   H. B. Stewart

W. Mclain

263 / HENRY B. STEWART TO WILLIAM McLAIN

City of Greenville, Liberia,   May 23, 1857

In my Last I intimated that his Excellency President Benson was then at the County of Mariland and would on his Return Give the Citizens of Greenville a visit. On the 11th inst. he Arrived here on the Government Schooner Lark, Commander, Capt. R. Cooper, and took Lodging at the mansion of the Hon. Edward Morris, General Superintendent, where a number of his warm hearted frinds Congratulated him, and Such another Shaking of hands! Never Before has the Citizens of Greenville manifested Such a Disposistion To do honour To the Chief Executive of their Country. Every heart Seems to of Been Lighted up with Joy from Every Sex and Every age. The Inquiry was heard: Is the President Come? Is he Come? Even the natives Seem To of Been affected in this Contratulatory. There are two Circumstances Connected with this Sensitive Show on the part of Citizens [that] may well be Stated, not that they Appreciated Less on any former visit of their President but it do Seem that it is one of the ordeals of afflictions that man Should [give] Due Respect To those that Rule over them, Especially when they Rule in the fear of God. The Latter has Been fully Seen in the Reign of S. A. Benson, and Becaus he was with us in the time of our Greatest Difficultes, and the next he is the President of Liberia and will be for the next two years. President Benson is a Stern adherent of the Constitution of '47; this is Evident in all his acts.

To Show a Peples Gratitude for the Pass and hopeing Better for the future, Party upon Party was Served for him. For the First two or three Days he was much Engaged in the Local matters necessarily Devol[v]ed on him from the Late war. On the 18th a Picknick was Served for him by the fair Sex when a number of them meet at the house of Mrs. R. D. Wath at 3 P.M. under a full Ban of musicians, marched up Johnston Street To the Lodgin of his Excellency with nine Bower of Garlans forming an Eliptic Arch, etc. Borne by two Ladies Each Beautifully trimed with the Ever Delightfull verdurous of Liberia, with bowels [bowls?] of flowers in Each hand and in the Centre 4 Stars Representing the 4 Counties of the Republic of Liberia with the Insignia in front Covering the President.

God Bless the President. In Reaching the house one of the Ladies, Mrs. J. L. Brown, Advanced in front meeting the President and in a Speach Repleat with Eloquence informing him that they were then Ready to Escort him. The Procession then Proceeded up Mississippi Avenue To the Residence of the Hon. J. L. Brown. Within a few Space of the Door the whole Procession halted when Mrs. M. A. Delamatter in an impressive Speach of much tast welcomed the Distinguished Gest. After the Relaps of a few moment *of Rest* a Chorus was formed in the Centre of the Parlour when A Beautiful Ode was Sung By these Standard Bearers, at which time the Last 4 Salute of Cannon utterd its Awful voice in the heavens, Denoting the 4 Counties of this Republic. The President Rising from his Seat and in his usual felitius maner Responded in Lofty Strain of Eloquence with interrupted Applauses for 15 or 20 minutes, After which the Party was then invited to the north End of the Dweling into a vestible of much Length. The first thing that meet our Eyes was a Large Lengthy table neetly Dressed with Every thing that the Eye and heart Could Desire that Could be got were on that table. All the various Luxury of Life, ham, winged fowls Dressed in Every Prepared stat[e], Pound Cakees, Etc. & all the other Little Dainties So Pecular to that

Seasin, got up on the Shortest notice. However, after a Blessing by one of the Rev'd, commenced the Cuting and Slaying [Slicing?], i.e. [consumption of food]. During the interval Sentiments and toast were Given of which Mr. J. Negle, Sen. Esq., Compliment the President on the Success that had attended his Administration and that it had met the heart[y] Approval of the Citizens of the County of Sinoe and also alluding to the Great Struggles of 1855, in Electing him to the Gubernatoral Chair and Assured him that his friends are now the Same to which the President Responded in his usual Sublimity Giving Satisfaction to the Entire Company and that he was the Same in heart and Principles, and After much Chitchating at a Late hour in the Evening, Cheered and Gladen, the whole Party Joined the Procession and thence up Mississippi Street under a Lively Band of musick to his Excellency's Lodging where a few hours after he attended another Party of Like Splendure which then awaited him at the house of Mr. John Barlow, Esqr., where he was Gorgeously Entertained for a very Late hour of the night. And at 6 A.M. the next morning he took Passage on the Government Schooner Lark for the Seat of Government and in the Language of a Liberia Stateman, thus has the People honoured the man of their Choice.   H. B. Stewart

P.S. I understand the Herald is stop for the pres[ent].

264 / HENRY B. STEWART TO RALPH R. GURLEY

Greenville, Sino, August 8, 1857

My Dear Sir: Your very acceptable favour of the 14the May Came Safe to hand and found us all in the Blessing of health and I may Say a Degree of Peace and Prosperity. And [I] am Sorry to here of your Being unwell. I hope are this Reaches you, you may Be Better. Your fine Ship arrived here Safe and has unloaded her Cargo and in a few hours will leave for the County of Mariland and will not Stop here on her Return. She Brought out three Small houses and I think Some Storage.[1] It is Scarcely needed for me to Say to you how it made our hearts gladen with the Prospects of in no Distant Day our feble hand will be again Strong then with more of the Sable Sons of ham. May they Be helpers in the great work in the Civillesation of Down troden Africa. I thank you for the very holsome advice given me in your kind Letter. I Receive it as from a Brother Beloved in the Lord. We have nothing to Discurage us Save that of our own Slothfulness in Grace. The Promises we have and they are Sure and Steadfast, Etc.

I have not yet Received an answer from Dr. Burgess. I have thought that I Being Such a stranger how would it do for you to Drop a Line or too to him. My Reposatory Comes Regularly. I tha[n]k your for the papers Sent me.

I shall write you again on matters of importance. In Great hast I Remain yours most Certainly in the Lord.   H. B. Stewart

Revd R. R. Gurley

265 / HENRY B. STEWART TO RALPH R. GURLEY

Greenville, Sinoe, Jan'y 20th, 1858

My Dear Sir: With many thanks to you for your Continued favours in writing me from time To time. I am under So many obligations To you that I shall never be Better able To Pay you than wishing that you may Ever have the Smiles of our heavenly father.

The Papers & Repository Came Safe via of Monrovia, Per Schooner Lark in advance of the Stevens. Myself and family are all in the Enjoyment of good health; may it find you the Same. My Dear Sir, it is indeed of very great Satisfaction To me for the variety of inteligences in these paper & more Especialy So as my family is Large and is very fond of Reading. We were much Disappointed in Seeing no Emigrants for Sino *Per M. C. Stevens.* The news that there was a famin in Liberia and Especially So in this County was Really unknown to us untill the Return of the Stevens and on that account none of the Emigrants Could be Persuaded to make Sinoe their home. If these Statements were Really So I would not Blame the Emigrant for not being willing to Choose such a Place for their home. The writter of Such opprobrious Statement is no frend to Liberia as he has But very Little Knowledge of Liberia in Africa. Of all Countries in the world I do think this is the Last one for a famine in its Strictis Sense. What a Country that Produce grows of its own accord. (This is the gratis Difficulty in geting the people to work, finding that they Can Eat with so Little Labour). That there are times of Scarcity none will or Can Deny, Such as this last Season owing to the Last war this County had undergon and the Scarcity of Geting Seed at the Right time. The Statement is unfounded So far as this County is Concerned for I was Eating new Rice in April & May. This County never had So much farming Done the Last year and that is now Doing By its Citizens. There Seams to be a general tendency in the minds of Some to Lower the Standard of this County. If other Settlement are in advance it is not from their industry. It is from their advantages, the means for [a] Seminary & the Existing of College, &c. This County has Keep up its Self by her own industry to the Present, and we do think that it is no more than Right that Something ought to Be Done to Strengthen her if it is only to Send us more Emigrants. As Desireous as I am for Emigrants I never was very favourable in Seeing them Come out in the Drys.

I Receved a very interesting Letter Per Stevens from Rev'd L. A. Sawyer, Westmoreland, N. York who wishes us Every sucess but Cannot Do any thing at Present. The Deranged State of things at home makes Doubtfull at Present.

I have not as yet Received an answer from Dr. Burgess. I hope you will not forget to write him and inform me.

You will no Doubt be Please with the very great present Sent the Church by the Massachusetts Sabbath School Society.[1]

The Lord I trust is working in the hearts of his people in our behalf for we were not without a Blessing the Last Sabbath in the Last year. An adult Received an Examination (Male) and in the Commencing of the new [year] our heart & Eyes was mad[e] Glad by this very Rich treasure of Knowledge above mentioned.

I am not without houp that all that is wanting will in Due time be given.

All the Reposatory has been Received, and I herewith Send my Subscri[ption] for the present year, $1.00.

No more but Remains yours truly in the Lord.　　　　　　H. B. Stewart

266 / HENRY B. STEWART TO WILLIAM McLAIN

Greenville, Sinoe County, Jan'y 21, 1858

My Dear Sir:　　As your fine Ship is now about Leaving for the States, I take Great pleasure in writing you hoping that it may find you well.

I had the pleasure for the first time in visiting this Splendid vesel of the Society. It is indeed a Donation [of value]. Here philanthropy is Seen not in words mearly but in Living action.

I had also the pleasure of Becoming acquainted with the Rev'd Mr. [A. M.] Cowan, agent as I Learnt of the Colonization Society in Kentucky.[1] He is certainly a vigilant observer of matters and things in general from a Cat To Dog. I think however he will gether more information than any that has yet preceded him.

There is [one] fault however I find in him. He is Like all new Comers, Expecting Really more than could posably be Expected.

To be acquainted with Liberia it Requires Experiance.

How far his visit will affect the intrest, the progressive interest, of this County time alone will tell. There is one thing Cirtan. Liberia or the Colonization Society gains nothing if the County of Sinoe is not Sustained. What I mean is that she Receive an Equal Ratio of Emigrants Equivalent of Strength, for without it, its Citizens Could not advance far from the Sea Board thereby Deprived of the Better Land To plant.

It is imposable for the farming Division To advance as it Should do [unless] the traiding Reaches nothing Shor[ter] than 10, 15, 20 miles interior. To Do this an increase of Emigrant is indispencably necessary. But why State I things that you are alredy acquainted with?

Particulars of affairs is not needed as yo[ur] agent will Carry them. I am Sorry however that our Physician has to Leave us. I hope not for good. O Sinoe, Poor Sinoe! I Remain yours truly,   H. B. Stewart

Revd Wm Mclain

267 / HENRY B. STEWART TO RALPH R. GURLEY

Rev'd R. R. Gurley   Greenville, Sinoe Co, July 16, 1858

My Dear frend: Your very interrestion Letter Came Safe to Hand by your Excellent Ship M. C. Stevens. It afforded us much Pleasure to hear of the Display of Divine Grace in your much favoured land of Gospel privailedge. It is Certainly gratifying to all who love to see Zion travel and Bring forth Sons and daughters into Glory. There have been more than an ordannary attention to the Subject of Religion for this Place. Many have united themselves with the People of the Lord and I trust Saveingly Converted.

The Difficulties that have attended Such a Display of a Sanctifying and Lasting opperation of Divine Grace upon the Lives of the People with its [blessings] you have not as a General thing, that is the distinguishing nature and Practical knowledge of true Godliness or in the language of that most Eminent Servant of the Lord, Rev. Jonathan Edwards, whose tretise on Religious affections was Presentted to me by the Late Rev. S. G. Cassels. He says tell we (or they) [to] Learn to Distinush between Saveing Experience and other affection, &c. This, however, I am happy to Say that many of our brethren in the ministry Labours to impress upon the mind of their People that a Right & corect knowledge of Divine truth is essential to Salvation. This is in strick conformity to the commission given by the great head of the Church, Go ye therefor and teach all nations, teaching them to observe all things whatsoever I have Commanded you, &c. The Prospect Cheers our heart for the future when we See the Untired Effort put forth by the Citizens in their Perseverance in the Literary instruction of their Children. The Sabbath Schools of all our Churches will testify that our aim is to perpetuate the Blessings and knowledge of the Christian Religion to our Children.

Together with this, the Blind has not been forgotten. I allude here to that most interresting School in our vicinity among the native Children under the Patronage of the M.E. Church taught by the Rev. E. Ward. This is a very Interresting opperation, more So when we take into Consideration the Rapid proggress it has made. Many of them are in their Second Syllable & Repeats the Lord's Prayer with perfect Ease.

You have, however, Denyed us of a very important Blessing in Depriving us of a medical aide. Never have I felt this so severly as in the Last Six month, in the Dislocation of my Daughter Elbow, from a fall. It Remained out of place for nearly five month, untill in the Provedance of God Dr. Delyions Stoped here on his way to Palmas. He was Kind Enough to place it back in its place. What the Result will yet be, I cannot tell. Together with other Sickness I will assure you it was very trying. The Deprivation of Emigrant is nothing to Compare with not having medicial attendance in Extreme Cases. So far as other matters are Conserned, Compareing the Present with the Past, we are on the improved State. Their are not that Scarcity and want. Farming buisness is Really beter. There is in this, as in all new Countries, those that are willing to sell their birth Right for a morsel of Bread. I never was more forceably struck with this fact than in Reading Capt. Hugh McCall history of the Early Setling of the State of Georgia. Men as a General thing Loves Ease and many will Do most any thing than Labor for the Comfort of Life, and Untell our Race Shall know how to Appreciate Civil, Religigious & Political Priviledges untrampeled in all bearings, their will be that Longing after the flesh poots of Egypt. The mandate is unalterable, by the Sweat of thy brow Shall they Eat Bread.

And now in Conclusion Suffer me to acknowledg the packages of papers you were so pleased to Send. I was Completely Dry for the want of Something to Refresh my mind. You know how much we Stand in need of them, in this far off Land.

I think you, through the multiplicity of buisness, have forgotten to Press the Claims of our Church to our frinds. I Did Suggest to you in one of my letters the proprity of your written to Dr. Burgess as we were Such great Strangers. I tha[n]k you for your favorable Expression in our Success. But, my Dear Sir, without meanes we Cannot Successfully & Effectualy progress fast. The Ends Cannot be met without Some meanes to obtain this. We are Entirely Dependent on our frinds. You know the great Difficulties in my leaving here for that purpose. All our Letters Seams as yet to be Unavailing Yours very truly,   H. B. Stewart

268 / HENRY B. STEWART TO RALPH R. GURLEY

Rev R. R. Gurley   Greenville, Sinoe, Co., Augt 10, 1860

My Dear and much Esteamed frind: The Limited time I have for writing will not Enable me to Say much. The Necessary Cares and fiting up my Son for the State presses very heavily upon me at this time. You will always here from me as heretofore.

Thomas Goes out in the Benson for Oberlin, from this to New York, through the Beneficent Care of Rev. Dr. R. Storrs of Brooklyn. He is now in his 15th year of age.

I meet my family all well.[1] The Church and Sabbath School Encourageingly progressing. Four stood [and] propounded for membership. Some 12 or more native Boys added to the Sabbath School.

All my things were Landed Safe, among these 150 Bibles & testaments, from the Mass. bible Society and as many Geography atlases, Arith[m]etic, Grammars, Dictionarys, Speling Books, Etc., from frinds in Boston, Providence and New York. 6 Volumes of henry's Commentary from Mrs. Dang of Boston, 50 plymouth hymn Book and Sabbath School Collection, Punchard Views of Congregationalism, the Congregation[al] Quarterly, Vol. 1, Lock Compilation Book, Sermon of Dr. Preston, history of Christianity first three Centuries, and many others too numerous to name. Yours very truly,　　　　　　　　　H. B. Stewart

269 / HENRY B. STEWART TO RALPH R. GURLEY

Rev. R. R. Gurley　　　　　　　　Greenville, Sinoe Co., March 16, 1861

Dear Sir:　　Yours per Ship M. C. Stevens, came safe to hand and would of Received an answer on her Return were it not that I Desired to inform you of what Disposision were made of the Recaptive africans that were Keep So Long on hand in this County, which has been the Cause of So much unesiness, and I may say of Strife and Contention.[1] I am happy, however, to Say that these Difficulties are Giving way, as I hope, for the better. On [March] 11 or 12 the Commissioners, on the part of the Government, Rev. James M. Priest, S. J. Crayton and [J. M.] Mountgomery, acting Jointly with the Probate Court, Commence apprenticing these people out. A few of the older ones will be Sent to the falls the present week, how many I am not prepared to Say. The whole number turned over to the General Superintendent by your Society agent [was] 296. It is thought that there are not that number now, as Some have been Shot and others got Drowned in makein[g] their Escape. Whatever may be Said of these People of being Lawless or Rebellious I have not Seen it. I have visited them from the Day of their Landing to the present. Many of them have been Regular attendance on Divine worship to my Church and Sabbath School Ever Since and are as yet a more orderly Set of people in time of Service I have never witnessed, which has been the occaision of frequent Remarks, that Such Raw heathens Could Remain for an hour

and [a] half So becomingly in the house of God. The uneasness, Sir, I alluded to, are to be attributed to the Disagreement of the Citizens, and not
the Recaptives. They are heathen. They were told Shortly after Landing
that they were to be taken in a body to the falls. Their was no Dissatisfaction with them in that arrangement. When this Change was made and
they were informed that they were to be sepperated, they immediately
question the Sincerity of our motive in Doing them Good. All who are
attall acquainted with the manners and Customs of the natives Knows
that they will Strenously hold you to your word, whilst they think it is
nothing for then to Cheat, Steal or tell a Lie.

As Regard my own Concerns, viz, the Church, we have Great Reasion
to Bless God for his manifold mercies to usward. We are Still Enjoying
the meanes of Grace. He hath not left us without a witness of his willingness to pour out his Spirit and Convert Sinners, which is the Chiefest ob-
ject of my ministry. Not a Communion Season has pass since my arrival
that some hast not been added to testify his willingness to Save Sinners.
My Sabbath School is Still in an incour[ag]ing State. We are now on the
Eave, as you are well aware, of that most Perplexing and Vexatious
Sea[so]n of another Letionaring Campain, which is So Deliterious to the
Church of Christ. You have been informed of the Late War at Mariland.
We have had also the pleasur of Dr. James Hall and D[a]ughter for a few
Days.[2] The Dr. was in fine Spirit, visited the falls twice, Did Every thing
[that] Laid in his power to have the falls [troubles] Settled.

My health are as Good as Could be Expected for one having So much
to Do.

My best respect to your Good family. Yours truly,   H. B. Stewart

270 / HENRY B. STEWART TO RALPH R. GURLEY

Greenville, Sinoe County, September 18, 1863

My Dear Friend: I have nothing special or new to write you; things
here remain the same, with little or no alteration; I think, however, a little towards a doing of something, a little more of a disposition towards
the farming line, whether from actual necessity of a sense of bettering
conditions in future, time will tell; there has been an increase in the farming operation over former years among the Liberians in such things as the
natural products of the county, rice, potatoes, etc. I am glad in saying
that our recaptives are getting on remarkably well with few exceptions;
here and there you may find a rude fellow that will steal. The company
that were sent to the settlement of Ashmun, under proper managers have
behaved themselves in every sense worthy of future hopes. In industry

and sobriety, they have not only maintained themselves, but in a great measure supplied the town of Greenville with the products of their industry. This I think is a great beginning for the better; as an illustration of this facts a few weeks ago they presented quite an imposing sight in our town under the command of Capt. R. S. Jones, Esq., for company drilling; it was a pleasing sight for me to see over eighty of these once raw heathens under the military command of our Government. Their deportment and orderly behavior won the respect of all. I understood from the Captain that there are in all over one hundred and fifty of them enrolled for military duty.

What an acquisition to this county! Those that were apprenticed out are doing well; their terms of service will expire on the first of the coming year. We were pleased with the company of our friend, Mr. Edward S. Morris of Philadelphia. Mr. Morris's plans of cleaning and preparing coffee, have attracted and stimulated the minds of many of our people; he has done great good in his visit to Sinoe. I am afraid, however, that the fond desires of our friends for the culture of cotton in Liberia will not to any exent be soon met, especially so in this county. In this I would not predict, as we know not what a day, or a year may bring forth. The M. C. Stevens has just left for Palmas, and will not on her return touch this place. She has, I learned, brought but a few emigrants, and some jacks; of course none could be expected for this place, as it would seem that Sinoe is to be the last to be served.

We would have been glad to have a few emigrants for the new Recepticle, 16 miles above this. This building is well nigh completed; it can now receive visitors. My son Thomas informs me that you had written him sometime back; when last heard of, he was doing well in his studies at Oberlin; we are well; thank you kindly for your favors; no letter come; remember me to Dr. McLain. I am, yours truly, H. B. Stewart

271 / HENRY B. STEWART TO WILLIAM COPPINGER

Greenville, Sinoe, Jan'y 22, 1867

Mr. Coppinger:[1]   The Ship Golconda with over 200 Emigrants arrived here on the 14th ult. and as far as [I]have Lernt, nothing Lost. The Company Seems to be well please with their new home. I Regret very much that measures were not taken in time to of Sent the greater part of them up to Ashmun Settlement near the falls, Sixteen miles from this place. It is my Dessided oppinion a better and healthyer place than on this Sandy Beach (as Such I have Spoken to those who has this Business in hand.) Especially So as I trust the tide of Emigration are again open for Liberia. There is Room for all. My Respect to our old friends, &c. Send us the Repository. Ind[ependent] Cong[regationa]l Church are Endeavoring to Do her part in this great work of Africks Redeemtion.

With Every Respect for your health and prosperity.   H. B. Stewart

272 / HENRY B. STEWART TO WILLIAM COPPINGER

Mr. William Coppinger,   Greenville,
Washington, D.C.   Sinoe, Jan'y 24, 1868

Dear Sir: The Golconda not Coming to this place prevented me writing by her on her Return. I was much Disappointed in the arrangement in the Society in not Sending any Emigrants to this place by her, Especially So as I have been Successful in my previous Desire to Commence a Settlement at Ashmun. Every preparation hast been made there for the Reception of Emigrants. The Company Sent out in January was Sent up there hast Done well for which I have been more than anxious to increase its numbers. Of the 66 that went to that Settlement there hast not been more than three Deaths, and those were infants. The Rest are all well and are doing well, went to work and hast a plenty planted to Sustain them before their Six months were up. And Some Seven or Eight houses built, whilst those that were Sent out in the first Company Remained on the beach are Discontented and Very poorly provided for. This was my fears as you will Remember in my Letter to you. At first the town of Greenville is no place for farming. It is a traiding place. Neither is there any good land for farming Shorter than 16 miles up the Sinoe River. The health too are far better. There is Scarcely any Danger of the fevers and, with proper Care and attention, none. This I assert from personal Experience and with Due Respects for the other Counties in the Republic, there are not a more healthy Location in Liberia.

I have been Lead to make this appeal to the Society and its friends because of a Letter from its agent at Monrovia to the Society agent at Greenville, viz. Mr. A. J. More, puting a Stop to any further preparations for Emigrants to this County. Are we to understand by this peremptory orders that no more Emigrants are to be Sent to this County? Or is the tide of Emigrants [to] Cease for the present? Or is it thought that the people of this place are Sinners above all that are in Liberia? I trust not. If the first Company that Came over in the Golconda were Dissatisfied and wrote back to their friends opprobrious Letters it was more the faults of the managers than the place or its Citizens. It having been my Lot to be the general Superintendent of the County over two years, I can Speak freely as Regards the attention of the Citizens to the Emigrants in that they were incessant in Sickness and in Death. And though I have no personal ill will towards Dr. Snowden, I new at the first that it was imposable that he Could Do Justice to both physician and agent. First, his health would not allow him. Secondly, I Did not believe he had a turn to manage Southerners on their first Entrance into this Country. Be that as it may, too much Care Cannot be paid to them in their Sickness. I know that all that may be Done, you canot please all, but Let Justice be Done according to promise. Some hast Left and gone to other Counties of the Republic. This is their privilege. There is an Evil too prevalent on the arrival of Emigrants to Dissuade them to this place or that place other than the place they Embarked for. This is wrong and I hope hereafter that the Society will Rectify this matter. As Regard myself, though I wish a greater number of Emigrants in this County to Strengthen us, I have a free and good will for all Liberia because I So Sincerely believe it is the only home for the Black man. The Negro nationality, Liberia, under her Lone Star Let me Live and Die and I ask no more.

I am, Sir, yours with much Respect,   H. B. Stewart

273 / HENRY B. STEWART TO WILLIAM COPPINGER

Mr. Wm. Coppinger   Greenville, Sinoe Co., August 17, 1868

My Dear Sir: Your Kind Letter Dated Savannah, Ga., M[a]y 2d, Came to hand yesterday. I was more than glad to hear from you and Especially the Cause of the Emigrants not Coming to this County. Many Reasons hast been Set up by others. Some thought it was the agent at Monrovia. Be this as it may, there is Some truth as Regards the Emigrants that Came over in '66. Every thing was not as it Should of been. Much of the blame is with the Emigrants. They Came over unfortunately at a time of high political Excitement. Went into it by party persuassion, from January to May and no Entreaties from older Citizens were of any avail. Not one of them from that time would Leave the Beach. The fever took them. Many of them Died from night Exposure. Their Rashions gave out, and not the best of medical attention [was available]. They became Dissatisfied and Knew not how to Remedy their Lost Cond[i]tion and with no inclination to work, Several of them Left for Grand Bassa Co[unty]. The Remainder of them, with a few Exceptions, are Recruiting and Bids fair to become real fine Citizens. [Concerning the] Company under the Leadership of Mr. Lewis Sherman, I have heard little or no Complaint. All of that people hast Settled to Ashmun Settlement and were Living in their own houses before July. Mr. Sherman hast not been well but is about; was to my Church Last Sunday Evening, Came Down to attend Court. It is now a Little pulling and haling in the Several Counties for Emigrants. As Regards of health, thre are very Little Differance;

the most is good treatment. Mr. Wyatt Madden Death was much Regretted by all, a good man. His Companions believed in him. By his Death, their Church hast met with a great Lost. Your Suggestion of my making a visit to the United States of America Strikes me Favorably for Several Reasons. First, I wants Rest. I have been preaching Every Sabbath for the last Eight years. Seconly, I have a Brother and three Sisters in Liberty County, Ga., with Some twelve or fifteen Children. In a Recent Letter of my Brother Dated Savannah, April 13, '68, he wishes to know from me Something of this Country. He is undesided about Coming to the Country. If my going over Could be of any avail, I would be very glad of the opportunity. In view of these facts, Could or would the Society give me a free passage over in their Ship, and also my Wife? If it Could be, as myself alone, I am not Connected with any missionary Society as Such, though I will have friends when I arrive. If these Ends Could be met, I would be Ready to Leave on the Return Ship, So as to be there the first of next Spring. The Golconda not Stoping here, the mail is my only Chance of writing you in time; and also if accepted please give the necessary instruction to your agent, Mr. Dennis. I am very Respectfully yours,   H. B. Stewart

EPILOGUE

Liberia has come a long way since the letters contained in this volume were written. It still has enormous problems in the form of poor health, low income, a high rate of illiteracy, and need for further integration of the tribal people into the economic, political, and social life of the nation.[1] But progress is being made, and the Liberians of American descent, who now comprise about 5 percent of the nation's population of approximately 1,500,000, are largely responsible for the country's achievement. Today, as in times past, they provide most of Liberia's political and social leadership.[2]

Survey of the files of the *African Repository and Colonial Journal* indicates that immigrants who were born free, numbering only about 4,500, provided more leaders than the 7,000 who were born in bondage. All of the republic's first five presidents, for example, were freeborn; indeed, no person born in slavery ever headed the Liberian government. This preponderance of free blacks in leadership positions seems to have been due to the advantage that they had in self-reliance, initiative, and experience acquired during prior years of sustaining themselves and their families. In Africa many of them established themselves in a relatively short time as artisans, tradesmen, farmers, and shippers, and thus laid a foundation for leadership in Liberian affairs. In 1831, during the infancy of the Liberian experiment, an agent of the American Colonization Society noted a difference between immigrants who had been born free and those who were ex-slaves. The latter, he stated, "having never been permitted to act or think for themselves . . . are in point of industry and intelligence far below the free people of colour, and really know not how to provide for their future wants."[3]

There were doubtless many exceptions. Ex-slaves such as those sent to Liberia after considerable preparation, by John McDonogh, the Blackfords, the Pages, and others, must have compared favorably in character and ability with the best of the free Negroes. Three or four ex-slaves whose letters appear in this volume are known to have become leaders in Liberia. Washington McDonogh became a member of the lower house of the Liberian legislature. James C. Minor, one of the Blackford group, became a judge. Of him a prominent member of the Liberian judiciary wrote in 1867: "Judge Minor is considered by the Bar to be one of the ablest Judges that ever sat upon the Bench in this Republic."[4] Sion Harris (possibly freeborn) became a member of the Liberian House of Representatives.[5] Seaborn Evans served as senator from Sinoe County from 1861 to 1863.[6] Among leaders of slave background for whom no letters were found were Lott Cary, one of Liberia's most outstanding pioneers, and the Reverend Robert F. Hill, who for ten years was a member of the Liberian legislature.[7] There must have been many other former slaves who achieved prominence in the land of their adoption. Certainly it seems reasonable to conclude on the basis of the letters reproduced in this volume that a majority of the rank and file of immigrants of slave background became good citizens and, as such, contributed substantially to the well-being and progress of Africa's oldest republic.

Appendix

ADMINISTRATIVE HEADS IN LIBERIA
1819-1978

*Representatives of the American Colonization Society
with one or more years of service*

Eli Ayres, 1821-1824
Jehudi Ashmun, 1824-1828
Joseph Mechlin, Jr., 1829-1833
John P. Pinney, 1833-1835
Ezekiel Skinner, 1835-1836
Anthony D. Williams,1836-1839
Thomas Buchanan, 1839-1841, Governor of the Commonwealth of Liberia
Joseph J. Roberts, 1841-1847, Governor of the Commonwealth of Liberia

Presidents of the Republic of Liberia

Joseph J. Roberts, 1847-1856
Stephen A. Benson, 1856-1864
Daniel B. Warner, 1864-1868
James S. Payne, 1868-1870
Edward J. Roye, 1870-1871
James S. Smith, 1871-1872
Joseph J. Roberts, 1872-1876
James S. Payne, 1876-1878
Anthony W. Gardner, 1878-1883
Alfred H. Russell, 1883-1884
Hiliary R. W. Johnson, 1884-1892
Joseph J. Cheeseman, 1892-1896
William D. Coleman, 1896-1900
Garrett W. Gibson, 1900-1904
Arthur Barclay, 1904-1912
Daniel E. Howard, 1912-1920
Charles D. B. King, 1920-1930
Edwin Barclay, 1930-1944
William V. S. Tubman, 1944-1971
William Tolbert, 1971 -

Notes

INTRODUCTION

1. The account of the American Colonization Society and its affiliates is based largely on Early Lee Fox, *The American Colonization Society, 1817-1840* (Baltimore, Md.: Johns Hopkins Press, 1919); Philip J. Staudenraus, *The African Colonization Movement, 1816-1865* (New York: Columbia University Press, 1961); Charles Morrow Wilson, *Liberia: Black Africa in Microcosm* (New York: Harper and Row, 1971); Harry Johnston, *Liberia*, 2 vols. (New York: Dodd, Mead and Co., 1906; reprint ed., Negro Universities Press, 1960); Archibald Alexander, *A History of Colonization on the Western Coast of Africa* (Philadelphia: William S. Matrien, 1846; reprint ed., Negro Universities Press, 1960); J. Gus Liebonow, *Liberia: The Evolution of Privilege* (Ithaca, N.Y.: Cornell University Press, 1969); Charles Henry Huberich, *Political and Legislative History of Liberia*, 2 vols. (New York: Central Book Co., 1947).   2. Auxiliary colonization societies were established in all states except Rhode Island, South Carolina, Arkansas, and Michigan. During the period 1833-1857 the Maryland State Colonization Society operated independently of the parent organization. A tabulation of annual shipments of blacks to Liberia, 1820-1866, was published in the *African Repository and Colonial Journal* 43 (1867): 109-17. (This source will be cited hereafter as *African Repository*.) This shows that 11,909 Negroes were transported between February 1820 and December 1866 by the American Colonization Society and 1,227 by the Maryland State Colonization Society during the years when it operated as an independent agency. Of the 11,909 transported by the American Colonization Society during this period 4,541 were born free, 7,054 were ex-slaves and the status of 314 was unknown. Virginia sent 3,733 blacks, and this was more than twice the number sent by any other state. In addition to the 13,136 sent under colonization society auspices, the United States government settled in Liberia 5,722 Africans captured from ships operating in violation of laws prohibiting trade in slaves.   3. Gurley's administrative duties were shared after 1840 by William McLain who served successively as clerk of the executive committee, treasurer, and financial secretary. When McLain was appointed financial secretary in 1858 Gurley became corresponding secretary. Gurley was born in Connecticut May 26, 1797, and graduated from Yale College in 1818. He made three trips to Liberia, in 1824, 1849, and 1867. He wrote three books, including a biography of Jehudi Ashmun. He died July 30, 1872. McLain, a native of Ohio, graduated from Miami University, Athens, Ohio, in 1831. After studying theology at Andover and Yale, he became minister of the First Presbyterian Church in Washington, D.C., and while holding that position he was appointed clerk of the executive committee of the American Colonization Society. He died in February 1873. See *African Respository* 49 (1873): 99-105, 230-31, and Huberich, *Political and Legislative History of Liberia*, 1: 323.   4. The periodical was issued monthly until April 1875 when it shifted to a quarterly basis.   5. All of the early agents were white, but black colonists, among them Elijah Johnson, Lott Cary, Anthony D. Williams, and George R. McGill, served as acting agents for considerable periods during the years 1822-1834.   6. Ashmun was born in New York in 1794. After graduating from Middlebury College in 1816 he entered the ministry. In 1819-1820 he edited religious journals, among them the *African Intelligencer*. His publication in 1821 of a memoir of Samuel Bacon, who had served as the principal agent of the American government for liberated Africans, stimulated in him a great interest in the colonization movement and called him to the attention of the American Colonization Society. In 1822 he left for Africa as a representative of the American Colonization Society, and his connection with that organization lasted until his death early in

1828. In 1826 he published a brief history of Liberia, a splendid source on the first two years of the American settlement in Africa. 7. Thomas Buchanan, born in Franklin County, N.Y., Sept. 19, 1808, was appointed governor of Bassa Cove in 1836 by the New York and Pennsylvania colonization societies. After eighteen months of service in that office he returned to the United States. In 1839 he went back to Africa to become first governor of the Commonwealth of Liberia. He served with distinction in that position until Sept. 3, 1841, when he died of fever. He was the last white to serve as chief administrative officer of Liberia. Huberich, *Political and Legislative History of Liberia*, 1:727. 8. Joseph Jenkins Roberts, an octoroon, was born of free parents in Norfolk, Va., Mar. 15, 1809. He migrated to Liberia with his widowed mother, two younger brothers, and two younger sisters on the *Harriet* in 1829. He established a trading firm which became one of the most prosperous in the colony. In 1841 he became the first black governor of Liberia and held that office until 1847 when he became the first president of the Republic of Liberia. He was reelected president in 1849, 1851, 1853, 1871 and 1873. He served for several years as president of the College of Liberia and as professor of jurisprudence and international law. One brother, John Wright, became a bishop and the other, Henry J., was a prominent physician. President Roberts died in Monrovia Feb. 24, 1876. Huberich, *Political and Legislative History of Liberia*, 1:770-71. 9. Penelope Campbell, *Maryland in Africa: The Maryland State Colonization Society, 1831-1857* (Urbana: University of Illinois Press, 1971), pp. 202, 223, 236. After Maryland in Africa became a part of the Republic of Liberia, blacks migrating from Maryland to Liberia went under the auspices of the American Colonization Society. 10. Samuel Wilkeson, an affluent real estate promoter of Buffalo, N.Y., was from 1838 to 1841 president of the board and chairman of the executive committee of the American Colonization Society and during most of this time he performed the duties of secretary of the society. Staudenraus, *African Colonization Movement*, pp. 237-38. 11. Stefan von Gnielinski, ed., *Liberia in Maps* (London: University of London Press, 1972), p. 10. 12. For an excellent discussion of the strife between settlers and natives see Svend E. Holsoe, "A Study of Relations between Settlers and Indigenous Peoples in Western Liberia, 1821-1847," *African Historical Studies* 4 (1971): 331-62. 13. Fox, *American Colonization Society*, p. 56. Thomas W. Shick in "A Quantitative Analysis of Liberian Colonization from 1820 to 1843 with Special Reference to Mortality," *Journal of African History* 12 (1971); 45-59, states that of 1,918 deaths among emigrants to Liberia, 1820-1842, some 896 or 45.7 percent resulted from fever, probably malarial, and that while 4,571 emigrants were sent to Liberia, 1820-1843, the number living in Liberia in 1843 was only 1,819. 14. Von Gnielinski, ed., *Liberia in Maps*, pp. 8-26. 15. *African Repository* 35 (1859): 3. 16. The letters of Sion Harris appearing in chapter 8 may represent an exception to this statement since Harris's status could not be definitely determined. His letters are included because they have the character and flavor of those written by correspondents known to have been recently emancipated and because of their vividness and informativeness. 17. When the editor of the *African Repository* published John B. Phillips's letter of May 19, 1849, to William McLain, treasurer of the American Colonization Society he omitted a statement critical of the food served on the ship that transported Phillips to Liberia. See original letter in the American Colonization Society Papers (hereafter cited as ACS Papers) in the Library of Congress and the edited version in *African Repository* 25 (1849): 231-32. In publishing Isaac Roberts's letter of Oct. 22, 1849, from Greenville, Liberia, the editor omitted this statement: "There is now a cry among the people. They have very little pork and very little flour in three weeks after [we] landed. At all event the provision is short." See original in the ACS Papers and printed version in *African Repository* 26 (1850): 60-61. Most of the letters in this volume were transcribed directly from original manuscripts in the Library of Congress. After I completed most of my research, the papers were microfilmed. In all instances in which I have been able to do so, I have traced the originals to the microfilm and cited them by reel and number. 18. For another example of humor, see Letter 218, which closes with a risqué anecdote related by Sion Harris to William McLain and J. W. Lugenbeel. 19. Very unusual among emigrants to Liberia was a Virginia white man, name unknown, who accompanied his black mistress and several of her children (only one of whom was said to be his) to Africa in December 1856. When American Colonization Society officials advised him not to make the trip, telling him that he could not hope for citizenship in Liberia and that he would have no white associates there, he replied that he was much attached to his "wife" and child and that he wanted to share their future. Nothing is known of the Liberian experiences of this family. James Hall, first governor of Maryland in Africa, accompanied the family to Liberia and talked with them during the voyage. He was a man of veracity. See Hall's account in "Voyage to Liberia" in *African Repository* 33 (1857): 297. For more about Hall see below, Letter 214, note 1. The Rev. A. F. Russell, also a credible authority, told of a similar instance in a letter to the *Liberia Herald*, Sept. 8, 1846. "A real unprejudiced white man we have yet to look on," he stated, "unless it be the Hon. Mr. Gray who followed a colored woman and her children to Liberia, married her, and lived and died happy." Quoted in *African Repository* 23 (1847): 181.

CHAPTER 1

Introduction

1. For an account of this remarkable woman's career, see L. Minor Blackford, *Mine Eyes Have Seen the Glory: The Story of a Virginia Lady, Mary Berkeley Minor Blackford, 1802-1896* (Cambridge, Mass.: Harvard University Press, 1954.   2. Ibid., p. 42.   3. Ibid., p. 23.   4. Ibid.   5. *African Repository* 43 (1867): 133.   6. The "Register of Emigrants, 1835-1837" in the ACS Papers shows that Abraham sailed from Norfolk on the *Virginia* June 16, 1844, and lists him as a teacher, age twenty.   7. Blackford, *Mine Eyes Have Seen the Glory*, pp. 60-61.   8. Blackford was still living, and active, in Cape Mount in 1870, though he had been captured and held prisoner for a short time in a war among the Vai. Svend E. Holsoe, "The Cassave-Leaf People; An Ethnohistorical Study of the Vai with Particular Emhasis on the Tewo Chiefdom" (Ph.D. diss., Boston University, 1967), p. 182.

Letter 1 (African Repository 9 [1833]: 126-27)

1. This reference is probably to ninety-one recaptured Africans taken from a slave ship and sent by U.S. authorities in August 1829 for settlement in Liberia. See *African Repository* 6 (1830): 49-51. Friction between the recaptured Africans and other colonists is suggested in a report by American Colonization Society agent Joseph Mechlin, stating that during a joint expedition of recaptured Africans and other colonists against the native forces of King Brumley and King Willy in March 1832, "recaptured Africans who could not be controlled" set fire to a captured town. *African Repository* 8 (1832): 129 ff. Referring specifically to recaptured Africans taken to Liberia on the *Pons*, the annual report of the American Colonization Society in 1847 stated that the colonists received the Africans cordially, took many of them into their houses, clothed them, fed them, and took steps for their education, "yet the citizens of Liberia have had a vast amount of trouble with these recaptives. They knew nothing of laboring for a living—they were destitute of moral principles—they were adverse to all kind of restraint—they were unwilling to submit to law, or observe order; hence, they were ready for any wickedness that offered itself. Many of them left the homes that were provided for them and wandered about in the neighborhood of the settlement, stealing whatever they could lay their hands upon, and committing all kinds of depredations. . . . We are, however, happy to state that many of them have conducted themselves with propriety, and that they are making rapid improvement in civilization. . . . They all express the most heartfelt gratitude for their deliverance." Ibid., 23 (1847): 76-77. 2. Colin Teage, a native of Virginia, purchased himself and his family and in 1821 migrated to Sierra Leone. Four years later he moved to Liberia where he became a prominent minister and engaged successfully in commerce. In 1835 he was pastor of the Second Baptist Church in Monrovia. He died Aug. 27, 1839, while returning from a visit to the United States. *African Repository* 29 (1853): 316; 11 (1835): 88; and 16 (1840): 47.   3. William Weaver migrated to Liberia from Petersburg, Va., in 1824. He supervised the establishment of the settlement at Grand Bassa and founded the town of Edina, named for Edinburgh, Scotland, in recognition of the kindness of that city's people to Liberia. He was a member of the Liberian senate, 1847-1849. He died Feb. 27, 1852. *Africa Repository* 28 (1852): 242.

Letter 2 (ACS Papers)

1. The reference apparently is to leather balls used by printers for applying ink to type.

Letter 3 (ACS Papers, microfilm, reel 153, no. 203.)

Letter 4 (ACS Papers, microfilm, reel 154, no. 72.)

1. Minor's reference is to an expedition of about 200 colonists, personally led by Governor Buchanan early in 1841, against King Getumbe (also spelled Gatoomba, Gatumba, and Gay Toombay) in retaliation for destructive raids conducted by Getumbe and his followers. Getumbe was defeated and his town destroyed. A period of peace ensued. See annual report of the American Colonization Society in *African Repository* 17 (1841): 41.

Letters 5 (ACS Papers, microfilm, reel 154, no. 90)

Letter 6 (African Repository 22 [1846]: 260)

1. Possibly Abraham was referring to Dr. J. W. Lugenbeel, a white Virginian, who went to Liberia in 1843 as an American Colonization Society agent and physician. His poor health forced his return to the U.S. in 1849. He continued in the service of the American Colonization Society and at the time of his death, Sept. 22, 1857, he was the society's recording secretary. *African Repository* 33 (1857): 318.

Letter 7 (African Repository 22 [1846]: 260-61)

Letter 8 (African Repository 22 [1846]: 261)

1. In December 1845 U.S. naval authorities, acting in accordance with a law of Congress of March 3, 1819, delivered at Monrovia 756 Africans, mostly Congoes, taken from the slave ship *Pons*. These and other "Recaptured Africans," as they were called, were settled at New Georgia, a site on the eastern side of Stockton Creek about five miles from Monrovia. Some of these liberated Africans were apprenticed to colonists from the United States who had become established as farmers or artisans in Liberia. See article "U.S. Agency for Recaptured Africans" in *African Respository* 22 (1846): 176 ff. Also see Dr. J. W. Lugenbeel, "Sketches of Liberia," ibid., 26 (1850): 208; and article "The Recaptured Africans," ibid., 34 (1858): 289-300. For the capture of the *Pons* and other slave ships see Peter Duignan and Clarence Clendenen, *The United States and the African Slave Trade* (Palo Alto, Cal., 1963), pp. 40 ff.

Letter 9 (African Repository 22 [1846]: 261-62)

Letter 10 (Maryland State Colonization Society Papers, Maryland Historical Society, Baltimore)

1. James B. McGill was one of four brothers who migrated from Baltimore. His father (the Rev. George McGill) and one of his brothers (Samuel F. McGill) arrived in Liberia in 1826 and his mother, three brothers, and two sisters arrived in 1831. The McGills became leaders in Liberia's business community. In 1856 James B. and Urias McGill headed the McGill trading firm in Monrovia and Dr. Samuel F. McGill and Roswell S. McGill directed the family establishment at Cape Palmas. *African Repository* 47 (1871): 287.

Letter 11 (Maryland State Colonization Society Papers)

Letter 12 (Blackford Family Papers, University of North Carolina)

Letter 13 (Blackford Family Papers)

1. The Reverend John Payne went to Liberia in 1836 to serve as a missionary for the Protestant Episcopal Church. He was consecrated bishop in July 1851. He returned to the United States on sick leave in 1869 but never regained his health. He died at his home in Westmoreland, Ky., in 1874. *African Repository* 28 (1852): 161; and 50 (1874): 372-73.

Letter 14 (ACS Papers, microfilm, reel 155, no. 88)

Letter 15 (Blackford Family Papers)

Letter 16 (African Repository 28 [1853]: 237)

Letter 17 (Blackford Family Papers)

1. Both Davis and Brown served in the Liberian legislature. Governor Thomas Buchanan wrote to the secretary of the American Colonization Society on Dec. 13, 1840, that Brown was "one of the very best men in the colony. . . . Of good sense, considerable talent as a speaker." Both men died in 1853. *African Repository* 17 (1841): 84; 24 (1848): 97; and 30 (1854): 250.

Letter 18 (ACS Papers, microfilm, reel 157, no. 90)

1. Edward Wilmot Blyden, a black born in the Danish West Indies, migrated to Liberia in 1851, when he was nineteen. He mastered several languages, including Greek, Latin, and English, and authored several books. In 1865 he became a professor in the College of Liberia. In the late 1870s he served as minister to England and ten years later he was Liberia's minister of the interior. Johnston, *Liberia,* 1:231, 260, 277, and 383. The best biographies of Blyden are: Thomas W. Livingston, *Education and Race: A Biography of Edward Wilmot Blyden* (San Francisco: Glendessary Press, 1975), and Hollis R. Lynch, *Edward Wilmot Blyden: Pan-Negro Patriot, 1832-1912* (London: Oxford University Press, 1967).
2. John Seys, a white preacher, went to Liberia in 1834 to superintend the missions of the Methodist Episcopal Church in West Africa. He founded and edited the newspaper *Africa's Luminary.* In 1839 he headed a faction which challenged the authority of newly appointed Governor Thomas Buchanan. He lost out in the rivalry but continued to be active in religious and secular affairs in Liberia until his return to the U.S. in 1870, two years before his death. See Staudenraus, *African Colonization Movement,* p. 241; and *African Repository* 48 (1872): 92.

CHAPTER 2

Introduction

1. Information about Cocke and his relations with his slaves was obtained mainly from Martin Boyd Coyner, "John Hartwell Cocke of Bremo: Agriculture and Slavery in the Antebellum South," (Ph.D. diss., University of Virginia, 1961), 2 vols.; and from Randall M. Miller, ed., *"Dear Master": Letters of a Slave Family* (Ithaca, N.Y.: Cornell University Press, 1978).   2. According to Randall Miller, Lucy, "although she married Jesse Skipwith . . . did not use his last name. Some of her children also went by the surname Nicholas." Miller, *"Dear Master",* p. 69, note 1.   3. Cocke to J. C. Cabell, Jan. 31, 1832, quoted in Coyner, "John Hartwell Cocke," 2: 305.   4. A copy of the certificate of emancipation is filed in the John Hartwell Cocke Papers, University of Virginia.   5. Cannon, Jones, James and Julia Nicholas, Sterdivant, and his three children, all belonging to the estate of Cocke's sister, Mrs. Sarah Faulcon, embarked from Norfolk on the *Mariposa,* June 7, 1842. On the manuscript roster of *Mariposa* passengers, Sterdivant is erroneously listed as Lucinda Stewart and his children are listed as Diana, Rose, and Leander Stewart. ACS Papers, microfilm reel 314.   6. Most of the letters, written from Liberia by members of the Skipwith family were published in Miller, *"Dear Master."*

Letter 19 (John Hartwell Cocke Papers, University of Virginia. Cited hereafter as Cocke Papers)

1. Felicia was Skipwith's six-year-old daughter.   2. The charge that American settlers enslaved natives was made repeatedly by colonists and by others. The charge was based in large part on the practice of natives apprenticing their children to colonists for training, or as security for loans. See *African Repository* 29 (1853): 278; and 59 (1883): 22. Apprentices were sometimes called "pawns." James Thomas Sabin, "The Making of the Americo-Liberian Community: A Study of Politics and Society in the Nineteenth Century Liberia" (Ph. D. diss., Columbia University, 1974), p. 150.

Letter 20 (Cocke Papers)

1. Sally Cocke was one of John Hartwell Cocke's daughters. In 1856 or 1857 she married Dr. Arthur Lee Brent.

Letter 21 (Cocke Papers)

Letter 22 (Cocke Papers)

1. Lewis Johnson, son of Elijah, one of Liberia's distinguished pioneers, ran several Baptist-sponsored schools in Monrovia.   2. Miss Evans conducted an elementary school in Monrovia.   3. The "wounds" referred to in this and several subsequent letters were probably sores caused by frambesia, a tropical skin disease also known as "yaws."

Letter 23 (Cocke Papers)

1. John J. Mathias was governor of the Bassa Cove settlement in 1837-1838. The lieutenant governor of Liberia in 1838 was Anthony D. Williams, born a slave in Virginia, who migrated to Liberia as a missionary in May 1823. He was vice-president of Liberia, 1850-1854. He died in 1860.   2. John Hartwell Faulcon, sixteen-year-old son of Sucky Faulcon, whom Cocke had emancipated and apprenticed to Peyton.

Letter 24 (Cocke Papers)

Letter 25 (Cocke Papers)

Letter 26 (Cocke Papers)

1. Erasmus was the brother of Peyton Skipwith.

Letter 27 (Cocke Papers)

1. Chief Jenkins of the Gola (or Gora) tribe went on the warpath in 1837-1838, in an effort to enlarge the territory under his control. On Jan. 28, 1838, Lt. Gov. Anthony D. Williams wrote American Colonization Society officials in Washington that Jenkins had recently made a raid on a Dei town and captured and murdered about two hundred persons and that Jenkins seemed determined to wipe out the Dei. Jenkins's aggressions were considered injurious to the peace and security of Liberian colonists. *African Repository* 14 (1838): 66.   2. For an account of the Logan-Harris difficulties with the natives, see *African Repository* 14 (1838): 251   3. Green Hoskin, a resident of Monrovia, was accused of dealing in slaves. When brought to trial he was acquitted for lack of evidence. *African Repository* 14 (1838): 165-66.

Letter 28 (Cocke Papers)

1. Lancelot Byrd Minor, son of John Minor of Topping Castle, Va., went to Africa as a missionary in 1837. He died at Cape Palmas, in 1843, age twenty-nine. Blackford, *Mine Eyes Have Seen the Glory: The Story of a Virginia Lady . . . 1802-1896*, pp. 37-38.

Letter 29 (Cocke Papers)

Letter 30 (Cocke Papers)

1. The Fisherman, or Fishmen, were a tribe whose principal occupation was fishing. Their settlements were scattered all along the Liberian coast. See George E. Brooks, Jr., *The Kru Mariner in the Nineteenth Century: An Historical Compendium* (Newark, Del.: Liberian Studies Association, 1972).   2. The Liberian flag, to which Skipwith refers, resembled the United States flag, with a cross substituted for the stars. Knowing that British and American captains would refrain from searching vessels flying colors other than their own, slave traders operating along the western coast of Africa carried flags of two or more countries. If a British ship approached, the slaver would hoist the American flag; if an American vessel came near, the slave trader would run up a Spanish or Portuguese flag. *African Repository* 18 (1842): 62.

Letter 31 (Cocke Papers)

1. *The Liberia Herald*, edited by John B. Russwurm and published in Monrovia, was founded in 1830. *Africa's Luminary*, edited by John Seys, was a Methodist periodical launched in 1839 in Monrovia.

Letter 32 (Cocke Papers)

Letter 33 (Cocke Papers)

1. For an account of the expedition against Getumbe in which Skipwith participated, see letter of Governor Thomas Buchanan to Samuel Wilkeson, secretary of the American Colonization Society, Apr. 6, 1840, in *African Repository* 16 (1840): 174-86. Getumbe, a chief of the Gola tribe, headed a federation of native groups in the Boporo region near the Saint Paul's River above Millsburg and about fifty miles inland from Monrovia. Skipwith was one of about 300 colonial militiamen organized by Buchanan and let by Joseph J. Roberts, a very able commander who was to become the first president of the Republic of Liberia. Buchanan wrote Wilkeson after the victory over Getumbe: "This is in all respects the most important expedition that has ever been undertaken by the Colony. . . . Gay Toombay is completely prostrated." See also Johnston, *Liberia*, 1: 179-81; Wilson, *Liberia*, pp. 51-52; and the annual report of the American Colonization Society in *African Repository* 17 (1841): 31.   2. For descriptions of the attack on Heddington, see *African Repository* 16 (1840): 194; and 17 (1841): 41. See also in chapter 8 Sion Harris's letter of Apr. 16, 1840. Harris was a participant in the fight.   3. Samuel Benedict migrated to Liberia from Georgia in 1835. In 1840 he was associate judge of the Liberian Supreme Court. He served as chief justice from 1847 until his death in 1854.

Letter 34 (Cocke Papers)

1. The missionary was John Seys. See Letter 18, note 2.   2. For a discussion of the African activities of the Cuban slave trader Don Pedro Blanco, see Johnston, *Liberia*, 1:164-65; and *African Repository* 33 (1857): 338-39.   3. Theodore Canot, whose real name apparently was Theophilus Conneau, was a native of Tuscany, whose checkered career included a period as a slave trader on the West African coast. See Svend E. Holsoe, "Theodore Canot of Cape Mount, 1841-1847," *Liberian Studies Journal* 4 (1971-72): 163-81. See also Theophilus Conneau, *A Slaver's Log Book; or, Twenty Years Residence in Africa* (Englewood Cliffs, N. J.: Prentice-Hall, 1976).

Letter 35 (Cocke Papers)

Letter 36 (Cocke Papers)

1. Nicholas, son of Lucy Nicholas Skipwith, addressed the envelope containing this letter to "General John H. Cockes." Erasmus Nicholas, brother of Peyton Skipwith, appears on the roster of *Mariposa* passengers departing Norfolk, June 7, 1842, as a twenty-four-year-old black liberated by Philip St. George Cocke, son of John H. Cocke. ACS Papers, microfilm, reel 314.

Letter 37 (Cocke Papers)

1. A report in the *Liberia Herald* of Mar. 31, 1843, stated: "On the 4th last this illustrious stranger revealed itself with unequalled splendor. This is the third comet we have seen, but neither of the others equalled this in the enormous length of fiery tail or splendor of brightness."   2. Dr. James Lawrence Day, a graduate of the Medical College of New Jersey, practiced medicine at Wilkes Barre, Pa., before going to Liberia in 1840. He was colonial physician until his retirement in 1843.

Letter 38 (Cocke Papers)

1. For provisions of Mrs. Faulcon's will affecting her slaves, see ACS Papers, microfilm, reel 314, "Extracts from Wills. . . . " p. 15. The slaves liberated by her will who went to Liberia on the *Mariposa* in June 1842 were James Nicholas, age thirty-two; Judy Nicholas, twenty; Richard Cannon, thirty-two; Peter Jones, thirty; Robert Leander Sterdivant, thirty; Diana Sterdivant, thirteen; Rose Sterdivant, seven; and Leander Sterdivant, five. See ACS Papers, microfilm, reel 314, "List of Emigrants by the *Mariposa*." As previously noted, the Sterdivants' last names erroneously appear on the list as "Stewart" and the father's first name appears as "Lucinda."

Letter 39 (Cocke Papers)

1. Skipwith's reference is to the African Squadron, created as a result of the Anglo-American treaty of August 29, 1842. The U.S. Government agreed to station a squadron of ves-

sels mounting at least eighty guns on the African coast to apprehend American slavers operating there. The squadron, never exceeding five vessels, was utterly unequal to the task of patrolling 3,000 miles of coast. The first commander of the squadron was Matthew C. Perry who held the position from May 1843 to Dec. 1844. See Warren S. Howard, *American Slaves and the Federal Law, 1837-1862* (Berkeley: University of California Press, 1963), pp. 40-43 and Appendix E.

Letter 40 (Cocke Papers)

1. Richard seems uncertain about the spelling of his name. His signature appears as Canon in this letter and as Cannons in the letter of Sept. 30, 1850. The spelling on the *Mariposa* list is Cannon.

Letter 41 (Cocke Papers)
Letter 42 (Cocke Papers)

1. The writer of this letter, Robert Leander Sterdivant, was one of the slaves liberated by the will of Mrs. Sarah Faulcon. On Sept. 21, 1841, John H. Cocke wrote William McLain: "Leander, who has 3 children, is a young man of exalted character and is of one of the best colored families I ever knew." ACS Papers.   2. The friend to whom Sterdivant refers is his recently deceased owner, Mrs. Sarah Faulcon.

Letter 43 (Cocke Papers)

1. Liberia's constitution, based on that of the United States, was drafted for the American Colonization Society by Simon Greenleaf, professor of law at Harvard and president of the Massachusetts Colonization Society. Anderson, *Liberia: America's Best Friend*, p. 80. 2. See Letter 8, note 1, for information on the *Pons*.   3. John, Charles, and Philip were sons of John H. Cocke. "Miss Coatny" was Sally Courtney, the wife of Philip St. George Cocke. The identity of Nancy Cavel is not known.

Letter 44 (Cocke Papers)
Letter 45 (Cocke Papers)

1. Lomax, whom Matilda married on Mar. 30, 1845, migrated to Liberia from Fredericksburg, Va., in 1829.   2. A news story in the *Liberia Herald*, July 17, 1846, stated: "A number of these people are living wild in the woods and at night come in town and carry off cattle, &c. . . . We have considerable sympathy for these people and the community in general would willingly assist in taking care of them—but such is the disposition of some of them that they prefer, notwithstanding you may lavish upon them much care and expense—to live a wild life in the woods . . . rather than live with the colonists where warm and comfortable quarters may be found."

Letter 46 (Cocke Papers)
Letter 47 (Cocke Papers)

1. Ellis was a self-educated preacher-teacher from Alabama. For information about him see below, introduction to chap. 8, note 2.

Letter 48 (Cocke Papers)

1. Hilary Teage, son of Colin Teage, born free in Virginia, migrated to Sierra Leone in 1821 and in 1825 moved to Liberia. After achieving success in commerce, he became a Baptist minister. He edited the newspaper *Liberia Herald* from 1835 to 1847. At the time of his death in 1853 he was Liberia's secretary of state. *African Repository* 13 (1837): 131; and 29 (1853): 258, 316.

Letter 49 (Cocke Papers)
Letter 50 (Cocke Papers)
Letter 51 (Cocke Papers)
Letter 52 (Cocke Papers)

1. Alison History was doubtless Archibald Alison's *History of Europe from the Commencement of the French Revolution in 1789 to the Restoration of the Bourbons in 1815*, 4 vols. (New York: Harper and Bros., 1842-1844).

Letter 53 (Cocke Papers)

Letter 54 (Cocke Papers)

1. In November 1851 Grando, a chief of the Fishmen tribe who previously had pretended friendliness toward the colonists, made a series of attacks on the settlements at Fishtown and Bassa Cove, burned many houses, and murdered and mutilated a number of settlers, including some women and children. In retaliation President Roberts led an expedition of colonists against Grando and his followers, defeated them, and restored peace. For accounts of the "Grando War" see *Liberia Herald*, Nov. 19 and Dec. 31, 1851; *African Repository* 28 (1852): 91-94; and 29 (1853): 37. John H. Faulcon, as his letter to Cocke of May 12, 1852, reveals, was a participant in the expedition against Grando.

Letter 55 (Cocke Papers)

Letter 56 (Cocke Papers)

1. The reference is probably to the Rev. John B. Pinney, a native of Baltimore, who after attending Princeton Theological Seminary became a Presbyterian minister. He went to Liberia as a missionary in 1833. For a short time in 1834 he served as chief administrator for the American Colonization Society in Liberia. He returned to the U.S. because of poor health and served at various times as American Colonization Society agent and corresponding secretary of the Pennsylvania and New York Colonization Societies. He died in Orlando, Fla., in 1882. *African Repository* 59 (1883): 35.   2. The Rev. Eli Ball went to Liberia in 1852 as an inspector of missions for the Southern Baptist Board of Missions. He criticized the American Colonization Society for maintaining settlers for as long as six months and for providing them with houses. See Miller, *"Dear Master,"* p. 109, note 2, Matilda Lomax's letter to John H. Cocke, May 19, 1852.

Letter 57 (Cocke Papers)

1. Susan [Sucky] Faulcon, who appears on the passenger list as Susan Cocke, age thirty-nine, along with her daughter Agnes, age eighteen, and her son George, age sixteen, embarked from New Orleans Dec. 31, 1852, on the *Zebra*. Cholera broke out among the passengers soon after the ship left port. The *Zebra* made an unscheduled stop at Savannah, Ga., so that the sick could obtain medical treatment. During the voyage from New Orleans and the sojourn at Savannah, the ship's captain, a mate, three seamen, and 36 of the 135 passengers died, among them Agnes Faulcon. The *Zebra* departed Savannah Feb. 10, 1852, and arrived in Monrovia late in March without further loss of life. See *African Repository* 29 (1853): 69-70 and 212.

Letter 58 (Cocke Papers)

Letter 59 (Cocke Papers)

1. Early in 1853, Boombo, a Vei chief, attacked towns over which chief Dwalu-Be (or Dwar-loo-Beh), also a Vei, ruled, and invaded Dei country, murdering Dei inhabitants and threatening Liberian colonists trading in the Little Cape Mount area. In March 1853 President Joseph J. Roberts sent an expedition of about 250 men to Little Cape Mount to protect the imperiled colonists and to apprehend the offending chief. Boombo was seized and imprisoned. See *African Repository* 29 (1853): 230-90; and 30 (1854): 101-3. See also editorial "Little Cape Mount" in *Liberia Herald*, Feb. 2, 1853; and the news story, "The Military Expedition," ibid., Mar. 2, 1853.

Letter 60 (Cocke Papers)

1. Henry W. Dennis emigrated from Maryland with his father in 1833. When he was sixteen he was virtually adopted by James B. McGill. In 1852, while still in the employ of McGill, he was appointed agent for the American Colonization Society in Monrovia and held that position until his death on June 11, 1876. He served in the Liberian legislature and for a time was secretary of the treasury. *African Repository* 52 (1876): 124-26

Letter 61 (Cocke Papers)

1. The varying signatures of Sucky Faulcon's three letters—April 20, 1853; Sept. 27, 1853; and August 21, 1857—and differences in handwriting and style indicate that the writing was done by three different persons.

Letter 62 (Cocke Papers)

Letter 63 (Cocke Papers)

Letter 64 (Cocke Papers)

Letter 65 (Cocke Papers)

1. Mary Diana Sterdivant was the daughter of Robert Leander Sterdivant. She was thirteen when she embarked for Liberia on the *Mariposa* June 7, 1842.

Letter 66 (Cocke Papers)

1. This was a cousin of John H. Cocke. He had been placed in charge of the Cocke plantation in Greene County, Alabama. See Coyner, "John Hartwell Cocke of Bremo," 2: 382. 2. James Skipwith did not depart for Liberia as soon as he anticipated. He arrived in Monrovia in 1857.

Letter 67 (Cocke Papers)

1. The war to which Sterdivant refers was in reality a series of clashes in late 1856 and early 1857 between Maryland colonists at Cape Palmas and the Grebo people, consisting largely of the Grahway and Cape Palmas tribes, who lived in the area. These conflicts derived in large part from errors of judgment on the part of Boston J. Drayton, governor of Maryland in Africa, in dealing with the natives. The natives eventually triumphed, and in so doing they inflicted enormous damage on the colonists. In response to an appeal from Drayton, the Liberian government in February 1857 sent to Cape Palmas a relief expedition of more than 100 volunteers commanded by ex-President Joseph J. Roberts. The presence of this force and the good offices of James Hall, former governor of Maryland in Africa, who accompanied the volunteers, enabled Roberts to arrange a peaceful settlement of the troubles. Sterdivant was a member of the expedition which, though small, was said to have included a general, two colonels, one major, and two captains. "The very large proportion of officers," according to Hall, "is very likely owing to the fact that most of [the] old Liberians were from Virginia, a soil somewhat prolific to the production of this genus." *African Repository* 34 (1858): 178-83. See also *Liberia Herald*, Feb. 18, 1857; and Penelope Campbell, *Maryland in Africia*, pp. 229-36. 2. The signer of this letter and the one that follows is obviously the same person who signed his letter of June 11, 1846, "Robert L. Sterdivant."

Letter 68 (Cocke Papers)

1. The reference to the three years of fighting is to the Cape Palmas war and the conflict at Sinoe which preceded it. See above, Letter 67, note 1.

Letter 69 (Cocke Papers)

1. Johnson, a native Liberian born in 1832, married Sarah Ann Roberts, daughter of President Joseph J. Roberts. Miller, *"Dear Master,"* p. 117, note. 2.

Letter 70 (Cocke Papers)

1. The writer of this letter is specified as Solomon Creecy, age sixty-five, in the list of emigrants who sailed from Baltimore on the *Mary Caroline Stevens* May 21, 1857, and from Norfolk May 28. This ship was named for the wife of John Stevens, a Boston philanthropist, who contributed $36,000 to the American Colonization Society for the construction of a packet ship to be used in transporting emigrants and supplies to Liberia. This vessel, which made her maiden voyage to Liberia in January 1857, was commonly called the *M. C. Stevens*. A description and drawing of the ship appears in ACS Papers, near the end of reel 314. The drawing is reproduced on p. 279 of this book. See also *African Repository* 33 (1857): 213. 2. Cary Charles Cocke, born in 1814, was John H. Cocke's youngest son.

Letter 71 (Cocke Papers)

Letter 72 (Cocke Papers)

1. J. W. Barraud, an officer of the *U.S.S. Cumberland* and a nephew of John H. Cocke, wrote Cocke from Monrovia November 12, 1857: "I made it a point to find out your former servants here and regret that I cannot give a very flattering account of them. . . . Matilda

. . . I saw and had a long talk with. . . . She seems to be tolerably contented and happy but said they did not *fare* half so well as at home which they still continue to deem old Virginny. She is living with her second husband and three children. I . . . was disapointed to find her inhabiting a miserable shanty in a low damp part of town, but she seemed and doubtless was thankful to Providence that matters were no worse. . . . I also saw old Suckey. . . . I asked her if she did not wish to be back. 'Oh, yes, sir,' said she, 'that I do.' Now you will probably ask why they are discon[ten]ted with freedom. Simply because they only enjoy *freedom to do nothing*. There is no work to be had. Every one performs what little is absolutely necessary to support sustenance for themselves and consequently there is no demand for labor." Barraud, whose comments were unduly pessimistic, gained "the painful impression that divested of the aid and counsel of the White Race, the American Negro ever will relapse into his original barbarism." His letter is filed with the Cocke Papers, University of Virginia.   2. Philip St. George Cocke was the second son of John H. Cocke.

Letter 73 (Cocke Papers)

1. James Skipwith, age twenty-three, a nephew of Peyton Skipwith, departed Norfolk on the *Mary Caroline Stevens* Nov. 12, 1857. *African Repository* 33 (1857): 356.

Letter 74 (Cocke Papers)

1. Molly Haynes, née Mary Diana Sterdivant, married George W. Haynes, presumably before November 1851. Information provided by Svend E. Holsoe.

Letter 75 (Cocke Papers)

Letter 76 (Cocke Papers)

Letter 77 (J. H. Cocke Papers, University of North Carolina, Chapel Hill)

1. Smith is James Skivring Smith. He received his medical education from Dr. J. W. Lugenbeel, Liberian colonial physician, and at Pittsfield (Mass.) Medical Insititute. He was Liberian senator, 1855-1863; vice-president, 1870-1871; and president, November 1871-January 1872. *African Repository* 24 (1848): 70; and information provided by Svend E. Holsoe. McGill is Dr. Samuel F. McGill, merchant and physician, the son of the Rev. George McGill. Dr. McGill migrated from Baltimore to Liberia in 1826. He received his medical education at Dartmouth. See *African Repository* 14 (1838): 360.

Letter 78 (Cocke Papers)

1. Stephen Allen Benson was president of Liberia for four terms, 1856-1864. For information about Joseph J. Roberts, see above, Introduction, note 8.   2. Carysburg (sometimes spelled Careysburg), named for a prominent pioneer colonist in Liberia, Lott Cary (or Carey), was established early in 1857 on an elevated site about twenty miles inland from Monrovia. Colonists who settled there enjoyed better health than those residing in the lower lands lying along the coast. See annual report of the American Colonization Society in *African Repository* 34 (1858): 68-70.

Letter 79 (Cocke Papers)

Letter 80 (Cocke Papers)

1. Skipwith's reference is to 318 Africans taken Aug. 21, 1858, near the coast of Cuba from the brig *Putnam* (with assumed name *Echo*) by Captain J. N. Maffit of the U. S. brig *Dolphin*. The captives were delivered into the custody of the U.S. marshal at Charleston, South Carolina. Later they were transported to Liberia on the frigate *Niagara*. On their arrival in Monrovia, in accordance with an agreement with the U.S. government, they were placed under the control of the American Colonization. Society. They society agreed to provide them with shelter, food, clothing, medical attention, and educational facilities for a period of twelve months and "to prepare them for the duties of civilized life." Thirty-two of the Africans died before leaving Charleston and seventy-one more on the voyage to Liberia. See annual report of the American Colonization Society in *African Repository* 35 (1859): 78-79.

Letter 81 (Cocke Papers)

Letter 82 (Cocke Papers)

1. This is the person who appears on the passenger list of the *Mariposa*, departing Norfolk June 7, 1842, as Leander Stewart [Sterdivant], age five. He was the son of Robert Leander Sterdivant.

Letter 83 (Cocke Papers)

Letter 84 (Cocke Papers)

1. Berthier Edwards was a field hand on Bremo plantation. Miller, *"Dear Master,"* p. 121, note 3.   2. Patsy was James Skipwith's wife. She and her children belonged to John H. Cocke's son, Dr. Cary Charles Cocke. John H. Cocke tried unsuccessfully to persuade his son to free Patsy and her children so they could accompany James to Liberia.

Letter 85 (Cocke Papers)

Letter 86 (Cocke Papers)

1. Skipwith's reference is to the blacks emancipated and sent to Liberia in 1856 by James Terrell of Albermarle County, Va. Miller, *"Dear Master,"* p. 135, note 1.

Letter 87 (Cocke Papers)

Letter 88 (Cocke Papers)

1. Persistent trouble between the Poe, Padae, and Garroway natives living near the northwest boundary of the Cape Palmas settlement was regarded as a threat to the peace and security of the colonists and caused President S. A. Benson early in 1861 to send an expedition to quell the disturbances. *African Repository* 37 (1861): 139, 161; and 38 (1862): 34.

CHAPTER 3

Introduction

1. Charles W. Andrews, *Memoir of Mrs. Anne R. Page* (Philadelphia: Herman Hooker, 1884), pp. 30, 47, 57-60.   2. Mary F. Goodwin, ed., "A Liberian Packet," *Virginia Magazine of History and Biography* 59 (1951): 73.   3. Cassada was the popular name for cassava, a shrub with edible roots. J. W. Lugenbeel, "Sketches of Liberia," in *African Repository* 26 (1850): 279.

Letter 89 (Charles W. Andrews Papers, Duke University)

Letter 90 (Charles W. Andrews Papers)

1. Page's reference may be to a fight between Liberian volunteers commanded by John N. Lewis and Elijah Johnson, and Natives led by Prince Bahgay late in 1839. The native force was subdued and Bahgay turned over to the Liberians four blacks intended for the slave trade; he claimed that other blacks in his possession had escaped. *African Repository* 16 (1840): 34-35. Lewis, a brother-in-law of President Joseph J. Roberts, was a member of the Liberian Constitutional Convention of 1847 and later served as secretary of state and as commander of the Liberian militia. Elijah Johnson was born a slave in Maryland. He migrated to Liberia in 1820 and fought beside Ashmun in defense of the beleaguered colony in 1822.

Letter 91 (Matthew Page Andrews Collection, Virginia Historical Society, Richmond)

1. The list of emigrants on the *Luna* departing Norfolk March 3, 1836, includes Peggy Potter, age twenty-three and her son William Nelson, age two. ACS Papers, microfilm, reel 312.

Letter 92 (Matthew Page Andrews Collection)

1. The conflict which Page recounts in this and the following letters occurred in March 1849, when an expedition of 350-400 Liberians attacked and destroyed Spanish slave-trad-

ing factories at New Cess and Trade Town. The slave traders were supported by a large force of native Africans recruited and commanded by the traders. The French ship that assisted the Liberians was the *Espado*. See *African Repository* 25 (1849): 244 and 249-250. The expedition, which was accompanied by President Joseph J. Roberts and commanded by General J. N. Lewis, consisted of two regiments. James C. Minor, adjutant of the First Regiment (see his letters in chapter 1), wrote a detailed account of the operation which was published in three installments in the *Liberia Herald* of June 25, July 27, and Sept. 28, 1849.

Letter 93 (Matthew Page Andrews Collection)

1. Page's account of the bee incident and other details of his narrative are confirmed by the third installment of Minor's report in the *Liberia Herald*, Sept. 28, 1849.   2. Twenty-five Congoes, recruited probably from recaptured Africans taken from the *Pons*, participated in the expedition. The slave traders and the native chiefs supporting them were said to have dreaded encounter with the Congoes. See first and second installments of James C. Minor's report in the *Liberia Herald*, June 25 and July 27, 1849.

Letter 94 (Matthew Page Andrews Collection)

Letter 95 (Matthew Page Andrews Collection)

Letter 96 (Mary F. Goodwin, ed., "A Liberian Packet," Virginia Magazine of History and Biography 59 [1951]: 83)

Letter 97 (Matthew Page Andrews Collection)

1. Tom Seigun was a quack medical theory set forth by Samuel Thompson in 1822 in a book entitled *A New Guide to Health*. Thompson held that all diseases were the effect of one general cause and could all be cured by botanic medicine. Robert Page had probably heard this theory discussed in his master's household and he may have hoped to use African herbs to combat native witch doctors.

Letter 98 (Matthew Page Andrews Collection)

Letter 99 (Matthew Page Andrews Collection)

1. The Rev. Jacob Rambo was an Episcopal missionary in Liberia and was active in educational affairs.

CHAPTER 4

Introduction

1. McDonogh outlined his plan in "A Letter of John McDonogh on African Colonization Addressed to the Editors of the New Orleans Bulletin, July 10, 1842." This letter is reproduced in the *African Repository* 19 (1843): 48-60.   2. Ibid., p. 54   3. On May 30, 1842, John McDonogh sent to William McLain a list of the seventy-nine blacks whom he was sending to Liberia on the *Mariposa*. In most cases he made a brief comment about the persons included in the list. This list, which is filed with the ACS Papers in the Library of Congress, will be cited hereafter as McDonogh list. In some instances names of correspondents do not appear in this list. This may be due to errors made in compiling the list or it may be attributable to the fact that some blacks changed their names after they arrived in Liberia. ACS Papers, microfilm, reel 314.   4. *African Repository* 49 (1873): 249. 5. This letter is filed in the ACS Papers, Library of Congress. George served as a captain of the first Liberian Regiment in an expedition of March 1849 against chiefs of New Cess and Trade Town who were engaged in the slave trade. *Liberia Herald*, June 25, 1849. In the 1850s George owned the Navy Hotel in Monrovia and was a partner in the business firm of Ellis and Johnson. Information provided by Svend E. Holsoe of the University of Delaware.

Letter 100 (McDonogh Papers, Tulane University, New Orleans, La.)

1. On the McDonogh list the writer of this letter appears as Gallaway, son of Judy, "a first rate Carpenter and Sugar Mill Builder, aged about twenty-two years."

Letter 101 (McDonogh Papers)

1. The McDonogh list states: "George Ellis . . . a Sugarmaker, Carter and Plowman understanding in all things and a man in whom every Confidence may be placed for honesty of purpose, aged about twenty-two years.

Letter 102 (McDonogh Papers)

Letter 103 (McDonogh Papers)

Letter 104 (McDonogh Papers)

Letter 105 (McDonogh Papers)

Letter 106 (McDonogh Papers)

1. This person appears on the McDonogh list as Augustine Lombard, "an Excellent Carpenter and Builder of Sugar mills, handy at all things, being full of talent, moral, honest and faithful, an excellent man twenty-one years of age." Either the compiler of the McDonogh list made a mistake or Augustine changed his last name after the list was made. 2. Andrew Dunford who was mentioned several times in the letters of the McDonogh blacks was apparently a neighbor and friend of McDonogh. 3. McDonogh in his list describes Phillis as "an Excellent woman, a Doctress, and understands all things, aged about fifty-two years." She was the mother of George R. Ellis McDonogh and Washington W. McDonogh.

Letter 107 (McDonogh Papers)

1. The *Renown* was wrecked at Porto Praia, Cape Verde Islands. All of the passengers were saved, but most of their provisions were lost. *African Repository* 20 (1844): 129. 2. According to the McDonogh list, McGeorge in 1842 was about twenty-five years old, "a Bricklayer, a Sugar Kettle Setter and Sugar Chimney Builder of Excellent character." In his list McDonogh wrote of McGeorge's father: "James, an African by birth, has been their [McDonogh slaves'] commander [overseer or driver]. [He] is a man in whom confidence may be placed for his honesty. [He] is a Brickmaker and is acquainted with plantation work."

Letter 108 (McDonogh Papers)

1. For information on the African Squadron, see above, Letter 39, note 1. 2. McDonogh's list characterizes James Gray as "an excellent man, a Carpenter and a man of all trades, aged about forty years."

Letter 109 (McDonogh Papers)

Letter 110 (McDonogh Papers)

Letter 111 (African Repository 23 [1847]: 263-64)

1. The only Mary appearing on the McDonogh list is specified simply as "Mary, wife of Simon, about twenty years of age."

Letter 112 (African Repository 23 [1847]: 260)

1. This must have been the man listed by McDonogh as "Richard, a minister of the gospel, aged about fifty years." 2. According to the McDonogh list "John, son of Elisa [is] an intelligent youth fourteen years old." His mother was depicted as "an Excellent woman, thirty-six years of age."

Letter 113 (African Repository 23 [1847]: 261)

Letter 114 (McDonogh Papers)

Letter 115 (African Repository 23 [1847]: 261)

1. McDonogh lists Bridget as "a woman of high moral character, thirty-two years of age."

Letter 116 (McDonogh Papers)

Letter 117 (McDonogh Papers)

Letter 118 (McDonogh Papers)

Letter 119 (McDonogh Papers)

Letter 120 (African Repository 23 [1847]: 264-65)

1. The only Nancy appearing on McDonogh's list is described thus: "Nancy, a Talented woman, capable of teaching a Common School and of Excellent moral character, twenty-two years." She may have been the sister of Gallaway Smith.

Letter 121 (McDonogh Paprs)

1. A Liberian physician, Dr. J. W. Lugenbeel, in an article "Native Africans in Liberia— Their Customs and Superstitions," published in *African Repository* 27 (1852): 311, stated: "It sometimes happens . . . that no particular person is accused; in which case it is incumbent on the gree-gree man, or [witch] doctor . . . to point out the culprit. The accused person is required to undergo the infallible ordeal of 'drinking sassa-wood.' . . . This drinking of sassa-wood, which is a universal test of witchcraft, consists in swallowing large quantities of the infusion of the bark of the sassa-wood tree, gulping it down until the distended stomach will not receive any more. If the person rejects from his stomach this poisonous infusion and lives, his innocence is established; but if he retains it, and consequently dies, his cruel tormenters are satisfied of his guilt."

Letter 122 (McDonogh Papers)

1. A notation on the back of this manuscript states: "This is a copy. The original was given to the Reverent Robert S. Finley, at his request, to publish."

Letter 123 (McDonogh Papers)

Letter 124 (McDonogh Papers)

1. John Aiken apparently was the person described thus in the McDonogh list: "Jack. Intelligent, honest, a Carter and somewhat of a sugar maker, a faithful man, aged nineteen years."

Letter 125 (African Repository 23 [1847]: 175-76)

1. James M. Priest was for twenty-seven years the pastor of the Presbyterian Church at Sinoe. He was vice-president of Liberia and president of the senate, 1864-1868, and at the time of his death, May 16, 1883, he was associate justice of the Liberian supreme court. *African Repository* 47 (1871): 37; 40 (1864): 138; and 60 (1884): 119.

Letter 126 (African Repository 23 [1847]: 176-177)

Letter 127 (African Repository 23 [1847]: 263)

1. Not on McDonogh list.

Letter 128 (McDonogh Papers)

Letter 129 (African Repository 23 [1847]: 265-266)

Letter 130 (McDonogh Papers)

Letter 131 (McDonogh Papers)

Letter 132 (McDonogh Papers)

1. Julia Smith may have been the person appearing on McDonogh's list as "Julia, wife of Augustine Lombard, aged 17 years" or she may have been "Judy, an excellent woman, a first rate midwife, a Spinner of Cotton and wool, &c, &c, aged about 50 years."

Letter 133 (McDonogh Papers)

Letter 134 (McDonogh Papers)

1. This is probably the person whom McDonogh lists thus: "Simon, a Sugar Maker, a ship Sawyer, a Carter and plowman, also a Brickmaker and understanding in the work of a Plantation generally, aged about twenty-two."

Letter 135 (McDonogh Papers)

Letter 136 (McDonogh Papers)

1. Henrietta Fuller, wife of James Fuller, described on McDonogh's list as "aged about thirty-eight years."

Letter 137 (McDonogh Papers)

1. Ralph R. Gurley made the second of his three trips to Liberia in 1849.

CHAPTER 5

Introduction

1. For information about the emancipation of the Ross slaves, their experience while awaiting the voyage to Africa, and litigation about their freedom, see Franklin L. Riley, ed., "A Contribution to the History of the Colonization Movement in Mississippi," in *Publications of the Mississippi Historical Society* 9 (1906): 411 ff. See also a brief history of the case involving the Ross Negroes in *African Repository* 18 (1842): 99-106.   2. A copy of Ross's will and three codicils appears in ACS Papers, microfilm, reel 314, "Extracts from Wills of Deceased Friends of the American Colonization Society," pp. 3-11. A legal document filed in the Isaac Ross Estate Papers at Mitchell Memorial Library, Mississippi State University, shows that the Ross slaves were called together on December 16, 1847, and told of the provisions of their late master's will. When asked individually their wishes concerning their future, all of them elected to be freed and sent to Liberia. I am indebted to Anne Wells, Manuscripts Librarian, Mitchell Memorial Library, for calling this item to my attention and providing a copy of it.   3. For a list of passengers transported on the *Nehemiah Rich*, see *African Repository* 24 (1848): 59-61; emigrants transported on the *Laura* are listed in *African Repository* 25 (1849): 118-21.   4. "Colonization and the Cholera," *African Repository* 25 (1849): 193.   5. Grandville Woodson, son of Pascal Woodson, was only sixteen when he migrated to Liberia in 1848 on the *Nehemiah Rich*.   6. Peter Ross was forty-four when he migrated to Liberia in 1848 on the *Nehemiah Rich*.   7. Gurley shared Peter Ross's low opinion of Isaac Wade. On Jan. 1859, in passing on one of Peter's complaints to William McLain, he stated: "I am in favor of sending this old man something. But you know the case better than I do. The cruelty and covetousness of the Executor of that Ross business is not to be described." ACS Papers, microfilm, reel 242, no. 225. 8. Gurley repeatedly wrote Peter Ross that no money was left from the Ross estate. Oct. 28, 1859, he wrote: "The property of your old master was taken by the heirs, much of it wasted . . . and none was left remaining for your benefits." ACS Papers, microfilm, reel 242, no. 287.

Letter 138 (Publications of the Mississippi Historical Society 9 [1906]: 405-6)

Letter 139 (Publications of the Mississippi Historical Society 9 [1906]: 400-401)

1. Hannibal Ross was sixty-two years old when he embarked for Liberia on the *Nehemiah Rich*.

Letter 140 (ACS Papers)

1. Sarah Woodson, wife of Pascal Woodson and mother of Grandville Woodson, was thirty-five when she sailed for Liberia on the *Nehemiah Rich*.

Letter 141 (Publications of the Mississippi Historical Society 9 [1906]: 401-2)

1. The writer of this letter appears on the passenger list of the *Nehemiah Rich* as Hector Ross, age seventy-one. The cholera victims to whom he refers were passengers on the *Laura* which departed New Orleans for Liberia Jan. 28, 1849.

Letter 142 (ACS Papers)

Letter 143 (ACS Papers)

Letter 144 (ACS Papers)

Letter 145 (ACS Papers)

Letter 146 (ACS Papers)

1. The reference is probably to A. M. Cowan, for twelve years an agent of the Kentucky Colonization Society. Cowan apparently represented the American Colonization Society temporarily in getting the Ross Negroes ready for shipment to Liberia. He visited Liberia in 1858 and wrote a book *Liberia as I Found It* (Frankfort, Ky.: A. D. Hodges, 1858), based on six weeks of travel in Liberia. In this book Cowan was critical of the colonists for not doing more to prepare Liberian natives for citizenship. *African Repository* 34 (1858): 193.
2. Woodson's first name appears as Paschall on the *Nehemiah Rich's* passenger list but he signed his letters Pascal Woodson. He was forty-five when he embarked for Liberia.

Letter 147 (ACS Papers)

Letter 148 (ACS Papers)

1. The war, or wars, referred to here and in subsequent letters, began in November 1855 and continued through June 1857. After a successful campaign by forces of the Liberian Republic, led by General J. N. Lewis, the chiefs who attacked the Sinoe settlements were required to pay heavy indemnities for the damage that had been inflicted by the natives. Annual report of the American Colonization Society in *African Repository* 33 (1857): 73. The native tribes involved in the attacks were the Grand Butaw and Little Butaw, the Sinoe, and the Blue Barre. For details concerning the destruction that they wrought and of the expedition that subdued them, see President S. A. Benson's message to the Liberian legislature in *Liberia Herald*, Dec. 3, 1856.   2. The name George Ross does not appear on the passenger list of either the *Nehemiah Rich* or the *Laura*. He was apparently Peter Ross's son but he generally (as in other letters in this chapter) used the name George Jones.

Letter 149 (ACS Papers)

Letter 150 (ACS Papers)

Letter 151 (ACS Papers)

Letter 152 (ACS Papers)

1. Horace Ross is listed as a thirty-two-year-old passenger on the *Nehemiah Rich* .

Letter 153 (ACS Papers)

Letter 154 (ACS Papers)

1. This person's name appears on the *Nehemiah Rich's* passenger list as York Ross, age thirty-five.

Letter 155 (ACS Papers)

Letter 156 (ACS Papers)

Letter 157 (ACS Papers)

Letter 158 (ACS Papers)

Letter 159 (ACS Papers)

Letter 160 (ACS Papers)

1. As previously stated, George Ross, who acted as the amanuensis of his father Peter Ross, signed the name of his father, who had been dead for over a year. Perhaps he assumed that Catherine Wade was not aware of Peter's death.

Letter 161 (ACS Papers)

CHAPTER 6

Introduction

1. See Memorandum of Agreement between W. W. Rice and the Louisiana Colonization Society, Feb. 11, 1851, in ACS Papers.   2. See "List of Emigrants by the Brig *Alida*" in *African Repository* 27 (1851): 153.

Letter 162 (ACS Papers)

1. The name James Rice does not appear on the *Alida's* passenger list or on W. W. Rice's Memorandum of Agreement with the Louisiana Colonization Society. Possibly the writer changed his name after arrival in Liberia.

Letter 163 (ACS Papers)

Letter 164 (ACS Papers)

1. James Patterson appears on the *Alida's* passenger list as a farmer, age forty-three. His wife Ginny was thirty-eight and their three children were Eliza (fifteen), Edmund, (twelve), and Milly (ten).

Letter 165 (ACS Papers)

1. The signers were doubtless Reuben Whittemore and Henry Brashear, listed on the *Alida's* passenger roster as farmers, ages twenty-two and twenty-six respectively.

Letter 166 (ACS Papers)

1. Henry Smith appears on the *Alida's* passenger list as a farmer, age forty.

Letter 167 (ACS Papers)

1. John B. Jordan was born in slavery in New Orleans. He was educated by his master, who made him a bookkeeper in his store and who eventually paid him a salary of $1,000 a year. He was emancipated by his master's will. Despite objections ot his wife and friends, Jordan migrated to Liberia in 1852, taking with him merchandise valued at several thousand dollars. The passenger list of the *Oriole* gives his age as thirty-five, that of his wife, Ollila, as twenty-three, and of his daughter, Emelina, as two. The editor of the *African Repository* in 1856 rated him as "one of the most enterprising farmers of Liberia" and "the most extensive sugar cane planter in Liberia." *African Repository* 28 (1852): 345; and 32 (1856): 229. 2. In a letter to Dr. J. W. Lugenbeel, Jan. 23, 1856, President Benson stated: "The five interior settlements of Bluntsville, Reedsville, Lexington, Louisiana and Farmersville have been depopulated except the soldiers stationed in each settlement to protect the few houses that have escaped the flames. The inhabitants have lost their property (crops inclusive) either by the flames or the pillaging and destructive hand of the enemy [Blue Barre, Sinoe, and Butaw tribes]; so that for the last two months five-sixths of the Americo-Liberian inhabitants have been objects of charity, depending for subsistence and clothing on the subscriptions taken up in the other two counties and an appropriation made by the Government." *African Repository* 32 (1856): 136.

Letter 168 (ACS Papers)

1. The only Reuben appearing on the *Alida's* passenger list, except for infant Reuben Brashear, is Reuben Whittemore, age twenty-two. The children mentioned in the postscript must have been born in Liberia. Possibly Reuben Whitemore changed his name to Reuben Rice.

Lettes 169 (ACS Papers)

1. Henry Smith appears on the *Alida's* passenger list as a farmer, age forty; the only Stephen listed is Stephen Filmore, farmer, age thirty; perhaps he changed his name to Stephen Rice.

Letter 170 (ACS Papers)

Letter 171 (ACS Papers)

1. Levi Seay appears on the *Alida's* passenger list as a farmer, age twenty.

Letter 172 (ACS Papers)

1. James Spriggs Payne was born in Richmond, Va., Dec. 13, 1819. He migrated to Liberia with his parents on the *Harriet* in 1829. He was ordained as a Methodist minister in 1840. He was elected president of Liberia in 1867 and again in 1875. In his obituary he is referred to as "of unadulterated African descent."*African Repository* 58 (1882): 90.

Letter 173 (ACS Papers)

1. Edward James Roye, a Negro of very dark skin, was born in Newark, Ohio, Feb. 3, 1815. After attending Ohio University in Athens, Ohio, he was engaged in the mercantile business for several years. He migrated to Liberia in June 1846 and entered the shipping business. He was said to be the first Liberian to carry goods in his own vessel to Europe. Eventually he became one of the wealthiest men in Liberia. He combined business with politics and in 1849 he became speaker of the house in the Liberian legislature. He founded the *Liberia Sentinel* and published that paper for about a year. He was chief justice of Liberia 1865-1868. He served as president of Liberia from January 1870 until he was deposed in 1871. He was accused of trying to extend the presidential term from two to four years in violation of the constitution and of corruption in connection with a loan of $500,000 that he negotiated in England. His death, under mysterious circumstances, was attributed to drowning while trying to make his way to a British ship anchored off the coast of Liberia. See Huberich, *Political and Legislative History of Liberia*, 2: 1258 and *African Repository* 46 (1870): 290; and 48 (1872): 41-46, 220.

Letter 174 (ACS Papers)

CHAPTER 7

Introduction

1. Douglas S. Freeman, *R. E. Lee* (New York: Scribner's, 1936), 4: 400. Freeman states that Lee in 1869 told the Reverend John Leyburn that he had received affectionate letters from former slaves who had gone to Liberia, but Freeman apparently was not aware that any of the letters had been preserved. 2. *African Repository* 31 (1855): 19. The editor of this journal stated that the letters of Burke and his wife to the Lees were sent to him, along with permission for their publication. He did not indicate by whom the letters were sent. Ibid., 32 (1856): 70; 34 (1858): 331; and 35 (1859): 213.

Letter 175 (ACS Papers, microfilm, reel 156, no. 50)

1. See "Emigrants by the Banshee . . . " in *African Repository* 30 (1854): 19-24. The four children who accompanied Burke and his wife were: Cornelia, age seven; Grandison, age five; Alexander, age three; and William, age four months.

Letter 176 (African Repository 31 [1855]: 19-20)
Letter 177 (African Repository 31 [1855]: 20-21)

1. The president of Liberia at this time was Joseph J. Roberts.

Letter 178 (African Repository 32 [1856]: 70)

1. Lee was superintendent of the U.S. Military Academy at West Point from August 1852 to March 1855, when he was sent to West Texas as lieutenant colonel of the Second Cavalry. 2. Beverly Page Yates, freeborn native of Virginia, migrated to Liberia in 1829, at age eighteen. He was active in Liberia's military affairs and in recognition of his achievement he was made colonel of the First Regiment, Liberia Volunteers. In 1852 he was appointed associate justice of the Supreme Court. In 1856 he became vice-president and in 1873 he was appointed commanding general of the Liberian Militia. *African Repository* 28 (1852): 109; 49 (1873): 107; and 59 (1873): 58.

Letter 179 (ACS Papers, microfilm, reel 157, no. 14)

1. This statement indicates that William, the infant whom the Burkes took to Liberia, must have died soon after Mrs. Burke's letter of Aug. 21, 1854, in which she stated that he was very weak from the acclimating fever. 2. Burke's reference is to the war of the settlers with the Sinoe, Butaw, and Blue Barre tribes during the period November 1855-June 1856. For reports on this conflict see *African Repository* 32 (1856): 136, 259; and 33 (1857): 73.

Letter 180 (ACS Papers, microfilm, reel 157, no. 73)

1. John Day was born in North Carolina in 1797. Apparently born free, he became a cabinetmaker. While a young man he was converted and became a Baptist minister. He migrated to Liberia in 1830 with his wife and four children. He became superintendent of the Baptist mission in Liberia and served for a time as chief justice of the Liberian Supreme Court. *African Repository* 35 (1859): 158; and 37 (1861):154-58.   2. Burke's reference apparently is to G. R. Ellis McDonogh who, as previously mentioned, became a hotel owner in Monrovia. See above, introduction to chapter 4, note 5.

Letter 181 (ACS Papers, microfilm, reel 157, no. 63)

1. Mrs. Lee suffered from chronic arthritis.

Letter 182 (ACS Papers, microfilm, reel 157, no. 107)

1. John Stevens was a Maryland philanthropist whose contribution of $36,000 to the American Colonization Society made possible the construction of the packet ship, *Mary Caroline Stevens*. See Letter 70, note 1.

Letter 183 (ACS Papers, microfilm, reel 157, no. 177)

Letter 184 (ACS Papers, microfilm, reel 158, no. 27)

1. George Washington Parke Custis, father of Mrs. Robert E. Lee and owner of the mansion, Arlington, died Oct. 10, 1857, at age seventy-six. *Dictionary of American Biography*, 5: 9-10.   2. The will of Custis provided for the emancipation of all his slaves within a period of five years following his death, and their removal from Virginia when they obtained their freeman. Robert E. Lee was made executor of the will. See R. R. Gurley to Wm. C. Burke, Feb. 26, 1858, ACS Papers, microfilm, reel 242, no. 8.   3. The White House, a plantation on the Pamunkey River in Virginia, was the property of George Washington Parke Custis. It was inherited at Custis's death by William Henry Fitzhugh Lee, grandson of Custis and son of Robert E. Lee. William Henry Fitzhugh Lee became a major general in the Confederate army. Ezra J. Warner, *Generals in Gray* (Baton Rouge: Louisiana State University Press, 1959), p. 184.

Letter 185 (ACS Papers, microfilm, reel 158, no. 114)

1. The will of William Henry Fitzhugh, dated March 21, 1829, provided that after the year 1850 his slaves were to be unconditionally free and allowed to go to whatever places they desired. As an encouragement to go to Liberia, the cost of their transportation was to be paid from Fitzhugh's estate and each of them was to be given the sum of fifty dollars in cash on arrival in Africa. See ACS Papers, microfilm, reel 314, "Extracts from Wills. . . . " pp. 52-54. Apparently none of the Fitzhugh slaves migrated to Liberia.   2. These were prefabricated dwellings erected for the housing of emigrants during their first six months in Liberia. See *African Repository* 33 (1857): 68.   3. The French slave ship to which Burke refers was the *Regina Coeli*. R. R. Gurley, secretary of the American Colonization Society, stated in the fall of 1858 that the account of the mutiny given by Burke in this letter was "more particular than anything we have seen." *African Repository* 34 (1858): 331. 4. As previously noted, "wounds" such as the one troubling Burke's daughter were probably caused by a skin disease known as "yaws."

Letter 186 (ACS Papers, microfilm, reel 158, no. 114)

Letter 187 (African Repository 35 [1859]: 213-15)

1. Gurley wrote to Burke, Oct. 29, 1858: "There has been some dissatisfaction and very improper conduct among several of these people since Mr. Custis' death, as I have been told by Mrs. Lee herself." ACS Papers, microfilm, reel 242, no. 105.   2. John Seys in 1859 was U.S. consul in Monrovia. While holding this position he was put in charge of establishing a new settlement at Carysburg on high ground in the interior about twenty miles from Monrovia. The newly arrived emigrants who settled there got along much better than those who took up residence in the lower coastal country. See *African Repository* 33 (1857): 33, 139, 194; and 34 (1858): 45. For further information about Seys, see Letter 18, note 2.

Letter 188 (African Repository 35 [1859]: 215)

1. Mary Ann, Catherine, and Agnes were daughters of Robert E. Lee and Mary Custis Lee.

Letter 189 (African Repository 35 [1859]: 215)

Letter 190 (ACS Papers, microfilm, reel 159, no. 162)

1. John H. Cheesman, a Baptist missionary and a judge, was drowned while crossing the Saint John's River in a canoe June 20, 1859. *African Repository* 35 (1859): 280.

Letter 191 (ACS Papers, microfilm, reel 159, no. 59)

1. This was probably Mrs. M. A. Ricks, widow of Sion Harris, several of whose letters were published in the *African Repository*. See *African Repository* 34 (1858): 136, 329-30; 36 (1860): 7; and 40 (1864): 6. Mrs. Ricks lived in the Clay-Ashland community.

Letter 192 (ACS Papers, microfilm, reel 159, no. 57)

Letter 193 (ACS Papers, microfilm, reel 159, no. 173)

Letter 194 (ACS Papers, microfilm, reel 160, no. 131)

1. The *Nightingale*, with 801 slaves captured by the U.S. man-of-war *Saratoga* near Cabendt, was brought into the Monrovia harbor on May 2, 1861. On July 4, 1861, President Benson stated that during the preceding year and a half, more than 4,000 recaptured Africans had been brought to Liberia. *African Repository* 38 (1862): 36.

Letter 195 (African Repository 39 [1863]: 132-33)

1. Daniel B. Warner was born free in Baltimore on April 19, 1815. He migrated to Liberia in the spring of 1823. Although he had never witnessed the construction of a ship, he entered the shipbuilding business and completed a sloop in 1843. Later he built four other vessels. Before his election as president of Liberia in 1864 he served as speaker of the house, secretary of state, and vice-president. After two terms as president he was twice reelected vice-president, in 1877 and 1879. In the late 1870s he served as agent in Monrovia of the American Colonization Society. He died in 1881. See *African Repository* 27 (1851): 81; 39 (1863): 247; and 57 (1881): 52. For information on Priest, see Letter 125 note 1. Boston J. Drayton migrated from Charleston, S. C., to Liberia in 1845, at age twenty-four. Before his unsuccessful candidacy for the presidency in 1863 he was governor of Maryland in Africa and superintendent of the Baptist Board of Missions in the Cape Palmas area. At the time of his death from drowning, Dec. 12, 1864, he was serving as chief justice. *African Repository* 41 (1865): 124-125. Asbury F. Johns was secretary of the treasury in President Warner's administration. *African Repository* 40 (1864): 137.

Letter 196 (African Repository 40 [1864]: 5-6)

1. Contraband was a term applied to slaves who came under Federal control during the Civil War. This usage is said to have originated with General B. F. Butler in Virginia in 1861, when he refused to return some fugitive blacks to their master on the ground that, having been used for the erection of Confederate fortifications, they were contraband of war and hence subject to confiscation. See Bell I. Wiley, *Southern Negroes, 1861-1865* (Baton Rouge: Louisiana State University Press, 1974), p. 175.

CHAPTER 8

Introduction

1. According to Tom W. Shick, *Emigrants to Liberia, 1820-1843: An Alphabetical Listing* (Newark, Del.: Liberian Studies Association in America, 1971), p. 43, Harris went to Liberia on the ship *Liberia* in 1830 at age nineteen. He was a carpenter-farmer from Knox County, Tennessee. Records do not indicate whether he was freeborn or an ex-slave.   2. Information about Ellis was obtained from the *African Repository*. See especially 23 (1840): 46-48, 294-95; 24 (1848): 161; and 46 (1870): 223.

Letter 197 (Maryland State Colonization Society Papers, Maryland Historical Society, Baltimore)

1. John H. B. Latrobe, son of the famous architect Benjamin H. Latrobe, was president of the Maryland State Colonization Society, and William McKenney was an agent of that organization.

Letter 198 (Maryland State Colonization Society Papers)

Letter 199 (Maryland State Colonization Society Papers)

Letter 200 (Maryland State Colonization Society Papers)

Letter 201 (Maryland State Colonization Society Papers)

Letter 202 (Maryland State Colonization Society Papers)

Letter 203 (ACS Papers, microfilm, reel 154, no. 37)

1. This letter, with spelling and grammar corrected, and with some other editing, was published in the *African Repository* 16 (1840): 195-97.   2. A half town was a village. It did not have a town chief but owed allegiance to the town from which its founder came. Information provided by Svend E. Holsoe.   3. Harris's statements about the mutilations were marked through in the manuscript and omitted from the published version. 4. Harris's account of the clash at Heddington and his role therein is corroborated by John Seys in his "Reminiscences of Liberia," *African Repository* 42 (1866): 216-18. Seys refers to Harris as "a brave and noble man."

Letter 204 (ACS Papers, microfilm, reel 154, no. 64)

1. John B. Pinney who had had to give up missionary service in Liberia owing to poor health, was at the time of Harris's letter serving as a traveling agent for the American Colonization Society in the U.S. For further information about him, see Letter 56, note 1.

Letter 205 (ACS Papers, microfilm, reel 154, no. 65)

1. The writers of this letter, Samuel D. Harris and his wife Polly Harris, were from Lexington, Va. They arrived in Monrovia on the *Liberia Packet* June 6, 1847. Apparently they had belonged to G. E. Dabney. Information provided by Svend E. Holsoe.

Letter 206 (ACS Papers, Microfilm, reel 154, no. 66)

1. Charles Stark, and Marshall Hooper and William Butler mentioned later in this letter, all slaves of Mrs. James C. Washington of Blakely, Va., left Baltimore Feb. 24, 1849, on the *Liberia Packet* and arrived in Monrovia Apr. 5. Information provided by Svend E. Holsoe.   2. J. N. Lewis was serving as an agent for the American Colonization Society in Montserrado County at the time Harris wrote this letter. For more information about Lewis, see Letter 90, note 1.   3. Esther Helms died on Apr. 28, 1849. Information provided by Svend E. Holsoe.

Letter 207 (African Repository 26 [1850]: 118-19)

1. Either Ellis or the editors of the *African Repository* made some slight errors in the Latin but a free translation of the quotation is: "Bless the Lord, oh my soul, and forget not his benefactions."

Letter 208 (ACS Papers, microfilm, reel 154, no. 137)

Letter 209 (ACS Papers, microfilm, reel 154, no. 164)

1. In the roster of emigrants by the barque *Huma* which left Savannah May 14, 1849, for Sinoe, Roberts is listed as a cooper and a Baptist preacher, age forty-seven, manumitted to go to Liberia. *African Repository* 26 (1850): 219.

Letter 210 (African Repository 27 [1851]: 2-4)

Letter 211 (ACS Papers, microfilm, reel 154, no. 175)

Letter 212 (ACS Papers, microfilm, reel 154, no. 176)

Letter 213 (African Repository 27 [1851]: 18)

Letter 214 (Maryland State Colonization Society Papers)

1. Hall, a graduate of the Medical School of Maine, went to Liberia early in 1831 to serve as colonial physician for the American Colonization Society. He returned to the U. S. in 1833, because of poor health. In the fall of 1833 he returned to Africa and served for three years as colonial physician and governor of Maryland in Africa. Later he entered the shipping business on the Liberian coast and served at the same time as general agent for the Maryland State Colonization Society. He was functioning in this dual capacity when Harris wrote him this letter. Harris apparently had had some contact with Hall during a visit to the United States in 1849. See Penelope Campbell, *Maryland in Africa*, p. 54 ff, and *African Repository* 18 (1842): 337.

Letter 215 (ACS, microfilm, reel 155, no. 67)

Letter 216 (ACS Papers)

1. Shick, *Emigrants to Liberia, 1820-1843*, p. 104, lists Edward White, age unknown, as an emancipated black from Louisiana who migrated to Liberia on the *Louisiana* in April 1835.

Letter 217 (ACS Papers, microfilm, reel 155, no. 120)

Letter 218 (ACS Papers, microfilm, reel 156, no. 16)

1. This letter, addressed to William McLain, treasurer of the American Colonization Society, and Dr. J. W. Lugenbeel, one of the society's agents in Liberia, is the last communication from Sion Harris that was found in the society's papers. He was killed by lightning while in bed in his home in the spring of 1854. He was a member of the Liberian House of Representatives at the time of his death. After Harris's death his widow, née Martha Ann Erskine, married Moses Ricks. She had arrived in Monrovia Feb. 17, 1830, on the same vessel, the brig *Liberia*, that carried Sion Harris. Four letters written after she married Ricks, and signed Mrs. M. A. Ricks, were published in the *Africa Repository* 34 (1858): 136, 329-30; 36 (1860): 7; and 40 (1864): 6.

Letter 219 (ACS Papers, microfilm, reel 155, no. 198)

1. Simon Harrison made the trip to Liberia on the *Banshee*, which departed Norfolk April 30, 1853. Harrison was a former slave, age fifty and literate. With him was his wife, Nice, age forty, and their three chilren: Daniel, age eleven; Matthew, age nine; and Martha, age six. The Harrisons were Presbyterians from the Choctaw Nation, "purchased by friends in New York and [in] the Choctaw Nation." See *African Repository* 29 (1853): 181; and ACS Papers, microfilm, reel 314, list of emigrants on the *Banshee*.

Letter 220 (ACS Papers)

1. Flournoy was born in Missouri June 1, 1826. He and his parents were sold by Solomon G. Flournoy to the Rev. Nathaniel Dodge, a Presbyterian missionary working among the Osage Indians. Dodge placed the Flournoys in the Harmony Mission and taught Phillip to read. After five years the family was emancipated and sent to Liberia on the *Mariposa*, which arrived in Monrovia Aug. 20, 1842. Phillip became a Presbyterian minister. *African Repository* 66 (1890): 62-63.

Letter 221 (ACS Papers)

1. Another person who labeled as false the charges of James and William Watson that they were mistreated in Liberia was A. M. Cowan, agent of the Kentucky Colonization Society, whose undated letter to the editor of the *Kentucky Commonwealth* was published in *African Repository* 34 (1858): 199-203. Cowan stated that the Watson men were ex-slaves of the late John Watson of Prince Edward County, Va. On their return to the United States, he stated, they complained of exorbitant prices in Liberia, of broken promises with respect to the amount of land they were to receive in Africa, and of the Liberian president's being engaged in the slave trade. "They have returned to slavery," Cowan added, "believing that freedom to the negro in Africa is the greatest curse that could possibly befall him, and that had the Liberians the means of getting away, seven-eighths of them would gladly return to the United States." Cowan declared these charges to be completely false, on the basis of his observing the men who made them during the voyage to Liberia, while they were there, and

on the return voyage to the United States.　2. According to information provided by Svend E. Holsoe of the University of Delaware, James W. Wilson, a slave preacher from Augusta, Ga., emancipated by D. Williams Marks, arrived at Cape Mount, Liberia, on the *Elvira Owen*, Aug. 9, 1856. He was asccompanied by his wife, Emma, and a child, Francis.

Letter 222 (ACS Papers)

Letter 223 (ACS Papers)

1. Tills belonged to the estate of Mrs. Margaret A. Reed, daughter of Isaac Ross of Mississippi. Executors for the estate were Stephen Duncan and Zebulon Butler. Apparently the money that Tills and the other Reed Negroes hoped to get from the estate was expended in litigation in which the estate was involved and in getting the blacks ready for the voyage to Liberia. See *African Repository* 18 (1842): 99-106; 20 (1844): 34. Tills's name does not appear on the passenger list of the *Lime Rock* but he very well may be the person listed with "Mrs. Read's people" among the *Renown* passengers as "George Washington Sillis," age twenty-two. See list of emigrants on the *Renown*, ACS Papers, microfilm, reel 314. For information on the Ross Negroes, see above, chapter 5.

Letter 224 (ACS Papers)

Letter 225 (ACS Papers, microfilm, reel 161, no. 4)

Letter 226 (ACS Papers, microfilm, reel 161, no. 16)

1. The name of Landon Williams appears on the list of immigrants landed at Tracy Receptacle from the ship *Mary Caroline Stevens* in 1857. He was forty-five years old and said to be in good health. ACS Papers, microfilm, reel 314.

CHAPTER 9

Introduction

1. Horland is the name as printed at the close of his two letters published in the *African Repository* 23 (1847): 279-81, but an article in the same journal, 28 (1852); 94, telling of his receiving a head wound in a fight with Chief Grando and a band of natives, gives the spelling as Harland.

Letter 227 (John M. McCalla Collection, Duke University, Durham, N.C.)

1. According to information provided by Svend E. Holsoe of the University of Delaware, Crawford, a carpenter, and his wife, Malinda, arrived in Monrovia on the brig *Ajax*, July 11, 1833.

Letter 228 (John M. McCalla Collection)

Letter 229 (Pattie Mordecai Collection, State Archives, North Carolina Division of Archives and History, Raleigh, N.C.)

1. Duncan Cameron and George Mordecai were executors of the estate of John Rex, to whom Malinda Rex had belonged. I am indebted to Memory F. Mitchell, Historical Publications Administrator, Department of Cultural Resources, State of North Carolina, for calling this letter to my attention and providing a xerox copy of it. For information about John Rex and his slaves, see Memory F. Mitchell and Thornton W. Mitchell, editors. "The Philanthropic Bequests of John Rex of Raleigh," *North Carolina Historical Review* 49 (1972): 254-79 and 353-76. Tom W. Shick, in *Emigrants to Liberia, 1820-1843*, p. 80, lists Malinda Rix, age forty, from North Carolina, arriving in Caldwell, Liberia, on the ship *Saluda*, September 1839. This is obviously Malinda Rex.

Letter 230 (African Repository 23 [1847]: 279-80)

1. The editor of the *African Repository* stated in a note accompanying this and Horland's letter of Jan. 19, 1846, that the two letters were published "without alteration or correction."　2. "Asbury Harland" was killed late in 1851, in a fight near Bassa Cove between the settlers and a group of about 300 members of the Fishmen tribe, led by Chief Grando.

Wesley "Harland" was seriously wounded in this encounter. *African Repository* 28 (1852): 94.

Letter 231 (African Repository 23 [1847]: 280-81)

Letter 232 (Shelby Family Papers, University of Kentucky, Lexington)

1. The passenger roster for the *Rothschild*, departing New Orleans Jan. 24, 1846, lists from the estate of Mrs. Jane Meaux of Kentucky (Thos. G. West, executor), Moses C. Jackson, age thirty-three, from Jessamine County; Amy, his wife, age twenty-six; and children: James, fifteen; Pegg, ten; Henry, four; and William, two. ACS Papers, microfilm, reel 314.

Letter 233 (Shelby Family Papers)

1. For information about Ellis, see above, chapter 8.   2. This reference is to the failure of the United States (until 1862) to recognize Liberia as an independent nation.   3. The passenger list of the *Rothschild* departing New Orleans Jan. 24, 1846, specifies that Nelson Saunders, age twenty-four, had been set free by Mrs. Sarah Fishback of Lexington, Ky. ACS Papers, microfilm, reel 314.

Letter 234 (Mississippi Quarterly 22 [Spring, 1969]: 151, "Letter from Liberia, 1848," ed. Terry L. Alford. Original in the Randolph-Sherman Papers, Mitchell Memorial Library, Mississippi State University)

1. I am indebted to Mr. Alford for calling this letter to my attention and making a copy of it available to me. Elisa Thilman was one of twenty-one slaves emancipated by Edward Brett Randolph and sent to Liberia in April, 1836, on the *Swift*.

Letter 235 (Cameron Papers, University of North Carolina, Chapel Hill)

1. Henry J. Roberts received his medical degree in the Pittsfield (Mass.) Medical Institute. He became the chief American Colonization Society physican in Liberia. *African Repository* 25 (1848): 70, 95.   2. The signature is virtually indecipherable. According to Svend E. Holsoe, the signer appears on the ACS List of Emigrants as Virgil Bannehan, freed by Thomas D. Bannehan of North Carolina.

Letter 236 (Gordon Family Papers, University of Kentucky, Lexington)

1. Jacob Harris appears on the passenger list of the *Nehemiah Rich*, departing New Orleans Jan. 7, 1848, as age twenty-four, from Kentucky. ACS Papers, microfilm, reel 314.

Letter 237 (Haynes Family Papers, Tennessee State Library and Archives, Nashville)

1. According to Svend E. Holsoe, the signer of this letter and of Letters 240 and 248 below, all from the estate of Christopher Houston of Giles County, Tenn., were sent to Liberia by Col. James S. Haynes of Camerville, Tenn.

Letter 238 (Georgia Historical Quarterly 24 [1940]; 253-54, "Liberian Letters from a Former Georgia Slave," ed. Charles S. Davis)

1. Evans, his wife, and four children, emancipated by Josiah Sibley, a merchant-planter of Richmond County, Ga., sailed from Savannah on the *Huma*, May 14, 1849. On the passenger roster, ACS Papers, microfilm, reel 314, they are listed as free, as apparently they were at the time of their migration.

Letter 239 (William M. Tillinghast Collection, Duke University, Durham, N.C.)

1. Hooper sailed from Norfolk on the *Liberia Packet* Jan. 26, 1850. He had previously visited Liberia in 1848. ACS Papers, microfilm, reel 314, List of Emigrants on the *Liberia Packet*, Jan. 1850, and on the *Amazon*, Feb. 5, 1848.

Letter 240 (Clay Family Papers, University of Kentucky, Lexington)

1. Mary Ann Clay and her niece, Lucy or Lucinda Clay (see Letters 241, 248) were emancipated by the will of Sidney B. Clay of Bourbon County, Kentucky. They sailed from New Orleans on the *Alida* Feb. 13, 1851. On the *Alida* passenger list (ACS Papers, microfilm,

reel 314) Mary Ann Clay appears as Mary Thomas, a cook, age nineteen . With her were two sons, ages three years and six months, both of whom died of fever shortly after their arrival in Liberia. Lucy Clay, also listed as a cook, age nineteen, was accompanied by an eight-month-old infant who died on the voyage. Two other slaves belonging to the estate of Sidney B. Clay refused to go to Liberia, vowing that they would drown themselves rather than go to Africa. They were taken to Texas and presumably remained in bondage. See A. M. Cowan to Brutus J. Clay, Jan. 10, 1851, and C. T. Field to Brutus J. Clay, Mar. 22, 1856. Clay Family Papers.

Letter 241 (Clay Family Papers)

Letter 242 (Haynes Family Papers)

Letter 243 (John R. Kilby Collection, Duke University, Durham, N.C.)

1. Randall Kilby arrived in Liberia as Randal Bunch, on the *Sophia Walker* July 30, 1854. Information provided by Svend E. Holsoe.

Letter 244 (Georgia Historical Quarterly 24 [1940]: 255-56, "Liberian Letters from a Former Georgia Slaves," ed. Charles S. Davis)

1. The conflict between the colonists at Sinoe and several tribes of that area began in November 1855 and was terminated by a peace imposed by President Benson in June 1856. See annual report of the American Colonization Society, *African Repository* 33 (1857): 73. See also Benson's message to the Liberian legislature in the *Liberia Herald*, Dec. 3, 1856.

Letter 245 (John Kimberly Papers, University of North Carolina, Chapel Hill)

1. Susan Capart, listed as Susan Capehart, sailed from Norfolk on the *Liberia Packet*, Jan. 26, 1850. List of Emigrants, ACS Papers, microfilm, reel 314.

Letter 246 (Gordon Family Papers)

Letter 247 (Ellis Malone Collection, Duke University, Durham, N.C.)

1. "Imigrants [sic] Landed in Tracy Receptacle from Ship M. Caroline Stevens, 3rd July 1857" includes the name "Henry Chavers," age twenty-five. ACS Papers, microfilm, reel 314.

Letter 248 (Clay Family Papers)

Letter 249 (Pettigrew Family Papers, University of North Carolina, Chapel Hill)

1. Tania was a broad-leaf plant about two feet tall with a bulbous root that resembled and tasted like an Irish potato.   2. According to information provided by Svend E. Holsoe of the University of Delaware, Richard McMorine, formerly known as Richard Blount, was a slave from Elizabeth City, N.C., who purchased his freedom with the aid of $500 from Anson G. Phelps of New York City, through John B. Pinney. He went to Liberia on the *Sophia Walker* which arrived in Liberia July 30, 1854. He was accompanied by his wife, Phebe, who was freeborn.

Letter 250 (Haynes Family Papers)

CHAPTER 10

Introduction

1. See "List of Emigrants by the Barque *Huma*" in *African Repository* 25 (1849): 218.

Letter 251 (ACS Papers, microfilm, reel 154, no. 121)

1. For information on James Priest, see Letter 125 note 1.   2. R. E. Murray, an agent in Liberia of the American Colonization Society, migrated from Charleston, S.C., in 1843. He represented Sinoe County in the convention that drew up the Liberian constitution of 1847. See Johnston, *Liberia* 1: 217; and *African Repository* 27 (1851): 335, 336.

Letter 252 (ACS Papers, microfilm, reel 154, no. 166)

Letter 253 (ACS Papers, microfilm, reel 155, no. 17)

1. J. W. Lugenbeel, "Sketches of Liberia," in *African Depository* 26 (1850): 209.

Letter 254 (C. C. Jones Papers, Tulane University, New Orleans, La.)

1. Charles Colcock Jones (1804-1863) was a prominent Presbyterian minister and planter of Liberty County, Ga. During the period 1850-1853 he was corresponding secretary of the Board of Domestic Missions of the Presbyterian Church. He worked long and hard for the evangelization of blacks and especially of his own slaves. In 1842 he published a book entitled *Religious Instruction of the Negroes*. For eighteen months in 1831-1832 he was minister of the First Presbyterian Church in Savannah, Georgia. Stewart may have met him during that period. Many of Jones's letters for the period 1854-1863 were published in *Children of Pride: A True Story of Georgia and the Civil War*, ed. Robert Manson Myers (New Haven, Conn.: Yale University Press, 1972).

Letter 255 (ACS Papers, microfilm, reel 155, no. 12)

1. Edward Hall, of Savannah, Ga., after purchasing his freedom and that of his wife and two brothers (William, age forty-four, and Cyrus, age thirty-three) migrated to Liberia on the *Baltimore* in the spring of 1851. Edward who was forty-eight at the time of his migration was said to have taken with him to Sinoe the first steam sawmill to be operated in Liberia. *African Repository* 27 (1851): 156; and 28 (1852): 67.   2. Stewart seems to be practicing his Latin by conjugating the verb *praepedio*, which means to tangle the feet, to hinder, to shackle. Apparently he means to state that more Savannah blacks, given the opportunity, will migrate to Liberia unless forcibly hindered.   3. The two Latin words means literally "well, better." So Stewart's meaning apparently is that the people are alive, well, and improving.   4. James Brown migrated to Liberia in 1836. He became a member of the town council of Monrovia and later moved to Sinoe County. He was a member of Liberia's first senate in 1847. Governor Thomas Buchanan wrote to the secretary of the American Colonization Society on Dec. 13, 1840: "One of the very best men in the colony is James Brown of Sinou. . . . He is a man of good sense, considerable talent as a speaker and is devoted heart and soul to America." See *African Repository* 12 (1836): 160; 17 (1841): 84; 24 (1848): 97; and 30 (1854): 251.

Letter 256 (ACS Papers, microfilm, reel 155, no. 124)

1. On Jan. 3, 1853, Jacob M. Snow, clerk of the newly established church, sent to McLain the following statement concerning organization of the Congregational Church in Liberia (ACS Papers, reel 155, no. 12 1/2):

Believing that you feel an interest in Every good institution of the day and Especially in the Cause of Evangelistical Religion, we have taken the Opportunity of sending you for publication a brief sketch of the Organization of the first Independent Congregationalist Church in this place. We deem a waist of time to Enter into all of the details that give rise to this Organization. Suffer us However to say to you that it is not the startling impulse of a day nor of a year, for previous to our comeing to this Country we imbided this form of Church Government, but not finding a Church here of the Same form of Government We as a matter of Course United Ourselves to the One that became the nearest until we could do better. Finally Brother H. B. Stuart having called upon the Bretheren that thought as He did and having obtaining their Consent to Unite in Church fellowship to Enjoy the Ordinances of God as we were taught, on Sunday September 19, 1852, Divine Service was held at the house of Brother H. B. Stuart and a sermon was preached by him to a very Respectable audience from Math. 18 Chap., 20 Verse for ever where two or three are gathered together there am i in the midst of them. At the Close of the Service it was Recommended that next Lord's day be Observed by us as a day of Fasting and prayer to God for a blessing upon our Undertaking & that a sermon be preached by Brother Stuart on the government of the Church. Through the Politeness of a friend who freely tendered to us a house of His Unoccupied, accordingly Sunday the 26 ult., Divine Service was there held and a Sermon was Preached from Isaah 40 Chap., 10 Verse, to a large and attentive Audience. At the Close of the Sermon we Covenanted with Each other in the Presence of Almighty God to obey him in all of the Audienances [ordinances] as he make known to us and Should further make known to us. Brother Henry B. Stuart was chosen to be our spiritual teacher and Brother David J. Hazzard was appointed as Deacon and Brother Jacob M. Snow Clerk.

The following names Constitute the above Church: Henry B. Stuart, David J. Hazzard, Jacob M. Snow, Ann Snow, Sarah A. Stuart, Rebecca C. Stuart, Margaret Stuart. And Here we Conclude by returning our thanks to our Friends and fellow Citizens for the very friendly feelings they have manifested towards us in assisting us in fitting up the house with Comfortable seats for we were not able of Ourselves. Also we take great pleasure in returning our Thanks to the members of the Baptist and Methodist Churches for their friendly visits with us. By Request the Following Gentlemen submit their names to be Placed Here as well Wishers to the Institution: Isaac Johnston, Stephen Britton, Wm. Cassiday, E. Hall, R. S. Jones, B. A. Payne, J. W. Brown, H. C. Hicks, Goldsmith Taylor, Rev'd R. E. Murray, Rev'd Isaac Roberts.

Greenville, Sinoe, October 5, 1852
Foreign Papers will Copy. Jacob M. Snow, Clerk

Letter 257 (ACS Papers, microfilm, reel 157, no. 28)

1. Stewart refers to the destructive raids on the Sinoe settlements late in 1855 by the Grand Butaw, Little Butaw, Sinoe, and Blue Barre tribes. Early in 1856 President Benson sent an expedition to Sinoe County to punish the aggressive tribes. The expedition restored peace to the area. See *Liberia Herald*, Dec. 3, 1856, message of President Benson to the Liberian legislature.

Letter 258 (ACS Papers, microfilm, reel 157, no. 18)

Letter 259 (ACS Papers, microfilm, reel 157, no. 62)

Letter 260 (ACS Papers, microfilm, reel 157, no. 72)

1. The Rev. Beverly R. Wilson was a freeborn black from Norfolk, Va. He headed the Methodist mission at Cape Palmas and was one of the signers of the Liberian Declaration of Independence. *African Repository* 11 (1835): 241; and 41 (1865): 63.

Letter 261 (ACS Papers, microfilm, reel 157, no. 95)

1. Matt. 18:15 reads: "Moreover if thy brother shall trespass against thee, go and tell him his fault between thee and him alone; if he shall hear thee, thou hast gained thy brother." Luke 17:3 reads: "Take heed to yourselves; if thy brother trespass against thee, rebuke him; and if he repent, forgive him."

Letter 262 (ACS Papers, microfilm, reel 157, no. 139)

1. This letter is headed by the word "Demonstration."

Letter 263 (ACS Papers, microfilm, reel 157, no. 143)

Letter 264 (ACS Papers, microfilm, reel 157, no. 179)

1. In the 1850s, if not sooner, American Colonization Society officials began to send to Liberia for reception of newly arrived emigrants, houses prefabricated in the United States. These receptacles, as they were called, were 96 feet long, 36 feet wide, and 2 stories high. The initial cost for each in 1856 was $6,600, freight for shipping $4,000, and erection in Liberia, $1,400. See annual report of American Colonization Society in *African Repository* 33 (1857): 68.

Letter 265 (ACS Papers, microfilm, reel 158, no. 17)

1. This reference is to a donation of 224 volumes, mostly religious, given by the Massachusetts Sabbath School Society, the receipt of which was acknowledged by Stewart on January 20, 1858. Stewart listed the books by author and title. See ACS Papers, reel 157, no. 16.

Letter 266 (ACS Papers, microfilm, reel 158, no. 20)

1. For information on Cowan see Letter 146, note 1.

Letter 267 (ACS Papers, microfilm, reel 158, no. 88)

Letter 268 (ACS Papers, microfilm, reel 161, no. 155)

1. Stewart apparently had been on a trip to the United States to obtain aid for his church in Liberia.

Letter 269 (ACS Papers, microfilm, reel 160, no. 69 1/2)

1. The forty-fourth annual report of the American Colonization Society contained a section on "Recaptured Africans" showing that 343 of these people had been landed in 1860 at Sinoe from the *Star of the Union (African Repository* 37 [1861]: 75). On October 1, 1860, President Benson stated: "We have landed in the Republic within about two months nearly four thousand receptives, for whom this government will have to render account in the future." Ibid., 38 (1865): 35. W. W. Schmokel in "Notes on Settlers and Tribes: The Origins of the Liberian Dilemma," *Western African History*, Boston University Papers on Africa (New York: Frederick R. Praeger, 1969), 4: 159, states that while the recaptured Africans were permitted to become citizens of Liberia, "they found themselves in a distinctly inferior social position." Schmokel also states that the system of apprenticeship amounted to "something very much like temporary slavery." Ibid., p. 166.   2. For more information on Hall, see Letter 214, note 1.

Letter 270 (African Repository 40[1864]: 7-8)

Letter 271 (ACS Papers, microfilm, reel 161, no. 7)

1. William Coppinger became secretary of the American Colonization Society in 1865.

Letter 272 (ACS Papers, microfilm, reel 161, no. 136)

Letter 273 (ACS Papers, microfilm, reel 161, no. 193)

EPILOGUE

1. According to Charles Morrow Wilson, *Liberia: Black Africa in Microcosm*, pp. 221-26, the tuberculosis infection rate in 1960 ranged from 60 to 70 percent of the population above thirty years of age, only about 15 percent of school-age children actually were in school, and in 1970 per capita income was only about $185 a year. The article on Liberia in *Encyclopedia Britannica* (15th edition, 1974, 10: 855) states that "the incidence of malaria is close to 100 percent."   2. J. Gus Liebenow in *Encyclopedia Americana* (1975 edition) 17: 298. Liebenow states that in the 1940s President William V. S. Tubman initiated reforms designed to end the social, political, and economic discrimination experienced by the tribal people who comprise the overwhelming majority of Liberia's population. His reforms established woman suffrage and gave to tribal people "the right to vote and be represented in the Senate and House of Representatives" and led to the appointment of tribal people to the cabinet and the supreme court. Ibid., pp. 301-2. In 1972, according to A. N. Woods, of the seventy members of the national legislature of Liberia, "more than half . . . are direct representatives of the tribal population." Von Gnielinski, ed., *Liberia in Maps*, p. 32.   3. *African Repository* 7 (1831): 260.   4. Ibid., 43 (1867): 133.   5. Ibid., 30 (1854): 228-29.   6. Information provided by Svend E. Holsoe.   7. *African Repository* 44 (1868): 278-80; and 53 (1877): 81.

Bibliographical Note

The basic sources for this study were the letters written by blacks who migrated from the United States to Liberia during the three decades preceding the American Civil War. Only those letters written by ex-slaves were included in this compilation, but many communications written by freeborn migrants were read and these provided useful information on transportation to Africa and life in Liberia.

During preparation of the volume inquiries were made at all major southern manuscript depositories in an effort to locate pertinent material. The largest collections of letters found were those contained in the John Hartwell Cocke Papers at the University of Virginia, the John McDonogh Papers at Tulane, the Ross-Wade Papers in the Mississippi Department of Archives and History, and the Blackford Family Papers, some of which are in the Southern Collection of the University of North Carolina, some at the University of Virginia, and some in private possession.

The American Colonization Society Papers in the Library of Congress contain a substantial number of letters written by migrants to Liberia. Most of these are to officials of the society but some are to former owners. This collection also contains much useful information in the form of reports and correspondence of the society's agents, both in the United States and in Liberia, reports and correspondence of civic and religious leaders and groups in Liberia, passenger lists of ships bound for Africa, correspondence of masters desirous of sending blacks to Africa, and communications from members of state colonization societies.

The papers of the Maryland State Colonization Society filed in the holdings of the Maryland Historical Society in Baltimore contain numerous letters of blacks sent to Liberia under the auspices of that organization but relatively few of them could be identified as communications of ex-slaves.

The Liberian Studies Association in America, whose headquarters are at the University of Delaware, has issued some important reference works pertaining to Liberia. These studies, published at the Department of Anthropology of that institution in a series of working papers edited by Svend E. Holsoe, include the following: number 1, *Bibliography on*

Liberia: Books, edited by Svend E. Holsoe (1971); number 2, *Emigrants to Liberia, 1820-1843: An Alphabetical Listing*, edited by Tom W. Shick (1971); number 3, *Publications Concerning Colonization*, edited by Svend E. Holsoe (1971); number 4, *Immigrants to Liberia, 1865-1904: An Alphabetical Listing*, edited by Peter J. Murdza, Jr. (1975); number 5, *Articles*, edited by Svend D. Holsoe (1976). The alphabetical listing of emigrants for 1820-1843, compiled from passenger lists, specifies for each person age, origin, status (freeborn or emancipated), literacy, occupation, cause of death, ship on which transported, and place and date of arrival in Liberia. Usefulness of this list was limited by the fact that many of the blacks whose letters are reproduced in this volume migrated in the period 1844-1860 (and hence were not included in the list); and even in the instance of those migrating in the period 1820-1843, names appended to the letters often do not appear on the list. The explanation may be that some migrants changed their names after their arrival in Africa.

Of serials, the *African Repository and Colonial Journal* (Washington, D.C., 1825-1894), published by the American Colonization Society, proved the most useful. This publication contained the society's annual reports, information about the activities of state and local colonization societies, reports and correspondence of governmental and church leaders in Liberia, correspondence of the society's agents in Africa and of American naval officials visiting Liberia, passenger lists of many of the ships transporting blacks to Africa, and letters of emigrants. The editors did not publish letters that were critical of the society and of the letters that they published they usually corrected spelling, grammar, and punctuation; they also deleted statements reflecting adversely on the society's activities. Even so, some of this correspondence is vivid and informative. Another useful serial was the *Liberia Herald*, published in Monrovia. Microfilm of imcomplete files of the *Herald* for the period 1842-1857 was borrowed on interlibrary loan from Yale University and from the University of Wisconsin.

Among books most helpful in editing the letters contained in this volume were: R. Earle Anderson, *Liberia: America's African Friend* (Chapel Hill: University of North Carolina Press, 1952); L. Minor Blackford, *Mine Eyes Have Seen the Glory: The Story of a Virginia Lady, Mary Berkeley Minor Blackford* (Cambridge, Mass.: Harvard University Press, 1955); C. C. Boone, *Liberia as I Know It* (Richmond, Va.: privately printed, 1929; reprint ed., New York: Negro Universities Press, 1970); Penelope Campbell, *Maryland in Africa: The Maryland State Colonization Society, 1831-1857* (Urbana: University of Illinois Press, 1971); Peter Duignan and Clarence Clendenen, *The United States and the African Slave Trade, 1619-1862* (Palo Alto, Cal.: Hoover Institution on War, Revolution, and Peace, 1963); Early Lee Fox, *The American Colonization Society, 1817-1840* (Baltimore, Md.: Johns Hopkins University

Press, 1919); Elizabeth Dearman Furbay, *Top Hats and Tom Toms* (New York: Ziff Davis, 1943); Stefan von Gnielinski, ed, *Liberia in Maps* (London: University of London, 1972); Arthur J. Hayman and Harold Preece, *Lighting up Liberia* (New York: Creative Press, 1943); Sir Harry H. Johnston, *Liberia*, 2 vols. (New York: Dodd, Mead, 1906, reprint ed., New York: Negro Universities Press, 1969); Randall M. Miller, ed., *"Dear Master": Letters of a Slave Family* (Ithaca, N.Y.: Cornell University Press, 1978); Philip J. Staudenraus, *The African Colonization Movement, 1816-1865* (New York: Columbia University Press, 1961); Charles Morrow Wilson, *Liberia: Black Africa in Microcosm* (New York: Harper and Bros., 1971); Charles Henry Huberich, *The Political and Legislative History of Liberia*, 2 vols. (New York: Central Book Co., 1947); J. Gus Liebenow, *Liberia: The Evolution of Privilege* (Ithaca, N.Y.: Cornell University Press, 1969).

Index

African fever, 5. *See also* American
freedmen in Liberia, health of; Liberia,
health in

African Luminary, 49, 51

African Repository and Colonial Journal,
2, 8, 312 n.17

Africans, native: character of, 206-7; life
of, 205-6; mutiny against crew of slave
ship, 202; strife among, 77, 321 n.1
(ltr 80); superstitions of, 138; war with
settlers, 156, 166, 170, 328 n.1 (ltr
148). *See also* American freedmen in
Liberia, relations with African natives;
Recaptured Africans; *and names of
individual tribes and chiefs*

African squadron, 127-35; effectiveness in
suppressing slave trade, 60, 317-18 n.1
(ltr 39). *See also* Slave trade

Agriculture. *See* American freedmen in
Liberia, aversion to agriculture; crops
of; farming activities of

Aiken, John, letter of, 140

American Colonization Society (ACS):
administrative structure, 1-3; attitude
of settlers toward, 64; failure to
provide adequately for emigrants, 282;
founding of, 1; and recaptured
Africans, 91, 321 n.1 (ltr 80); and
slaves of Isaac Ross, 155-59; and
slaves of William Rice, 176-89;
summary history of, 1-3

American freedmen in Liberia: apprentice
African natives, 141; artisans, 40, 51,
53, 64, 117, 134, 191, 255, 258;
attitude toward African natives, 57,
67, 242; attitude toward American
Civil War, 184, 211-12; attitude
toward ACS, 211-12; attitude toward
former masters, 226, 250, 264-66, 271-
72; aversion to agriculture, 6-7; books
requested by, 112, 164, 166, 180, 264;
character of, 8-9, 11-12, 122-23, 131,
175-76, 184, 203, 228, 231-33, 243,
246, 254-55, 257-58, 262, 270, 275,

277, 282, 287, 298, 300, 306; churches
of, 130, 147, 149, 258, 261-62, 271;
clothing of, 30, 103, 133-34, 140, 149,
163, 170, 273; compared with freeborn
settlers, 308-9; crops of, 109, 110, 260,
263-64, 275; discrimination against
women, 75, 273; and education, 39,
94, 106-9, 150, 159, 162, 171, 176,
185, 192-95, 216, 218, 228, 232-33,
245, 262-64, 270, 281, 283-87, 291,
300; and rumored enslavement of
African natives, 36, 315 n.2 (ltr 19);
and family ties, 70-71, 101, 111-14,
120, 130, 133-34, 136, 147, 149, 160,
164, 193, 217, 219-20, 239, 247, 253,
259, 261, 267, 274, 286, 291, 307;
farming activities of, 53, 55, 60, 64,
92, 125, 130-32, 135, 140-42, 144, 153,
179, 194, 206, 208, 214, 225-26, 234-
37, 246, 252, 263-64, 275, 277, 288,
298, 300, 303, 305; food of, 5-6, 22,
32, 39, 51, 76, 101, 161-62, 178-79,
183, 190, 245, 252, 273, 275, 277-79,
322 n.3 (introduction); hardships of,
85, 92, 156, 159, 165-70, 175-76, 180-
82, 185, 197, 217-18, 227, 239, 247,
252-53, 273, 278, 282, 301, 320 n.1 (ltr
72), 328 n.2 (ltr 167); health of, 7, 24,
65, 96, 111-12, 156-60, 162, 169, 177-
80, 184-85, 190-91, 212-13, 226, 230,
235, 239, 245-46, 251, 253, 256-59,
261, 265-68, 272, 288, 305-6, 323 n.1
(ltr 97); housing of, 151, 191, 201,
209, 213, 242-43, 255, 264, 268, 276,
287-88, 297, 304-5, 330 n.2 (ltr 185),
338 n.1 (ltr 264); humor of, 10, 241,
269; hunting activities of, 278; and
leadership in Liberia, 308-9; and
livestock, 133, 142, 144, 163, 183; and
miscegenation, 312 n.19; numbers of,
1; pride in Liberia, 80, 91, 94-95, 115,
132, 142, 153, 156, 162-65, 167, 175,
197, 213, 226, 229, 233, 242-43, 245,
258, 263-64, 270, 272, 280, 286-87,

Grebos, 83, 320 n.1 (ltr 67); war with Garroway, Padae, and Poe tribes, 99, 322 n.1 (ltr 88)
Carter, Peter, letter of, 157
Cary, Lott, 309
Carysburg settlement, 90, 94, 96-97, 201, 204, 321 n.2 (ltr 78)
Chaver, Henry, letter of, 272
Cheesman, John H., 209, 331 n.1 (ltr 190)
Churches, 17, 22-23, 51, 192, 195-96, 199, 201, 208. *See also* American freedmen in Liberia, and religion; *and individual denominations*
Clay, Brutus J., letters to, 265, 266, 273
Clay, Henry, 188
Clay, Lucinda (Lucy), 335 n.1 (ltr 240); letters of, 266, 273
Clay Mary Ann, 335 n.1 (ltr 240); letter of, 265
Clay-Ashland settlement, 188, 192
Cocke, Anne (Barraud), 33
Cocke, John Hartwell, 5, 33-34; letters to, 36-38, 40, 43, 48, 51-55, 58-62, 68-83, 85-89, 91-93, 96, 99
Cocke, Louisa (Maxwell) Holmes, 33; letters to, 42, 46
Cocke, Sally Faulcon. *See* Brent, Sally Faulcon (Cocke)
Congos, 67, 108, 210, 323 n.2 (ltr 93), 331 n.1 (ltr 194). *See also* Recaptured Africans
Congregational church in Liberia, 288-90, 294, 305, 337 n.1 (ltr 256)
Conneau, Theophilus, 55, 317 n.3 (ltr 34)
Constitution, 31
Coppinger, William, 339 n.1 (ltr 271); letters to, 304-6
Cowan, A. M., 165, 299, 327 n.1 (ltr 146)
Crawford, George, 334, n.1 (ltr 227); letters of, 251, 252
Creecy, Solomon: emigration to Liberia, 85; letters of, 85, 87; and religion, 87; and temperance, 87
Crocker, Lewis Gary (Little Bassa chief), 196
Custis, George Washington, death of, 198, 330 n.1 (ltr 184); emancipates slaves in will, 199, 330 n.2 (ltr 184)

Dabney, G. E., 225-26
Davis, W. W., 31
Day, James Lawrence, 58, 317 n.2 (ltr 37)
Day, John, 195, 246; sketch of, 330 n.1 (ltr 180)
De Counsey, Mrs. Caroline, 203
Dei (Dey) tribe, 220
Dennis, Henry W., 78; letter to, 96; sketch of, 319 n.1 (ltr 60)

Drayton, B. J., 213
Duaga, King, 107-8
Dwalu-beh (Dwar-loo-beh), 77, 319 n.1 (ltr 59)

Edina settlement, 63
Edwards, Berthier, letter to, 95
Ellis, H. W., 145, 148, 258; early life in U.S., 216; letters of, 228, 231
Episcopal church in Liberia, 27, 115
Erskine, H. W., 229
Evans, Seaborn, 309; letters of, 263, 269

Faulcon, John H.: apprenticed to Peyton Skipwith, 34, 41; criticism of, 10, 97; and education, 68; and family ties, 75; health of, 89; letters of, 68, 74, 80, 89; pride in Liberia, 80; relations with John Hartwell Cocke, 75, 89; as soldier, 74; work of, 75
Faulcon, Mrs. Sally, 35
Faulcon, Sucky (Susan): criticism of, 10, 97; emigrates to Liberia, 34; family of, 76, 319 n.1 (ltr 57); and family ties, 76, 79; hardships of 321 n.1 (ltr 72); letters of, 76, 78, 85; reaction to Liberia, 76, 79; and religion, 36, 77, 85-86
Fishback, Susan, letter to, 258
Fisherman tribe: attacks Grand Bassa settlement, 48; attacks settlements at Fishtown and Bassa Cove, 74, 319 n.1 (ltr 54)
Fitzhugh, William Henry, 201
Flournoy, Phillip F., letter of, 244; sketch of, 333 n.1 (ltr 220)
Fuller, Henrietta, 9; letter of, 153

Garrison, William Lloyd, 3
Getumbe (Gatoomba, Gaytoombay, Gaytoombah), 23; attacked by settlers, 52, 54; attacks Heddington, 220
Gibson, Jacob, letter of, 216
Glover, Titus, 177, 179; hardships of, 181, 187; letters of, 178, 181, 186; pride in Liberia, 177, 181; and religion, 10, 181; relations with African natives, 181; relations with former master, 178-79
Gola (Gora) tribe, 43, 77
Goodwin, Mary F., 101
Gordon, N. M., letters to, 261, 271
Gotora (Gotola, Goterah): attacks Heddington, 220-23; death of, 53, 222
Graham, Violet, letter of, 262
Grahway tribe, 83, 320 n.1 (ltr 67)
Grand Bassa, 5, 17
Grand Butaw tribe, 166, 181, 289-90

Grand Cape Mount, 5, 96
Grando, Chief, 74, 319 n.1 (ltr 54)
Gray, James, letter of, 126
Grebo tribe, 83, 320 n.1 (ltr 67)
Greenville settlement, 5
Gurley, Ralph R.: letters to, 13-14, 17, 18,
    20, 31, 166-69, 171, 173, 193-200, 207-
    14, 289, 290, 292, 293, 297, 298, 300-
    303; secretary of ACS, 2; visits
    Liberia, 153, 229; writes John
    McDonogh, 119

Hall, Edward, 286
Hall, James: letter to, 236; sketch of, 333
    n.1 (ltr 214); visits settlement at
    Greenville, 303
Hall, Stephen, letters of, 219
Hall, Thomas, letter to, 262
Hance, Alexander, 215; letters of, 216,
    217
Harris, Jacob, letters of, 261, 271
Harris, Martha A., 238; letters of, 230,
    237; remarriage of, 333 n.1 (ltr 218)
Harris, Polly D., letter of, 225
Harris, Samuel D., letter of, 225
Harris, Sion, 215; attitude toward African
    natives, 235; builds brick house, 240;
    catches boa constrictor, 236-37;
    character of, 220-23, 227, 241; death
    of, 333 n.1 (ltr 218); elected to
    Liberian legislature, 227; and family
    ties, 240-41; farming activities of, 234,
    236-37, 240; health of, 224; humor of,
    241; hunting activities of, 236; letters
    of, 220, 224, 226, 229, 234, 235, 236,
    240; pride in Liberia, 224, 226-27, 236;
    and religion, 220, 222, 254; repels
    attack on Heddington, 220-23; serves
    in Liberian.legislature, 309; and trade,
    240; visits U.S., 224, 226
Harrison, Simon, 333 n.1 (ltr 219); letter
    of, 241
Haynes, Dicy, letter to, 262
Haynes, James, letters to, 262, 267, 278
Haynes, Molly. See Sterdivant, Mary
    Diana
Heddington, attacked by African natives,
    53, 220-23
Hill, Robert F., 309
Hooper, A.B., letter of, 264
Hopewell plantation in Alabama, 34
Horland, Wesley, 250; letters of, 254, 255

Jackson, A., letter of, 143
Jackson, Mary, letters of, 129, 143
Jackson, Moses, letter of, 256
James, Diana (Skipwith). See Skipwith,
    Diana
Jefferson, Charles, letters of, 267, 278

Jenkins, Chief, 43, 316 n.1 (ltr 27)
Johns, A. F., 213
Johnson, Elijah, 104, 322 n.1 (ltr 90)
Jones, Charles Colcock: letter to, 285;
    work for evangelizing slaves, 337 n.1
    (ltr 254)
Jones, George, letters of, 173, 174
Jordan, John B., 181; farming activities
    of, 328 n.1 (ltr 167)

Kennedy, Thomas, letter to, 267
Kentucky in Africa, 229, 259
Ker, John, 156; letters to, 157-59
Kilby, John R., letter to, 268
Kilby, Randall, letter of, 268
Kimberly, John, letter to, 270
King, Mary, letter of, 249

Lansay, Paul F., letter of, 219
Latrobe, John H. B., letters to, 216, 218,
    219
Lee, Mary (Mrs. Robert E.): illness of,
    196, 198; letters to, 190, 192, 203, 206
Lee, Robert E., 8, 188, 193, 196; letters
    to, 190, 203, 206
Lewis, John N., 150; accused of trade
    monopoly, 227; in war against African
    natives, 104, 106
Liberia: artisans in, 40, 51, 53, 64, 86, 93,
    102-3, 108, 112, 220, 255, 258;
    churches in, 94, 195, 199, 224, 226,
    228-29, 243, 246, 282, 284-86, 288-90,
    294, 300-305; climate of, 6, 128, 194,
    201, 205-7, 229, 231, 276, 285;
    constitution of, 63; crops of, 64, 70,
    83, 92, 142, 144, 206, 208, 212, 254,
    272, 275, 304; depression in, 85, 90,
    92, 194, 199; farming in, 55, 60, 90,
    92, 108-9, 110-12, 191, 206, 208, 214;
    flag of, 49, 316 n.2 (ltr 30); and
    foreign trade, 31, 230; founding of, 1;
    government and politics of, 63, 163-
    64, 167, 187, 193, 213, 254, 259, 288,
    296, 303, 306, 310; governors of, 310;
    health in, 38-40, 65, 96, 123-24, 128,
    133, 139-40, 153, 212; history of, 1-4,
    308, 309, 339 nn. 1, 2; hunting in,
    236; land ownership ordinances of, 20;
    livestock in, 6, 39, 53, 56, 205, 208,
    225, 235-37, 275; mail service in, 29;
    map of, 12; name of, 1; pests in, 6;
    presidents of, 310; prices in, 64, 97,
    191-200, 219, 273; prosperity of, 127;
    rainfall in, 6; relations with Brazil, 28;
    relations with England, 27, 30, 64,
    264; relations with France, 28, 202,
    264; relations with Spain, 227;
    settlements in, 255-56, 260; slave trade
    in, 106-8, 202, 227; timber in, 225,

254; trade in, 110, 287, 300, 304; in twentieth century, 308, 309, 339 nn. 1, 2; wages in, 53, 70, 72, 92; wars in, 4-5, 156, 176, 181-83, 194, 289-90; wild life in, 133, 142, 258

Liberia Herald, 14, 17, 20, 25, 29, 49, 51

Little Butaw tribe, 166, 181, 289-90

Lomax, Matilda. *See* Skipwith, Matilda (Lomax, Richardson)

Lugenbeel, J. W: letter to, 240; sketch of, 314 n.1 (ltr 6); writes articles on Liberia, 284

McCalla, John M., letters to, 251, 252

McDonogh, Augustine Lamberth, letters of, 124, 131, 136

McDonogh, Bridget, letter of, 133

McDonogh, David, 118

McDonogh, Galloway Smith, letters of, 119, 127

McDonogh, George R. Ellis: character of, 119, 145; death of, 195; health of, 132, 139; letters of, 120, 124, 132, 133, 139, 142, 144-46, 152, 154; relations with former master, 121, 132, 140, 143, 145-46; and religion, 120, 143, 145-46; success in Liberia, 119, 132, 140, 146

McDonogh, Henrietta Fuller, letter of, 153

McDonogh, John, 8, 248; African experiences of his former slaves, 117-53; letters to, 119-53; plan of emancipation, 116-17; sketch of, 116

McDonogh, Julia Smith, letter of, 149

McDonogh, Nancy Smith, letters of, 136, 150

McDonogh, Simon Jackson, letter of, 151

McDonogh, Washington W., 9; character of, 118, 129, 142, 148; health of, 128, 139, 141; journey to Liberia, 121; letters of, 121-23, 128, 138, 139, 141, 147, 148, 151; marriage of, 153; missionary work of, 118, 129, 138-39, 142, 147; pride in Liberia, 142; relations with African natives, 129, 138, 141; relations with former master, 129, 139, 141-42; religion of, 138, 141-42, 148-49, 153; sketch of, 118

McGeorge, James, letters of, 125, 134, 135 n.1 (ltr 10)

McGill, James B., 63; success in Liberia, 314 n.1 (ltr 10)

McGill, Samuel F., 89, 321 n.1 (ltr 77)

McKenny, William, letters to, 216, 217, 219

McLain, William, connection with ACS, 311 n.3; letters to, 174, 189, 203, 210, 224-26, 228-35, 239-49, 281, 283, 286, 288, 291, 295, 299

McLain, Mrs. William, letters to, 230, 237

McMorine, Richard, letter of, 274

McParrhan, Richard, letter of, 274

McParrhan, Virgil P., letter of, 260

Maffit, J. N., 321 n.1 (ltr 80)

Malone, Ellis, letter to, 272

Mary Caroline Stevens, 279, 320 n.1 (ltr 70)

Maryland in Africa, 2; attacked by Grebos, 83, 320 n.1 (ltr 67)

Maryland State Colonization Society: withdraws from ACS, 2; papers of, 8

Masons, formation of lodge in Liberia, 29

Matthias, J. J., 40

Mechlin, Joseph, 5

Methodists, 22, 23, 224, 262, 271, 300-301. *See also* American Freedmen in Liberia, churches of

Minor, James Cephas: achieves prominence in Liberia, 14, 308-9; attitude toward African natives, 28; death of, 14; difficulty in obtaining land, 21; effort to establish mercantile business, 305; letters of, 15, 17, 18, 20, 23, 25, 26, 28, 29-31; member of Masonic lodge, 29; pride in freedom, 17; printer for *Liberia Herald*, 14, 18; relations with African natives, 16; and religion, 16

Minor, John, 13; letters to, 15, 29

Minor, Lancelot B., 13, 46, 53

Minor, Lucy Landon (Carter), 13

Minor, Mary Ann, 13; letters of, 25, 31

Miscegenation, 241, 312 n. 19

Mississippi Colonization Society, 3

Mississippi in Africa, 3, 5

Mitchell, Henry M., 29

Monroe, James, 4

Monrovia: appearance of, 255-56, 260, 264; named for President James Monroe, 4; population of, 255-56

Moore, James M., letters to, 254, 255

Mordecai, George, 334 n.1 (ltr 229)

Morris, Edward, 295-96

Murray, R. E., 282, 336 n.2 (ltr 251)

New Cess (New Cesters), 106

New Hope plantation in Alabama, 34

New York Colonization Society, 3

Nicholas, Erasmus: letter of, 56; visits U.S., 62, 67

Page, Mrs. Anne (Randolph), 100

Page, Charles W., 100; letters to, 102-15

Page, John M., Jr., letter of, 110

Page, John M., Sr., letters of, 103, 113, 114

Page, Robert M., letters of, 102, 108, 112

Page, Solomon S., letters of, 105, 107

Page, Thomas M., letter of, 111

Palm oil, 57-58. *See also* American freedmen in Liberia, crops of; food of

Liberia, 33, 36; family of, 33, 67; family ties, 56, 65-66; health of, 37-39, 40; letters of, 36-38, 40, 43, 45, 48, 51-55, 59, 63, 65; pride in Liberia, 66; reaction to Liberia, 36-37, 52; religion, 35, 51, 55, 66-67; sketch of life in Liberia, 35; war against African natives, 52-53; work of, 40, 51, 64

Skipwith, Richard, letter of, 98

Slaves in U.S., relations with masters, 8

Slave trade, 24-25, 49, 51-52, 60, 91, 106-8, 202, 210, 227, 316 n.2 (ltr 30), 322 n.1 (ltr 92). *See also* Liberia, slave trade in

Smith, Frances, letter of, 184

Smith, Gerrit, withdraws from ACS, 3

Smith, Henry, letters of, 180, 182-84

Smith, James K., 89; sketch of, 321 n.1 (ltr 77)

Sterdivant, Leander, 5, 35, 315 n.5

Sterdivant, Mary Diana (Haynes), 35; letters of, 82, 88

Sterdivant, Robert Leander, 33; character of, 62, 318 n.1 (ltr 42); letters of, 62, 83; reaction to Liberia, 62; relations with African natives, 63, 83; relations with Cocke family, 62, 318 n.1 (ltr 42); service with U.S. navy, 70-71, 74, 90-91, 97

Sterdivant, Rose, 35

Sterdivant, William Leander, 35; as carpenter, 84, 93; letter of, 93

Stevens, John: attitude of settlers toward, 299; and *Mary Caroline Stevens*, 330 n.1 (ltr 182)

Stewart, Henry B.: character of, 280-81; emigrates to Liberia, 280-82; education of children, 283, 302; and family ties, 286, 307; founds Congregational church in Liberia, 288, 289-90, 294, 337 n.1 (ltr 256); health of, 285, 293; letters of, 281-307; pride in Liberia, 280-81, 291, 306; reaction to Liberia, 282-83; relations with African natives, 281, 302-3; and religion, 280, 283, 285, 290-92, 300, 307

Tappan, Arthur, 3

Teage, Colin, 17, 31; death of, 49, 51; sketch of, 313 n.2 (ltr 1)

Teage, Hilary: death of, 80; sketch of, 318 n.1 (ltr 48)

Thilman, Elisa, letter of, 259

Tillinghast, Samuel, letter to, 264

Tills, George Washington, letters of, 247, 248

Trade Town, 106, 322 n.1 (ltr 92)

Tubman, William V. S., 339 n.2 (epilogue)

Vanbonn, Jacob, Grand Bassa chief, 196

Vey (Vai, Vei) tribe, 77; attacks Heddington, 220

Virginia colonists and claims of superior status, 6

Virginia Magazine of History and Biography, 101

Wade, Mrs. Catherine, letters to, 158, 160, 163, 174

Wade, Isaac R.: character of, 156, 326 n.7; contests will of Isaac Ross, 155; letters to, 161, 162, 165, 170, 175

Walker, York, letters of, 170, 175

Warner, D. B., 213

Watson, James, 244-45, 333 n.1 (ltr 221)

Watson, William, 244-45, 333 n.1 (ltr 221)

Watts, Phillis, 125

Weaver, William, 17; sketch of, 313 n.3 (ltr 1)

West, Elliott, letter to, 256

Wheeler, Susan, letter to, 22

White, Edward Z., letter of, 239

Whittemore, Reuben, letter of, 180

Wilkeson, Samuel, letters, to, 18, 220

Wilkins, Samuel, letter to, 18

Williams, A. S.: lieutenant governor of Liberia, 40; sketch of, 316 n.1 (ltr 23)

Williams, Anthony D.: attitude of settlers toward, 253; visits U.S. 64

Williams, Landon, 334 n.1 (ltr 226); letter of, 249

Wilson, A. D., 195

Wilson, Beverly R., 293; sketch of, 338 n.1 (ltr 260)

Wilson, James W., 216; letters of, 240, 244, 246

Woodson, Grandville, letters of, 158, 161, 162, 163

Woodson, Pascal, letter of, 165

Woodson, Sarah J., letters of, 158, 160

Yates, Beverly, vice-president of Liberia, 193; sketch of, 329 n.2 (ltr 178)